Ethics in Marriage and Family Therapy

Edited by   Robert Henley Woody
Jane DiVita Woody

Published by the American As ociation

for Marriage and Family Therapy

Washington, D.C.

The American Association for Marriage and Family Therapy promotes and advances the common professional interests of Marriage and Family Therapists.

This document is published by:

The American Association for Marriage and Family Therapy

1133 15th Street NW #300

Washington, DC 20005-2710

(202) 452-0109

TABLE OF CONTENTS

ABOUT THE CONTRIBUTORS

Dorothy S. Becvar, Ph.D., M.S.W., is President and CEO of the Haelan Centers (St. Louis, MO). In AAMFT, she is a Clinical Member and Approved Supervisor.

O. Brandt Caudill, J.D., is an Attorney at Law and Partner of the Law Firm of Callahan, McCune & Willis, L.L.P. (Los Angeles and San Diego, CA).

Wayne H. Denton, Ph.D., M.D., is Associate Professor and Director of the Marital and Family Therapy Clinic for the Department of Psychiatry & Behavioral Medicine at the Wake Forest University School of Medicine (Winston-Salem, NC). In AAMFT, he is a Clinical Member and Approved Supervisor.

Brian Jory, Ph.D., is Associate Professor and Director of Family Studies at Berry College (Mount Berry, GA). In AAMFT, he is a Clinical Member and Approved Supervisor.

Colleen Margaret Peterson, Ph.D., is Clinical Assistant Professor and Director of the Center for Individual, Couple & Family Counseling at the University of Nevada, Las Vegas (Las Vegas, NV). In AAMFT, she is a Clinical Member and Approved Supervisor.

Cheryl L. Storm, Ph.D., M.A., is Professor in the Department of Marriage and Family Therapy at the Pacific Lutheran University (Tacoma, WA). In AAMFT, she is a Clinical Member and Approved Supervisor.

Stephanie R. Walsh, M.S., is a Doctoral Candidate in Marriage and Family Therapy at the Virginia Polytechnic Institute and State University, and Doctoral Intern in the Department of Psychiatry & Behavioral Medicine at the Wake Forest University School of Medicine (Winston-Salem, NC). In AAMFT, she is a Student Member and Supervisor-in-Training.

Jane DiVita Woody, Ph.D., M.S.W., is Professor of Social Work at the University of Nebraska at Omaha (Omaha, NE). In AAMFT, she is a Clinical Member and Approved Supervisor.

Robert Henley Woody, Ph.D., Sc.D., J.D., is Professor of Psychology and Director of the School Psychology Training Program at the University of Nebraska at Omaha, and an attorney in private practice (Omaha, NE). In AAMFT, he is a Fellow.

PREFACE

The world is more complicated and fast paced today than at any time in history. Communication—global communication, on a mass or a personal level, is instantaneous. Pagers are passé; we now use email and cell phones. Video or satellite phones are on their way. Wireless communication, with no wait, is part of our present, not part of our future.

In the midst of these technological and accompanying cultural changes sits the enterprise of therapy—marital and family therapy. It is essentially a low-tech activity—conversation designed to help individuals, couples, and families assign meaning, change behavior, and improve the quality of their lives. We do that through a combination of science and art; from diagnosis and treatment in the use the medical model, to tapping people's most deeply held sense of the spiritual and sacred. Though the world changes, much of the mystery of hearts and minds meeting in relational and healing conversation is essentially timeless.

Yet those therapeutic conversations, timeless as they may be, occur in this context of vast change—and those changes do impact the processes of therapy in profound, yet still undefined ways. And the context is not just that of communications technologies. The way mental health services are financed has changed dramatically as well. Risk management and liability concerns loom larger than previously. Many therapists have moved to a more collaborative model of therapy from those that might now be considered more paternalistic or hierarchical. Consumer groups have found their voice as advocates for recipients of care. Even the profession of marriage and family therapy itself has changed—it now stands as an equal partner to other disciplines in terms of the rights and responsibilities marriage and family therapists hold. We are no longer an "emerging" profession. We are fully part of the regulatory and practice context in North America.

In light of all these changes, it becomes critical to examine, at a broad level, the parameters of ethical practice in marriage and family therapy. How do we create a conceptual map for thinking about

1) the domains of activity in which therapists engage;

2) the parameters which must be considered in defining what constitutes ethical practice; and

3) what, in fact, is considered within the realm of ethical practice in this current context—what is clearly outside of ethical practice—and where are the gray areas that require special attention and care?

AAMFT offers this book as the starting point for thinking and talking about these issues: "the map of the world as we know it at this time." However, while it offers markers for ethical practice in a number of areas, it is not simply a "how-to" book, nor a book with easy and defined answers. Rather, it provides room for thought—for a continued building of a conceptual map for ethical practice for marriage and family therapy.

On behalf of AAMFT, I'd like to thank the editors, Bob and Jane Woody, and all of the contributors, for their work. It is our hope that, through this contribution, ethical practice will be furthered, and further discourse and development of ideas about ethical practice will be advanced. May we all focus on not only the Hippocratic concept of doing no harm, but also on the goal of being at the leading edge of thought and practice in a competent and ethical manner.

ETHICS, PROFESSIONALISM, AND DECISION MAKING: A THEORETICAL AND PRACTICAL PERSPECTIVE

1

Robert Henley Woody and Jane DiVita Woody

This chapter offers background for understanding and applying professional ethics in marriage and family therapy in general and for the special issues covered in the chapters of this book. The discussion reviews the societal trust and obligations associated with being a professional, the inevitable linkage between ethics and values in therapy, models of ethical analysis that can promote ethically defensible decisions, and practical guidelines for integrating ethical principles from the AAMFT ethics code in day-to-day practice.

CONTENTS
Professionalism
The Intertwining of Values and Ethics
Ethical Decision Making
Integrating Ethical Concepts and Principles into Day-to-Day Practice
Conclusion

Marriage and family therapy practitioners know that ethical dilemmas in practice are real and common; still these are not typically at the top of their priority list for study or contemplation. The goal of this chapter and this book is to put ethics front and center in practice. Both new and experienced clinicians can benefit from gaining a clear sense of the most common ethical issues and dilemmas, how to resolve them when they strike, how to recognize them in their early stages, and, most importantly, how to prevent them.

As marriage and family therapists have expanded their client base and the range of emotional, behavioral, and interactional problems that they treat, the complex family, mental health, and societal issues involved often create similarly complicated ethical and legal constraints and challenges. Yet ethics complaints against marriage and family therapists and other mental health professionals continue to involve the most obvious and blatant violations. For example, dual relationships, especially romantic or sexual relationships with clients, remain a primary reason for disciplining therapists in all mental health professions.

At the same time, an increasing number of complaints involve true ethical dilemmas in which more than one judgment might be defensible. In a child visitation example, a therapist who had worked closely with a family in therapy believed that the father's intention to move some three hundred miles away would be detrimental to the couple's three-year old son. This opinion was based primarily on the therapist's understanding of cognitive and emotional needs for this stage of the child's development. The father had a very close relationship with his son and indicated that he would be talking with him on the phone regularly and making frequent visits to see him so as to not upset the child's usual routines. The therapist adamantly tried to get the father to review his decision in light of her explanation of the child's need for more frequent contact. On consulting a colleague, the therapist heard another "professional" viewpoint. The colleague emphasized the father's needs along with those of the child; that is, the father was devoted to the child, gained much identity from parenting, and could be expected to benefit from keeping the frequent and close contacts that his son needed at this age, while also giving the child the stability of staying in his mother's custody.

As this example shows, more than one judgment on an ethical concern may be defensible on various grounds. Therapists who work with problems such as child custody, child abuse, and domestic violence encounter a plethora of potential ethical issues that demand a blend of competence, skill, and familiarity with ethics and the law.

Professional codes of ethics, and specifically the AAMFT Code of Ethics (reprinted in full in Appendix A), are essential to ensure a high standard of professional service in the field of marriage and family therapy. Such codes are a formal mechanism to maintain and strengthen the public's trust in the profession of marriage and family therapy, which takes seriously its responsibility to clients/consumers and affirms its commitment to put the welfare of the public and service users first. The AAMFT Code of Ethics provides a standard for the AAMFT membership and all those who practice marriage and family therapy, regardless of their organizational membership (although non-members have no formal obligation to adhere to the Code). Thus, true to its leadership as a professional association, the AAMFT serves an important societal function by setting forth a formal code of ethical standards for practitioners to know and apply in their day-to-day practice.

Contemporary ethical issues facing marriage and family therapists demand a high degree of consciousness and thought, however, that goes beyond referring to a code of ethics in the midst of an ethical dilemma. To clarify and promote this important intellectual process, this chapter discusses: (1) the nature of professionalism, (2) the inter-twining of values and ethics in practice, (3) the process of ethical decision making, and (4) the integration of ethical concepts and principles into day-to-day practice.

PROFESSIONALISM

As a professional organization, AAMFT (and its current ethics code) has evolved within a changing sociocultural context that defines the mission and responsibilities of mental health practitioners. Society sanctions professionals and awards them certain status and privileges, but it also mandates that their services meet standards in accord with ever-changing public policy.

The category of "professional" has evolved from the time-honored role of "trustees" of socially important knowledge, a designation that fell only to those who fulfilled strict criteria. These criteria included extensive study and training, specific skills for putting knowledge into practice, and integrity to assure that the services rendered would be in the best interests of society. Allowing therapists to provide expert opinions in child custody cases is one of the best examples of the union between knowledge and integrity.

During the last century, the role of the professional has undergone further refinement and more precise definition. Specifically, the professional must assiduously commit to: serving the welfare of others (before self); improving knowledge and enhancing the results of practice, such as through research; and maintaining conduct that does not jeopardize or cause harm to the recipients of the professional services. One therapist lamented that the prohibition in the licensing law against assigning clients to an unlicensed assistant resulted in a loss of possible income. By expressing this view, the therapist revealed a failure to realize that the protection of the consumer, the basis for the licensing law, was deemed more important than entrepreneurship.

Following up on the preceding example, the privilege of being a professional includes social status and financial opportunity that often translates into above-average income. Brint (1994) has noted that the idea of professionalism is intertwined with the development of modern capitalism. Thus, "expert professionalism needed no sharp distinction from business enterprise, and it required less separation from the idea of pursuing trade for a profit" (p. 9). In other words, society accepts that the professional's social benevolence does not contradict the desire for income and other personal benefits. Nonetheless, the welfare of the public, such as the imposition of quality control through licensing laws and adherence to ethics codes, must always be honored above financial incentive.

From the preceding paragraph, it is obvious that marketplace issues must not dominate decision making in mental health services. Marriage and family therapy—like medicine, psychology, counseling, and social work—is not simply an entrepreneurial enterprise. Professional services that are dedicated to the welfare of human beings place "considerable emphasis upon special moral commitments made through ethical responsibilities to its clients." That is, financial factors cannot subvert dedication "to a distinctive set of ideals and standards of conduct" (Preister, Vesper, & Humphrey, 1998, p. 5).

Because of the peerless importance of protecting the welfare of consumers of mental health services, the privilege and status of being a professional do not insulate the practitioner from continued scrutiny. Society expects professionals to fulfill their commitment to provide beneficial services that meet agreed-upon standards. In this regard, professional associations, such as the AAMFT, have an important role to play both for their members and for society. Their foremost purposes include inculcating and furthering new knowledge; promoting benefits for the public and adherence to law; and promulgating guidelines, standards, and ethics that will assure proper, reasonable, and reasoned conduct by and among the membership.

Because professionals have not always conducted themselves properly or enjoyed a sterling reputation with the public, providing standards for and scrutiny of professional conduct is a critical mission for professional associations. The relatively few errant practitioners have caused grave concerns among their professional colleagues as well as among the general public about how to control unacceptable conduct. Consequently, a major dimension of professionalism and of professional associations has become creating and enforcing a code of ethics to regulate practitioners.

Early on, the preferred approach was for the profession to regulate itself. Indeed, sociologists held that professionals were best prepared to monitor practitioners. Etzioni (1969), for example, argued that "the individual professional has the ultimate responsibility for his professional decision." Professionals were assumed to be "basically responsible to their conscience (though they may be censured by their peers and in extreme cases by the courts)" (p. x). Within this framework, the primary means for safeguarding the public from nonprofessional conduct and assuring quality care for service recipients was the professional association's code of ethics and the practitioner's commitment to continued learning and honing of skills. In other words, a code of ethics implies "a social contract with the public that purports to balance professional privilege with responsibility and a commitment to consumer welfare" (Koocher & Keith-Spiegel, 1998, p. 27).

The financial cost imposed on a professional association for maintaining and enforcing an ethics code has created a contemporary problem. Some professional associations have chosen to discontinue adjudicating complaints, relying instead on governmental regulatory agencies (i.e., licensing boards) or courts of law to provide service users with recourse against allegedly errant practitioners. An important question now is whether this step signals a trend toward professional associations' abdicating the societal mandate to promulgate and promote ethics for their members. AAMFT has not, however, moved in this direction, and still adjudicates complaints.

With or without adjudication of complaints, it is a matter of fact that relying solely on a professional association to enforce a code of ethics has proved to be woefully inadequate. In the past twenty-five years, safeguards from other sources have emerged, most notably actions from governmental regulatory agencies, such as licensing boards, and legal actions, such as malpractice claims.

In spite of this change, the code of ethics promulgated, promoted, and enforced by a professional association continues to be the cornerstone for decision making and self direction by practitioners and for monitoring and regulating the members of the profession. In fact, the other consumer protection sources, such as licensing boards and courts of law, rely, to varying degrees, on the relevant discipline's code of ethics to derive the standard of care that will be applied in the regulatory or legal proceedings. Certain state governments have even adopted legislatively the code of ethics from a professional association to use as the legal standard for licensees in the profession, which indeed appears to be a trend. Such procedures allow the licensing boards to determine whether to sustain the allegations of wrongdoing and impose disciplinary sanctions or punitive actions. As Koocher and Keith-Spiegel (1998) stated, "Despite wide variations in length and specificity, the functions of most professional ethics codes echo similar themes: (1) to promote the welfare of consumers served, (2) to maintain competence, (3) to do no harm, (4) to protect confidentiality and privacy, (5) to act responsibly, (6) to avoid exploitation, and (7) to uphold the profession through exemplary conduct" (p. 27).

THE INTERTWINING OF VALUES AND ETHICS

Although there is debate as to whether all of therapy is laden with values, the brief discussion here agrees with Tjeltveit (1999), who accepts that values permeate therapy, primarily because all therapy involves value-laden goals.

First, consider that practitioners work toward accomplishing both rather general therapy goals as well as those that are specific to remedying the client's problems. Thus therapists and their clients have ideas about what are good and desirable human behavior, effective human functioning, good mental health, good relationships, and so on. Values permeate these concepts because they posit what are good and desirable human goals. As an example, a couple who seeks therapy for the wife's severe depression will typically want to see therapy bring about a change in her degree of depression as well as improve her functioning in the marriage and with all members of her family. Presumably, the therapist will negotiate goals that will be congruent and agreeable to all involved and that will create no ethical dilemmas. But the potential for an ethical problem is always present. For example, what if significant differences emerge during the course of therapy between the husband's, the wife's, and the therapist's views on what would be acceptable improvement in the couple's sexual relationship? At this point, the therapist and the client couple must go back to the drawing board, and renegotiate the goals for the treatment plan.

Consider the case of a therapist who, when treating a couple with conjoint and individual sessions, is asked by each spouse in his or her individual session to keep secrets from the other spouse. The husband wants to continuing having affairs without the wife's knowledge, and the wife wants to continue abusing drugs and engaging in prostitution. This example raises obvious questions about values, such as each partner's value assumptions about marriage and the values that undergird most models of marital and couple therapy, not to mention the therapist's personal values that might emerge. It is a large question as to whether this client system could negotiate treatment goals and a plan without focusing on values. In addition, the risky behavior of both spouses creates the specter of potential legal problems for the therapist. If one spouse should suffer a negative consequence because the therapist did little or nothing to counter the risky behavior, the potential for malpractice liability for the therapist might arise. For reasons relating to both quality of treatment and risk management, the therapist might be faced with terminating the treatment (perhaps referring each spouse to seek individual therapy).

The foregoing example points to another way in which values and ethics connect. Ethics cannot be separated from any profession's knowledge base (which is likely quite diverse and drawn from various scientific fields), professional values, intervention methods, and the required therapist self-awareness that are so important in all forms of therapy. Consider how the various models promulgate the "right" or "desirable" outcomes of therapy and the "right," "best," or "most effective" methods for achieving these. Thus cognitive-behavioral models assert that changes in both client thinking and behavior are the vehicle to remedy symptoms and problems. Other therapy models, however, emphasize the interpersonal relationship between client and therapist and see this relationship as having the best potential to help the client experience changes that can carry over to real life problems and symptoms outside the therapy room. With family problems, the various family therapy models hold value assumptions about what constitute "good" or "healthy" family or marital functioning and what are the "best" interventions to help clients reach these goals.

Perhaps one of the most complicated issues of all is whether therapists influence the values of clients. It seems reasonable to assert that this kind of influence is inevitable in therapy and therapists should understand that it comes with the territory. As Tjeltveit (1999) aptly explained, "Because we do influence the values of others . . . , we have a professional responsibility to reflect with great care on the values and ethical theories that we hold . . ." (p.12).

The inevitable intertwining of values and ethics points to several practical steps to assure that professional services and decisions are ethically defensible. First, it is important for marriage and family therapists to seriously consider ethical convictions and ethical theory and "the reason for holding certain ethical convictions as opposed to others" (Tjeltveit, 1999, p. 7). Second, therapists should also be willing and prepared to carry out sophisticated analyses of values and related ethical problems as these emerge in therapy. Third, therapists should take guidance on ethical matters, both to prevent and remedy ethical problems, from their profession's established code of ethics. Finally, therapists can fine-tune their ethical decision-making abilities by considering and applying established models of ethical decision making to resolve ethical dilemmas, such as those discussed in the next section.

ETHICAL DECISION MAKING

Ethics codes are purposefully structured and worded to provide general guidance. The primary underlying tone is philosophical rather than pragmatic. Recently, however, ethics codes have become more specific, especially about critical areas of practice; that is, rules target practice sectors that are most often linked to therapeutic errors, misconduct, and malpractice.

Morals and values are inherent to the principles, standards, or rules in an ethics code: "Ethics is traditionally a branch of philosophy that deals with moral problems and moral judgments" (Koocher & Keith-Spiegel, 1998, p. 4). Consequently it is no surprise that professional codes of ethics include such moral concepts as autonomy, beneficence, non-malfeasance, justice, and fidelity (Beauchamp & Childress, 1979). These same concepts appear as ethical principles for guiding, for example, psychologists: doing no harm, respecting autonomy, benefiting others, being just, being faithful, according dignity, treating others with caring and compassion, pursuit of excellence, and accepting accountability (Koocher & Keith-Spiegel, 1998). Clearly, as suggested above, therapeutic services and the ethics that apply to them are not value-free (Tjeltveit, 1999).

Whatever the stated ethical principles and standards for a mental health profession, they will be tempered by the practitioner's beliefs, preferences, and characteristics that impact one's interpretation of and adherence to the ethics code. Not only will practitioners within a given profession differ among themselves as individuals, they may also differ from other critical sources, such as clients and the general public (Stiles, Shapiro, & Barkham, 1993), as well as differ from the collective wisdom of public policy and government. For example, various chapters in this book deal extensively with the many ethical concerns that arise from differing perspectives of clients' problems and conditions (the complexities of therapy with children in Chapter Six, violence and dangerousness in Chapter Seven, and sexuality and spirituality in Chapter Eight).

Appropriate ethical decision making becomes central when the practitioner faces a situation that might constitute a dilemma. At that point, the practitioner must conduct a careful analysis that will produce a sound and defensible ethical course of action. There is no one prescription for making ethical decisions; however, several models merit consideration.

At its most simple conception, analysis for ethical decision making requires a step-by-step procedural approach. It is necessary to dissect the theoretical and professional components of the given scenario, order the components for relevance or importance, consider alternatives or modifications, and, finally, accept a course of action. These steps constitute a process of decision analysis that offers significant benefits:

It [decision analysis] can help us make the best possible decision in a given situation. Moreover, it can help us to clarify our values, that is, the preferences among possible outcomes by which we judge what the best decision might be. Decision analysis can also be used to build logic and rationality into our intuitive decision making—to educate our intuition about probabilities and about the paths of contingency by which our actions, in combination with chance or "outside" events, lead to outcomes. (Gutheil, Bursztajn, Brodsky, & Alexander, 1991, p. 41)

A similar model of decision analysis includes five components: "(a) acknowledging the decision, (b) listing the pros and cons, (c) structuring the decision (including development of a decision 'tree' to graph decisional paths and subsequent decisional branches, (d) estimating probabilities and values, and (e) calculating expected value" (Cottone & Claus, 2000, p. 276).

Taking a more pragmatic approach to resolving ethical dilemmas within marriage and family therapy, J. Woody (1990) identified specific components that impact practice and merit analysis: ethical theories; professional codes of ethics; counseling theories; the sociolegal context in which the therapeutic services occur; and the personal/professional identity of the therapist. This approach is congruent with and includes the procedural steps of decision analysis mentioned above, specifically, identifying and weighting the claims of the different components. In addition, concepts of ethics and morality permeate the components of general ethical theories, professional codes, and the character of the professional.

A model that gives primary emphasis to moral development and producing moral behavior suggests four components in this process: (1) interpreting the situation according to how the action affects the welfare of others; (2) formulating a course of action that embraces the moral ideal for the particular situation; (3) after considering alternatives, selecting a moral ideal to act upon; and (4) executing and implementing the chosen moral ideal (Rest, 1984). Viewed a bit differently, Rest aligns the moral components with sensitivity, judgment, motivation, and character. This focus on moral/ethical concepts is similar to J. Woody's (1990) analysis of the importance of the personal/professional identity of the marriage and family therapist. The practitioner's character is central since this mediates the entire decision-making process. For example, a therapist who knowingly uses false information on an insurance form (e.g., stating that reimbursable individual therapy was provided, when in fact it was nonreimbursable marriage therapy with a couple) to enable the couple to wrongfully collect insurance reimbursement has allowed his or her own character flaw to denigrate the therapeutic intervention. Such a decision lacks a full ethical analysis and is detrimental to the clients, the therapist, the profession, and society. To summarize, it is essential that the therapist possess the above-stated virtues of sensitivity, judgment, motivation, and character to do an impartial analysis of a dilemma and reach an ethical decision.

Clearly, practicing in an ethical manner and resolving complex ethical dilemmas demands a high level of competence and integrity. This responsibility calls for ongoing professional development, personal awareness, and willingness to learn about and carry out the steps for making ethical decisions and analyzing complex moral issues that involve oneself as part of the equation. The marriage and family therapist who sincerely commits to a high level of ethical practice and decision making will reap the benefits of providing clients with quality care and of managing the risks of practice in a sound manner. Cottone and Claus (2000) provided a useful summary of the steps or stages in various practice-based ethical decision-making models.

In the real world of everyday practice, following procedures for decision making and moral analysis, such as those briefly noted above, can help produce the right ethical decision. For example, in the earlier situation, the therapist filed false information, possibly based on the faulty notion that the clients' receiving insurance reimbursement would outweigh the fraud. Yet other ethical principles were ignored; namely, the obligation to adhere to honesty and not promote the therapist's interests, such as the financial benefit from keeping paying clients. Within the framework of decision making and moral analysis, other practical steps can also help. In the following list suggested by Koocher and Keith-Spiegel (1998), the editors' comments in brackets show how the steps fit or mesh with the other decision-making procedures or components mentioned above.

1. Determine that the matter is an ethical one (p. 12) [dissect the various components];

2. Consult the guidelines already available that might apply to a specific identification and possible mechanism for resolution (p. 13) [e.g., specific principle or principles in the ethics code, legal constraints];

3. Consider, as best as possible, all sources that might influence the kind of decision you will make (p. 13) [ethical theories, sociolegal context, theories of therapy, therapist's personal/professional identity];

4. Locate a trusted colleague with whom you can consult (p. 14) [e.g., dissecting and gaining insight into all components];

5. Evaluate the rights, responsibilities, and vulnerability of all affected parties (including, if relevant, an institution and the general public) (p. 14) [ordering of importance, relevance of components];

6. Generate alternative decisions (p. 14) [considering alternatives, modifications];

7. Enumerate the consequences of making each decision (p. 14) [estimating probabilities and expected values];

8. Make the decision (p. 14) [executing, accepting a course of action]; and

9. Implement the decision (p. 14) [implementing the choice and ongoing evaluation].

As Koocher and Keith-Spiegel (1998) pointed out (see p. 15), following these steps toward making good ethical decisions means that the practitioner will allow time to collect and think about the needed information, identify the person or entity to whom one owes primary allegiance, strive to maintain a calm demeanor and objectivity, and continue with ongoing evaluation to allow for any needed corrections in resolving the dilemma.

Reduced to its essence, ethical decision making centers on the idiosyncratic elements of the particular practice dilemma, as processed mentally and emotionally through the professional and personal qualities of the therapist. Whether deciding on a clinical strategy or a means for resolving an ethical dilemma, the "decision making consists of an unpredictable mix of intuition and rationality" (J. Woody, 1990, p. 144).

Sometimes, of course, intuition and rationality may be in conflict. Upon being threatened by a client, a therapist chose to not include any of the threats in the clinical notes, although the threats were certainly relevant and material to the treatment, for fear that the client would see the entries and become violent. Aside from the need to have a record of the threats for purposes of risk management, the information would also be relevant to current treatment and any subsequent treatment source. By disregarding what must be included in clinical records, the therapist seemingly allowed emotionalized intuition to override reasoning, which would support the need for entries for clinical, risk management, and legal purposes.

Still other conditions unique to marriage and family therapy add to the burden of making sound ethical decisions. First, the client system is often a couple or family, a reality that means the therapist will have a relationship with all persons involved. This condition can elicit countertransference reactions that lead to aligning more strongly with some family members than with others. For example, some therapists tend to identify too much with a child or the "underdog" in a relationship. Second, even when the welfare of the family or the relationship is the appropriate focus of therapy, clarity about this obligation sometimes changes. When conditions emerge, such as child abuse, spouse battering, or the decision to divorce, flexibility is needed to renegotiate the treatment plan. Third, further complications may arise from the fact that many family problems are infused with values, and these can cause even the most seasoned therapist to feel the rush to assert personal values, a reaction that must be held in check. Marriage and family therapists are likely to hold strong personal values on such issues as extramarital sexual affairs, divorce, cohabitation, anonymous sex, family violence, child sexual abuse, and so on. In addition, many therapists struggle to maintain the needed objectivity when clients present these problems. The ethical challenge is to enable clients to gain information and insight for use in arriving at their own autonomous personal decisions that fit with their own value system (Cottone, Tarvydas, & House, 1994).

These additional conditions that are unique to marriage and family therapy make it even more critical to acknowledge that the therapist's own professional competence and personal character have a great impact on ethical decision making. Inevitably, the practitioner's personal beliefs, values, morals, needs, and preferences are potential influences that may or may not serve the welfare of clients or promote ethical decisions: "Ultimately ethical practice is moderated through and driven by the self as opposed to being driven by external variables" (Garfat & Ricks, 1995, p. 397). To conclude on the issue of the personal-self influences on ethical decision making, Cottone and Claus (2000) explained: "Attributes necessary for this self-driven ethical practice include self-awareness, ability for critical thinking, willingness to take personal responsibility, openness to alternative choices, and ability to monitor and implement feedback subsequent to ethical actions" (p. 281).

INTEGRATING ETHICAL CONCEPTS AND PRINCIPLES INTO DAY-TO-DAY PRACTICE

In the practice of marriage and family therapy, ethics should not be an afterthought or a philosophical endeavor that one considers only rarely and reluctantly, when all else fails. Ethical concepts and principles make the most sense and bring the most benefits when they are completely integrated into day-to-day clinical practice. By following a few practical steps, therapists can increase their consciousness about ethical issues, prevent the most blatant ethical violations, and be prepared for resolving complex ethical dilemmas that are bound to arise in today's changing social environment.

1. Do a careful analysis of your practice to determine the most common client problems encountered or types of clients served.

2. Review the knowledge base upon which you rely for understanding, assessment, and intervention relevant to the problems and clients and the inherent value assumptions of the knowledge base.

3. Review your preferred models of therapy and their inherent values about the process of helping clients, the therapeutic relationship, intervention strategies and their consistency with ethical concepts, principles, and the AAMFT Code of Ethics (and for therapists with identity with more than one mental health discipline, other relevant codes of ethics).

4. Do an ethical analysis of any professional book you read or seminar you attend to explore potential ethical issues and how the book or seminar leader accounts for these. (Relevant to this point, a recent examination of 11 contemporary textbooks dealing with theories and methods of family therapy revealed that only 6 of the 11 books indexed the term "ethics.")

5. Talk with colleagues, supervisors, and staff about ethical issues in marriage and family therapy.

6. Be vigilant about monitoring your personal/professional identity, including personal problems, handling countertransference with clients, difficult clients, etc.

7. Seek and use formal and regular supervision/consultation from a well-respected professional who is competent in your area(s) of practice.

8. Become familiar with legal mandates in your jurisdiction and how they impact on your most common areas of practice and interface with the ethical responsibilities of therapists.

9. Consider the procedures and routines that characterize your practice group, agency, or organization and whether these are congruent with and make possible the routine adherence to ethical standards.

10. When facing an ethical dilemma, act quickly to seek professional and legal consultation and begin the process of rational analysis, following one of the models outlined previously, to reach a decision that is ethically defensible.

11. Keep the AAMFT Code of Ethics handy, read it thoroughly, and refer to it often, not just in the midst of an ethical crisis. Visit the AAMFT website (aamft.org) and seek other resources for assistance with ethical and legal concerns.

12. Never believe all that you hear; some professionals who are poorly informed about ethical and legal matters and who write for publication and/or teach classes or seminars may actually disseminate incorrect information. If you read or hear something that just does not pass your intuition-rationality test, seek additional information to confirm or disconfirm the message you doubt.

CONCLUSION

The origins of marriage and family therapy are diffuse, but may well have started in historic times with the elders of a tribe advising a couple to behave in a certain way or else they would be banished or killed. It is likely that this sage advice from the elders came about when a couple acted in a manner that created jeopardy for the tribe, such as by not doing their share of hunting and gathering, or by subjecting their children to conditions that could hinder their growth as healthy and productive members of the tribe. The tribal elders probably dealt with the psychological aspects of the tribe's members, since cultural anthropologists report that even prehistoric people transitioned "from treating bodily ills to ministering to mental anguish" (Bromberg, 1975, p. 2).

In modern times, society has deemed that marriage and family therapists are professionals, a status that requires, of course, that all would-be practitioners fulfill the criteria established by public policy and law. Although the study of marriage and family therapy was initially pursued within other mental health professions (e.g., psychiatry, psychology, social work, and mental health and pastoral counseling), marriage and family therapy today is a distinct profession.

Public policy, law, and government have declared the AAMFT to be the senior organizational guardian of the profession. The AAMFT promulgates professional guidelines and standards (e.g., via a code of ethics); offers continuing education and training to upgrade knowledge and skills (including through conferences, publications, and accreditation); and engages in public service (e.g., advocating legislation that will benefit society). Also, the AAMFT has accepted the role of monitoring the profession, through adjudicating ethical complaints, although this function applies only to its dues-paying members.

As a professional organization, AAMFT is an invaluable resource for all professionals who practice marriage and family therapy. As suggested above, besides the formal Code of Ethics, a variety of resources are available through its publications, training opportunities, and website to assist marriage and family therapists and other mental health practitioners with professional, ethical, and legal concerns and standards.

REFERENCES

Beauchamp, T. L., & Childress, J. F. (1979). Principles of biomedical ethics. Oxford, England: Oxford University Press.

Brint, S. (1994). In an age of experts: The changing role of professionals in politics and public life. Princeton, NJ: Princeton University Press.

Bromberg, W. (1975). From shaman to psychotherapist: A history of the treatment of mental illness. Chicago: Henry Regnery.

Cottone, R. R., & Claus, R. E. (2000). Ethical decision-making models: A review of the literature. Journal of Counseling & Development, 78 (3), 275–281.

Cottone, R. R., Tarvydas, V., & House, G. (1994). The effect of number and type of consulted relationships on the ethical decision making of graduate students in counseling. Counseling and Values, 39, 56–68.

Etzioni, A. (Ed.). (1969). The semi-professions and their organization. New York: Free Press.

Garfat, T., & Ricks, R. (1995). Self-driven ethical decision-making: A model for child and youth care. Child and Youth Care Forum, 24 (6), 393–404.

Gutheil, T. G., Bursztajn, H. J., Brodsky, A., & Alexander, V. (1991). Decision making in psychiatry and the law. Baltimore: Williams and Wilkins.

Koocher, G. P., & Keith-Spiegel, P. (1998). Ethics in psychology: Professional standards and cases (2nd ed.). New York: Oxford University Press.

Preister, S., Vesper, J. H., & Humphrey, F. G. (1998). The evolution of a professional ethics code. In G. W. Brock (Ed.), Ethics casebook (pp. 5–19). Washington, DC: American Association for Marriage and Family Therapy.

Rest, J. R. (1984). Research on moral development: Implications for training counseling psychologists. Counseling Psychologist, 12, 19–29.

Stiles, W. B., Shapiro, D. A., & Barkham, M. (1993). Research directions for psychotherapy integration: A roundtable. In J. C. Norcross (Ed.), Research directions for psychotherapy integration: A roundtable. Journal of Psychotherapy Integration, 3, 91–131.

Tjeltveit, A. C. (1999). Ethics and values in psychotherapy. London: Routledge.

Woody, J. D. (1990). Resolving ethical concerns in clinical practice: Toward a pragmatic model. Journal of Marital and Family Therapy, 16, 133–150.

PROTECTING AND BENEFITING THE CLIENT: THE THERAPEUTIC ALLIANCE, INFORMED CONSENT, AND CONFIDENTIALITY

2

Jane DiVita Woody and Robert Henley Woody

This chapter focuses on the overriding ethical obligation of marriage and family therapy in terms of its responsibility to clients, which is to advance their welfare by providing beneficial services while also protecting their rights. The discussion demonstrates why the first three ethical principles from the AAMFT Code—Responsibility to Clients, Confidentiality, and Professional Competence and Integrity—are intricately connected and essential to the task of rendering beneficial, effective, and ethical therapeutic services. This analysis sets the stage for subsequent chapters that deal in detail with specific types of client problems and concerns that often give rise to ethical risks and dilemmas.

CONTENTS

Providing therapeutic services to families and individuals carries a significant ethical burden. Most specifically, the overriding obligation is to protect and benefit the client. Because therapy is a highly complex process with many dimensions, especially when multiple persons are part of the client system, practitioners need to constantly monitor whether their services are, in fact, both "doing good" and "doing no harm." To carry out this obligation and not rely merely on good intentions, therapists can draw on established ethical principles within marriage and family therapy.

Speaking most directly to the general goal of advancing the client's welfare are the first three principles in the AAMFT ethics code: I: Responsibility to Clients, II: Confidentiality, and III: Professional Competence and Integrity. These ethical concepts are interrelated and contribute to making sure that therapeutic services advance the welfare of families and individuals in accord with professional standards, while also respecting their rights.

This chapter will highlight several aspects of these first three principles by discussing the following topics: responsibility to clients; basic tenets of the therapeutic contract; informed consent; the therapeutic relationship; and confidentiality. Later chapters will also deal with these same ethical principles, but in the context of specific client problems or situations (e.g., Chapter Six on children in therapy, Chapter Seven on violence, abuse and dangerousness, and Chapter Seven on moral, spiritual, and sexual issues). Multiple relationships, although mentioned in this chapter, are such a serious threat to client welfare that they are covered separately and in detail in Chapter Three.

RESPONSIBILITY TO CLIENTS: PUTTING CLIENT WELFARE FIRST

In the AAMFT ethics code, Principle I, Responsibility to Clients specifies that marriage and family therapists have to, as the primary responsibility in their therapeutic services, put the welfare of families and individuals first. Various subprinciples indicate how the therapist must safeguard clients' welfare and rights, and assist clients in making appropriate use of professional services.

Putting the client's welfare first is a general ethical principle that must be brought to life for each unique client situation. The subprinciples in Principle I suggest that therapists are vulnerable to losing focus on the client's welfare if and when they shift toward their own self-centered needs or biases. This type of unethical motivation or inclination also connects to Principle III, Professional Competence and Integrity, which delineates the ability and means that a therapist must have in order to advance the client's welfare. Consequently, meeting this central responsibility to clients demands simultaneous attention to several points in Principle III, specifically those that deal with the importance of a strong knowledge base, skills, and integrity.

The nature of therapeutic or clinical services derives from an implicit contract between the client and helper. Namely, the client pays a fee or is otherwise entitled to service that should promote his or her welfare, and the therapist agrees to provide the service with this focus. This broadly defined contract is the substance of Principle I, but further detailed safeguards within that principle aim to protect clients from therapists who might lose sight of the client's welfare. Those safeguards most directly relevant to the immediate therapeutic process include

The right to non-discrimination;

The right to give informed consent;

Protection against potential exploitation by the therapist's involvement in dual relationships, multiple roles, or efforts to further his or her own interests;

Protection against sexual intimacy between current client and therapist;

Protection against the risks involved in sexual intimacy after two years following termination of therapy;

The right to make their own decisions about marriage and intimate relationships; and

The right to services that are reasonably beneficial.

These safeguards serve as a "reminders list" that alerts therapists to the fact that, although in most cases the good intentions of the helping professional are securely in place, the potential exists for therapy to veer away from its primary responsibility to clients. These subprinciples make it clear that the client is entitled to certain rights, benefits, and protections.

One way to understand why the specific guidelines are necessary is to acknowledge that the nature of the therapeutic process itself can lead to confusion as to what actions, decisions, and behaviors will potentially benefit each unique client. Central to the therapeutic process is the therapeutic relationship that develops between the therapist and client.

To varying degrees, all theoretical approaches to marriage and family therapy acknowledge the importance of the therapeutic relationship. By definition, the therapist is one member of this typically intense and intimate relationship that poses a potential risk to the client's welfare. In reality, the marriage and family therapist inevitably functions within the relationship, allowing influence by his or her professional self and personal self. The personal self includes the therapist's values, needs, and character; and these qualities have the potential to compromise, either blatantly or subtly, the required faithful focus on the client's welfare. The professional self is supposed to operate within the relationship in a way that monitors the personal self. This critical process presumably flows from the qualities of professional competence and integrity that can assure that the client's welfare remains primary. In other words, the well-trained marriage and family therapist brings an integrated, cohesive total self that has a constructive influence on the therapeutic relationship.

It is easy to see why advancing the welfare of clients depends heavily on professional competence and integrity. Before the client can even give informed consent, the marriage and family therapist must have the level of competence to apply the appropriate knowledge and skills for assessing the problem, negotiating the focus and goals, and offering an appropriate treatment plan (note that R. Woody, 1991, provides information about treatment planning). Presumably the therapist would believe that the plan offers an effective way to advance the client's welfare.

Professional knowledge and skills also bear on the quality of effective and non-discriminatory service that all clients deserve. Similarly, understanding the complexities and risks inherent to therapeutic relationships demands theoretical knowledge and translating this into therapeutic skills that benefit rather than exploit the client.

All aspects of the therapeutic process—whether assessment, implementing strategies for change, or monitoring the therapeutic relationship—demand of the professional a sound knowledge base and a commitment to ongoing personal self awareness and scrutiny. These characteristics are essential for rendering effective, beneficial services, and for identifying issues that conflict with the primary responsibility to clients or that impair the professional judgment needed to stay focused on the client's welfare.

BASIC TENETS OF THE THERAPEUTIC CONTRACT

Several of the most fundamental ideas in the AAMFT ethics code that aim to insure the primacy of the client's welfare closely resemble basic human rights and reflect the nature of the therapeutic contract. The client is entitled to:

(1) therapeutic services that are non-discriminatory;

(2) autonomy or the right to make one's own decisions (with a specific emphasis on decisions about intimate relationships, marriage, divorce, etc., which are common concerns in therapy); and

(3) the right to receive reasonably beneficial services.

In other words, the client surrenders some degree of autonomy, but not all, by participating in therapy and, in return, has the right to expect that the therapist will show respect and offer beneficial help that remains focused on the client's welfare. The marriage and family therapist, receiving appropriate payment (compensation) and compliance with the agreed upon-therapeutic contract, provides the service according to these terms.

Sometimes a marriage and family therapist fails to meet even these most basic tenets of the therapeutic contract. The therapist may lose sight of his or her required faithful dedication to the client's welfare and may instead allow, consciously or unconsciously, personal needs or interests to take over. This occurrence signals a failure in the responsibility to promote the client's welfare and a failure in professional competence and/or integrity.

NON-DISCRIMINATION IN THERAPEUTIC SERVICES

In the AAMFT ethics code, Subprinciple 1.1 states: "Marriage and family therapists provide professional assistance to persons without discrimination on the basis of race, age, ethnicity, socioeconomic status, disability, gender, health status, religion, national origin, or sexual orientation." A violation of this subprinciple could be blatant or subtle. A blatant violation would be refusing service to a client based on one's own personal values or biases, such as refusing to continue therapy upon learning that a married client is involved in a homosexual relationship (Brock, 1998). This therapeutic stance has been deemed unethical and a clear ethical violation because it reflects discriminatory bias that calls for consultation or supervision rather than the act of terminating the client.

The substance of this subprinciple, as quoted above, seems to demand more of marriage and family therapists than monitoring for whether they harbor personal biases that may produce blatant discrimination or refusal of services. This ethical concept connects to competence and integrity as well. Because therapeutic services to all types of clients should be beneficial, therapists have an obligation to maintain competence and to stay abreast of new developments in the field, which includes understanding the dynamics of diverse client life conditions and situations.

Using these ethical concepts as an aspirational goal and for preventing potential violations, therapists can monitor themselves for subtle discrimination that may lead to inferior services that do not meet the standard of promoting the client's welfare. In other words, the therapy may not reflect sufficient professional knowledge of the client's characteristics or sensitivity to these in relation to presenting problems. Offering a poor quality of service that is not beneficial and may reflect discrimination could trigger an ethics complaint. This issue is exemplified in the following case example.

<u>Adam and Andrew</u>. Adam and Andrew, a gay couple in their late 20s, went to see a marriage and family therapist about Adam's panic symptoms that had begun with his new job and the couple's recent move to a new state. Adam's problems were creating a strain on his relationship with Andrew, who went to treatment with Adam to support him.

In the initial session, the marriage and family therapist focused on their gay identity: when they came out, how long they had been together, and how they got along. By the end of the session, the therapist had not asked Adam about the specific panic symptoms he had experienced—their severity, how long he had been experiencing them, when and where they occurred, or how he coped with them. When the therapist attempted to set the next appointment, Adam said he would not be returning.

In the case of Adam and Andrew, the therapist failed to apply relevant knowledge and skills for assessing the client's presenting mental health problem and instead focused on his sexual orientation. The emphasis, perhaps based on the hypothesis that Adam's sexual orientation was the cause of the problem, apparently interfered with the therapist's ability to hear and acknowledge the client's major reason for seeking professional services. Whether the therapist's conduct of the session came from a subtle bias about gays or from lack of knowledge about both gays and mental health symptoms, the client clearly felt that the session was not beneficial and did not reflect therapeutic competence. Minority persons often voice the complaint about therapists in general, "It should not be my responsibility to educate therapists about my condition, race, orientation, etc."

THE CLIENT'S RIGHT AND RESPONSIBILITY TO MAKE PERSONAL DECISIONS

A basic assumption of interpersonal therapy, regardless of which professional discipline provides it, has long been that clients have the right and responsibility to make their own personal decisions. Yet for logical and understandable reasons, many qualifiers and exceptions surround this assumption; and often more questions than answers abound.

In the AAMFT ethics code, Subprinciple 1.8 states

> *Marriage and family therapists respect the rights of clients to make decisions and help them to understand the consequences of these decisions. Therapists clearly advise the clients that they have the responsibility to make decisions regarding relationships such as cohabitation, marriage, divorce, separation, reconciliation, custody, and visitation.*

This ethical guideline specifically emphasizes that therapy helps clients make their own decisions. The second statement calls for therapists to "advise" clients of their responsibility to make their own decisions about "relationships." The implication is that this reminder to clients is needed because of the possibility that some clients may want therapists to make decisions for them and because some therapists might too readily oblige. It is important to note the specific focus given to decisions about intimate and marital relationships, their dissolution, and related decisions affecting children.

This additional warning no doubt also speaks to another piece of therapeutic reality; namely, relationship problems are a common issue in marriage and family therapy; and, moreover, intimate relationships involve many value-laden assumptions held by society, clients, therapists, and theories of human behavior and therapy. In other words, the risk is high for therapists to influence client values about intimate relationships in an inappropriate way and perhaps infringe on their right to make personal decisions about these. Beyond the fact that clients hold the "right" to make personal decisions, most models of therapy also assume that a therapeutic process that empowers clients to make their own informed decisions benefits them. In the short-term, the clients reach a decision that should help resolve a problem. In the long-term, the process should strengthen them for future problem solving and decision making.

The ethics involved in the client's right to make personal decisions encompasses not only ethical principles but also values, virtues possessed by or desired for therapists and clients, and value assumptions within various theories of human behavior and theories of therapy. The following case example illustrates many of these complex issues and ethical risks around the client's right to make decisions.

Deanna. Deanna, a 40-year old Caucasian woman, went to a family counseling agency because "she needed someone to talk to." She reluctantly began by saying that, about one month before, she got divorced from Tom, her husband of 21 years. It was the first marriage for both of them, and they had two teenage sons, Brad (19) and John (16). She said she loved her sons very much, but about 8 months prior, she moved out of the house and left them with their dad while she decided about the divorce. She felt very guilty about that, but she still saw them regularly. She said everything about her life was "up in the air."

Deanna said the worst thing right then was that she'd had an abortion two months before and she "couldn't deal with this." It was all she thought about: "For me it was wrong, but what else could I do? I got pregnant with a man that I hardly knew, even before I was divorced. How could I face my husband and sons with that? My husband would have found out. I work for him as his office manager, and I'm going to continue. It's the only job outside the home that I have ever had since we were married, and Tom knows that he couldn't hire a trustworthy employee to do the job I do."

Deanna went on to explain that she had met Sean (age 37) shortly after she had separated from her husband. They met at a bar, and after several drinks, she invited him to her apartment, where they had sexual intercourse. She never told him about the pregnancy or abortion. Since then they continued to spend a lot of time together, and Sean began to resent the time she wanted to spend with her sons,. He wanted her to move in with him, and talked of marriage and having a family. He was unemployed at the time, and had quit two jobs in the previous six months. He bitterly complained that he lost his family as a result of his divorce. Deanna worried then about what would happen if Sean ever found out that she had been pregnant by him and had had an abortion.

Deanna said that she did not really know why she went for the appointment since she did not see any way out, and she could not really afford it. Toward the end of the interview, Deanna asked the therapist directly whether she should continue the relationship with Sean. At the next session, Deanna began by saying that she thought she might be pregnant again.

The case of Deanna presents a client facing many personal decisions that appear in the first session and others that would likely arise in the course of therapy. She had already made some decisions—to divorce Tom, to have unprotected sex with Sean, to have an abortion, to keep it a secret, to keep working for her husband, to spend time with Sean, and to keep having unprotected sex with him. Other possible future decisions were whether and how to spend time with her sons, whether to move in with Sean and contribute financial support to this unemployed partner, and whether to continue the relationship with him.

As suggested in Chapter One, values permeate therapy because all therapy involves value-laden goals. In therapy, "good" or "desirable" goals, behaviors, and outcomes for clients are primarily expressed in not so much moral terms but as "psychological virtues," such as the client will become more "effective or successful in life," have "improved mental health," be more "insightful," have "healthy relationships," etc. (Tjeltveit, 1999). Thus with Deanna, one client goal to be negotiated might be for her to consider more consciously the range of choices she has, including the relationship with Sean, and to evaluate choices in terms of all of her needs, and attempt to predict the consequences of different choices. Another goal might be for her to pursue behaviors that improve her sense of well being, mood, happiness, and the kind of relationship she wants with her sons and her ex-husband.

Because of so many value-laden issues and the emotionality surrounding these matters, this case is fraught with numerous ethical risks to the client's right to make personal decisions. For example, Deanna appears either uninformed or conflicted about protecting herself from pregnancy and sexually transmitted diseases. If her overall well being, mood, and happiness are goals, this issue merits careful exploration, information, and promoting decision-making. These therapeutic methods should result in a meaningful decision, whereas the therapist's direct advice for Deanna to go get birth control, to stop having sex with Sean, or to insist that Sean use condoms would be an ethical mistake, as well as probably ineffective. The same analysis applies to the decision that Deanna faces about Sean. Although research on divorce documents the vulnerability of persons in the early stages of divorce, it also finds that new social and love relationships help divorced persons who are experiencing low self esteem. In other words, making a decision about the relationship with Sean also calls for both informing Deanna about divorce adjustment and guiding her to explore and evaluate what she needs in this present relationship and possibly future relationships. Again, direct advice from the therapist as to whether she should continue the relationship would be a therapeutic mistake and an ethical violation.

Violations of the client's right to make personal decisions are probably more common than marriage and family therapists prefer to acknowledge. Clients often suggest to a new therapist, as well as to family and friends, that therapists have told them in direct terms what they should do; e.g., "go back to your wife," "you need to divorce the guy," "don't go back," "you should stop the visits," and "there is no reason for you to move out of that house." Although not all clients are equally credible when it comes to reports about previous therapy, such comments suggest that client decisions are fraught with ethical minefields.

Marriage and family therapists need to monitor closely whether they are becoming strongly aligned with the client's making a certain choice regarding a personal decision. The stronger the therapist's emotional reaction, the more likely it comes from within his or her own personal experience or values—rather than based on authoritative theory and research—and the greater the risk for an ethical violation.

Under these emotional circumstances, even the marriage and family therapist who is striving to maintain neutrality and allow the client to arrive at the decision may say the wrong thing out of personal frustration. This occurrence means that the therapist is not giving priority to the client's welfare. Life decisions belong to the client, and the therapist's comfort level should not take center stage without regard to helping the client explore and evaluate the expected benefits of different choices.

Obviously, a high level of clinical judgment must go into working with clients who are struggling with critical life decisions. Sound clinical judgment draws upon knowledge, theory, skills, and personal awareness and integrity. Clinical judgment plays a part in every aspect of therapy: selecting and applying intervention strategies that are expected to help with the client's problem, evaluating progress, identifying barriers, redefining goals, and monitoring self for whether one is providing beneficial and ethical therapy.

Both professional competence and integrity must be on active duty to help marriage and family therapists make sound clinical judgments that prevent their over-stepping and pushing a decision on a client. A strong commitment to this ethical principle is necessary since marriage and family therapists may use theoretical rationales and methods to mask their more personal motivations for asserting inappropriate influence on a client's decision making.

Another reason a marriage and family therapist may infringe on the client's right to make decisions is the lack of adequate behavioral science knowledge about a matter being dealt with in therapy. For a therapist to function adequately, it is important to have knowledge of research on life stages, normal transitions, health risks, and family crises (e.g., divorce, separation, or custody/visitation arrangements). Without up-to-date, accurate, academically based knowledge, a therapist's personal moral/religious beliefs and personal experience are more likely to fill the knowledge vacuum.

Working effectively for the client's welfare requires a solid body of academic knowledge about human behavior and problems. Combining academic knowledge, practice skills, and professional integrity enables the marriage and family therapist to carry out this central responsibility to the client. The integration of academic knowledge, practice skills, and professional integrity is reflected in the following case.

  Ben and Barbara. Ben and Barbara, both age 40, went to a therapist on referral from another therapist who felt frustrated by the couple's situation and unable to be helpful. Ben was involved in an extramarital sexual affair, his second in the past six months. These behaviors had occurred following his recovery from quadruple bypass surgery. Although Barbara wanted to work on the marriage, Ben indicated that he was not ready to end the affair and that Barbara should use therapy to deal with her own sexuality. Ben had no intention, however, of moving toward divorce, and he did not want Barbara to mention their marital problems to anyone in their families.

The therapist agreed to do individual work with each partner. Ben attended six sessions, then stopped going. Barbara continued and remained focused on herself and her marriage. She reported that Ben had later gone to see another therapist who told him, during their one and only session, that he should go back to Barbara and that he was ruining his life and marriage. Barbara continued to work with Ben in their joint business and to live in the same house with him.

Only gradually, over a period of months, did Barbara begin to make small decisions, such as not covering for Ben in their joint business, asking him to move out, deciding on a visitation schedule for him with their child, moving to another house of her own, and consulting an attorney. Barbara's actual decision to divorce and to take all the necessary steps to finalize it was a process that took nearly two years.

The foregoing case shows two therapists whose frustration or personal values led them to push a decision on Ben (which he promptly ignored). The third therapist enabled Barbara to deal with all the complexities in her life, to evaluate her options, and to move at her own pace in making and executing major life decisions.

Stated bluntly, a therapist should not make a direct recommendation about clients' life decisions. Rather, enabling the client to consider and evaluate information and options is more likely to produce a decision that the client understands and accepts, regardless of the outcome.

THE CLIENT'S RIGHT TO BENEFICIAL SERVICES

The concept of beneficial services is suggested in two places in the AAMFT ethics code. First, it appears under the broad Principle I: Responsibility to Clients, which tells marriage and family therapists to "make reasonable efforts to ensure that their services are used appropriately." This guideline is quite general. It implies that the marriage and family therapist give professional consideration first to the nature of services that will benefit the client; and second, to evaluating that the professional services are meeting the intended goal of helping the client.

In general, this guideline suggests several possible standards of practice for marriage and family therapists. They should offer treatment services that are professionally judged as potentially appropriate to the client's idiosyncratic problems and needs. Therapists should recognize when other types of services are needed or more pressing than therapy; for example, medical, legal, residential or inpatient, or specialized treatment such as for addictions, etc. Also, therapists should assist in obtaining services, as specifically required by Subprinciple 1.10, and take special care not to "abandon or neglect clients" in this process as required by Subprinciple 1.11).

As a starting strategy, therapists should develop a treatment plan with which to evaluate progress and the client's appropriate use of services. They should monitor for ineffective interventions or those that cause deterioration in the client's situation and, of course, discontinue these and seek alternate methods. They should also monitor whether one family member consciously distorts or sabotages the therapeutic contract, violates it, or inappropriately uses the treatment process against another family member or other person.

The second reference to beneficial services in the AAMFT ethics code appears in Subprinciple 1.9. It states, "Marriage and family therapists continue therapeutic relationships only so long as it is reasonably clear that clients are benefiting from the relationship." This guideline means that therapeutic services should clearly benefit clients, and it would seem to apply from the beginning to the end of the process. Here the specific focus, however, appears to warn against continuing beyond a point when the therapist should be more carefully evaluating whether the professional services are beneficial and still focused on advancing the client's welfare. It also conveys that an ethical breach occurs if the therapist ignores the client's situation and need, and therapy moves toward benefiting the therapist, be it financially, socially, or emotionally.

Failing to heed the larger intent of this subprinciple—whether at the beginning or end stages of therapy—carries serious ethical risks. It means that the marriage and family therapist is accountable for monitoring the client's progress at all times and at all stages. Monitoring implies that the therapist pays close attention to whether the services are actually benefiting the client. Evaluating for benefits requires a careful assessment, a treatment plan, specific interventions, obtaining feedback on outcomes, and evaluating the client's progress from the interventions provided. These are components that will allow evaluation of actual benefits from the beginning of therapy to an agreed-upon end point.

Ethical violations can occur when therapy continues without a clear therapeutic contract that defines the nature of problems, goals, and consciously and conscientiously applied therapeutic interventions. In the unfortunate circumstance in which clients lack such clarity, they may continue to appear for sessions with little sense of their purpose. Although intended to be therapeutic, the discussions may come to resemble a social interaction in which the marriage and family therapist seems to function as a friend. The therapist appears to have given up on providing a meaningful therapeutic experience that focuses on remedying the client's problems. Such a situation could evolve from the loss of focus on agreed-upon client goals, lack of competence, or the failure of the therapist's integrity. Regarding integrity, therapists must make sure that they "do not use their professional relationships with clients to further their own interests" (Subprinciple 1.7) and that they "continue therapeutic relationships only so long as it is reasonably clear that clients are benefiting from the relationship" (Subprinciple 1.9).

Therapists should seek direct feedback as to the clients' views of the therapy and whether it is helpful. It is essential to document the benefits that clients report and both their positive and negative views of therapy or the therapist.

On a national television talk show, the host and guests all gave examples of how each of their respective therapists had, in some way, kept him or her in treatment beyond any legitimate reason. These consumers gave examples of how the therapist attempted to extend the number of treatment sessions, presumably for financial gain (or possibly for the ego gratification for providing treatment to a celebrity).

Marriage and family therapy sessions typically and appropriately review how the services are proceeding (e.g., bringing positive changes in the client's life, relief from symptoms and problems, and improvement in mood and life relationships); and the outcomes are used to further guide interventions. Beyond documenting good results, therapists should also explore directly for client's potential doubts and complaints about therapy. Promptly dealing with and resolving these can prevent later ethical problems. If a good resolution is not possible, then the therapist has an ethical obligation to evaluate whether therapy should continue, can still be beneficial, or needs to be terminated along with a referral to another therapist.

INFORMED CONSENT

Informed consent is another ethical principle that supports therapists in carrying out their overriding responsibility to provide therapy that advances the welfare of clients through providing beneficial services and through protecting their rights. As this discussion argues, obtaining informed consent should be seen as a procedure that strengthens the therapeutic endeavor, not as an imposition on the therapist's autonomy.

The concept of informed consent is a familiar one, and the general public encounters it regularly in medical services. The AAMFT ethics code offers an extensive set of guidelines for obtaining clients' consent to therapeutic services. Since the previous AAMFT ethics code (AAMFT, 1998) mentioned informed consent only in the context of requiring clients' written consent before videotaping, audio recording, or permitting third party observation (which also remains), the following current Subprinciple 1.2 merits close attention:

Marriage and family therapists obtain appropriate informed consent to therapy or related procedures as early as is feasible in the therapeutic relationship, and use language that is reasonably understandable to clients. The content of informed consent may vary depending upon the client and treatment plan; however, informed consent generally necessitates that the client: (a) has the capacity to consent; (b) has been adequately informed of significant information concerning treatment processes, procedures; (c) has been adequately informed of potential risks and benefits of treatments for which generally recognized standards do not yet exist; (d) has freely and without undue influence expressed consent; and (e) has provided consent that is appropriately documented. When persons, due to age or mental status, are legally incapable of giving informed consent, marriage and family therapists obtain informed permission from a legally authorized person, if such substitute consent is legally permissible.

This multifaceted stance merits special study, acceptance, and implementation by every marriage and family therapist.

Clarifying the Basics of Informed Consent

Subprinciple 1.2 safeguards clients by making sure that they are capable of consenting, that they understand how the process of therapy is expected to help them, that they freely and without undue influence express consent, and that consent is documented. On the one hand, some degree of flexibility seems permitted from the statement that the content of informed consent may vary depending upon the client and treatment. On the other hand, specific elements of consent are also present and deemed to be essential.

It is notable that Subprinciple 1.2 mentions a treatment plan. This statement assumes the presence of a treatment plan, without stating, however, that there must be a treatment plan. This interpretation also finds support in a later statement suggesting elements of a treatment plan; namely, that to consent, the client must have been adequately informed with "significant information concerning treatment processes and procedures" and "informed of potential risks and benefits of treatments for which generally recognized standards do not yet exist."

Clearly, this guideline implies the need for and value of a treatment plan but is still general enough to allow for the therapist's judgment about what constitutes "significant" information about treatment procedures and processes. It does require thought, however, about which treatments do not have generally recognized standards for benefits and risks, but again seemingly relies on the therapist's competence and integrity for determining which treatments might fall into this category and what constitutes "generally recognized standards." Chapter Nine comments that the following might fit that category: Eye Movement Desensitization Reprocessing (EMDR), Thought Field Therapy (TFT), and Breath Work. Relatedly, techniques for hypnosis and recovered memories of abuse are also controversial, and seemingly lack recognized standards (Knapp & VandeCreek, 1997).

There is no requirement per se for a written, signed consent, but the procedures for obtaining consent must use language that is reasonably understandable to clients; and the client's expressed consent must be documented, presumably in the client's file. For example, in cognitive-behavioral models, including marital and family interventions, the straightforward feedback/assessment discussion presented to clients might meet the standards for informed consent, along with notes showing the client's acceptance of or compliance with the ongoing tasks or homework that the therapist presents to them. As "early as feasible in the therapeutic relationship," the therapist should have some focused verbal discussion with the client about the plan for therapy and should obtain the client's agreement to this. Perhaps the most acceptable and preferred option might be the presence of a written treatment plan in the client's file and ongoing documentation of the client's expressed consent and active participation or cooperation with the plan.

Informed consent in the AAMFT ethics code is not a protection limited solely to the beginning stages of marriage and family therapy, and it may need to be obtained at various points in therapy. Clients' goals for being in therapy can change, and, accordingly, therapy procedures and processes may change. For example, marriage and family therapists may routinely use several different models of treatment and a variety of formats in working with couples and families. This is true in several models of couple therapy that routinely use both conjoint and individual sessions. In such cases, partners need to know whether all sessions are focused on improving their relationship, whether sessions might involve an intensive focus on emotions or on setting homework tasks, whether a spouse's presence is required for dealing with the relationship within the context of so-called "spouse-aided therapy," such as for helping a partner with agoraphobia, etc. If therapy goals and formats change, obtaining further independent informed consent is needed.

Updating the client's consent would be wise, perhaps even essential, if the focus shifts from, say, couple therapy to individual therapy. A couple would need to understand the purpose of this shift, the goals for partners if they are in individual therapy, whether treatment will return at some point to couple therapy, and the limits of confidentiality. If individual therapy does not remain clearly connected to the couple's relationship or if one partner's individual personal goals become the focus, an ethical response is to tell clients that one of the risks of individual therapy is that it may result in a further weakening of the relationship. The ethical therapist would want the client to know this information that is relevant to consenting to individual therapy under these circumstances. This situation is different from the obligation to explain risks and benefits for treatments for which no generally recognized standards exist (an issue noted above).

Similarly, although a child's problems may bring a family to therapy, sometimes the focus shifts to working with parents around such problems as their relationship, sexual concerns, mental health disorders, etc. A reverse shift may also occur, with children entering into therapy following previous sessions that focused on marital or couple issues.

Needless to say, if the treatment plan undergoes change, clients need a clear understanding of the new focus so that they can, in fact, give informed consent. The information that is needed for informed consent will, of course, depend on the person's characteristics (e.g., explaining the treatment plan to a child would be different from explaining it to an adult).

The issue of informed consent becomes complicated with models of therapy and strategies that are not designed to be shared with or explained to clients. For example, the potential success of some strategic and solution-oriented strategies appears to depend on not explaining techniques to clients. The AAMFT ethics code relies on the therapist's competence and integrity for deciding what might be "significant information concerning treatment processes and procedures" to provide clients before they give their consent. Given this general guideline, there are bound to be differences of opinion among professionals on exactly what constitutes "significant" information.

An example of an intervention strategy based on withholding explanation was the subject of an ethical/legal critique several years ago (Woody & Woody, 1988). The case, reported by Bobele (1987), focused on a woman in her mid-30s who was involved with her boyfriend with whom she fought. He was repeatedly violent and had twice fired shots in her direction. The treatment team deliberately chose not to respond to her fear, and ignored the data about the boyfriend's violent, impulsive history, as told by the woman. The final statement of the intervention with her was: "You may have to stand in front of his loaded gun and let him pull the trigger so that he will understand that you love him so much you would be willing to give up your life to prove your love for him" (p. 231).

In this case, the Bobele team gave the directive without further explanation to increase the chance that its very extremeness would paradoxically lead the client to see the problem in a new context. The theoretical assumptions of such strategies are in apparent contradiction to the ethical guideline that clients should understand the therapeutic "processes and procedures" and freely give informed consent to these (Woody & Woody, 1988, p. 134; also see Bobele, 1988, for a reply to the preceding article). Professionals will likely continue debating which treatments need to be discussed before clients give consent because they do not have generally recognized standards for benefits and risks. The AAMFT ethics code demands that the individual practitioner consider the issue and seek guidance from both the professional literature and from supervision.

Informed consent becomes more complex in situations in which the client or one family member perhaps is quite opposed to participating in therapy, or is required to participate because of legal mandates. For example, a husband may say that he wants no part of therapy, although he is willing for his wife to attend; or an adolescent may refuse to attend with the family; or a perpetrator may be court-ordered to attend therapy for sexual abuse of a family member. In such cases, the therapist often uses persuasion to gain cooperation—but the persuasion must not reach the level of undue influence or coercion. Under these circumstances, a wise course would be to make sure the client gives consent according to all of the conditions stated above.

Beyond the Basics of Informed Consent

The issue of informed consent affects cases in which a third party requests service for a person or entity, who may be either willing or involuntarily constrained to attend. Subprinciple 1.13 states, "Marriage and family therapists, upon agreeing to provide services to a person or entity at the request of a third party, clarify, to the extent feasible and at the outset of the service, the nature of the relationship with each party and the limits of confidentiality." Such a circumstance involves asserting that one's primary responsibility is to the client, offering a clear treatment plan, and obtaining informed consent from the party or parties that have the right to consent.

Although a third party requests the service (and perhaps pays for it), the marriage and family therapist owes primary allegiance to the client(s) in therapy and is responsible to work to promote that client's welfare. Obtaining freely given consent according to all of the guidelines in Subprinciple 1.2 would be especially important in such a case. For example, an insurance company, or an attorney representing a client in a lawsuit or custody battle might request therapy for a client for various purposes, such as to assess the impact of an injury on a person's marital relationship or family, to strengthen emotional and cognitive functioning in preparation for a court appearance, etc.

The marriage and family therapist needs to have a clear contract with the third party at the outset to specify the therapist's role and obligations. This contract is essential if the therapist is to obtain a meaningful and freely given informed consent from the client. It allows the therapist to ensure that the client understands the nature of the therapy (specifically a treatment plan), accepts the terms of the third party's involvement, and freely gives consent.

Given the intrusion of managed care and insurance companies into the healthcare industry, the marriage and family therapist may encounter conflicting expectations. For example, although the client may want, need, and expect certain things in treatment, the third-party source may specify something different (e.g., the treatment modality, the number of authorized sessions, the release of confidential information, etc.).

If a therapist gets caught in the conflict between differing expectations from a client and a third-party payment (or other non-client) source, an ethical dilemma may arise. The bottom line is three-fold.

(1) The third-party source, even if it is making the payment, cannot negate the rights of the person who receives the professional service.

(2) The primary allegiance of the therapist should be with the person(s) who participate(s) in the professional service.

(3) The duty to take legal action, when there is a deadlock or stalemate, rests with the client and the third-party payment source, not the marriage and family therapist.

Clearly, the practitioner should carefully adhere to the ethical obligations discussed previously and prevent getting caught in a dispute or legal fray.

As an ethic, the responsibility to obtain informed consent for treatment is a new and important ethical obligation for marriage and family therapists. As such, it may elicit concerns about how to implement it, along with all the many other demands of therapeutic services. Once again, as this chapter has argued throughout, therapists cannot meet their responsibility to advance the client's welfare without a high level of commitment to professional competence and integrity. These qualities will guide the practitioner on how to gain consent in an effective and ethically sound manner.

Clearly, professional knowledge of theory and practice must guide the process of assessment, and considerable therapeutic competence and skill are necessary to translate a treatment plan into ordinary language to present to the client. Integrity plays a role here also because the therapist must truly value the client's right to give consent and not see this as any infringement on professional autonomy. In fact, the basic ethical concept of justice can be instructive: if the therapist were in the role of client, he or she would no doubt want and claim the right to consent to treatment. (See Chapter Nine, which recommends the use of a written form that the client signs as documentation establishing the client's informed consent.)

THE THERAPEUTIC RELATIONSHIP

Many of the subprinciples under Principle I, Responsibility to Clients, convey guidance about situations in which the therapeutic relationship veers off course and starts to benefit the therapist rather than advancing the welfare of the client. Some examples include dual relationships, sexual intimacy with clients, and professional relationships that further the therapist's own interests. Since the basics of professional education emphasize the healing qualities of the relationship, such violations represent serious failure on the part of the therapist. The causes involved in such ethical lapses are many and complex (see Chapter Three, which deals with multiple relationships in marriage and family therapy). As background before discussing these and the AAMFT ethic code's subprinciples, the discussion here briefly reviews the nature of the therapeutic relationship.

Regardless of the theory of therapy, the relationship between the marriage and family therapist and the client implies qualities of a sanctuary. This term denotes a haven from demands and manipulation by others for personal gain at the expense of the client's needs. Although some therapeutic approaches, such as cognitive-behavioral therapy, give less importance to the therapist-client relationship than insight-oriented models, still the nature or conditions of that unique relationship are essential to psychological change. For example, while Lazarus (1981) denied the curative aspects of the therapist-client relationship, he nonetheless acknowledged the value of "client-therapist compatibility," and advised the multimodal therapist to accommodate the unique personal qualities of the client (p. 30). Of course, with insight-oriented theories such as client-centered or object relations/self therapy, the therapeutic relationship is essentially the vehicle of client change (Elson, 1986; Henry, Moffitt, Caspi, Langley, & Silva, 1994; Teyber, 2000). As Trull and Phares (2001) put it, "For some, the nature of the relationship or therapeutic alliance between patient and therapist is the single element most responsible for the success of psychotherapists" (p. 299).

With theories of therapy and professional education placing so much emphasis on the therapeutic power of the relationship, a central question is why practitioners might subvert its noble aims and potential for benefiting the client. Several reasons merit consideration.

ALLIANCE ISSUES UNIQUE TO MARRIAGE AND FAMILY THERAPY

In many practice situations, the marriage and family therapist has a treatment commitment to multiple clients, such as several family members or a couple, rather than to a single person. This condition complicates the nature of the therapeutic relationship. Consequently, it demands a high level of professional competence in the form of academic knowledge and practice skills and a similarly high level of integrity in the form of personal character, maturity, and even wisdom.

Ongoing at any moment is "the therapist's relationship with each family member, with each subsystem, and with the family as a whole" (Nichols & Schwartz, 1998, p. 519). Clearly, the marriage and family therapist has the onus of dealing with more relationship factors than would commonly be present in the treatment of an individual only. In this dynamic and ever-changing context, the therapist must be able to monitor the role that his or her self plays in these relationships and the concomitant interactions, while also monitoring the relational system within the family.

The therapist's professional and personal self constitutes a central component in the newly created therapeutic social system. He or she functions as both a participant and observer, a fact that complicates the role of monitoring self. The therapist's personal characteristics come to bear on both roles. Specifically, "what the therapist does reflects not only what he or she believes, but also who he or she is"; thus "personal style will have a large impact on his or her posture with families" (Nichols & Schwartz, 1998, p. 479). Other aspects of the therapist's self that operate within therapy include "the personality of the therapist" (Worden, 1999, p. 179) and the therapist's "view of human nature" (Nichols & Schwartz, 1998, p. 481).

Given the presence of the highly personal self-related factors in the therapeutic relationship, professional competence and integrity become critical ingredients for keeping the therapeutic relationship as it should be, namely, devoted to advancing the welfare of the family and its members. A variety of academic knowledge bases can assist in this process.

One of the great values of object relations/self theory is its focus on the deep-level psychic needs of both the client and the practitioner. When the marriage and family therapist's self and functioning in relationships are impaired, he or she may excessively or obsessively approach others, even clients, for support, admiration, love, control, etc., in an attempt to heal developmental wounds or disown personal deficits. Under such circumstances, the marriage and family therapist experiences strong countertransference coming from his or her own issues. A life-long commitment to self-awareness and personal growth is essential in monitoring the therapeutic relationship and avoiding ethical violations. Participating in an ongoing regimen of supervision is recommended for monitoring the quality of one's therapeutic services. (See Chapter Four for further discussion of supervision for marriage and family therapists.)

While monitoring for his or her own personal countertransference issues, the marriage and family therapist must also manage the transference responses of family members toward the therapist and toward each other (Elson, 1986; Teyber, 2000). The family's relational system has long been the focus of marriage and family therapy models. Professional competence demands the use of theoretical knowledge for understanding of the systemic characteristics and dynamics within the family in treatment. It is necessary to understand system and subsystem structure and functioning, the impact of the sociocultural environment on families, and the interface between the family system and the individual (J. Woody, 1992).

Other concepts may also be useful for unraveling the interplay between family dynamics, the moral context, and the therapeutic alliance. For example, the theoretical principles of relational ethics set forth in the contextual-theory view of Boszormenyi-Nagy (1987) hold that relational ethics bind each family member's welfare with that of the welfare of all other family members. Relational ethics "have to do with the dynamics of the family and the degree to which there is concern for and consideration of the welfare of others within the family" (Becvar & Becvar, 2000, p. 169).

As the previous discussion suggests, moral issues, which are usually unacknowledged, are pervasive in virtually all types of therapy, but are especially apt to emerge in marital and family therapy. Marriage and family therapists must filter their own moral personae and the moral context of the family through the lens of theoretical models and strategies, which in turn have moral components.

A high degree of professional competence in applying relevant theories of therapy, in conjunction with professional integrity, bolstered by the AAMFT ethics code, can help marriage and family therapists stay attuned to the complex alliance issues unique to marriage and family therapy. Because the therapist has a dual responsibility to the family system as well as to the individuals, maneuvering back and forth between these therapeutic alliances can create ethical challenges. For example, the therapist needs to gain a balanced understanding of the family's and each individual's dynamics; carefully assess family members' commitment to each other's welfare; participate, in accord with client goals, to strengthen family bonds within the client system; show concern for the interests and welfare of all family members, while also remaining aware of any serious oppression of individuals within the family system. The therapist must also continually monitor for imposing personal values and self needs or interests above the interests and welfare of clients. In all of these therapeutic activities the unique alliance issues call for vigilance to be sure the therapist stays on track to work for the agreed-upon therapeutic and client goals.

THE CROWD IN THE THERAPY ROOM

With the ongoing development and evolution of theories and strategies of marriage and family therapy, therapists must consider the impact of and possibly intervene with systems outside the immediate therapeutic alliance with the family system. Treatment strategies have often focused on including not only extended family but also neighborhood/community contexts and the peers of youths in therapy (Speck & Attneave, 1973; Laszloffy, 2000).

In an approach called "community family therapy," Sells (2000) drew on the model of settlement houses in which families receive services designed and run collaboratively by both residents and outsiders (presumably professionals). A given family session might include ten or more people, such as elders, neighbors, peers, and ministers to help a parent and child with the family's problems. Many ethical concerns arise with this expanded concept of traditional therapy, and they merit careful attention if professional practitioners are part of the intervention "team." Among the most important concerns are the professional's responsibility for the welfare of the client versus the responsibility of community helpers, maintaining central focus on a given client or client family, the nature of the therapeutic relationship, the nature of a treatment plan under this format, informed consent, and confidentiality.

Even without innovative strategies that bring in a network of persons as therapeutic aides, therapists have always had to consider the presence and power of outside agents or contexts that impact the family in treatment and potentially dilute the power of the therapeutic relationship. For example, therapists may rightly need to incorporate issues and other professional personnel relevant to schools, youth placement sources, child protection agencies, the criminal justice system, and domestic legal actions and the courts. Often one or several of these systems are significant factors in a couple's or family's problems, and as such, they complicate the ethical obligations involved in the therapeutic alliance and in providing treatment.

Other potential threats to the sanctity of the therapeutic alliance come from the often-intrusive stance taken by payment sources such as insurance companies and HMOs. The widely accepted sense of uniqueness and privacy accorded to the therapeutic alliance appears diluted by current trends in public policy and law that increasingly demand the therapist's clinical records. These factors complicate the task of building and maintaining an effective therapeutic alliance; the professional must constantly strengthen competency and integrity to stay the course and give primacy to the client's welfare.

As an example of an invasion of the therapeutic alliance by a third-party payment source, a therapist provided treatment to a couple, in which the female refused to allow release of her clinical records to the managed care company. In turn, the managed care company withheld payment to the therapist. Company officials pointed out that they had approved the therapist as a provider, in part, on condition that she submit records upon request, and that they had granted the client services, in part, on condition that she allow her clinical records to be sent to the third-party payment source. Stymied by the intractability of the female client and the managed care company, the therapist resigned from the managed care panel, telling the female client that she could begin making self-payments or the therapist would refer her to a different therapist.

This examination of the therapeutic relationship provides an important backdrop for the following analysis of the AAMFT ethics code's Principle II: Confidentiality. Besides the therapeutic relationship, the previously discussed sections will also help with the duty to maintain confidentiality. That is, adhering to the principles and subprinciples relevant to confidentiality comes more easily when marriage and family therapists remain firm and faithful to their responsibility to clients and work within a clear therapeutic contract to which clients give informed consent.

CONFIDENTIALITY: ETHICAL OBLIGATIONS

Just as with informed consent, the ethical principle of confidentiality is essential if therapy is to carry out its primary responsibility to advance the welfare of families and individuals. The importance of confidentiality to this goal stems from the nature of the therapeutic contract. That is, the client agrees to reveal highly personal information—thus placing himself or herself in a vulnerable position—on condition that the therapist agrees to provide help for these personal matters and at the same time respect the client's rights, such as the right to privacy and the right not to be harmed. (See Chapter Nine for a detailed discussion of confidentiality in terms of day-to-day practice management and procedures.)

Because the highly personal communications inherently place the client in a vulnerable position, society accepted that there would be societal benefits from protecting these communications and assuring that they remain within the confines of the therapeutic relationship. According to both theory and research, confidentiality is assumed to be essential to the effectiveness of therapy:

Confidentiality is the cornerstone of the psychotherapy process. Therefore, patients have the right to be guaranteed the protection of the confidentiality of their relationship with a psychologist, except when laws or ethics dictate otherwise. (Cantor, 1998, p. 189)

The mental health professions are, however, being mandated legally to weaken confidentiality and to become (perhaps unwillingly) participants in situations that may be counter to the clinical interests of their clients (Bollas & Sundelson, 1995).

Privileged communication and confidentiality both came from the right of privacy, but the two terms are distinguishable:

Confidentiality is the ethical duty to fulfill a contract or promise to clients that the information revealed during therapy will be protected from unauthorized disclosure.

Privileged communication is a client's legal right, guaranteed by state statute, that confidences originating in a therapeutic relationship will be safeguarded during certain court proceedings. Even if counselor-client relationships are not privileged by statute, counselors still owe clients the ethical obligation of confidentiality. (Arthur & Swanson, 1993, p. 7)

In the AAMFT ethics code, Principle II deals with confidentiality. The legal concept of privileged communication, however, will arise when the marriage and family therapist provides testimony or records for legal proceedings.

Guidance from the AAMFT Ethics Code

Regarding confidentiality, the AAMFT ethics code offers significant guidance to practitioners. Understanding the guidelines, some of which are quite specific, can help marriage and family therapists manage confidentiality issues to protect their clients and their own practice.

Marriage and family therapists have an ethical responsibility to clarify confidentiality issues, to do so early, to do so repeatedly as circumstances may require, and to include not only the client in this clarification but also other interested parties. Subprinciple 2.1 states

Marriage and family therapists disclose to clients and other interested parties, as early as feasible in their professional contacts, the nature of confidentiality and possible limitations of the client's right to confidentiality. Therapists review with clients the circumstances where confidential information may be requested and where disclosure of confidential information may be legally required. Circumstances may necessitate repeated disclosures.

This subprinciple emphasizes that the therapist has the specific obligation to review any confidentiality matter, including possible and actual exceptions, to ensure that the client has full understanding.

Subprinciple 2.2 of the AAMFT ethics code specifies in general terms the ethically and legally safe procedures to follow for the exceptions to confidentiality. Thus, disclosure of client confidences may not take place "except by written authorization or waiver, or where permitted or mandated by law." Specific exceptions due to legal mandates are not mentioned as they were in the 1998 AAMFT ethics code (such as to prevent clear and immediate danger to a person or persons). The reason is that legal jurisdictions vary on such mandates; however, the AAMFT ethics code requires the marriage and family therapist to assume responsibility for knowing the applicable jurisdictional law and to use attorney advice for exceptions. For example, mental health records and information may not be confidential if the client is connected to a threat of physical harm to self or others; alleged abuse or neglect of a protected class of person, such as a child or a disabled or a senior person; a possible mandatory hospitalization; or a court order for any reason. (For situations of abuse, violence, and dangerousness, Chapter Seven discusses in detail the therapist's ethical and legal obligations.)

The major emphasis throughout Subprinciple 2.2 is on gaining the client's written authorization, including from individual family members competent to provide it. It specifically warns against the use of a client's verbal authorization: "Verbal authorization will not be sufficient except in emergency situations, unless prohibited by law." With regard to disclosing "information" to any source outside the treatment context, this cannot be done "without written authorization from each individual who is competent to execute a waiver."

When it comes to sharing information within the client unit, the guideline again specifies obtaining written permission of that individual; however, some further interpretation is needed as the guideline states that the "therapist may not reveal any individual's <u>confidences</u> to others in the client unit . . . ." The term <u>confidences</u> is not as broad as <u>information</u> and should be clarified between the therapist and client. For example, is all information discussed in an individual session considered confidential or only that which the client says is confidential and not to be shared? The need to clarify these details also relates to informed consent as well as to the therapist's ability to provide effective therapy.

Because both confidentiality and informed consent are interrelated and need to be discussed early in treatment, therapists should deal with both of these issues at the beginning of treatment and not wait for an ethical problem to arise. When working with a couple, a marital unit, a family with small or adolescent children, or perhaps even grandparents, foster parents, or guardians, it is essential to define what is meant by "confidences" to each individual client. The therapist and clients need to agree on this term and also on any limitations on confidentiality, not only those mandated by law, but also those that the therapist might set to provide effective treatment. Then if a situation arises of revealing one person's confidences to others in treatment, the terms of the understanding are in place, but the signed authorization of each individual is still required.

Presumably, even a child must give written permission for what can be revealed within the treatment unit, as the phrase "competent to execute a waiver" is <u>not</u> attached to the guideline on sharing confidences within the treatment unit. Among the most common issues pertaining to confidences for adult partners or family members that may require clarification are: extramarital affairs, commitment to the relationship, sexual activities/preferences/orientation, criminal activities, substance use, and mental states suggesting the risk of violence and dangerousness to self or others. Common issues relating to confidences of children and youth in therapy may include sexual activities/preferences/orientation, mental states suggesting the risk of violence and dangerousness to self or others, and other behaviors that pose potential risks to the child's health and welfare, e.g., truancy, substance use, gang affiliations, etc. (See Chapter Six for discussion of a family therapy model that does not promise confidentiality to aggressive teenagers who are in family therapy.)

To summarize, when the treatment unit includes couples or a family, the prudent therapist will address confidentiality issues clearly and in a straightforward manner early on and take guidance from the AAMFT ethics code, the law, and principles of effective therapeutic intervention. The code is clear about the importance of early and specific, possibly repeated, disclosure to clients regarding all aspects of confidentiality; obtaining written authorization for any disclosure of confidences both to outside sources and to those inside the couple or family unit; and awareness that legally permitted or mandated reasons for exceptions to confidentiality exist. Note that the marriage and family therapist is responsible for knowing about the reasons for these exceptions, although they are not specified in the ethics code.

If there is any potential conflict between the legal and ethical aspects of confidentiality, the Preamble for the AAMFT ethics code states, "Marriage and family therapists comply with the mandates of law, but make known their commitment to the AAMFT Code of Ethics and take steps to resolve the conflict in a responsible manner." (Note that Chapter Six explains potential conflicts between law and ethics regarding the rights of children.)

Another guideline (Subprinciple 2.6) deals in detail with the obligation to maintain confidentiality in specific terms as would apply when a marriage and family therapist consults with colleagues or referral sources. Again, the client's prior written consent is necessary to disclose any "confidential information that could reasonably lead to the identification of the client." In addition, disclosure is limited to only the information necessary for the purposes of consultation.

Confidentiality in Mandatory or Compulsory Treatment

Over the past decade, therapists from all mental health disciplines have become increasingly involved in providing treatment services that are mandatory or compulsory. Such treatment may be required by a variety of sources, for example, the courts, correctional institutions, employers, public human services agencies, attorneys, and insurance companies. The common denominator is that the source has some degree of control over the client (or the client is cooperating, albeit sometimes reluctantly, with the referral source) and thus can require the therapy. Clients mandated to attend therapy may be children, adolescents, adults, or entire families.

Therapists who provide mandatory treatment may work in a variety of settings and encounter a similar variety of client problems. Publicly-funded community agencies, solo practitioners, and private practice groups sometimes contract with the mandating source to provide therapy. Typical problems include those associated with alcohol and drug dependency, driving offenses, youth and adult sex offenses, juvenile antisocial behavior, child abuse and neglect, traumatic job experiences, and mental health problems alleged in legal and insurance claims.

In providing mandatory treatment, therapists need to pay close attention to their ethical obligations to the client, be cognizant of any requirements from the referring or collaborating referral source, and discharge all obligations in a planned and ethical manner. The three primary ethical obligations discussed in this chapter remain the same: providing therapy that aims to advance the client's welfare, obtaining informed consent, and maintaining confidentiality.

Since the compulsory element of treatment may potentially impact all of these obligations, the therapist should, prior to initiating treatment, clarify his or her role and responsibilities with the referral source and the nature of any reports or communications that are required (Koocher & Keith-Spiegel, 1998). Specifying the therapist's role and details about what type of information may be released is essential if the client is to give a true informed consent to treatment. This information also allows the client to provide a valid signed waiver for the release of only the specific type of information noted on the waiver. In other words, the client receives adequate "precounseling notification" of the conditions of treatment and of any required legal or clinical consultation (Cottone & Tarvydas, 1998).

This is sound guidance because, legally there is reason to question the propriety of having someone waive confidentiality without his or her knowing what will be released before the information is actually created. For risk management purposes, it is wise to have the client sign a document acknowledging that clarification has been and the situation is acceptable to the client.

To summarize, in situations of mandatory treatment and mandated release of certain client information, the therapist needs to carry out the ethical obligations of gaining informed consent and obtaining the client's written waiver. Still, there may be occasions in which clients do not want confidential information released, yet find that this is mandated. For example, the court may order parents involved in a custody dispute to participate in evaluation or therapy, specifying that each parent's mental health information (which would otherwise be confidential) will be released to the court and attorneys. In a situation in which a client disputes the court mandates, this type of dispute should remain primarily with the client and his or her attorney to use legal procedures to pursue a remedy.

SUMMARY OF CONFIDENTIALITY OBLIGATIONS

A final important guideline relevant to confidentiality in the AAMFT ethics code details the obligation to store, safeguard, and dispose of client records to maintain confidentiality and to do so "in accord with applicable laws and professional standards" (Subprinciple 2.4). A separate subprinciple, 2.5, specifically applies this same duty in the case of a marriage and family therapist's closing the practice or moving, or in the case of the death of the therapist, "Subsequent to the therapist moving from the area, closing the practice, or upon the death of the therapist, a marriage and family therapist arranges for the storage, transfer, or disposal of client records in ways that maintain confidentiality and safeguard the welfare of clients."

To adhere to these subprinciples, therapists must pay close attention to important everyday office procedures and practices. These include keeping accurate, complete, and up-to-date records; storing them in locked files; training staff who handle client files in the rules of confidentiality; and safeguarding records in cases of office-sharing or having a home-based office. Although these may seem like mundane tasks, they are essential to assuring a high quality of care for clients and sound risk management for the therapist.

Breaches of confidentiality and the ethical and legal dilemmas surrounding them are a common source of ethical complaints and legal actions against marriage and family (and other) therapists. Although the AAMFT ethics code offers rather specific subprinciples and guidance on the issues, further background information may help practitioners better understand confidentiality and make a commitment to implement practice actions to meet this ethical requirement. (See Chapter Nine for practical guidance on confidentiality and subpoenas in terms of day-to-day practice management and procedures to assure adherence to the ethical and legal obligations relevant to confidentiality.)

CONFIDENTIALITY: THEORY, THE LAW, AND THE CHANGING PRACTICE ENVIRONMENT

Confidentiality is one of the most critical and complex components of marriage and family therapy. It is important for therapists to understand how confidentiality as an ethical principle has evolved and continues to change as a result of legal theory, public policy, and the changing practice environment.

LEGAL THEORY UNDERLYING CONFIDENTIALITY

Historically, public policy and, thus, the law, have always deemed the relationship between the therapist and client as unique and deserving special protection. In order for the content of the therapeutic process to qualify for such protection:

(1) the communications must originate in a confidence that they will not be disclosed; (2) this element of confidentiality must be essential to the full and satisfactory maintenance of the relation between the parties; (3) the relation must be one which in the opinion of the community must be sedulously fostered; and (4) the injury that would inure to the relation by disclosure of the communications must be greater than the benefit thereby gained for the correct disposal of litigation. (Wigmore, 1940, p. 531)

As evidenced in the quote, "the opinion of the community" is relevant in determining whether or not particular communications deserve to be considered confidential.

For decades, the law supported that communications occurring between therapist and client merited confidentiality and legal protection, and statutes were passed accordingly. In about the mid-1970s, the idea of guaranteeing absolute confidentiality for the communications within therapy began to change. Especially noteworthy was the case of Tarasoff v. Regents of the University of California (1976), which held that protecting the public from harm may supercede the right to protection of confidentiality for what a client tells a therapist. That is, the therapist may have a duty to breach confidentiality and warn others of a client's expressed intention to cause physical injury. (See Chapter Seven for an extensive discussion of the Tarasoff case.)

Subsequent to the Tarasoff case, a myriad of other cases have dealt with the principle of duty to warn, and it has been tested, refined, and distinguished in a host of jurisdictions. VandeCreek and Knapp (1993) provide a useful review of cases relevant to life-endangering patients.

The changing context of the delivery of mental health services may also weaken the concept of confidentiality. Pressures and intrusions by third-party payment sources, professional licensure regulators, and legal sources can become extreme as they seek more and more information that should rightly be held in confidence. For example, in a complaint against a mental health practitioner, the licensing board often asks for all client records; these may contain information about family members who had no role in initiating the complaint. In spite of a source's seeming power or authority or simply its overwhelming pressure, therapists must never lose sight of the client's right to confidentiality. They must regard any request for access to client records as a red flag alert to confer with an attorney.

THE RIGHT OF PRIVACY

In the acclaimed book, The Right to Privacy, Ellen Alderman and Caroline Kennedy (1995) pointed out correctly that

The word "privacy" does not appear in the United States Constitution. Yet ask anyone and they will tell you that they have a fundamental right to privacy. They will also tell you that privacy is under siege. (p. xiii)

Although the Constitution does not establish a right to privacy, "the Bill of Rights is, by its very nature, a broad affirmation of personal privacy because it limits the government's power to interfere with individual liberty" (Hendricks, Hayden, & Novik, 1990, p. xii).

The right of privacy, which is the basis for according confidentiality to the therapeutic alliance, was apparently first mentioned by legal scholars Warren and Brandeis (1890) in a Harvard Law Review article. They proposed that the invasion of privacy constituted an actionable tort. Perhaps in part because of this scholarly source, the right of privacy was created subsequently by judicial construction. That is, judges ruled in specific cases in a manner that established that persons had a right to privacy that should be protected from governmental intrusion. Berman, Greiner, and Saliba (1996) pinpointed several Constitutional amendments that were precursors for judicial establishment of a right of privacy, notably the First, Third, Fourth, Fifth, Ninth, and Fourteenth Amendments. (See R. Woody, 2001, for details and cases.)

Although created by judicial decisions, the right to privacy has achieved the status of being a "fundamental" right: "Since the right of privacy is a 'fundamental right' and thus triggers strict scrutiny of any ordinance or statute that directly regulates the exercise of that freedom, these cases reflect judicial rulings on the validity of regulatory interests advanced by states and localities and whether such regulatory measures are narrowly tailored" (Ducat & Chase, 1992, p. 530). This means that, as a fundamental right, there must be a compelling reason for invading a person's right to privacy, which could include information contained in health-related records.

The right of privacy connotes that the individual, such as the client who receives marriage and family therapy services, can place limitations on others' invading their lives: "Privacy is important because it preserves and protects individuals as they exercise their freedom to develop their personal identity, choose their values, and shape the course of their lives" (Smith-Bell & Winslade, 1995, p. 145).

In practice, the marriage and family therapist must constantly commit to guarding the privacy rights of clients. There may be unreasonable attempts by others to access information about a client. For example, since employment-related insurance is paying for treatment, an employer may want to know if an employee is progressing in therapy. Family members may inappropriately assert that they should have access to a particular family member's information, such as parents wanting to know what their adult son or daughter said about substance abuse during an individual session. The therapist should help a client carefully consider the decision to agree to reveal information. For example, an adult son or daughter might authorize release of all clinical information to a disturbed parent, even though it is likely that the parent will abuse the client because of the information.

Staff members of the clinical practice need to guard carefully information about clients, including their identities, and take precautions against inadvertent violations of confidentiality. Thus it may be unwise for a secretary to talk to a client on the telephone about his or her clinical information when there are other clients in the waiting room who can hear the conversation. Also, a "domestic violation" of confidentiality might occur if a therapist who talks about cases at home unintentionally mentions details that reveal or suggest a client known to a family member (R. Woody, 1999). Although therapists may appropriately discuss their work in general or types of clients or problems they see, they must consciously guard against situations where confidentiality is treated carelessly.

INTRUSIONS ON AND EXCEPTIONS TO THE RIGHT OF PRIVACY

Today, despite its strong legal protection, "privacy is under siege" (Alderman & Kennedy (1995, p. xiii). The three primary sources of concern seem to be the insurance industry, the government, and the legal system. As will be discussed, each of these sources has a legitimate need and potentially a right to confidential information, such as about a client receiving marriage and family therapy; but the challenge to the practitioner is to avoid undue release of confidential information. Therefore, from the outset of professional services, the marriage and family therapist should help the client recognize the limits of confidentiality, as per Subprinciple 2.1: "Therapists review with clients the circumstances where confidential information may be requested and where disclosure of confidential information may be legally required."

To understand the use of confidential information by the insurance industry, consider the following: "Both to establish an applicant's eligibility for health, life, and disability policies and to process claims under such policies, insurance companies require extensive medical information from the patient's physicians and psychiatrists and from his hospital records" (Hendricks, Hayden, & Novik, 1990, p. 157). The insurance industry has reportedly maintained (since 1902!) a medical information databank that allows insurance companies to exchange medical data.

Because many of the marriage and family therapist's clients will be covered by a health insurance policy, the act of preparing entries in the clinical record should be determined, in part, by what the practitioner believes is necessary and appropriate for the insurance company to access. In some instances, an insurance company may demand more information than is justifiable. It is wise to always allow the client to review entries and to be involved in any decision to release clinical information that could be detrimental to the client's welfare.

Now that mental health professionals are regulated by the government, there must be concern about unwarranted sources obtaining information beyond what is legally justifiable. For example, if a licensing complaint is filed against a marriage and family therapist, the investigator or prosecutor for the licensing board may obtain records that the client or collaterals would not want released. In turn, through inadvertence or otherwise, the licensing board sources might release the information to another agency, such as a national coordinating source for licensing boards. Perhaps this kind of usage serves a positive purpose, but it also potentially infringes on the confidentiality rights of the persons who are receiving marriage and family therapy.

On its face, a licensing law for mental health practitioners (including, of course, licensed marriage and family therapists) is honorable. Such laws are intended to protect clients and practitioners alike. Thus, the release of certain amounts and kinds of information can, no doubt, be justified. The problem arises when the justifiable purpose is subverted, such as by a governmental unit of any kind requiring and acquiring information that constitutes over-breadth or overreaching.

If a government unit, such as the investigative office associated with the licensing board, determines that another agency or source has a need to know (e.g., to advance justice or a governmental purpose), information that was intended to be used for one confidential purpose may flow elsewhere for use for another purpose. Of course, licensed practitioners of marriage and family therapy must abide by statutes and regulations, such as (in some, perhaps most, jurisdictions) mandatory reporting of clients being treated who engage in child or senior abuse or threaten to imminently inflict physical harm on others; or another licensed mental health practitioner and the name of a client involved in an inappropriate activity (e.g., a romantic or sexual relationship). However, the aforementioned possibilities for mandatory reporting will vary among jurisdictions. Although it seems that such mandatory reporting has an honorable purpose, it still represents a governmental acquisition of confidential information that is linked to the right of privacy.

Because the government is subjected to the political force of public policy (which may be influenced by financial interests), there are laws that accommodate access to personal information that was once protected. A person may release information thinking or expecting that it will be confidential, only to learn later that a governmental unit has declassified it and the information is now available to the public. For example, a surprising amount of information about college students or about professionals holding licenses can be obtained by anyone. As another example, personal information about divorcing persons, such as financial statements, is commonly considered to be public record. It is appalling how much information about the children of divorced parents is available in the public records from the court. Simply because the information is held by a government unit does not automatically make the acquisition of personal or confidential information appropriate.

Marriage and family therapists must diligently seek to limit the release of confidential information to all sources, including governmental units, to what is legally justifiable and in the best interests of the client. This may necessitate action to affect the law. Consider Subprinciple 6.7, which states, "Marriage and family therapists are concerned with developing laws and regulations pertaining to marriage and family therapy that serve the public interest, and with altering such laws and regulations that are not in the public interest."

Therapists must also be concerned about the release of confidential information to the legal system. Increasingly, the statutory law and judicial decisions are tending toward requiring release of personal records, such as about mental health services, for legal proceedings. For example, if welfare of a child is at issue in a divorce case, the modern trend is to make historical information about each parent discoverable for evidentiary purposes. Even if the client opposes the release of confidential information, the current legal trend seems to be to elevate above the personal right to privacy the contribution that the confidential information will make to the legal proceedings.

In this day and age, whether right or wrong, the mental health records of clients can be readily obtained for legal purposes by issuing a subpoena or obtaining a court order. More than in the past, the rules for legal discovery appear to be expanding, such as for applying the power of the subpoena; and judges increasingly seem ready to issue a court order mandating release of mental health records. In other words, public policy and the law now tend to elevate the legal need for mental health records above the person's right to keep the records confidential. Although there are differences between jurisdictions on this matter, in some instances, when testifying in a legal case, the health-care provider will have to provide names of cases, and perhaps even the records, of other clients of his or hers who are not involved in the current case (albeit that, depending on the situation, there may be an opportunity to redact or remove identifying information). R. Woody (2001) provided details about the exceptions to and the erosion of the right of privacy, and the accessing of mental health records by insurance companies, the government, and the legal system.

The case of Jaffee v. Redmond (1996) deserves special attention. It helps define the confidentiality applied to the communications between the marriage and family therapist and client. To give the bottom line at the outset, the communications are still protected by public policy and law, but it is not an absolute protection. In the Jaffee case, the United States Supreme Court recognized that the effectiveness of therapy was dependent, to some degree, on confidentiality, and disclosure of confidential information deserved potential protection by the legal concept of privileged communication. However, potential protection is not the same as absolute protection.

The Jaffee ruling does not "remove all ambiguity" (Newman, 1996, p. 44) or answer all of the questions (Smith, 1996), and it cannot assuredly be generalized to other cases (Melton, Petrila, Poythress, & Slobogin, 1997). It does, however, affirm that society, through public policy and law, still believes that there is merit to allowing the possibility of privileged communication or confidentiality for what transpires between marriage and family therapists and their clients.

This discussion of the intrusions on or exceptions to confidentiality is intended to show how the client's privacy right is not absolute. Nonetheless, the therapist's ethical duty to maintain client confidentiality remains primary, although one must carefully consider governmental requests for confidential information.

The best practical advice is to adopt a two-pronged approach. First, when in doubt, the marriage and family therapist should re-read Principle II (and its subprinciples) closely, which offers detailed guidance. Second, if the detailed guidance does not seem to offer clear direction and more assurance seems necessary, the marriage and family therapist should consult with an attorney for what the particular jurisdiction may legally require and for options for meeting both the ethical obligations and legal mandates.

RECOMMENDATIONS FOR DEALING WITH LEGAL PROCESS

The following five recommendations briefly exemplify how therapists should approach situations involving requests from outside sources to obtain confidential information about a client. To follow these recommendations, the therapist may need to seek legal counsel to assist in interpreting the legal mandate. (See Chapter Nine for further discussion of the legal and ethical complexities surrounding confidentiality and subpoenas.)

First, even if there is a seeming legal exception (e.g., a subpoena), the therapist should seek the written authorization from the client to honor the legal exception (e.g., "I hereby authorize my therapist, Dr. B. F. Freud, to honor the subpoena dated_____"). The written authorization should specify what type of confidential information is to be released (e.g., "any and all documents pertaining to the treatment that I received from Dr. Sigmund Skinner"), the purpose for releasing the information (e.g., "the legal action to which I am a party"), the name and address of the marriage and family therapist, the name and address of the source that will receive information, and an affirmation that the authorization was given with mental competency, knowledge of purpose, and voluntarily, free from undue influence or duress.

Second, whenever a legal process seeks a client's confidential information and the client does not readily approve of the release of the information, the therapist should encourage the client to consult with his or her attorney about the possibility of countering the attempt by, say, a motion to the court for a protective order (which could lead to a judicial determination of whether or not the confidential information has to be released).

Third, the therapist should not slip into the role of quasi-legal advisor or advocate of a particular outcome. Rather the therapist should accomplish an appropriate purpose by supporting the client to take responsible action on the matter.

Fourth, legal exceptions to confidentiality involve complicated adversarial matters such as divorce, custody, child abuse reporting requirements, child placement, dangerousness, involuntary services, criminal charges, and so on. Consequently, the therapist should be familiar with the relevant laws in the jurisdiction of practice; however, obtaining legal advice about possible exceptions to confidentiality remains the prudent course of action. Since the AAMFT ethics code offers no details on how the marriage and family therapist should respond to legal process or how or when to advise a client about obtaining legal consultation, the practitioner should study this issue. This approach should produce criteria for making his or her own determinations about legal process and when to support the client's seeking legal counsel.

Fifth, when preparing confidential information for release, either as records or testimony, the therapist must be totally honest, and not omit information that he or she may think will be disadvantageous to the client. Stated differently, the therapist should release all information that is specified by the legal source and/or authorized by the client, regardless of whether it will strengthen or weaken the client's legal interests. The therapist is not to make judgments about the substance of information to be put in the clinical records, except that it is relevant and material to the therapeutic objectives encompassed by the treatment plan. The client's attorney, not the practitioner, has the duty to advocate the legal interests of the client.

The scope of this book does not provide for complete coverage of the necessary contents of written authorizations or all of the legal aspects of releasing confidential information, such as when faced with a subpoena or court order. However, in addition to the discussion in Chapter Nine, useful information on these subjects can be obtained through the AAMFT's Legal Risk and Management Consultation Plan on the Association's web site (aamft.org) and from the following sources: American Psychological Association (1996a, 1996b), Koocher (1998), and R. Woody (2001).

CONCLUSION

This chapter has discussed the overriding ethical obligation of marriage and family therapists in terms of their responsibility to clients, which is to advance their welfare by providing beneficial services while also protecting their rights. Carrying out this responsibility can be best accomplished by understanding and adhering to the first three ethical principles from the AAMFT Code—Responsibility to Clients, Confidentiality, and Professional Competence and Integrity. All three principles are intricately connected and essential to this task of providing beneficial, effective, and ethical therapeutic services. With the understanding gleaned from this integrated analysis, the reader has a sound framework for subsequent chapters that deal in detail with specific types of client situations and issues that often give rise to ethical risks and dilemmas.

References

Alderman, E., & Kennedy, C. (1995). The right to privacy. New York: Alfred A. Knopf.

American Association for Marriage and Family Therapy. (1998). AAMFT code of ethics. Washington, DC: Author.

American Psychological Association. (1996a). Statement on the disclosure of test data. American Psychologist, 51 (6), 644–648.

American Psychological Association. (1996b). Strategies for private practitioners coping with subpoenas or compelled testimony for client records or test data. Professional Psychology: Research and Practice, 27 (3), 245–251.

Arthur, G. L., & Swanson, C. D. (1993). Confidentiality and privileged communication. Alexandria, VA: American Counseling Association.

Becvar, D. S., & Becvar, R. J. (2000). Family therapy: A systemic integration (4th ed.). Boston: Allyn and Bacon.

Berman, H. J., Greiner, W. R., & Saliba, S. N. (1996). The nature and functions of law (5th ed.). Westbury, NY: Foundation Press.

Bobele, M. (1987). Therapeutic interventions in life-threatening situations. Journal of Marital and Family Therapy, 13, 225–239.

Bobele, M. (1988). Reply to "Public policy in life-threatening situations." Journal of Marital and Family Therapy, 14 (2), 139–141.

Bollas, C., & Sundelson, D. (1995). The new informants: The betrayal of confidentiality in psychoanalysis and psychotherapy. Northvale, NJ: Jason Aronson.

Boszormenyi-Nagy, I. (1987). Foundations of contextual therapy. Collected papers of Ivan Boszormenyi-Nagy. New York: Brunner/Mazel.

Brock, G. W. (Ed.). (1998). Ethics casebook. Washington, DC: American Association for Marriage and Family Therapy.

Cantor, D. W. (1998). Patients' rights in psychotherapy. In G. P. Koocher, J. C. Norcross, & S. S. Hill (Eds.), Psychologists' desk reference (pp. 189–191). New York: Oxford University Press.

Cottone, R. R., & Tarvydas, V. M. (1998). Ethical and professional issues in counseling. Upper Saddle River, NJ: Simon & Schuster.

Ducat, C. R., & Chase, H. W. (1992). Constitutional interpretation (5th ed.). St. Paul, MN: West.

Elson, M. (1986). Self psychology in clinical social work. New York: Norton.

Hendricks, E., Hayden, T., & Novik, J. D. (1990). <u>Your right to privacy</u> (2nd ed.). Carbondale & Edwardsville, IL: Southern Illinois University Press.

Henry, B., Moffitt, T. E., Caspi, A., Langley, J., & Silva, P. A. (1994). On the "remembrance of things past": A longitudinal evaluation of the retrospective method. <u>Psychological Assessment, 6</u>, 92–101.

Jaffee v. Redmond, 116 S. Ct. 1923 (1996).

Knapp, S. J., & VandeCreek, L. (1997). <u>Treating patients with memories of abuse: Legal risk management</u>. Washington, DC: American Psychological Association.

Koocher, G. P. (1998). Basic elements of release forms. In G. P. Koocher, J. C. Norcross, & S. S. Hill (Eds.), <u>Psychologists' desk reference</u> (pp. 467–469). New York: Oxford University Press.

Koocher, G. P., & Keith-Spiegel, P. (1998). <u>Ethics in psychology: Professional standards and cases</u> (2nd ed.). New York: Oxford University Press.

Lazarus, A. A. (1981). <u>The practice of multi-modal therapy</u>. New York: McGraw-Hill.

Laszloffy, T. (2000). Awesome allies: Tapping the wisdom of an adolescent's peers. <u>Family Therapy Networker, 24</u> (1), 71–81.

Melton, G. B., Petrila, J., Poythress, N. G., & Slobogin, C. (1997). <u>Psychological evaluations for the courts: A handbook for mental health professionals and lawyers</u> (2nd ed.). New York: Guilford.

Newman, R. (1996). Supreme Court affirms privilege. <u>American Psychological Association Monitor, 27</u> (8), 44.

Nichols, M. P., & Schwartz, R. C. (1998). <u>Family therapy: Concepts and methods</u> (4th ed.). Boston: Allyn and Bacon.

Sells, S. P. (2000). It takes a village: Reclaiming our youth through community family therapy. <u>Family Therapy News, 31</u> (4), 8–10.

Smith, S. R. (1996). U.S. Supreme Court adopts psychotherapist-patient privilege. <u>Bulletin of the American Academy of Forensic Psychology, 17</u> (1), 1 & 11–15.

Smith-Bell, M., & Winslade, W. J. (1995). Privacy, confidentiality, and privilege in psychotherapeutic relationships. In D. N. Bersoff (Ed.), <u>Ethical conflicts in psychology</u> (pp. 145–150). Washington, DC: American Psychological Association.

Speck, R. V., & Attneave, C. (1973). <u>Family networks</u>. New York: Pantheon.

Tarasoff v. Regents of University of California, 551 P.2d 334 (1976).

Teyber, E. (2000). <u>Interpersonal process in psychotherapy</u> (4th ed.). Belmont, CA: Wadsworth/Thomson Learning.

Tjeltveit, A. C. (1999). Ethics and values in psychotherapy. London: Routledge.

Trull, T. J., & Phares, E. J. (2001). Clinical psychology: Concepts, methods, and profession (6th ed.). Belmont, CA: Wadsworth/Thomson Learning.

VandeCreek, L., & Knapp, S. (1993). Tarasoff and beyond: Legal considerations in the treatment of life-endangering patients (Rev. ed.). Sarasota, FL: Professional Resource Press.

Warren, S. D., & Brandeis, L. D. (1890). The right to privacy. Harvard Law Review,4, 193.

Wigmore, J. H. (1940). Evidence (3rd ed., 10 vols.). Originally published in 1913, vol. 3 rev. 1970, vol. 4 rev. 1972, by J. H. Chadbourn. Boston: Little, Brown.

Woody, J. D. (1992). Treating sexual distress: Integrative systems therapy. Newbury Park, CA: Sage.

Woody, J. D., & Woody, R. H. (1988). Public policy in life-threatening situations: A Response to Bobele. Journal of Marital and Family Therapy, 14 (2), 133–137.

Woody, R. H. (1991). Quality care in mental health: Assuring the best clinical services. San Francisco: Jossey-Bass.

Woody, R. H. (1999). Domestic violations of confidentiality. Professional Psychology: Research and Practice, 30 (6), 607–610.

Woody, R. H. (2001). Psychological information: Protecting the right of privacy. Madison, CT: Psychosocial Press (International Universities Press).

Worden, M. (1999). Family therapy basics (2nd ed.). Pacific Grove, CA: Brooks/Cole.

CHAPTER THREE
MULTIPLE RELATIONSHIPS

3

Colleen Margaret Peterson

This chapter offers information for understanding and managing the complexity of multiple relationships. The discussion reviews the philosophical underpinnings and rationale for the avoidance of multiple relationships, summarizes data on the prevalence of multiple relationships, describes problematic aspects of multiple relationships, and recommends guidelines/precautions to consider when such relationships are unavoidable.

CONTENTS

In all forms of mental health services, a primary ethical issue is that of multiple relationships. Since treatment should be solely for the personal benefit of the service recipient (i.e., the client), with the quid pro quo for the therapist being financial compensation and the client's cooperation with treatment, the therapist is precluded from using the treatment relationship to satisfy his or her own personal needs. When a therapist has contacts with a client that go beyond the therapy relationship, such as socializing with a client, a multiple relationship has occurred. Ethically and legally, a therapist should avoid multiple relationships involving a client. This chapter examines multiple relationships; recognizes that certain multiple relationships are unavoidable but must, nonetheless, be managed professionally; and offers guidance for avoiding inappropriate multiple relationships.

TERMINOLOGY

In order to provide clarity, the terms used in this chapter are defined. For the purpose of discussion, the terms therapist, marriage and family therapist, family therapist, and clinician are used interchangeably.

As do other mental health professionals, marriage and family therapists function in a variety of professional roles, in accord with their education, training and experience (Sonne, 1994). These include such roles as therapist, supervisor, researcher, employer, consultant, professional association officer, or expert witness. Simultaneously, the therapist has a life that involves relationships with other persons not included in the categories above. That is, therapists function in numerous roles related to the personal, social, and business or financial aspects of their lives (e.g., as a family member, friend, church member, social acquaintance, or sexual partner, etc.). As will be discussed in a later example, the therapist (a professional role) who decides to hire a current or former client for any job, either in the home or in the office, has added a nonprofessional relationship with the client, that is, a business/financial arrangement.

A multiple relationship is defined as a situation in which the family therapist functions in roles associated with a professional relationship with a client and also assumes another definitive and intended role that is not inconsequential or a chance encounter (Sonne, 1994). The multiple relationship may be concurrent or consecutive. The term "multiple relationships" evolved from "dual relationship" because it was found to be more descriptive. Most of the relationships that these concepts refer to have multiple aspects rather than just two. These two terms are used interchangeably in this chapter. A multiple relationship involves a professional role and another non-professional role; this is different from multiple professional roles, as discussed in Chapter Six in regard to child custody legal disputes.

A professional boundary is conceptualized as a frame or limit that demarcates what is included or excluded from the therapeutic relationship (Gutheil & Gabbard, 1993; Haug, 1999; Peterson, 1992). Boundaries specify what is allowed and what connotes a safe connection in order to meet client needs (Peterson, 1992). This idea includes the structure and content of therapy, as well as the professional responsibilities and behaviors that appropriately help clients (Haug, 1999; Peterson, 1992). Boundaries regulate where the therapist ends and the client starts; they mark the territory between the parties engaged in the therapeutic relationship (Peterson, 1992).

In a discussion of boundaries, it is helpful to make the distinction between a boundary crossing and boundary violation. A boundary crossing is a non-pejorative term that indicates a departure from an accepted clinical practice that may or may not be harmful to the client. A boundary violation, on the other hand, is a departure from clinical practice that places the client or therapeutic process at risk (Smith & Fitzpatrick, 1995). Not all boundary crossings are harmful, and therefore not violations.

Related to the construct of boundaries is the ability a person has to influence another person or events: power. Power has the potential to be both helpful and harmful to those involved. This is particularly the case when there is unequal power between the parties involved and when one person has the ability to impose his or her will over others (Haug, 1999). Factors that contribute to power differences include such things as one's role, sex, education, and socioeconomic status. Peterson (1992) described therapists' professional power as being derived from four sources: societal ascription, expert knowledge, client expectations, and personal power. Through granting licenses to practice, society charges and grants professional the right to use their knowledge and power to benefit others. The actions of therapists are "credible because their role is sanctioned and protected by law and buttressed by social institutions" (Peterson, 1992, p. 36).

TYPES OF MULTIPLE RELATIONSHIPS

Multiple relationships vary in terms of the following: the type of relationship, the frequency, the duration, the degree of intimacy involved, whether the relationship is sexual or nonsexual, and whether the relationship is concurrent with or follows termination of therapy. Sexual intimacy between a therapist and client is expressly prohibited by the AAMFT ethics code (Subprinciple 1.4), and sexual relationships with former clients are prohibited for "two years following the termination of therapy or the last professional contact" (Subprinciple 1.5). At this point the following discussion of multiple relationships will focus predominantly on those of a nonsexual type.

In a study of 63 psychologist-respondents, Anderson & Kitchener (1996) identified eight categories of non-romantic, nonsexual post-therapy relationships with clients. These eight categories are as follows.

(1) Personal or Friendship Relationship. In this category, therapists and former clients moved beyond social acquaintance to a closer, more intimate relationship, with the therapist being more personally invested in the relationship. This type of relationship reflected a more personal connection between therapist and client or the client's having access to the therapist's private life. An example of this category would be the situation in which a former client marries a friend of the therapist's spouse and the two couples socialize together.

(2) Social Interactions and Events. Interactions and events included in this category ranged from a onetime occurrence (e.g., attending the wedding of a former client) to social activities that were ongoing. Two subcategories were identified: circumstantial (little or no prior planning on either the former client's or therapist's part) and intentional (therapist or former client initiated some action to invite contact or ensure interaction).

(3) Business or Financial Relationship. Relationships within this category were either (a) exchanging money between the therapist and the former client for the former client's expertise or assistance (e.g., hiring a former client) or (b) joining areas of expertise that brought in money (e.g., having a business together).

(4) Collegial or Professional Relationship. With the relationships described in this category, the therapist and former client held positions or assumed roles that were essentially equal in power and were more likely to be focused on external professional or business issues. An example of this type of relationship is the situation in which a professor (therapist) provides therapy to another university professor (in another department) and the two later work together on university committees.

(5) Supervisory or Evaluative Relationship. Supervisory or evaluative in nature, these types of relationships were typically characterized by the therapist's having a role that required him or her to oversee or evaluate the former client's performance in a clinical or academic setting. A situation that illustrates this kind of relationship is that of an instructor for a therapy course who has a student who was previously seen at the counseling center where the instructor supervised the therapist who provided services to the student.

(6) Religious Affiliation Relationship. The main type of interaction within this category was that in which the therapist and client attended the same church; however, it also included interactions that involved working together on church committees or social contact at church functions or after a service. As an example of this category, a therapist serving as a church officer had treated the child of a couple, who subsequently became active in the same church and worked on several church committees with the therapist.

(7) Collegial or Professional plus Social Relationship. The difference between this category and the "collegial or

professional" relationship is the presence of additional social contact. These social contacts occurred in a variety of settings. This would be, for instance, a situation in which a former client enters a training facility where the therapist is a faculty member, the former client later joins the same faculty, and the two find themselves working on the committees and attending social gatherings together.

(8) Workplace Relationship. In this category, the therapist and former client found themselves as either professional peers or employees at the same workplace. An example of this type of multiple relationship happening circumstantially is that in which a therapist leaves one agency to work for another, only to find that a former client had recently been hired as part of the office staff. An example of this type of relationship happening intentionally is that in which the parent of a former client, who was involved in family therapy sessions with her child, is hired as office help.

Other types of multiple relationships not specifically included in the eight categories identified by Anderson and Kitchener (1996) include being romantically and/or sexually involved with clients or former clients, bartering of goods for services, and accepting expensive gifts. With regard to multiple relationships with clients, the consensus appears to be that sexual relationships with clients are unethical and harmful to clients (Bouhoutsos, Holroyd, Lerman, Forer, & Greenberg, 1983; Gabbard, 1989; Pope, 1988, 1990). Although there is little research regarding the effects or benefits of multiple relationships with clients, the generally accepted stance in the field is that therapists should exercise caution in developing additional relationships with clients.

PREVALENCE OF MULTIPLE RELATIONSHIPS

In a survey of 4,800 psychologists, psychiatrists, and social workers, Borys and Pope (1989) examined the ethical beliefs and practices of these mental health professionals as they pertain to dual relationships. A majority of the professionals in this survey reported that they believed dual relationships to be unethical under most conditions; and most reported that they had rarely or never engaged in such behaviors. Of the behaviors indicative of a multiple relationship included in the survey, only five behaviors were rated as never ethical by a majority of respondents. These were—in order of greatest level of perceived unethicalness—sex with a current client; selling a product to a client; sex with a client post-termination; inviting clients to a social event; and providing therapy to an employee. There was no behavior that was universally identified as being unethical (Borys & Pope, 1989).

In a similar survey adapted for marriage and family therapists, Brock and Coufal (1994) examined the ethical beliefs and practices of marriage and family therapists. The results indicated that a majority of respondents (at least 90%) never engaged in the following multiple relationships with clients: petting and/or intimate kissing with client; disrobing in the presence of a client or clients; becoming sexually involved with a former client within one year of termination; borrowing money from a client; and terminating therapy in order to have sexual relationship. In addition, a majority of respondents (90%) indicated that the practices of engaging in petting and/or intimate kissing with a client and disrobing in the presence of a client or clients were absolutely unethical.

Among mental health professions, multiple relationships, particularly those including romantic or sexual involvement with clients, are the most frequent reason for disciplinary action by professional associations and regulatory bodies. In a review of AAMFT Code of Ethics violations by category, Stanley (2001) reported that the largest category had to do with multiple relationships (40%), of which 65% of the violations involved sexual or romantic attraction and behavior.

RATIONALE FOR AVOIDANCE OF MULTIPLE RELATIONSHIPS

Regarding boundary violations in professional relationships, Peterson (1992) described the underpinnings for the roles of professionals and asserted that contemporary professionals "are secular shamans who preserve, protect and treat our minds, our bodies, our souls, and our relationships with each other" (pp. 13-14). Intrinsic to the shaman perspective is that the shaman acts in the best of interest of those whom he or she helps.

Building upon the perspective of the professional as derived from shaman, Peterson (1992) elaborated on the point that society sets professionals apart, elevating them to privileged positions of power and allowing them to influence and manage the lives of clients. Because of this position of power and influence, it becomes even more critical that professionals respect the boundaries of their relationship with clients and not violate the trust and confidence bestowed upon them. The position requires that professionals, therapists included, exercise restraint and vigilance to make sure that the client's best interests come before those of the professional. The therapist who is acting in the client's best interests will exercise self-restraint and avoid situations that might give way to the temptation to abandon the needs of the client and further the therapist's own interests.

Because of the tremendous power that marriage and family therapists have, boundaries become essential to the therapeutic process in that they protect the space that must exist between the parties, and they control the power differential in the relationship (Peterson, 1992). Boundaries regulate therapist-client interactions, define the elements needed to produce a safe, consistent and predictable environment, and lower the risk to clients.

In their review of theory and research regarding therapist-client boundary issues, Smith and Fitzpatrick (1995) identified several principles that are foundational for the concept of boundary regulation in therapy. The first is that of abstinence, where therapists refrain from self-seeking and personal gratification in the therapeutic process. Part of this principle is that the only acceptable quid pro quo of the therapeutic relationship is the fee the therapist receives for professional services. A second principle is that of neutrality. Following this principle, therapists focus on the client's agenda and refrain from sharing unsolicited personal opinions in therapy. A third principle states clinicians strive to foster the client's independence and autonomy. When therapeutic boundaries based upon these principles are formed, a sense of safety exists for the client: he or she knows that the therapist will act in the client's best interests and allow the client to address his or her personal issues without fear of negative repercussions.

Another theory that provides a rationale for the avoidance of multiple relationships is psychodynamic theory. With concepts of transference and countertransference, it emphasizes the often-unconscious role the therapist plays in the client's fantasy life. Part of the process of therapy is to work through issues from the past, most often with powerful authority figures or caregivers. Sometimes this process may lead the client to have tender or erotic feelings toward the therapist, not due to the person of the therapist, but because of the context of therapy. When such feelings arise, the psychodynamically trained therapist helps the client understand those feelings apart from the therapist. The psychodynamic viewpoint maintains that transference does not end with the termination of therapy and that it is impossible for a therapist and former client to ever have a relationship of equality. According to this concept, it would be unethical to enter into a relationship with a client upon termination of therapy.

In a summary of the obligations of psychologists relevant to nonsexual relationships with former clients, Pipes (1997) offered eight reasons for limiting such relationships. The reasons and a brief description follow.

(1) Former clients may need to return to therapy. Being entangled in another type of relationship will cause difficulties if the client wants to resume treatment.

(2) There are a variety of clients who often remain vulnerable following termination. These clients would seem highly susceptible to exploitation.

(3) Some clients have very strong feelings about their former therapists. These strong feelings make the likelihood of poor decision-making high. With these strong feelings, can a client, even with "informed consent," be prepared for the possibility of not being able to return for therapy with the former therapist?

(4) Because former clients may request therapists to furnish records or testify in court on their behalf, it is important for therapists to maintain their objectivity as much as possible.

(5) There are clear theoretical reasons for assuming that recipients of clinical services should be able to trust that the therapist has no intentions other than to further the welfare of the client. How can the welfare of clients be ensured if they worry about the kind of relationship they might have with their therapist following termination?

(6) There can be obvious modeling effects if prospective clients see the therapist involved in post-therapy relationships with former clients (e.g., clients may think this is normal and expect to have personal, social, and/or business relationships with their therapists).

(7) There can be significant effects on former clients who establish post-therapy relationships with their former therapists if the relationship "goes bad."

(8) There are often legal reasons for avoiding post-therapy nonsexual relationships. Because state boards vary in their interpretation of ethical standards, and because legal statutes vary from state to state, it is clear that the safest approach to a post-therapy relationship is to use caution and discretion when contemplating entering one. Before adding any additional roles or relationships to the therapeutic relationship with clients, therapists should be aware of laws and regulations pertaining to the issue in the jurisdiction in which they practice.

PROBLEMATIC ASPECTS OF MULTIPLE RELATIONSHIPS

What is there about multiple relationships that make them problematic? Why is it that professional codes of ethics advise therapists to avoid multiple relationships? The answer is the belief that engaging in additional relationships puts the therapeutic relationship and the client at risk, and that conflicting roles and boundary violations could precipitate impaired therapist judgment and exploitation of the client.

ROLE THEORY AND MULTIPLE RELATIONSHIPS

In her seminal article on what makes dual relationships so problematic, Kitchener (1988) used role theory to explain the difficulties that arise in dual relationships when one person is involved, simultaneously or sequentially, with role categories that conflict or compete. She proposes that it is the conflicting or competing roles that become problematic and identifies three specific guidelines for differentiating between dual relationships that have a high versus a low probability of leading to difficulty.

Kitchener's (1988) first guideline is that "as the incompatibility of expectations increases between roles, so will the potential for misunderstanding and harm" (p. 219). Thus, when role expectations are incompatible or compete, there is often confusion about how one should behave. When these expectations are unclear or conflict, there is greater potential for feelings of frustration, confusion and anger, which in turn could lead to actions that could be harmful. An example of this is the conflicting roles of a therapist who also hires the client as a receptionist. This situation becomes problematic because the employer role places the therapist in a position to evaluate the employee's work performance. In the therapist role, on the other hand, the therapist is in a position to facilitate growth and maintain confidentiality. The expectations associated with these roles/positions, the expectation for growth and confidentiality, and the expectation of evaluation and work performance, could at times conflict. If the receptionist is not meeting the employer's expectations and the client's self-esteem and personal growth are tied to her having a job, the therapist who hired the client is in a dilemma: whose needs does he meet, his or the client's?

The second guideline is that "as the obligations of different roles diverge, the potential for divided loyalties and loss of objectivity increases" (Kitchener, 1998, p. 219). For example, whereas the main obligation of marriage and family therapists is to meet the needs of clients, as a friend or business associate the obligations tend to be more reciprocal, with the expectation that one's own needs, as well as the friend's needs, will be met. The problem in confusing these roles is that there may be confusion as to the underlying intentions. For instance, if a therapist and client are trading services, and the therapist determines that the client should continue in therapy, the client may wonder if the therapist's decision is based upon the client's needs or upon the therapist's desire to continue to receive the client's exchanged services.

Kitchener's (1988) final guideline is that "as the power and prestige between the professional's and the consumer's roles increase, so does the potential for exploitation and an inability on the part of the consumers to remain objective about their own best interests" (p. 219). Consider, for instance, a situation where a client, a skilled mechanic, is on probation and court-ordered for treatment and the therapist has the client working on his vintage car for minimum wage because the client, due to his background is having difficulty finding work. If the client begins to feel used, does he stay in treatment for fear of retaliation and a negative report to his probation officer, or does he stop working for the therapist if he thinks that is what is best for him?

In a discussion of potentially problematic dual relationships, Keith-Spiegel and Koocher (1985) noted that relationships that include such things as bartering of goods for services, socializing with clients, and accepting expensive gifts from clients may involve conflicts of interest, or the appearance of conflicts that could compromise the therapist's effectiveness. In the case of bartering goods for services, if a therapist provides services in exchange for a client doing the landscaping on her new house, what happens if the therapist finds the work unsatisfactory? What if a major disagreement ensues if the therapist voices dissatisfaction while the client thinks the work is fine? How might that impact their therapeutic working relationship? Subprinciple 1.3 of the AAMFT ethics code speaks clearly to these issues: "Marriage and family therapists are aware of their influential positions with respect to clients, and they avoid exploiting the trust and dependency of such persons . . . and make every effort to avoid conditions and multiple relationships with clients that could impair professional judgment or increase the risk of exploitation."

PSYCHOLOGISTS' VIEWS OF PROBLEMATIC AND NON-PROBLEMATIC MULTIPLE RELATIONSHIPS

In a study of psychologists' post-therapy experiences with clients, Anderson and Kitchener (1996) asked about the types of relationships the participants had experienced with clients (discussed earlier), and further asked them to categorize the relationships as either ethically problematic or not ethically problematic. Participants were also asked to describe their rationale for categorizing the relationship the way they did. The majority of participants who described social interactions and events, business and financial relationships, and workplace relationships with clients indicated that they saw these as ethically problematic. The majority of participants who described collegial or professional relationships with clients and collegial or professional relationships plus social relationships with clients did not see them as ethically problematic. For personal or friendship and supervisory or evaluative relationships, an equal number of participants saw these as ethically problematic and not ethically problematic.

In describing why they had categorized relationships as ethically problematic or not, therapists gave a variety of reasons. With the not ethically problematic relationships, they reported several factors: having already ended the therapeutic relationship, agreeing that if the client wanted to resume therapy, he or she would seek another therapist, assuring communication about needs and feelings, maintaining boundaries of each relationship and compartmentalizing the separate aspects, the passing of considerable time since termination, and having a discussion of the post-therapy relationship before entering it. For those who saw the various multiple relationships as ethically problematic, they reported several reasons: a belief that the therapist-client relationship continues after termination, the potential for role expectations and conflict, the power differential, knowledge about the former client influencing the therapist's objectivity, transference issues, and increased risk of exploitation. Another distinction that emerged, particularly with social relationships, was that circumstantial interactions were seen as less ethically problematic than were intentional interactions.

RESEARCH REGARDING THE EFFECTS OF MULTIPLE RELATIONSHIPS

Therapists' sexual involvement with current clients appears to be rare, and this may be related to the clarity of ethical and legal prohibition. In the Borys and Pope (1989) national study of mental health professionals, less than one percent of respondents reported engaging in sexual behavior with clients. There is, however, reason to question self-reports of this kind. As noted earlier, the most frequent reason for disciplinary action by professional associations and regulatory bodies is for multiple relationships. Stanley (2001) reported that the largest category of violations of the AAMFT ethics code had to do with multiple relationships—40%, of which 65% of the violations involved sexual or romantic attraction and behavior. It appears that the actual prevalence of professionals' engaging in sexual behavior with clients is unknown.

Sexual relationships between therapist and client have been shown in the literature to be harmful to clients (Bouhoutsos et al., 1983; Pope, 1990). Of the 559 clients in their study who were sexually involved with their therapists, Bouhoutsos and colleagues (1983) reported that 90% experienced adverse effects. This negative impact ranged from affecting the client's emotional, social, and sexual adjustment, to negative feelings about the experience, a negative impact on his or her personality, and a negative impact on the client's sexual relationship with his or her primary partner.

In describing the negative effects of therapist-client sexual involvement, Pope (1988) reported that it commonly results in a distinct clinical syndrome, which he calls the "Therapist-Patient Sex Syndrome." He explains that this syndrome shares similar symptoms with sexual abuse, child abuse, Post-traumatic Stress Disorder, Battered Spouse Syndrome, and Rape Response Syndrome. Just like these other syndromes, with Therapist-Patient Sex Syndrome, the appearance of adverse effects may be delayed. The 10 aspects that Pope (1988) identified as characteristic of this syndrome are ambivalence; feelings of guilt; sense of emptiness and isolation; sexual confusion; impaired ability to trust; identity, boundary, and role confusion; emotional lability; suppressed rage; increased suicidal risk; and cognitive dysfunction. These adverse effects, and the severity of most of them, attest to the harm that clients experience when their therapists are sexually involved with them.

CALL TO EMBRACE THE COMPLEXITIES OF MULTIPLE RELATIONSHIPS

Aside from sexual relations with clients, there is a lack of research demonstrating the harm or helpfulness of multiple relationships. While some professionals hold firmly to the position that multiple relationships are damaging and should be avoided at all cost, others argue that such relationships provide family therapists and clients the opportunity to enlarge their capacity for more complex human interaction (Bograd, 1992). This view fits with the postmodern approaches to therapy, which emphasize the importance of the therapeutic relationship being collaborative and egalitarian and which minimize or deny therapist power. Those who argue for acceptance of multiple relationships tend to believe that it would be safer to humanize and democratize the relationship than to fortify themselves with professional expertise and higher authority (Bograd, 1992). By being human and engaging with clients in a variety of ways, the therapist's power advantage is lessened; by having more information about the therapist, a client has more power.

In the same vein, Ryder and Hepworth (1990) argued that some aspects of dual relationships are ubiquitous and impossible to eliminate and that the absolute elimination of such relationships would not be good. They further argued that rather than focusing on eliminating multiple relationships, more focus should be given to addressing the status and power differences that underlie exploitation. They further stated that by addressing these issues and also by permitting others to have more power and equality, marriage and family therapists, particularly with faculty-graduate student relationships, model and facilitate the ability to navigate the inevitability of complex relationships and to interact as equals.

As a result of the attention given to sexual involvement with clients and the criticism that perhaps therapy professionals were being too rigid in their avoidance of dual relationships, there emerged a distinction between sex with current clients and sex with former clients. This distinction began to be reflected in the ethical codes of many professional associations (American Association for Marriage and Family Therapy, 1991, 1998; American Counseling Association, 1995; and American Psychological Association, 1992). Whereas sexual intimacy with current clients was expressly prohibited, the standard for sex with former clients became a prohibition for two years following termination of therapy. The current AAMFT ethics code prohibits sexual intimacy "for two years following the termination of therapy or last professional contact" (Subprinciple 1.5). This same subprinciple also encourages marriage and family therapists to not engage in sexual intimacy with former clients and clarifies that if a therapist does choose to engage in such a relationship, the burden is upon the therapist to demonstrate that there is no exploitation or injury to the former client or his or her family.

UNAVOIDABLE MULTIPLE RELATIONSHIPS

As discussed previously, there are those who argue that in some cases multiple relationships are unavoidable. This situation is particularly true for therapists who practice in small, rural communities, or with minority populations, and for therapists who are clergy and/or who work in religious settings. The inevitability and complexity of multiple relationships in rural communities has received considerable attention (Brownlee, 1996; Catalano, 1997; Faulkner & Faulkner, 1997; Hargrove, 1986; Schank & Skovholt, 1997; Stockman, 1990). Unlike clinicians practicing in large urban areas where they are able to maintain anonymity, those working in rural and small communities face unique challenges. In these settings, practitioners face three characteristics: the impact of greater distances and the sparse population; the formal and informal social and political units associated with living and working in smaller communities; and the multiple levels of personal and professional relationships (Brownlee; Faulkner & Faulkner; Hargrove).

A typical issue for those living in rural areas is the great distance between communities. As a result, to adapt to the relative isolation, members of these small communities have developed interdependence. These multiple levels of relationships impact the services therapists provide when, for example, the only choice for shopping is the client's store, or when the therapist's children attend the same school or are friends with clients or a client's children. Another difficulty is the fact that rural therapists have limited options for referring clients to other service providers (Brownlee, 1996). Additionally, the longer a therapist resides in the community, the more interaction the therapist will have with community members, and the more difficult it becomes to separate professional and personal relationships. In rural communities, there is a cultural and social expectation of overlapping relationships and that "everybody knows everybody" (Faulkner & Faulkner, 1997).

In addition to rural communities, therapists who are a part of small communities often have difficulty avoiding multiple relationships. An example of such overlapping relationships is that of a therapist, the only mental health professional in his community, and a physician, also the only one in the community. During the time that the therapist was in the community, he referred many clients to the physician to rule out physical problems related to a variety of problems for which clients presented in the therapist's office (e.g. depression, panic attacks, sexual problems). The physician in turn referred many patients to the therapist. The therapist and physician developed a good professional relationship, and both served on the board for the rural hospital in their community. When the physician began having difficulty with one of his children, he and his family sought family therapy from the therapist. Other than this local therapist, the nearest family therapist was located 250 miles away. To seek services form this other professional would be a hardship on the physician because of his work schedule and his constantly being on-call. This situation evokes many ethical concerns and questions. What should the family therapist do? How should he respond to the request? What if the physician insists that he knows the therapist and trusts him and does not want to see anyone else?

Another context in which therapists may have difficulty avoiding multiple relationships is with minority groups. Clients frequently choose a therapist because he or she is a part of a shared community and as a result perceives "reciprocity of respect" (Adelman & Barrett, 1990; Berman, 1985). This type of situation includes not only therapists from minority racial or ethnic backgrounds, but also includes gay and lesbian therapists. The ethical dilemma of being known and setting personal boundaries within these small communities can be even more complex and daunting for these therapists. In discussing the dilemmas for lesbians working in lesbian communities, Smith (1990) asserted that the success of a therapist's being a part of a community while still maintaining the necessary and important boundaries depends on the therapist's sense of self and level of personal sustenance. As for all therapists, and particularly within small communities, therapists need to make sure that their social, emotional, and sexual needs are met through relationships with friends, colleagues, family, partners, or others—not with clients. When a therapist's needs are not being met by nonclient sources, the press to satisfy needs in the therapy session can tempt or lead therapists to cross and violate boundaries with clients that they would not if their needs were being met appropriately.

In recent years, attention has been given to collaboration between family therapists and religious leaders (Weaver, Koenig, & Larson, 1997) and clinicians working in religious settings (Geyer, 1994; Rotz, Russell, & Wright, 1993). This trend warrants discussion of issues specific to multiple relationships in this arena, especially because marriage and family therapists report the most religious involvement of mental health professionals (Bergin & Jensen, 1990) and the often "small world" within a religious setting. In discussing ethical complexities for clergy therapists, Haug (1999) recognized that clergy family therapists are particularly vulnerable to problems in the area of multiple relationships. Their vulnerability is due to differences in professional training for the two areas (clergy and family therapy), as well as to the differences in role expectations associated with the two professions. Haug further elaborated that these challenges stem from numerous sources: clergy education that may not include ethical and professional issues; entrenched gender dynamics and traditions within religious cultures; idealized public images of clergy that may not match private reality; socialization of clergy to demonstrate warmth and friendliness through contact with parishioners (including visits at home, in the hospital, or over lunch) to the point of being almost over-involved; and the lack of clarity regarding job descriptions and criteria for success. These aspects of socialization can contribute to the clergy therapists' lack of boundaries, lack of appropriate self-awareness/monitoring, and the unrealistic assessments of their abilities and competencies (Haug, 1999).

ETHICAL DECISION MAKING AND PRECAUTIONS FOR MULTIPLE RELATIONSHIPS

While the AAMFT ethics code provides general guidelines, it does not provide clear and specific direction for each and every situation that may arise for therapists. It is up to therapists as individuals to assess and evaluate clinical situations and choose behavior they believe is the most ethical, legal, and beneficial to the client. This type of decision making is part of the therapist's overall professional responsibility to clients (Principle I) and professional competence and integrity (Principle III). To meet these ethical obligations, therapists need to either adopt an existing ethical decision making model or to formulate/adapt one of their own. (Readers are referred to Chapter One for discussion of general ethical decision-making models.)

A MODEL FOR AVOIDING EXPLOITATIVE MULTIPLE RELATIONSHIPS

What follows is a discussion of Gottlieb's (1993) ethical decision-making model specifically for multiple relationships. There will also be some guidelines, cautions, and questions for therapists to consider with regard to engaging in multiple relationships—before, during, and after reaching such a decision.

Building upon the ethical decision-making models of others (Haas & Malouf, 1989; Woody, 1990) and Kitchener's (1988) guidelines regarding role theory and dual relationships, Gottlieb (1993) developed a model for avoiding exploitative dual relationships. Because this model is designed specifically for addressing the ethical dilemmas in multiple relationships, regardless of the professional context, it is described in detail.

Underlying Gottlieb's model (1993) are seven assumptions. First, the model applies to all aspects of a professional's work, whether it is with clients, students, or supervisees. Second, the goal of avoiding multiple relationships, although aspirational, is unrealistic in certain circumstances. Third, all multiple relationships should be evaluated for potential harm because of the inherent risk. Fourth, although not all multiple relationships are exploitative and some are even beneficial, if there is the potential for harm, they must be avoided. Fifth, the model is intended to increase the therapist's awareness of relevant issues and make recommendations for possible courses of action. Sixth, the dilemmas addressed in the model are for professionals who are considering adding another relationship, not for situations where the multiple relationship already exists. Finally, when considering the dimensions of the model, the therapist is to take the perspective of the consumer, not that of the professional.

Gottlieb's model (1993) is based on three critical dimensions of the ethical decision-making process: Power, Duration of the Relationship, and Clarity of Termination. Power refers to the amount of power the therapist has in relation to the consumer. Duration of the Relationship has to do with the time involved and relates to power, in that power increases over time. Power is low when the relationship is brief, but increases as the relationship continues. Clarity of Termination refers to the consumer's perspective of how long the professional relationship will continue.

Is it clear that there was termination or is there the assumption that the therapist's obligation to the consumer will never end? Is it a one-time contact or an ongoing situation?

Each of the dimensions in the Gottlieb model is divided into three areas on a continuum. For power, there are low, mid-range, and high levels. In the category of low power, there is little or no personal relationship; for mid-range power, there is a clear power differential, but the relationship is circumscribed; and with high power, there is a clear power differential with profound personal influence possible. For duration, there is brief, intermediate, and long. For brief duration, there is single or few contacts over a short period of time; for intermediate duration, there is regular contact over a limited period of time; and for long duration, there is continuous or episodic contact over a long period of time. In the termination dimension, there are the specific, uncertain, and indefinite categories. For specific termination, the relationship is limited by time externally imposed or by prior agreement of parties who are unlikely to see one another again. For uncertain termination, the professional function is completed but further contact is not ruled out. Finally, with indefinite termination, there is no agreement regarding when or if termination is to take place.

Figure 1: Dimensions for Ethical Decision-making

POWER

Low	Mid-Range	High
Little or no personal relationship or Persons consider each other peers (may include elements of influence)	Clear power differential present but relationship is circumscribed	Clear power differential with profound personal influence possible

DURATION

Brief	Intermediate	Long
Single or few contacts over short period of time	Regular contact over a limited period of time	Continuous or episodic contact over a long period of time

TERMINATION

Specific	Uncertain	Indefinite
Relationship is limited by time externally imposed or by prior agreement of parties who are unlikely to see each other again	Professional function is completed but further contact is not ruled out	No agreement regarding when or if termination is to take place

From "Avoiding Exploitative Dual Relationships: A Decision-Making Model," by M. C. Gottlieb, 1993, Psychotherapy, 30, p. 44.

These dimensions and corresponding categories, essentially a three-by-three grid, are used to aid assessment when a professional is contemplating an additional relationship to the already existing professional relationship. To follow the model, the first step involved is assessing the current relationship, from the consumer's perspective, according to the three dimensions. Questions include: How great is the power differential? How long has the relationship lasted? Has the relationship clearly ended? If the responses to two or three of these questions fall to the right side of the grid (in the high, long or indefinite categories on the dimensions), the potential for harm is high and the additional relationship should not be added. If, however, the answers to the questions fall to the left side of the grid (in the low, brief, or specific categories), one should move to the next level of assessment.

The second step of the model involves asking the same questions of the contemplated relationship as were asked of the current relationship in step one. Again, if the answers fall to the right side of the grid, then the relationship should be considered too risky and should be rejected. If the answers do not fall to the right side of the grid, but instead fall on the left side, the relationship may be permissible, and the therapist can then move on to step three.

If both the current relationship and the additional relationship fall in the left-to-moderate range on the dimensions, then the third step of Gottlieb's model is for the therapist to look at both relationships and examine them for role incompatibility. If the roles associated with the two relationships are highly incompatible, then the contemplated additional relationship should not occur. If in examining the roles, the therapist finds them to have low incompatibility, then he or she may proceed with the additional relationship.

It is important, when a therapist proceeds with the relationship, to follow through with step four, consulting with a colleague, and step five, discussing the decision with the consumer. A colleague familiar with all the circumstances of the parties involved would be the ideal choice for the consultant. In reviewing the decision with the consumer, the therapist should review the entire ethical decision-making process and the potential risks and/or adverse consequences. With this step, if the consumer chooses to engage in the additional relationship, he or she does so with informed consent. It is important that the consumer give adequate consideration to the issues. If the consumer is not willing to give it the attention it requires, then he or she should be considered at risk, and the contemplated additional relationship should be rejected. Consider the analysis that follows.

A family therapist considered initiating a friendship with the parents of a child who attended a workshop on self-esteem that the therapist gave at the high school. In this case the therapist had high power, but for a brief, clearly defined period of time, and the termination was unambiguous (step one). The new relationship (friendship), although indeterminate in duration and having an uncertain termination, would have a minimal power differential if at all (step two). Both of these relationships fell to the left on the model dimensions; so the therapist then examined the role incompatibility. Since the roles were seen as having low incompatibility, the therapist discussed the situation with his colleague. Because the colleague was a co-worker and also gave frequent workshops at the same high school, the colleague was aware of the specific circumstances. She did not see a problem if the therapist were to become friends with the couple, and she encouraged the therapist to explore the option with the couple. The therapist met with the couple, explained the ethical decision-making process and its various aspects, and asked them if the relationship was something they wanted to pursue. The therapist and the couple agreed to enter a friendship.

ANALYSIS OF BOUNDARY FACTORS IN MULTIPLE RELATIONSHIPS

In their discussion of role boundaries in clinical practice, Gutheil and Gabbard (1993) identified some specific boundaries that clinicians should consider when contemplating multiple relationships. The first boundary is that of time, which defines the limits of the session and provides structure. If clinicians are considering unusual adaptations to the beginning or ending of sessions (starting or stopping late or early), they should exercise caution because this indicates a susceptibility to crossing a boundary. This particular boundary violation is one of the most common in sexual misconduct cases. For example, therapists who become involved sexually with clients often fall into a pattern of scheduling the client with whom they are involved as the first or last client of the day, typically when office staff is not present, and when they have flexibility to give the client a little more time than the usual therapy hour.

The second boundary Gutheil and Gabbard (1993) encourage therapists to consider is that of place and space. Aside from the accepted standard treatments that involve treatment outside of the usual therapist office, such as systematic desensitization or in-home family therapy, family therapists should exercise caution if they are considering doing home visits, meeting over lunch, or giving a client a ride home. In those cases, involving clear therapeutic directives, where treatment occurs outside the normal therapeutic locations, therapists should be sure to document the professional literature supporting their approach, the clinical rationale, and the risk-benefit aspects of the treatment.

Because money defines the business aspect of the therapeutic relationship, it is important for therapists to keep in mind that the fee received by the therapist for services is the only generally accepted and appropriate material gratification for his or her clinical work. Gutheil and Gabbard (1993) remind therapists that trouble begins when they stop thinking of therapy as work; therapists should discuss and follow through with fees for therapy services. If the fee becomes burdensome, therapists should discuss options with the client rather than simply allowing the billing to lapse or allowing a debt to mount. Gutheil and Gabbard discourage bartering because it blurs the boundary between payment and gift. (See Chapter Nine for a discussion of the risks associated with allowing client debt to go unpaid and the risks of using collection services.)

Regarding the issue of gifts and favors, Gutheil and Gabbard (1993) warn that clinicians need to exercise discretion. When therapists give gifts or ask favors, however small, they place unidentified obligations on the patient. Gutheil and Gabbard provide several examples: a therapist who offers a tissue to a crying client in a very nice leather case, telling the client to keep it; a client who returns the therapist's library books; and a therapist who sends flowers to a client who had struggled with infertility but who eventually gave birth to a child. Although many would consider such behaviors as non-problematic, Gutheil and Gabbard assert that such behaviors are outside the classic boundaries of the therapeutic relationship and are boundary violations. Subprinciple 3.10 of the AAMFT ethics code also addresses this issue, stating that "marriage and family therapists do not give to or receive from clients gifts of substantial value or . . . gifts that impair the integrity or efficacy of the therapeutic relationship."

The other boundaries that Gutheil and Gabbard (1993) encourage therapists to monitor in their risk management efforts are language, self-disclosure, and physical contact. Therapists are encouraged to consider the language they use, particularly client names, with their associated levels of intimacy and what messages the language used sends to clients. The same is true for self-disclosure. When a therapist indulges in even mild forms of disclosure, he or she should engage in careful self-scrutiny, because this conveying of information is often burdensome to clients. Therapists need to be clear regarding the therapeutic rationale and usefulness of self-disclosure, because inappropriate self-disclosure is a boundary violation that the legal system often uses to bolster claims of sexual misconduct. The reasoning is that if a client knows so much about the therapist's personal life, then the two of them must have been intimate.

The last boundary Gutheil and Gabbard (1993) discuss is that of physical contact. In today's litigious climate, even humane interventions that involve touch need to be documented to prevent them from being misconstrued. If operating from current risk-management principles, therapists should be aware that the handshake is the limit of physical contact. Gutheil and Gabbard suggest that most hugs from clients should be discouraged by tactful, gentle ways that include words, body language, and positioning. Consider the example of a therapist who, instead of engaging the client in the therapeutic work of dealing with the resentment and loss of her deprived childhood, hugs the client to comfort her. The hugging is an attempt to provide the physical contact that would typically be offered by a caring parent. The client being hugged may assume, or feel entitled to, more demonstrations of caring and affection. When physical contact between clinician and client occurs, the distinction in the therapeutic relationship between the symbolic and the concrete is lost.

CONCLUSION

When it comes to multiple relationships, the AAMFT ethics code provides clear direction. With regard to current clients, "sexual intimacy" is prohibited. With regard to former clients, "sexual intimacy" is prohibited for two years after termination, with the burden upon the marriage and family therapist to ensure that there is no exploitation. With regard to non-sexual multiple relationships with clients and former clients, the AAMFT ethics codes is less prescriptive. Given the ongoing debate as to whether one should avoid multiple relationships at all costs or embrace their complexity and inevitability, some therapists may perceive flexibility about the issue of their interactions with clients. Nevertheless, it is in the therapist's best interest to think through carefully his or her position on multiple relationships and consider such variables as power, boundaries, roles, and how these variables fit with the therapist's practice context and theoretical orientation.

It is up to therapists to be responsible professionals and monitor themselves when it comes to multiple relationships. This requires that they be aware of themselves (integrity, competence) and keep any of their personal issues or self-serving behaviors in check. Therapists do this by making sure that they are appropriately connected to significant others, family, friends, and colleagues, and that their own needs are being met through these interactions and not through clients.

When therapists find themselves vulnerable and at risk, they seek appropriate support and guidance through consultation with colleagues, supervision, and/or personal therapy. These steps are critical to avoid multiple relationships, and even more so in those instances when a therapist is involved in an overlapping or multiple relationship. If the therapist is not self-aware, he or she cannot know whether actions arise out of self-interest or out of thoughtful pursuit of the best interests of the client. This self-monitoring is also critical in the area of boundaries if the professional is to avoid boundary crossings that continue down the "slippery slope" to boundary violations. By engaging in careful self-awareness, therapists can recognize the issues and ethical dilemmas involved in multiple relationships, become willing and able to use ethical decision-making models, and allow themselves ample time for appropriate reflection and planning. All of these steps can facilitate ethical practice with minimal risk.

REFERENCES

Adelman, J., & Barrett, S. E. (1990). Overlapping relationships: Importance of the feminist ethical perspective. In H. Lerman & N. Porter (Eds.), Feminist ethics in psychotherapy (pp. 87–91). New York: Springer.

American Association for Marriage and Family Therapy. (1991). AAMFT code of ethics. Washington, DC: Author.

American Association for Marriage and Family Therapy. (1998). AAMFT code of ethics. Washington, DC: Author.

American Counseling Association. (1995). Codes of ethics and standards of practice. Alexandria, VA: Author.

American Psychological Association. (1992). Ethical principles of psychologists and code of conduct. Washington, DC: Author

Anderson, S. K., & Kitchener, K. S. (1996). Nonromantic, nonsexual post-therapy relationships between psychologists and former clients: An exploratory study of critical incidents. Professional Psychology: Research and Practice, 27, 59–66.

Bergin, A. E., & Jensen, J. P. (1990). Religiosity of psychotherapists: A national survey. Psychotherapy, 27, 3–6.

Berman, J. R. S. (1985). Ethical feminist perspectives on dual relationships with clients. In L. B. Rosewater & L. E. A. Walker (Eds.), Handbook of feminist therapy: Women's issues in psychotherapy (pp. 287–296). New York: Springer.

Bograd, M. (1992, November/December). The duel over dual relationships. Family Therapy Networker, 16, 33–37.

Borys, D. S., & Pope, K. S. (1989). Dual relationships between therapist and client: A national study of psychologists, psychiatrists, and social workers. Professional Psychology: Research and Practice, 20, 283–293.

Bouhoutsos, J., Holroyd, J., Lerman, H., Forer, B. R., & Greenberg, M. (1983). Sexual intimacy between psychotherapists and patients. Professional Psychology, 14, 185–196.

Brock, G. W., & Coufal, G. (1994). A national survey of the ethical practices and attitudes of marriage and family therapists. In G. W. Brock (Ed.), AAMFT ethics casebook (pp. 27–48). Washington, DC: American Association for Marriage and Family Therapy.

Brownlee, K. (1996). The ethics of non-sexual dual relationships: A dilemma for the rural mental health professional. Community Mental Health Journal, 32, 497–503.

Catalano, S. (1997). The challenges of clinical practice in small or rural communities: Case studies in managing dual relationships in and outside of therapy. Journal of Contemporary Psychotherapy, 27, 23–35.

Faulkner, K. K., & Faulkner, F. A. (1997). Managing multiple relationships in rural communities: Neutrality and boundary violations. Clinical Psychology: Science and Practice, 4, 225–234.

Gabbard, G. O. (1989). Sexual exploitation in professional relationships. Washington, DC: American Psychiatric Press.

Geyer, M. C. (1994). Dual role relationships and Christian counseling. Journal of Psychology and Theology, 22, 187–195.

Gottlieb, M. C. (1993). Avoiding exploitative dual relationships: A decision-making model. Psychotherapy, 30, 41–48.

Gutheil, T. G., & Gabbard, G. O. (1993). The concept of boundaries in clinical practice: Theoretical and risk management dimensions. American Journal of Psychiatry, 150, 188–196.

Haas, L. J., & Malouf, J. L. (1989). Keeping up the good work: A practitioner's guide to mental health ethics. Sarasota, FL: Professional Resource Exchange.

Hargrove, D. S. (1986). Ethical issues in rural mental health practice. Professional Psychology: Research and Practice, 17, 20–23.

Haug, I. E. (1999). Boundaries and the use and misuse of power and authority: Ethical complexities for clergy psychotherapists. Journal of Counseling & Development, 77, 411–417.

Keith-Spiegel, P., & Koocher, G. P. (1985). Ethics in psychology. Hillsdale, NJ: Lawrence Erlbaum.

Kitchener, K. S. (1988). Dual role relationships: What makes them so problematic? Journal of Counseling and Development, 67, 217–221.

Peterson, M. R. (1992). At personal risk: Boundary violations in professional-client relationships. New York: Norton.

Pipes, R. B. (1997). Nonsexual relationships between psychotherapists and their former clients: Obligations of psychologists. Ethics & Behavior, 7, 27–41.

Pope, K. S. (1988). How clients are harmed by sexual contact with mental health professionals: The syndrome and its prevalence. Journal of Counseling and Development, 67, 222–226.

Pope, K. S. (1989). Therapist-client sex syndrome: A guide for attorneys and subsequent therapists for assessing damage. In G. O. Gabbard (Ed.), Sexual exploitation in professional relationships (pp. 39–56). Washington, DC: American Psychiatric Press.

Pope, K. S. (1990). Therapist-patient sexual involvement: A review of the research. Clinical Psychology Review, 10, 477–490.

Rotz, E., Russell, C. S., & Wright, D.W. (1993). The therapist who is perceived as "spiritually correct": Strategies for avoiding collusion with the "spiritually one-up" spouse. Journal of Marital and Family Therapy, 19, 369–375.

Ryder, R., & Hepworth, J. (1990). AAMFT ethical code: "Dual relationships." Journal of Marital and Family Therapy, 16, 127–132.

Schank, J. A., & Skovholt, T. M. (1997). Dual-relationship dilemmas of rural and small-community psychologists. Professional Psychology: Research and Practice, 28, 44–49.

Smith, A. J. (1990). Working with the lesbian community: The dilemma of overlapping relationships. In H. Lerman & N. Porter (Eds.), Feminists ethics in psychotherapy (pp. 92–96). New York: Springer.

Smith, D., & Fitzpatrick, M. (1995). Patient-therapist boundary issues: An integrative review of theory and research. Professional Psychology: Research and Practice, 26, 499–506.

Sonne, J. L. (1994). Multiple relationships: Does the new ethics code answer the right questions? Professional Psychology: Research and Practice, 25, 336–343.

Stanley, L. (2001). Do all ethics complaints end in termination of membership? Family Therapy News, 32, 8–9.

Stockman, A. F. (1990). Dual relationships in rural mental health practice: An ethical dilemma. Journal of Rural Community Psychology, 11, 31–45.

Weaver, A. J., Koenig, H.G., & Larson, D. B. (1997). Marriage and family therapists and the clergy: A need for clinical collaboration, training, and research. Journal of Marital and Family Therapy, 23, 13–25.

Woody, J. D. (1990). Resolving ethical concerns in clinical practice: Toward a pragmatic model. Journal of Marital and Family Therapy, 16, 133–150.

RELATIONSHIPS WITH SUPERVISEES, STUDENTS, OTHER PROFESSIONALS, EMPLOYEES, AND RESEARCH SUBJECTS

4

Cheryl L. Storm

This chapter discusses a variety of ethical issues that present challenges as marriage and family therapists participate in relationships with supervisees, students, employees, research subjects, and other professionals. Drawing on postmodern concepts, it first covers how values embedded in the ethics code are reflected in these relationships and challenges that occur as marriage and family therapists carry out supervision, teaching, research, and their overall professional life with colleagues and the community. Guidelines are offered for avoiding or at least significantly reducing problems in the honoring of these values. Further discussion focuses on the special nature of the relationships and roles involved in supervision, research, and professional life, and offers guidelines for maintaining ethically informed relationships with the various stakeholders.

CONTENTS

Many marriage and family therapists engage in several professional roles, all of which demand that they have ethical relationships in these various contexts. As Chapter One in this book conveys, maintaining ethical relationships goes well beyond referring to a code of ethics when an ethical dilemma occurs. Ethical decisions are "…relational—they have to do with taking a clear stand and, in doing so, defining a relationship between self and other" (Flemons, Green, & Rambo, 1996, p. 45).

This chapter focuses specifically on ways the profession defines ethical relationships of marriage and family therapists with a key group of stakeholders: supervisees, students, other professionals, employees, and research subjects. The standards of the AAMFT ethics code for these relationships will be highlighted and common ethical concerns in these relationships will be discussed. When there have been public debates about what constitutes ethical practices, these too will be noted. The ethics code is one way that marriage and family therapists have of knowing consensual ethical standards, while debates on ethical issues represent efforts to develop and change universal consensual ethical standards (Hirschorn, 1999). Vignettes purposively illustrate typical situations that are designed to spark thoughtful consideration by readers.

THE INFLUENCE OF POSTMODERN IDEAS ON ETHICS

Several postmodern therapists, most notably Anderson (in press), Gergen (in press), and Swimm (in press), have proposed an alternative view of ethics that places the idea of relationship central to ethical practice. This view explores "the social construction of ethics that is local to the therapeutic process and relationship between the client and therapist [and other stakeholders]" (Swimm, in press, p. 1, brackets added). She further proposes all participants as collaborators in mutually defining ethical standards and actions. As Chapter One in this book notes, the idea of including the perspectives of those involved has always been a crucial part of ethical decision making. The new element in this way of thinking about ethics is that participants are co-creators of the process every step of the way. Thus, information about the AAMFT ethics code would be discussed with participants, along with a myriad of other reactions, ideas, beliefs, values, and possibilities. Together participants figure out what is ethical given the particular issue being faced at this point in time and place.

In the traditional view of the process for determining ethical standards, professionals as experts gather information about other stakeholders' (e.g., clients', other related professionals', community members') viewpoints and then consider their perspective when setting standards. A postmodern view of ethics may fundamentally change this process by increasing conversations about ethical issues among all stakeholders, including typically marginalized groups. Such discussions would take place on an ongoing basis and would likely result in consensual universal ethical standards in the field that are more fluid and apparent to all involved. These then could become the standards in ethics codes that would be more known to all stakeholders, including clients, since all would have been integral in the process. Because these ideas are in the infancy, the implications for the field are just emerging.

The following sections include, among other concepts, the influence of postmodern ideas in general on the relationships of marriage and family therapists with the stakeholders discussed in this chapter. Readers are encouraged to consider additional ways in which this alternative postmodern view of ethics could influence their relationships with these stakeholders.

HONORING ETHICAL VALUES IN RELATIONSHIPS WITH SUPERVISEES, STUDENTS, OTHER PROFESSIONALS, EMPLOYEES, AND RESEARCH SUBJECTS

In the next sections, values that are embedded in the ethical code are considered as they pertain to marriage and family therapists' carrying out of supervision, teaching, and research, and how those values pertain to the therapist's overall professional life with colleagues and the community. An ethical dilemma based on an actual situation is used to illustrate the challenges that can occur as marriage and family therapists try to honor these idealized values. The actual resolution of these dilemmas involved significant time, discussion among a variety of individuals, a multifaceted plan of action, and emotional stress on the part of all participants. Although each case example tends to highlight a particular stakeholder group, a similar dilemma could easily occur in a different context with a marriage and family therapist serving in another professional capacity. Guidelines are suggested to help readers facilitate the honoring of these values while preventing or at least reducing problems and hopefully avoiding similar situations.

RESPECTING THE RIGHTS OF OTHERS: DEVELOPING RESPECTFUL RELATIONSHIPS

The idea of respecting the rights of others has always been important to marriage and family therapists (Principle I). It has, however, meant something different to marriage and family therapists than to other types of therapists, because marriage and family therapists are always dealing in the realm of relationships. Marriage and family therapists cannot not consider the rights of multiple individuals at once. Hence, considering the multiple views of, for example, supervisees, clients, and supervisors simultaneously or research subjects and researchers at the same time is part of being respectful.

The postmodern movement has begun to spark new interest in looking at the quality of marriage and family therapists' relationships with clients and other stakeholders (e.g., Moules, 2000). See, for example, the special issue on postmodern supervision in the Journal of Systemic Therapies, edited by Storm (1995), and recent literature on student-teacher relationships (Morrison, 1997); supervisory relationships (Fine & Turner, 1997; Gardner, Bobele, & Biever, 1997; Turner & Fine, 1995); and research relationships (Clark, Jankowski, Margee, & Springer, 2000; Morris, Gawinski, & Joanning, 1994). Across these relationships, the authors generally encourage marriage and family therapists to form collaborative relationships, especially those that validate multiple perspectives and give attention to decreasing any differential in power that exists in the relationships. For example, in the supervision literature many authors suggest ways for supervisors to flatten the hierarchy in the supervisory relationship while still assuming their ethical responsibility of gatekeeping for the profession (Fine & Turner, 1997; Flemons et al., 1996; Turner & Fine, 1995).

Ethical decision-making models recommend that when marriage and family therapists find themselves in ethical binds, they should consider multiple perspectives—the differing views of those involved that may result from each person's unique point of view (e.g., Zygmond & Borhem, 1989). Over time, the field of marriage and family therapy has increasingly acknowledged that the views about what is considered respectful can vary widely depending on contextual variables such as culture, ethnicity, gender, sexual orientation, race, professional setting, and so on. For example, the AAMFT ethics code allows bartering with supervisees if they request it (Subprinciple 7.5), which recognizes that in some cultures bartering may be a preferred way of contracting for professional services, whereas refusing to barter may be seen as disrespectful.

Case Example: When Rights Collide. Hernandez, in his supervisory role in the mental health center, is approached by one of his employees, Betty, who is a fully credentialed therapist. Betty's clients, a mother and teenager, report that the father has recently converted to a religion that believes homosexuality is sinful. The teenager recently told his parents he was gay. The parents are now arguing a lot about the teenager's homosexuality, and the teenager is increasingly depressed because he had been very close to his father in the past. Betty asks Hernandez how to proceed, especially since her religious beliefs coincide with the father's about homosexuality. Hernandez, who is gay but has not shared this with his colleagues, resonates with the mother and son's pain and wonders how Betty would feel if she knew the truth about him.

In this case, when one considers the rights and perspectives of the various stakeholders, the differences appear quickly. According to the AAMFT ethics code (Principle IV), Hernandez is not to exploit the trust of his supervisees. Betty may feel betrayed if (when) Hernandez shares with her that he is gay, especially since she has been openly confiding with him about her beliefs about homosexuality. Betty may believe she has a right to know about the sexual orientation of the person she reports to and to request a new supervisor and/or to transfer the clients if she is required to support the mother and teenager's view of homosexuality. According to the AAMFT ethics code (Principle I), Betty is to provide services without discriminating and to refrain from treating clients outside of her competency (Subprinciple 3.11). Hernandez is painfully aware of the employment discrimination that homosexuals frequently face and prefers to be cautious about disclosing his sexual orientation to persons in the workplace, especially since he did not select those who report to him. He may believe that he has a right to maintain his privacy in this area of his life. The mother and teenager may take comfort in knowing that Hernandez is involved in the case, or they may want a different therapist if they know Betty's beliefs. The father may decide to participate in the therapy if he knows that Betty is open to , or shares, his religious beliefs. Additional perspectives are also important. For example, according to the AAMFT ethics code (Principle I), the rights of clients are to be respected; and research indicates that gay clients prefer to work with therapists who are accepting of homosexuality (Long, 1997).

Suggested Guideline: Seeing From All Sides. When ethical dilemmas arise, such as in the case above, a wise course of action is to hypothesize about the views of the various people involved from their respective positions, to spend time considering "what if" scenarios, and to consult with a variety of individuals representing different stakeholders. Many clinicians and supervisors may be able to draw on their own experience in hypothesizing various perspectives. They know what it is like to be not only a therapist or supervisor, but also a student, a supervisee, a community member, and perhaps a clinic director, a faculty member in an educational program, an administrative supervisor, a researcher, and a research subject. These diverse experiences in multiple stakeholder groups create the advantageous context whereby therapists have a window into the perspectives of the various stakeholders. In an actual ethical dilemma, however, both the supervisor and supervisee should still involve as many other stakeholders as possible in the ethical issues of that unique situation. In addition, they may consider further the postmodern view that would include collaborating with all participants by carefully and fully discussing matters and jointly determining decisions and actions. In the vignette above, considering the perspectives of the family, Hernandez, Betty, agency representatives, experienced professionals working with gay and lesbian issues, spiritual/religious advisors, and other families who have experienced similar conflict in their family relationships will lead to the best plan for resolution of the dilemma.

DOING NO HARM: BENEFITING THOSE WE WORK WITH

One of the values that seems to be universally accepted within the field is that marriage and family therapists must strive to benefit those with whom they work, whether they are clients, students, supervisees, research subjects, or colleagues (Principle I). However, determining what is beneficial and what is harmful represents a real challenge in practice because, as noted earlier, individuals' perspectives may vary widely from one another. The vignette below illustrates this challenge in the context of supervision of a student during a marriage and family therapy internship in which the supervisor must be concerned about the welfare of the client family and the welfare of the supervisee.

Case Example: Doing No Harm: But To Whom? Anita, a supervisor, is confused after reviewing the case file of a family being seen by Rhonda, a supervisee who is doing her masters' degree internship in the agency. The agency records seem to imply that more sessions have occurred than what appear in the case file. The family seems to be benefiting from Rhonda's work. Johnny's school problems have decreased significantly since Rhonda has facilitated a working relationship between the family and his school. Anita questions her supervisee who states that she did in fact provide a couple of extra sessions without charging the clients, because the family is having difficulty coming up with the agency fee. Rhonda states that she has progress notes in another file at home because she knows it is her ethical responsibility and agency policy to document sessions. She further states that her religious beliefs require her to do all she can for the family. Rhonda is also pleased that the family's neighbors have now called asking for services from her. However, she quickly senses that Anita seems concerned, even upset, about the situation.

In this scenario, who is harmed and who is benefited? Each of these stakeholders may answer this question differently. The family could feel beholden to Rhonda because of the special treatment they received that affects, perhaps even harms, the therapeutic relationship. Or the family may simply be grateful they have received the help they needed. The agency may be pleased that the clients received quality services and that the clients' neighbors are now seeking services from them. Or the agency may be concerned that their reputation in the community has been harmed since they are not complying with local standards for documentation and fees. The agency may even be concerned that there is legal liability. Some professionals may rejoice in the effectiveness of Rhonda's work, whereas others may criticize Rhonda's actions for being outside the parameters of professional standards and thus harmful to the profession.

Anita's responsibility is to take reasonable steps to ensure that Rhonda provides professional services according to the AAMFT ethics code (Subprinciple 4.5). If Anita, in her gatekeeper role, takes action that leads to Rhonda's dismissal from her training program, Rhonda could be harmed in being prevented from pursuing her career dream. If, however, this incident is an indication of Rhonda's overall ethical reasoning, future clients and the profession may be harmed if Anita allows Rhonda to continue in the field without an adequate supervisory intervention. Anita's supervisory responsibility as gatekeeper places her in a powerful position.

Suggested Guideline: Consider the Best and Worst Possibilities. Using the previously suggested guideline of considering multiple viewpoints, therapists will cast the largest net for obtaining ideas about potential complications or harm, as well as possible benefits and solutions by considering and including all participants. Ultimately, there are advantages to processing decisions accordingly when the answer is (as it often is) less than clear about the potential benefits and potential harm. Therapists can then make the most informed decisions possible, take whatever steps are possible to reduce the potential for harm, and be clear within themselves and with others regarding why they did what they did. Therapists may find that the most difficult situations are more easily handled when everyone involved has been an active participant in the process. Using this guideline in the previous scenario, Anita will need to initiate a process for determining a course of action by discussing the situation with Rhonda, with the internship site representatives, and with other colleagues in the marriage and family therapy program such as the program director. A decision will need to be made about how to handle the fees and to talk with the family about the situation. Rhonda's willingness to reflect on her ethical decision-making ability and the degree to which she takes responsibility for the situation will greatly affect the outcome.

DISCLOSING RELEVANT INFORMATION: INFORMED CONSENT

There seems to be agreement in the field that, in the context of therapy, therapists, students, and supervisees should inform clients about their qualifications (Subprinciples 1.2 and 4.4). There is less agreement in the literature regarding what information students and supervisees should provide clients about the supervision process. For example, a few supervisors argue that a client should be given the supervisor's name and contact information (Bernard & Goodyear, 1992); but most supervisors believe that the knowledge that a supervisor is involved is enough information.

It is generally suggested that a prudent policy is for supervisors to develop thorough, specific written contracts that disclose relevant information about the process of supervision with supervisees (Prest, Schindler-Zimmerman, & Sporakowski, 1992; Storm, 1997). Suggested areas to cover in contracts are outlining the logistics of supervision; clarifying the supervision relationship; identifying supervision goals; describing supervisory methods; reviewing clinical issues; delineating the requirements of credentialing bodies, employers, and educational institutions; and specifying evaluation procedures. The ethics code requires supervisors to disclose to supervisees their financial practices (Subprinciple 7.2). Supervisors are strongly encouraged to inform their supervisees when personal and family information is central to their preferred supervision process. Braverman (1997) and Atkinson (1997), for example, have developed an informed consent document for this purpose.

When the experience or training of the supervisee is substantial or increases during the supervisory period, it appears that less specific and more generic information is given about supervision, as long as an honest appraisal is given of the marriage and family therapist's qualifications and services (Subprinciples 8.1, 8.6, 8.7, and 8.8). Therapists who are employed by an agency or group practice and who receive supervision as part of their professional position may not receive as much detail about the supervisory process as students who are practicing for the first time in their internship sites. However, a detailed contract is advised for therapists who contract for private, self-paid supervision. When therapists obtain supervision in pursuit of new skills or areas of specialization, they should also be asked to provide detailed information about their training and competencies within this new area (Subprinciple 4.4).

Disclosure of relevant information also applies to research. Informed consent within the research context may pose special challenges. Sometimes fully informing participants about all aspects of the study might seemingly defeat the purpose of the research. If research subjects are not fully informed, then researchers must weigh the possible negative consequences against the benefits that they and others may receive from the research results. The AAMFT ethics code requires researchers to inform research subjects fully of any information that "might reasonably be expected to influence willingness to participate" (Subprinciple 5.2). When making the decision about what information should be told to research subjects, and if fully explaining the study may negatively affect the research, researchers are to consult with knowledgeable colleagues to ensure research participants are not being taken advantage of (Subprinciple 5.1). Therapists who do research are also typically required to submit all studies with human subjects for review by institutional review boards, which serve as watchdogs for assuring that subjects receive full and adequate information for making an informed choice.

In addition, researchers are to respect the right of potential subjects to decline participation and to realize that it may be difficult for potential subjects to decline to participate if the researchers are in a position of influence or authority (Subprinciple 5.3). This situation especially applies to clients receiving therapy from researchers or when the research subjects are children.

    <u>Case Example: Can We Really Say No?</u> Jansen is one of the members of a research team who is studying conjoint therapy for couples who have had an incident of domestic violence. The team has had more difficulty than expected in finding clients who meet the criteria set for research subjects. Since Jansen knows several couples she is

seeing in her small private practice that could participate in the study, she decides to tell her clients about the study. She tells them that their participation is voluntary, that it will not make a difference to her, and she asks them to think about it before deciding. She further says that she believes there will be no potential harmful effects to them but offers extra sessions to them should they experience negative reactions due to the sensitive nature of the topic. Jansen is delighted that both of her couples agree to participate. Jansen and the couples are conscious of the time being used to discuss the study, and they keep the discussion short.

Unbeknownst to Jansen, one of the couples saw their participation as a way of obtaining extra therapy sessions at no charge and had already decided to request the sessions since they find Jansen's time with them so helpful. The other couple initially disagreed about participating but did not share this with Jansen; the wife finally decided to participate at her husband's urging. Both partners did not want to disappoint Jansen, since her enthusiasm for the study clearly came through to them when she talked about it.

This vignette raises the question: To what degree did therapeutic context become an obstacle to the couples' truly being informed about the study and understanding the positive and negative ramifications of participating in it? From her perspective, Jansen tried very hard to set up the context whereby the clients could say no, to build in a safeguard if any negative effects occurred to them, and to refrain from using their therapy time for her own purposes of finding research subjects. However, she was in need of research subjects so seeing potential problems could be understandably difficult. From the clients' point of view, they trusted Jansen to keep their best interests in mind, they wanted to maintain a positive relationship with her, the potential for extra sessions at no charge was inviting, and they were anxious to get on with the session. Consequently, discussing the study in detail did not seem warranted.

<u>Suggested Guideline: Take Time to Talk</u>. In recent years postmodern ideas have served as an impetus for therapists to be more open and disclose more information with others on an ongoing basis regarding their reactions, biases, and rationales. This trend towards being more open and disclosing more with others encourages more in-depth conversations about ethical matters and more dialogue. Informed consent is more than providing information but involves truly considering the matter at hand from multiple perspectives. For example, if Jansen had followed this guideline more closely, she would have taken far more time to explore with the clients and with others the potential effects on the couples participating in the research, and perhaps even offered the couples an opportunity to discuss their participation with another colleague, researcher, or even other research participants. This approach of consciously being more open with others may very well be the key to the desired end result: informed clients, students, supervisees, and research subjects.

SERVING OTHERS' INTERESTS: CAUTIOUSLY ENGAGING IN MULTIPLE RELATIONSHIPS

During the mid-eighties the issue of multiple relationships was debated in the field because of a concern that multiple relationships can easily result in relationships that serve the self-interests of marriage and family therapists at the expense of others involved. Nonsexual/nonintimate multiple relationships are believed to be inherent in supervision (Ryder & Hepworth, 1990), and a lot of attention has been devoted to this topic in the supervision literature. Marriage and family therapists encourage rather than avoid <u>nonsexual</u> multiple relationships with supervisees and students, such as co-authoring a paper, conducting research together, or attending meetings together, because they believe these joint endeavors are critical in socializing and mentoring new professionals (Ryder & Hepworth).

Although historically the AAMFT ethics code prohibits providing therapy to students or supervisees, several authors (e.g., Freidman, 1994; Peterson, 1992; Peterson, Tomm, & Storm, 1997; Tomm, 2000) have debated the pros and cons of providing therapy to supervisees and students; and some authors have called for a change in the ethical code (e.g., Freidman, 1994; Tomm, 2000). One viewpoint is that supervisors must address the personal and family lives of students and supervisees as part of the training process and that this focus could be seen as "therapeutic" (e.g., Aponte, 1994; Freidman, 1994). Another argument, such as from Tomm, cites an "ethic of caring" (Peterson et al., 1997) in which there are certain circumstances when a supervisor should provide therapy to supervisees. In contrast, Peterson (1992) argues that providing therapy to supervisees while fulfilling the supervisory role of a gatekeeper for the profession leaves supervisees at great personal risk.

Current supervisory practice seems to be that supervisors are wise to avoid becoming therapists for their supervisees, but they have wide latitude to focus on the interface of their supervisees' personal and professional lives (Storm, Todd, Sprenkle, & Morgan, 2001). This practice abides by the ethics code and is consistent with most supervisors' belief that good supervision requires them to address, to some degree, the personhood of supervisees.

Marriage and family therapists seem to endorse at a philosophical level the prohibition in the ethics code regarding sexual relationships with supervisees and students "during the evaluative or training relationship between the therapist and supervisee or student" (Subprinciple 4.3). They also seem to accept that supervisors and teachers assume the responsibility to ensure that no harm occurs if they engage in sexual relationships with former supervisees and students. At the same time, most marriage and family therapists know of at least one couple whose relationship blossomed when one of the members was a supervisor or teacher of another. Therapists are human beings, preventing people from falling in love is nearly impossible, and most marriage and family therapists acknowledge that there is a difference between sexual harassment and mutual caring (Bernard & Goodyear, 1992). Typically, in situations where an attraction develops with a desire to act on it, most marriage and family therapists try to honor the ethical code by going public with their situation and asking for advice from their colleagues in how to pursue a relationship in an ethically informed manner.

Due to "their influential positions," marriage and family therapists have been given the responsibility by the AAMFT ethics code to make sound decisions about engaging in multiple relationships with supervisees, students, and research subjects. If therapists develop such relationships, the ethics code requires that they proactively take steps to avoid "exploiting the trust and dependency" of these stakeholders (Subprinciples 4.1 and 5.3). There is also recognition that clients of researchers who are asked to be research subjects are especially at risk (Subprinciple 5.2). There is recognition in the field that ethical decision making in these situations is much more easily read about than done (Peterson et al., 1997; Storm, 1998).

The AAMFT ethics code also states that marriage and family therapists avoid taking on a student or supervisee with whom one had a pre-existing relationship (Subprinciple 4.6), and avoid providing "services that create a conflict of interest that may impair work performance or clinical judgment" (Subprinciple 3.4). Some of the reasons for these guidelines become evident in the vignette below.

    <u>Case Example: A Special Relationship.</u> Jane, an MFT Program Director, is asked by faculty and supervisors to intervene with a student, Steven, who is not doing well in his classes and not transitioning well to his internship site. In fact, the internship site is threatening to cancel Steven's placement because their clients are not being served well and his documentation is overdue. The other faculty and supervisors are frustrated that Jane has not responded to the earlier warning signs that Steven was not living up to program expectations.

Jane remembers when Steven applied to the program. As his former therapist, Jane knew Steven better than the other applicants and she felt confident in her vote to accept him into the program. Steven had excellent experience since he was employed as a case manager in a local mental health center where he planned to continue working while in school. Once accepted, he became a strong supporter of the program and helped the university clinic set up a lucrative contract with his center. Problems began when he started his internship and he did not adjust his professional life to make room for the time needed for his internship. Jane hoped that her long-term relationship with Steven would help them work through this hurdle, but she was nervous during the meeting with him because she had to take a strong stand that something needed to change. Although Steven expected Jane to address the problems he was having in class and at his internship, he was shocked with her strong stance. How could Jane of all people not understand his situation? He had trusted her with the most intimate details of his life, and now she was turning on him and not giving him the room he needed to reach his goals. Steven had hoped that Jane would grant him extra time to fulfill the internship requirements. After all, she was the Program Director! Since he had even gone to bat for her program in his own agency during contract negotiations, Steven felt Jane should go to bat for him with the other faculty and internship site.

The pre-existing relationship between Jane and Steven affected all of the involved stakeholders. Since Steven had acknowledged his therapy with Jane in his application materials, the admissions committee was able to talk with Jane and had more than the usual amount of information upon which to base its initial decision. The prior relationship had contributed to Jane and Steven's entering into a business relationship that benefited the program. However, the "special" unique quality to their relationship led each to expect certain actions from the other. Jane expected that Steven would not challenge program expectations and would cooperate with her in the same way that he had as a client. Steven expected that Jane would give him special consideration because she knew his intentions were sound, and he trusted her to help him reach his goals.

Suggested Guideline: Prepare for the Worst and Hope for the Best. Overall, therapists are wise to tread lightly in engaging in multiple relationships with supervisees, students, research subjects, and other colleagues. Peterson et al. (1997) proposed specific guidelines for making sound decisions regarding engaging in multiple relationships in supervision, and these seem to be useful across stakeholder relationships. They suggest that marriage and family therapists should carefully weigh the possible enhancements and complications of these relationships with involved parties (if appropriate) and with others; embrace the idea that it is their responsibility to prevent harm; consider the gender configuration of participants; and assess the role of power in the relationship in making the decision about whether to engage in a multiple relationship. Therapists who decide to engage in a multiple relationship should do considerable self-reflection throughout the relationship and have fallback plans and safeguards. Taking these steps would seem to be following the spirit of the AAMFT ethics code. If Jane and Steven had followed the suggestions above, they would have acknowledged the ways their pre-existing relationship could influence them in their new roles and the change in their relationship that would occur if a business agreement with Steven's agency was pursued. As a result, they could have explored ways to address these effects, found ways to maintain a more positive relationship, and insured a better educational experience for Steven.

HONORING OTHERS' PRIVACY: CONFIDENTIALITY

The idea of confidentiality is at the core of the therapeutic relationship and extends to relationships with supervisees, students, and research subjects. Because clients consent to have their therapy recorded in some way (i.e., in writing and/or taped), or observed by other students, supervisees, colleagues, researchers, or employees, they must be able to trust therapists as caretakers of their information. Similarly, supervisees who enter into supervision and share their struggles in their work and the ways their own personal and family experiences affect their clinical work also must be able to trust that their confidences will be honored. The same ethical guideline of protecting privacy and honoring confidentiality applies to research subjects. This principle is essential out of respect for research participants and to encourage them to provide the honest, reliable information that is the backbone of research.

There are several emerging phenomena that affect confidentiality. First, Storm et al. (2001) noted that the supervisory relationship seems to have become less private than in the past; perhaps because marriage and family therapy has moved into the mainstream of mental health services, with supervisees often receiving supervision within their places of employment. They suggest that the profession and supervisors more clearly state the limits of confidentiality and privacy with supervisees. Second, marriage and family therapists are increasingly using technology such as the Internet, e-mail, and cell phones in teaching (Gale et al., 1995; Maggio, Todd, & Chenail, in press; Thomas, 1999); supervision (Ambrose, 2000; Long & Storm, in press); and research. These electronic innovations create a growing concern about safeguarding personal information and promising confidentiality for clients, students, supervisees, employees, and research subjects. (Electronic communications and telehealth services are discussed in Chapters Nine and Ten.) Third, the mapping of the humane genome has created new questions (Clark, 1998): Who is privy to genetic information within families when the information has serious implications for other family members, and who outside the family, such as employers and medical personnel, can have access to information?

Marriage and family therapists have the responsibility of maintaining client confidentiality by obtaining written permission from all involved for the process of coordinating treatment with other professionals. And in situations where marriage and family therapists wish to consult with other professionals about a specific case, they take steps to protect the identity of the clients. In supervision, as in therapy, marriage and family therapists must obtain written permission from supervisees, students, or research subjects in order to refer them to other resources and to share information that could lead to their identification, such as by talking with consultants (Subprinciple 2.6). The notable exception is that supervisors in educational or training settings can exchange information with those individuals who share in the educational and training responsibility (Subprinciple 4.7). To recapitulate, unless they have obtained prior written consent, marriage and family therapists do not share information that could "reasonably lead to the identification of a client, research participant, or supervisee" (Subprinciple 2.6). Furthermore, information shared should be kept to what is necessary to accomplish the specific purpose of the consultations. (Confidentiality issues with regard to clients, including mandated clients, are covered in Chapter Two.)

Case Example: Unintended Disclosure of Information. During a break at a local conference, Carlos seeks out Barbara for an informal conversation about two of her supervisees who have applied for a job at his agency. He asks Barbara, "How is Jonathan Grey doing?" Barbara replies with a smile: "Jonathon is a highly skilled clinician. As an African American, he has really helped us understand therapeutic relationships between our predominantly white therapists and the African American population we serve. He is particularly skilled at engaging clients, and follow-up reports from them indicate that he's very effective. Any agency hiring him will get a great asset." Carlos continues, "What about Kevin Stanton?" Carlos immediately notices that Barbara pauses and seems guarded in her response. She replies, "Kevin is also doing well." Barbara quickly changes the subject because she does not want to convey any information about Kevin's recent marital and financial problems. He is handling them well but they are difficult for him nonetheless. Barbara hopes that her supervisees will sign releases for her to contact Carlos with a formal reference. Carlos, who was considering hiring Barbara's supervisees, decides to offer a position to Jonathon and not to Kevin. He wonders about what problems Kevin may be having in his work.

Without intending to, Barbara has given an informal employment reference endorsing one of her supervisees over another for a position. The employer, Carlos, walks away with an inaccurate conclusion about Kevin's abilities based on what the supervisor has said and the impressions he drew from her nonverbal reactions, as well as from what she did not say. Consider the positions of the involved stakeholders. Barbara and Carlos' intentions are noteworthy. As a supervisor, Barbara wishes to mentor her supervisees by helping them attain professional employment, honor her supervisees' confidences, and abide by the ethics code. In her response, she tries to be general in her comments without giving much specific information and quickly extricates herself from the conversation. Carlos desires solid information so that he can hire the best person for his agency. Both supervisees will undoubtedly appreciate any assistance Barbara can offer in obtaining employment. In this scenario, Jonathon would be pleased to have Barbara's input lead to his employment, but he would not like to be in Kevin's situation in the future. Kevin, if he knew, would probably be upset about the conclusions Carlos drew, and may even wish that Barbara had shared more about his current circumstances. At the very least, he probably would have liked to make the decision himself about what gets said to whom.

Suggested Guideline: Keep a Tight Lip Unless Written Permission Is Obtained. Generally, therapists are most likely to honor confidences in their relationships with other stakeholders when they do two things. First, openly discuss the limits of confidentiality with supervisees, students, research subjects, employees, and colleagues. This includes informing them under what conditions information about them has to be released such as when mandated by law. Second, ask with whom supervisees, students, and research subjects would like them to talk, and then obtain a written release. Barbara and both her supervisees would have been better served if she had indicated to Carlos that she would be happy to talk about any of her supervisees once she had releases. When technology is used, special care needs to be taken to know the risks that the technology poses for maintaining confidentiality, to use it only when participants are fully informed, and to use it in a way to insure as much privacy as possible (Long & Storm, in press).

TREATING OTHERS WITH DIGNITY: RESPECTFUL COLLABORATION

Over the years, marriage and family therapists have been called upon to be more cautious about claims of effectiveness as therapists and as supervisors (Storm et al., 2001). Because marriage and family therapy claims to be different from other mental health professions due to the underlying epistemology, its practitioners are sometimes passionate about their beliefs and work. As a result, they may unknowingly and unintentionally alienate other stakeholders.

Case Example: Who Is the Best Therapist for the Job? In the initial session, Samson sees a single parent mother who requests help with her parenting because she is overwhelmed. Both of her children are having trouble in school, and she is in conflict with the children's father over what to do. The children are already seeing a therapist at another agency. Samson, who has a passion for family therapy, tells the mother that some therapists are not trained to see families and that he believes all family members should be involved in therapy in this situation. The mother cancels the appointment with the children's therapist and leaves a message that she will be seeing someone else. At the next session, Samson is surprised to hear that the other therapist was a classmate of his in his marriage and family therapy program and that the mother herself had, in fact, requested that the other therapist begin individual therapy sessions with her children.

From Samson's point of view, he wanted to help this mother. In his enthusiasm to help, however, he may have unknowingly sabotaged the work of a colleague and deprived the family from the help that was needed. The mother may have concluded from what Samson said that the therapist seeing her children was incompetent or at least not trained well. The therapist already involved with the family may feel excluded and harbor some resentment toward Samson.

   Suggested Guideline: Explain Carefully. It is important to refrain from acting as if the profession of marriage and family therapy has all the answers, or that a marriage and family therapist is the best practitioner for a given clinical situation. There are significant differences in the ways that therapists do their work and in the training received by therapists. Explaining these differences as preferences based on beliefs may be more respectful to both clients and professional colleagues, and ethical and effective collaboration may bring a beneficial solution for all persons involved. Although switching therapists may have been the best alternative for the family in the previous situation, a more ethical and effective approach would have been to engage in a careful discussion with the mother and to develop a plan that included the therapist who was already involved.

CONTRIBUTING TO THE COMMON GOOD: MAKING A DIFFERENCE IN THE PROFESSION AND THE COMMUNITY

There are many ways in which marriage and family therapists can make a difference and contribute to the profession and community. These ways range from serving on work groups within their own professional setting or locale to improve services to those in need, to participating in AAMFT organizational activities, to developing clinical innovations, to making a contribution via conducting research or publishing new ideas. The AAMFT ethics code includes the following ways for marriage and family therapists to make a difference: participating in activities without financial remuneration (Subprinciple 6.6); working on laws in the public interest (Subprinciple 6.7); and encouraging public participation in the delivery of professional services and the regulation of marriage and family therapists (Subprinciple 6.8). If a conflict exists between the ethics code and organizational practices, marriage and family therapists who are employed in the organization can contribute to the profession by making known their commitment to the AAMFT ethics code and by making efforts to resolve differences in a way "that allows the fullest adherence to the Code of Ethics" (Subprinciple 6.1).

Many marriage and family therapists are devoted to research or clinical practice or to formulating theoretical conceptualizations about family therapy; as a result they make a contribution to the profession and community by writing about their work. One ongoing challenge for writers is to credit ideas and innovations appropriately (Subprinciple 6.2, 6.3, and 6.4). The trouble with ideas is that they build one upon another, evolve in conversations, and cannot belong to one person for long. For example, only wordings, not ideas, can be copyrighted. Who contributes what is not always clearly evident as can be seen in the vignette that follows. Once their work is published, marriage and family therapists have a responsibility to take reasonable steps to insure that the organizations that promote and advertise their work are doing so appropriately (Subprinciple 6.5).

   Case Example: Who Had the Idea First? In reading a blind review of a paper for a journal, Bob began to believe he was reading an article written by Tony, a former doctoral graduate student. The ideas were an expansion of some work that Tony and Bob had done together while Tony was a student in the marriage and family therapy program. Bob called Tony, and Tony proudly claimed authorship of the article. Tony had appreciated Bob's mentoring and believed that he had given Bob appropriate credit by referencing Bob's work liberally in the paper and by thanking him for his contribution on the first page. He believed that Bob's contributions to the original ideas were part of his responsibility as a faculty member. Tony was upset that Bob, who was well respected in the field, would question his ethics. Bob, on the other hand, felt ripped off, thinking that Tony had exaggerated his own contribution to the original ideas. Bob was also under pressure at that time to publish in order to build his case for tenure at his university.

In this situation, Tony claimed the ideas as his own, while Bob saw the ideas as a spin-off of their previous collaboration and not so different from those they had discussed between them. Being respectful to one another requires that writers take extra care in including all of those who have contributed to the work that is being described, perhaps even keeping others aware of writing projects. When writing about case examples from supervision or teaching (even when disguised or an amalgamation of several cases), some marriage and family therapists ask the original participants to review the cases and give them the option of being anonymous or identified.

Suggested Guideline: Find a Talent to Contribute to the Profession. The earlier generation of marriage and family therapists sacrificed to carve out a place for marriage and family therapists to practice. It is imperative for the profession that each generation of marriage and family therapists do the same for the next generation of therapists by finding a way to use their unique talents to make a difference. It may be helpful for marriage and family therapists to keep in mind that they are working together to build something greater than any one person's contribution. If this view is taken, it naturally leads to marriage and family therapists recognizing all those who have contributed before them and to realizing that there will be others that will reshape their contributions. If this view had been foremost in the individual's minds in the preceding vignette, Tony would have involved Bob from the start in discussions about the paper and Bob would have encouraged Tony to reshape and develop his own ideas without needing to involve Bob.

ETHICALLY INFORMED RELATIONSHIPS WITH OTHER PROFESSIONALS

There has been less written about marriage and family therapists' specific ethical responsibilities to other professionals than there has been about the other stakeholder groups covered in this chapter. However, marriage and family therapists endorse the idea that it is critical to develop effective relationships with other professionals to provide quality services. Good working relationships allow therapists to coordinate treatment of their cases with other professionals; to consult with other professionals about their work; and to collaborate in developing creative services, interventions, and peer support groups for practitioners.

To summarize the main points above, the AAMFT ethics code notes several responsibilities that encompass contacts and relationships with other professionals. Marriage and family therapists have the ethical responsibility to maintain confidentiality for their clients, supervisees, students, employees, and research subjects by obtaining written permission. Without written permission, they must refrain from sharing information about clients, supervisees, students, employees, and research subjects if there is the likelihood that the individuals could be identified. When consulting with professional colleagues, information shared should be limited to what is needed to accomplish the goals of the consultations. This is especially a challenge since informal conversations among colleagues about clients, essentially on-the-spot consultations, are often a means for therapists to relieve their frustrations or anxiety about cases. Identifying clearly the purpose for discussing a case with another professional, and sharing only information that the other person needs to know to understand the situation may help marriage and therapists follow this guideline. Marriage and family therapists provide professional services within their level of expertise and present their credentials, training, and competencies accurately to the public, professional referral sources, and others. They follow any laws about the reporting of unethical conduct of colleagues (Preamble). Finally, they avoid conflicts of interest whenever possible and disclose any potential conflicts of interest that may exist.

Ethically Informed Relationships with Students, Supervisees, and Employees

<u>Ethical Decision Making in Supervision.</u> For several reasons, decision making about ethical matters in supervision is often more complex than resolving ethical concerns in clinical work. First, supervisors must consider their responsibility to supervisees and their gatekeeping role for the profession. In addition, they have a responsibility to assure that the supervisee's clients receive services at a professional level. They also have an ethical responsibility to the community (Storm, 1998; Storm & Haug, 1997; Storm et al., 2001). Third, they must carry out these responsibilities while operating one step removed from the practice of the therapy in question. Fourth, supervisors must answer the question: Am I acting as a responsible, ethical supervisor according to the standard of care for supervision?

Regarding this latter point, several authors have argued that this step is critical if supervisors are to make informed ethical decisions that address supervisory legal liability (e.g., Heath & Engleberg, 2000; Huber & Peterson, 2000; Storm & Engleberg, 2000; J. Woody, 1990). (See Chapter Nine on practice management for a discussion of the liability associated with supervision.) But what is the standard of practice for supervision? Storm et al. (2001) proposed that the typical practices of supervisors seem to differ in some significant ways from the standard of practice for supervision described in the AAMFT ethics code, the marriage and family therapy supervision literature, and the standards for Approved Supervisors of AAMFT. Table 1 offers a suggested set of best practices for supervision aimed at defining more clearly the standard of practice for supervision (Storm et al., 2001).

Table 1 - Suggested Best Practices

Supervision In General
-   Due to the lack of support, we believe supervisors, including ourselves, need to be more modest with supervisees, consumers, and the community at large about their effectiveness and to be realistic about what supervision can and cannot accomplish. This particularly applies to supervisory claims regarding the effectiveness of supervision, the protection of consumers, the success of their own and their supervisees' preferred therapy approaches, and the degree to which supervisors actually serve as gatekeepers for the profession.
-   If supervisors are to be maximally effective as gatekeepers and thus protect consumers, it may be useful to join as a community to serve in this function.
-   It can be helpful to clearly define what responsibilities we are personally and professionally agreeing to assume when we take on the role of supervisor, and to have the specifics of the supervision process spelled out in a written, formal contract that is periodically reviewed.
-   Due to the public and legal view that supervisors are overseeing supervisees' entire caseloads, it appears that the best practice is to abide by the consensus, and to insist that supervision is frequent and extensive enough so supervisors can responsibly oversee supervisees' caseloads.

Contextual Sensitivity
-   Sharing of contextual influences within supervision, and taking note of contextual influences regularly in all cases promotes contextual sensitivity in supervisors and supervisees, and can create a context of permission for those influences less evident to emerge.
-   It can be useful to recognize the ways professional settings influence supervisory practice, and select the best supervisory practices for the supervisor's particular setting.

Supervision Philosophy
- The articulation of a supervision philosophy can contribute to theoretical consistency, and it can be useful to pay attention to the theoretical fit of particular supervisory structures and supervision formats to achieve goals which are important within a given model of supervision.
- A closer examination of the differences for all supervisors between therapy and supervision may be highly useful in identifying some issues that are paramount for particular models.
- Research suggests giving major emphasis to the supervisory relationship (rather than overvaluing technique).
- Because there does not appear to be a universal developmental sequence for supervisees, we propose that supervisors individualize their supervision to the specific needs of each supervisee based on what supervisees say they need.

The Supervision Relationship
- Supervisors and supervisees alike appear to need clarity regarding the degree to which the supervisory relationship is private and the degree to which information is shared. Perhaps the best practice is for supervisors and supervisees to be as personal and intense as is appropriate for the particular context.
- Making power issues transparent, rather than assuming that it is possible to make them disappear, may be the best practice.
- Supervisees may have difficulty being candid in their feedback; so supervisors who pay attention to the characteristics of the relationship or the supervisory context that make it difficult for them and proactively seek and respond to supervisee feedback may have the best supervisory relationships.

Methods and Interventions
- The selection of the best supervisory formats and structures may be dependent on such factors as the theoretical preferences of participants, learning goals of supervisees, professional setting in which supervision occurs, and so on, and can be selected accordingly.
- Raw data and self-report sources of information add value to the supervision process, albeit in differing ways; both sources have constraints and limitation, and both sources influence the supervision process. Supervisors may wish to continually reexamine the value of differing sources of information in supervision for the fit with their philosophies of supervision.

Note. These ideas are discussed more fully in the paper, Gaps between MFT Supervision Assumptions and Common Practices, by Storm et al. (2001) published in the Journal of Marital and Family Therapy.

The Supervisor's Ethical Responsibilities. There are several literature reviews that deal with the supervisor's ethical responsibilities (Storm, 1998; Storm & Haug, 1997). These reviews draw upon the AAMFT ethics code, AAMFT Approved Supervisor guidelines (AAMFT, 1999), trends in regulatory laws, and the supervision literature. As noted earlier, supervisors are seen as having simultaneous ethical responsibilities to clients, supervisees, the community, and the profession. A primary obligation is that supervisors are to be proactive in protecting clients' welfare, rights, and best interests. This stance includes ensuring that clients are informed consumers about therapy and supervision and that they receive reasonable care from supervisees. In addition, supervisors, in various ways, aid their supervisees to construct and maintain ethical relationships with their clients. Supervisors interweave ethical issues during discussions about cases, guide supervisees in resolving ethical dilemmas when they occur, model ethical practice in their supervision relationships, and serve as an ethical eye watching over their supervisees' overall clinical practice and conduct.

Supervisors are responsible to supervisees for providing timely and adequate supervision, maintaining supervisee confidentiality, and giving timely feedback and evaluations. Supervisors assess readiness for supervision by determining if supervisees have the necessary basic information and skills, including training in ethics, to begin clinical practice. A respectful relationship is promoted by informing supervisees about the supervisor's preferred ideas regarding therapy, supervision, and the supervision context. Supervisors are to convey respect for their supervisees' uniqueness, dignity, and right to hold values, attitudes, and beliefs different from their own. They are to be sensitive to contextual variables in supervision and therapy and proactive in resolving differences if they occur in supervisory relationships. Supervisors who discuss the importance of practice according to the AAMFT ethics code are insuring that they and their supervisees have an agreed-upon code of ethics as a basis for their work together.

Supervisors perform a significant role for the profession by preparing the next generation of therapists. As supervisors serve as the gatekeepers for the profession, they protect the reputation of, and public confidence in, the profession. With both postgraduate trainees and students and interns within marriage and family therapy training programs, supervisors ensure that these practitioners are adequately prepared to provide quality care to consumers, and that they are professionals who represent the profession well. Further, supervisors recognize the extent of their own abilities, and seek appropriate consultation and training so that they themselves are adequately qualified to perform their responsibilities.

All of the above responsibilities apply regardless of the context in which supervision takes place and the supervisee's status as a student, postgraduate supervisee, or employee. Some ethical responsibilities, however, may be more of an issue for a supervisor in a particular setting or at a particular point in time during supervision. For example, supervision of beginning therapists (whether students completing internship requirements as part of educational and training programs or employees in an agency) carries with it significant ethical responsibilities. Like all of the other helping professionals, marriage and family therapists have convinced consumers and other professionals that therapists who are in training can practice because there is a supervisor overseeing therapy behind the scenes (Slovenko, 1980). The supervisor's close guidance serves two goals: to assure that supervisees meet standards for "good enough" service, and to protect clients from what partially trained clinicians may not know they do not know. In contrast, supervisors play a different role when they supervise therapists who are either meeting the requirement for supervised postgraduate practice for marriage and family therapy regulatory laws, or are employees within their agencies. In this case, supervisees are typically more advanced therapists who are practicing more autonomously. Supervisors' preferred theoretical ideas are also associated with certain types of ethical dilemmas. Table 2 summarizes some of the typical issues that arise in the context of particular settings, models of practice, or points in time.

Little is known within marriage and family therapy or psychotherapy in general about whether supervision actually increases ethical behavior on the part of therapists or protects clients (Storm et al., 2001). The belief that supervision is a critical process in developing ethical marriage and family therapists is based on intuitive common sense and supervisees' accounts of the usefulness of supervision in helping them handle ethical issues.

Table 2 - Typical Ethical Issues

In Professional Settings
- In agency supervision, how do supervisors balance roles of administrative and clinical supervision?
- In privately contracted supervision, how do supervisors obtain adequate information and influence?
- In educational supervision, how do supervisors translate supervision into the academic culture?

In Developing Relationships
- Are supervisors willing to assume the degree of responsibility involved?
- Is there a consummate fit between supervisor and supervisee?
- Will supervisors engage in a situation where they are in multiple relationships?
- Is there a clear contract between supervisors and supervisees?

In Supervising Therapy
- Where should supervisors draw the line between therapy and supervision?
- How can supervisors ensure clients will receive reasonable care?
- How can supervisors prevent supervisees from becoming their "puppets"?
- How do supervisors maintain their competency?
- How do supervisors recognize supervisees' limitations and provide the needed guidance?
- When doing live supervision or using tapes of therapy sessions, how do supervisors ensure client's confidentiality?
- When supervising more than one supervisee, how do supervisors honor supervisees' confidentiality?

In Preferred Ideas
- Psychoanalytic Model and Intergenerational Approaches: Where is the line between therapy and supervision? How are clients assured of reasonable care?
- Symbolic Experiential and Systems Models: How do supervisors prevent supervisees from becoming "puppets" at the expense of supervisee development?
- Integrative Models: How do supervisors stay always up-to-date with theory and research?
- Postmodern Ideas: How do supervisors address supervisees' limitations and provide enough guidance?

In Gatekeeping
- Are clinicians ready for supervision?
- Are consumers receiving reasonable care?
- What should supervisors do when supervisees are not doing well?
- How do supervisors protect consumers while providing the opportunity for supervisees to learn?

Ethically Informed Relationships with Research Subjects

<u>Ethical Challenges in Research.</u> The major purpose of research is ultimately to benefit all consumers by helping therapists understand the therapy process and determine effective intervention and practices. This noble purpose may make it easy to adopt the view that the benefits of any research study outweigh the risks to individual

research subjects. Researchers, however, must think ethically as they weigh the common good against the risks to the individual research subjects. Because it can be difficult to do this in isolation, most researchers who study human subjects are required to present their research to institutional review bodies that assist researchers in determining the balance and in meeting ethical standards. If such a body does not exist, researchers are to consult extensively with colleagues. Even so, Fontes (1998) noted researchers often face ethical issues:

. . . alone with their consciences. Many ethical decisions will be based on the amount of overnight tossing-and-turning that a researcher can tolerate. Therefore all researchers are morally obligated to think deeply about ethical issues, to discuss these issues with others, and to keep their moral compasses delicately tuned, even if all researchers' compasses do not point in precisely the same direction. (p. 53)

THE RESEARCHER'S ETHICAL RESPONSIBILITIES

There are excellent reviews of the ethical responsibilities of researchers (e.g., Reynolds, 1979). Overall ethical responsibilities of researchers include the following. Researchers must consider the risks and benefits to research subjects when designing their studies. Each research method has specific unique ethical issues associated with using it. For example, in the context of marriage and family therapy, see the literature on ethical issues in doing qualitative research (LaRossa, Bennett, & Gelles, 1981; Piercy & Fontes, in press); ethnographic studies (Newfield, Sells, Smith, Newfield, & Newfield, 1996); outcome research (Aradi & Piercy, 1985; Jurich & Russell, 1985; Lyness & Sprenkle, 1996); observation research (Bussell, 1994); and cross-cultural research (Fontes, 1997, 1998; Piercy & Fontes, in press).

A couple of illustrations show how ethical issues arise when specific methodologies are used. Researchers using qualitative methods may find it hard to convey the spectrum of risks to clients before the research begins because the procedures used and the nature of the inquiry evolve as the research progresses. Researchers doing outcome research often wrestle with how to minimize harm to subjects in control groups who do not receive the benefits of the treatment being studied. Many of the referenced authors offer creative solutions to the ethical dilemmas posed by the various methodologies.

Research subjects are to be informed about the potential harm and benefits of participating and about the study so that they can make an informed decision about whether they wish to participate. If fully informing research subjects may negatively affect the research results, researchers must consult with others and determine what information research subjects need to know to make an informed decision. If some information is to be withheld from participants, researchers must determine what is the potential harm of doing so. If there is potential harm associated with participating in any research, investigators are to build in safeguards and offer something to counter the negative effects. Because researchers are often privy to personal information, research subjects' rights to confidentiality must be honored. There is, however, a difference between anonymity and confidentiality, and the purpose of the research and its design may call for one over the other. Researchers must take care to insure that the identities of research subjects are protected.

Researchers must pay attention to the contextual variables of the research subjects and the context in which the research is being conducted. Fontes (1997, 1998), discussing cross-cultural research, suggested paying special attention to understanding the context, the sensitivity of the topic being studied, the meaning of the research to the individuals and the community, the intended use of the results, and the effect of the research on the individuals and communities. These guidelines constitute sound advice to all researchers.

CONCLUSION: THE GOLDEN RULE

As suggested throughout this chapter, there are several means by which therapists can promote respectful, transparent, and collaborative relationships with professionals, supervisees, students, employees, and research subjects. The most critical components include: purposively discussing the situation from each stakeholder's perspective; weighing the pros and cons of various responses; taking the time to disclose preferred ideas, biases, values, and practices; honoring confidences and others' privacy; and being balanced about the superiority of the marriage and family therapy perspective as compared with other professions or models of practice. The most simple, but compelling guideline for relationships between all involved persons or stakeholders is probably the golden rule: Do unto others as you would like them to do unto you.

REFERENCES

Ambrose, H. (2000). Therapy and supervision in the age of the internet. In Readings in family therapy supervision (pp. 124–126). Washington, DC: American Association for Marriage and Family Therapy.

American Association for Marriage and Family Therapy [AAMFT]. (1999). American Association for Marriage and Family Therapy Approved Supervisor designation: Standards and Responsibilities. Washington, DC: Author.

Anderson, H. (in press). Ethics and uncertainty: Brief unfinished thoughts. Journal of Systemic Therapies.

Aponte, H. (1994). How personal can training get? Journal of Marital and Family Therapy, 20, 3–15.

Aradi, N., & Piercy, F. (1985). Ethical and legal guidelines related to adherence to treatment protocols in family therapy outcome research. American Journal of Family Therapy, 13, 60–65.

Atkinson, B. J. (1997). Informed consent form. In C. Storm & T. Todd (Eds.), The reasonably complete systemic supervisor resource guide (p. 11–15). Needham Heights, MA: Allyn & Bacon.

Bernard, J., & Goodyear, R. (1992). Fundamentals for clinical supervision. Needham Heights, MA: Allyn & Bacon.

Braverman, S. (1997). The use of genograms in supervision. In T. Todd & C. Storm (Eds.), The complete systemic supervisor: Context, philosophy, and pragmatics (pp. 349–362). Needham Heights, MA: Allyn & Bacon.

Bussell, D. (1994). Ethical issues in observational family research. Family Process, 33, 361–376.

Clark, W. (1998). Genetics: What should MFTs know? Family Therapy News, 15, 17.

Clark, W., Jankowski, P., Margee, & Springer, N. (2000). Searching for a fit: Utilizing a co-research team as a qualitative method of analysis. Journal of Systemic Therapies, 19, 56–64.

Fine, M., & Turner, J. (1997). Collaborative supervision: Minding the power. In T. Todd & C. Storm (Eds.), The complete systemic supervisor: Context, philosophy, and pragmatics (pp. 217–228). Needham Heights, MA: Allyn & Bacon.

Flemons, D., Green, S., & Rambo, A. (1996). Evaluating therapists' practices in a postmodern world: A discussion and a scheme. Family Process, 35, 43–56.

Fontes, L. (1997). Conducting ethical cross-cultural research on family violence. In G. Kantor & J. Jasinski (Eds.), Out of darkness: Contemporary perspectives on family violence (pp. 296–312). Thousand Oaks, CA: Sage.

Fontes, L. (1998). Ethics in family violence research: Cross-cultural issues. Family Relations, 47, 53–61.

Freidman, E. (1994). Letter to the editor. Supervision Bulletin, 7, 4 & 7.

Gale, J., Dotson, D., Huber, M., Nagireddy, C., Manders, J., Young, K., et al. (1995). A new technology for teaching/learning marital and family therapy. Journal of Marital and Family Therapy, 21, 183–191.

Gardner, G., Bobele, M., & Biever, J. (1997). Postmodern models of family therapy supervision. In T. Todd and C. Storm (Eds.), The complete systemic supervisor: Context, philosophy, and pragmatics (pp. 217–228). Needham Heights, MA: Allyn & Bacon.

Gergen, K. (in press). Relational process for ethical outcomes. Journal of Systemic Therapies.

Heath, A., & Engleberg, S. (2000). Legal liability in supervision: An interview with AAMFT legal counsel. In Readings in family therapy supervision (pp. 162–164). Washington, DC: American Association for Marriage and Family Therapy.

Hirschorn, D. (1999). Postmodern ethics and our theories: Doing therapy versus being therapists. Journal of Systemic Therapies, 18, 18–41.

Huber, C., & Peterson, C. (2000). MFT supervision: Evaluating and managing critical issues. In Readings in family therapy supervision (pp. 160–161). Washington, DC: American Association for Marriage and Family Therapy.

Jurich, A. P., & Russell, C. (1985). The conflicts between the ethics of therapy and outcome research in family therapy. In L. L. Andreozzi (Ed.), Integrating research and clinical practice (pp. 90–97). Rockville, MD: Aspen Systems.

LaRossa, R., Bennett, L., & Gelles, R. (1981). Ethical dilemmas in qualitative family research. Journal of Marriage and the Family, 43, 303–313.

Long, J. (1997). Sexual orientation: Implications for the supervisory process. In T. Todd & C. Storm (Eds.), The complete systemic supervisor: Context, philosophy, and pragmatics (pp. 59–71). Needham Heights, MA: Allyn & Bacon.

Long, J., & Storm, C. (in press). Training standards, supervision, and training issues in marriage and family therapy. In C. Cole, A. Cole, & V. Frusha (Eds.), Marriage and family therapy in the new millennium. Iowa City, IA: Geist Russell.

Lyness, K., & Sprenkle, D. (1996). Experimental methods in marital and family therapy research. In D. Sprenkle & S. Moon (Eds.), Research methods in family therapy (pp. 241–263). New York: Guilford Press.

Maggio, L., Todd, T., & Chenail, R. (in press). Teaching family therapy in an electronic age. Journal of Systemic Therapies.

Morris, J., Gawinski, B., & Joanning, H. (1994). The therapist-investigator relationship in family therapy research. Journal of Systemic Therapies, 13, 24–28.

Morrison, N. (with Hunt, T., Natoli, D., & DiTiberio, J.). (1997). Narratives of change: Teaching from a social constructionism perspective. Journal of Systemic Therapies, 16, 83–92.

Moules, N. (2000). Postmodernism and the sacred: Reclaiming connection to our greater-than-human worlds. Journal of Marital and Family Therapy, 26, 229–240.

Newfield, N., Sells, S., Smith, T., Newfield, S., & Newfield, F. (1996). Ethnographic research methods: Creating a clinical science of the humanities. In D. Sprenkle & S. Moon (Eds.), Research methods in family therapy (pp. 25–63). New York: Guilford Press.

Peterson, M. (1992). At personal risk: Boundary violations in professional-client relationships. New York: Norton.

Peterson, M., Tomm, K., & Storm, C. (1997). Multiple relationships in supervision: Stepping up to complexity. In T. Todd & C. Storm (Eds.), The complete systemic supervisor: Context, philosophy, and pragmatics (pp. 253–271). Needham Heights, MA: Allyn & Bacon.

Piercy, F., & Fontes, L. (in press). Teaching qualitative decision-making in qualitative research: A learning activity. Journal of Systemic Therapies.

Prest, L., Schindler-Zimmerman, T., & Sporakowski, M. (1992). The initial supervision checklist (ISSC): A guide for the MFT supervision process. Clinical Supervisor, 10, 117–133.

Reynolds, P. (1979). Ethical dilemmas and social science research. San Francisco: Jossey-Bass.

Ryder, R., & Hepworth, J. (1990). AAMFT ethical code: "Dual relationships." Journal of Marital and Family Therapy, 16, 127–132.

Slovenko, R. (1980). Legal issues in psychotherapy supervision. In A. Hess (Ed.), Psychotherapy supervision: Theory, research, and practice (pp. 453–473). New York: Wiley.

Storm, C. (Ed.). (1995). Special issue on postmodern supervision. Journal of Systemic Therapies, 14.

Storm, C. (1997). The blueprint for supervision relationships: Contracts. In T. Todd & C. Storm (Eds.), The complete systemic supervisor: Context, philosophy, and pragmatics (pp. 272–282). Needham Heights, MA: Allyn & Bacon.

Storm, C. (1998). Defensive supervision: Balancing ethical standards with vulnerability. In G. Brock (Ed.), Ethics casebook (pp. 173–190). Washington, DC: American Association for Marriage and Family Therapy.

Storm, C., & Engleberg, S. (2000). Supervising defensively: Advice from legal counsel. In Readings in family therapy supervision (pp. 165–166). Washington, DC: American Association for Marriage and Family Therapy.

Storm, C., & Haug, I. (1997). Ethical issues: Where do you draw the line? In T. Todd & C. Storm (Eds.), The complete systemic supervisor: Context, philosophy, and pragmatics (pp. 26–40). Needham Heights, MA: Allyn & Bacon.

Storm, C., Todd, T., Sprenkle, D., & Morgan, M. (2001). Gaps between MFT supervision assumptions and common practice: Suggested best practices. Journal of Marital and Family Therapy, 27 (2), 227–239.

Swimm, S. (in press). Foreword to special section on process ethics. Journal of Systemic Therapies.

Thomas, F. (1999). Creating local knowledge in an electronic community: A learning project. Journal of Systemic Therapies, 18, 69–76.

Tomm, K. (2000). Defining supervision and therapy: A fuzzy boundary. In Readings in family therapy supervision (pp. 171–172). Washington, DC: American Association for Marriage and Family Therapy.

Turner, J., & Fine, M. (1995). Postmodern evaluation in family therapy supervision. Journal of Systemic Therapies, 14, 57–69.

Woody, J. (1990). Resolving ethical concerns in clinical practice: Toward a pragmatic model. Journal of Marital and Family Therapy, 16, 133–150.

Zygmond, M., & Borhem, H. (1989). Ethical decision-making in family therapy. Family Process, 28, 269–280.

COMPETENCE AND INTEGRITY:
ETHICAL CHALLENGES FOR TODAY AND THE FUTURE

5

Wayne H. Denton and Stephanie R. Walsh

This chapter challenges both practitioners and the profession by exploring certain unstated but logical implications inherent in the ethical principle of competence. Although fairly detailed guidelines for the therapist's integrity are stated in professional ethics codes, the issue of competence is typically mentioned in more general terms. A major focus of the discussion is to demonstrate that competence inevitably connects to the primary ethical responsibility to advance the client's welfare. The logical implications of this assumption raise important questions about the process of clinical decision making in general, and the selection of intervention models and methods in specific for advancing the client's welfare. The movement toward evidence-based practice within the various helping professions addresses many of these questions and creates new ethical challenges for the day-to-day practice of marriage and family therapists and for the profession as a whole.

CONTENTS

Discussions of ethics do not often focus on debating the basic competence of the practitioner, if one understands competence to encompass primarily professional knowledge and skills. The idea that a therapist will possess an appropriate level of competence for the treatment role seems to be mostly assumed. This position may connect to the important role that the helping professions play in monitoring and accrediting the educational and training programs that produce practitioners for their various disciplines. Although ethics codes often detail and proscribe behaviors that directly relate to professional integrity, much less attention is given to professional competence in the sense of the level of knowledge and skill that are required for ethical practice. For example, the AAMFT ethics code (various subprinciples in Principle III) speaks in detail about competence and integrity as might be affected by personal problems of the therapist, conflicts of interest, harassment, exploitative behavior, and accepting gifts. Another issue relevant to integrity also appears under responsibility to clients (Principle I); namely, multiple relationships and roles and sexual relationships with clients.

Because other chapters in this book cover in detail issues of professional integrity and its potential violations, the focus in this chapter will be primarily on competence in regard to professional knowledge, skills, and clinical decision making. (See Chapter Three for a full discussion of multiple relationships. The values, personhood, and character of the therapist, all issues relevant to integrity, are also discussed in Chapters Two and Seven.)

Several new trends in the theory and practice of therapy are gaining momentum and are bound to influence thinking about the field and raise concerns. Many of these newer ideas are noted in this book and are important to discuss. The AAMFT ethics code requires therapists to "pursue knowledge of new developments" (Subprinciple 3.1). They are further advised that, when they "are developing new skills in specialty areas, . . . to ensure the competence of their work and to protect clients from possible harm" (Subprinciple 3.7). An overall prudent guideline is that practitioners must be aware of new developments, learn about them in detail, evaluate them carefully, and implement them in practice only with suitable training and supervision. These guidelines are suggested in regard to issues covered in this book such as spirituality and sexuality, the moral dimensions of family life, family violence, and the sometimes-conflicting needs of children and parents.

The issue of maintaining and upgrading one's professional competence in the context of knowledge and skills becomes extremely complex in the face of society's current knowledge and technological explosion. New and rapid changes in the scientific understanding of human behavior and remedies for human problems create extreme demands on professionals "to know about everything." As a result, training programs have, in fact, continued to expand the curricula that students must learn. And practitioners are expected to apply and process a great deal of knowledge when providing therapeutic help to a given client. One logical question is: what knowledge bases and what skills can be expected to apply to and help a given client's problems and how does one make these clinical decisions? This question seems highly relevant to the ethical principle "to advance the welfare of families and individuals" (Principle I).

An important trend in mental health services that bears on these questions and on the ethical issue of professional competence is that of evidence-based practice. This chapter confronts the issue of clinical decision making as an ethical issue. It proposes that the goals of marriage and family therapists should relate to the psychological or relational goals clients present that can be addressed through the usual skills learned by family therapists during the course of training. It further proposes the type of skills that may meet the ethical requirements of competence are those for which there is some evidence of their efficacy—a position that has been referred to as an "ethics of evidence" (Miké, 1999). Therapists have an ethical obligation to become aware of this movement as a major "new development" in the field (Subprinciple 3.1). The chapter concludes with suggestions for moving towards evidence-based practice.

CONFRONTING QUESTIONS OF ETHICS AND COMPETENCE IN DECISION MAKING

The AAMFT Code of Ethics states that marriage and family therapists advance the welfare of families and individuals (Principle I), but how does a family therapist decide what constitutes the welfare of a family and, then, how to best achieve that goal? Consider the following case example.

Case Example: Kay, Ben, and Family. Kay and Ben arrived for their scheduled appointment with their two daughters, 16-year old Jennifer and 13-year old Christie. The parents reported concern about Jennifer whose previously excellent grades had turned into failing marks. They discovered she had been binge-drinking alcohol and had been with some other youths that broke into a house. The parents were worried that Jennifer might be clinically depressed. Jennifer talked about the difficulty of being "different" in her school because her family did not belong to the majority ethnic group in their community. The therapist noticed that the parents often disagreed in their answers to questions, and she perceived a thinly veiled hostility between the two. Ben had recently been laid off from a local factory when his company transferred its manufacturing operations to another country. As a result, the family was experiencing financial hardship. As the session drew to a close the therapist wondered to herself what she should recommend to the couple in terms of continued treatment.

Kay and Ben's family was dealing simultaneously with scholastic, substance abuse, mood, conduct, marital, cultural, economic, and financial problems. In which of these problems should the therapist attempt to intervene, and in what order? What should be the goals of the therapy? Furthermore, what types of interventions should she use to try to achieve these goals?

The following sections confront these questions head-on, in the context of the case example above and others, and further discuss the ethical considerations involved in family therapy processes, goals, and outcomes. The underlying position is that that the welfare sought after for families and individuals should "generally stick closely to clients' stated goals and therapists' training" (Tjeltveit, 1999, p. 203).

EVIDENCE-BASED PRACTICE: A NEW ETHICAL FRONTIER

Traditionally, many therapists (and even the profession as a whole) have not tended to view the topic of efficacy as an ethical issue. To best advance the welfare of families and individuals, the discussion here proposes that the profession of marriage and family therapy has an ethical obligation to begin to move towards a standard of evidence-based practice. As noted earlier, this stance has been referred to as the ethics of evidence (Miké, 1999). This section discusses what evidence-based practice consists of and arguments that have been made against it.

ETHICAL ISSUES IN PSYCHOTHERAPY OUTCOMES

Scientific interest in the outcomes of interventions is a relatively recent event in the delivery of health care (Miké, 1999). An ethical question that outcomes research cannot answer, however, is what the goal of an intervention should be. In the case example presented above, a question to confront is what should be the goal of family therapy for Kay and Ben's family. Tjeltveit (1999) has defined a therapy goal as what one or more stakeholders want or intend to happen in therapy while therapy outcomes are what actually happens, which may or may not correspond to stakeholders' goals (p. 189). He has further proposed the term "mental health" as a summary for all individual psychotherapy goals while noting the limitation that a consensus definition of that term has not been possible (Tjeltveit, 1999, p. 199). The term "mental" refers to the mind and so, by definition, "mental health" refers to individuals. Family therapists, of course, may work with an individual but may also work with couples or families. This latter situation suggests two options: that the family therapist has several clients or that the relationship might be the client. Thus, family therapists might have the goal of "mental health" when working with an individual or the goal of "relational health" when working with a relational system of people.

Defining couple or family health would be as daunting a task as the definition of mental health since such definitions would vary from one model of family therapy to the next. For example, a structural family therapist might say that a healthy family is one with appropriate boundaries, functioning subsystems, and an intact hierarchy (e.g., Minuchin, 1974). A transgenerational family therapist might say that a healthy family is one in which the members are well differentiated, experience low anxiety, and are in good emotional contact with their families of origin (e.g., Bowen, 1978). A narrative family therapist might object to the very idea of trying to differentiate normal from abnormal at all (e.g., White, 1995).

The AAMFT ethics code avoids the pitfalls of trying to define mental health and/or relational health and simply states that family therapists "advance the welfare of families and individuals." Since a family therapist is to advance the welfare of a family or individual, it can be said that "welfare" is the desired outcome of therapy. For this discussion, "welfare" refers to the desired goal of family therapy whether it is with individuals, couples, or families.

Tjeltveit (1999) states that mental health "has to do with facts about how human beings function psychologically, but also with ideals about how human beings best function, or should function" (p. 198). Thus, concepts of mental health are "rooted in both science and ethics" (p. 198). Likewise, if the goal of family therapy is to advance the welfare of clients, then "welfare" is an outcome that "should" occur and so, likewise, there is an ethical component to welfare. It is therefore appropriate that the outcome of therapy be considered from an ethical perspective. In addition, the responsibility to make sure that the therapy is beneficial and to monitor outcomes is suggested in the AAMFT ethics code: "Marriage and family therapists continue therapeutic relationships only so long as it is reasonably clear that clients are benefiting from the relationship" (Subprinciple 1.9).

Mental and relational health does not exhaust the list of possible ethical goals for family therapy. Johnson (2001) discussed other ethical issues as they have appeared in the family therapy literature. These include solving issues such as racial divisions, world hunger, overpopulation, pollution of the environment, and so on. Johnson argued that family therapists, in the course of standard family therapy training, have not been "offered the tools with which to attack human discord on a national or global scale as we might be, for example, if we were trained as international mediators or foreign service workers" (p. 3). Tjeltveit (1999), likewise, has cautioned that therapists may at times combine mental health with other ethical goals. At the extreme, he warned that "therapists can use 'mental health' (at times in uncritical ways) to further particular ethical or political causes, to delineate one region within the heterogeneous realm of normality as the sole or best region for those seeking mental health" (p. 201). Johnson (2001) has referred to some of these other goals described in the family therapy literature as demonstrating "messianic tendencies" (p. 3).

Tjeltveit (1999) has proposed that the relationship between concepts of mental health and other ethical ideals can be understood as occurring along a spectrum "from mental health as freedom <u>from</u> serious psychological problems (mental disorders) to freedom <u>for</u> some state of positive mental health. Concepts of positive mental health range from limited ('minimalist') criteria for determining therapy goals or evaluating outcome, to criteria that are extensive ('maximalist'), criteria that fully flesh out the meaning of human flourishing" (p. 201). This line of thought suggests that "welfare" can be considered on a similar spectrum ranging from welfare as freedom <u>from</u> individual or relational disorders (the minimalist position) to freedom <u>for</u> some state of positive mental or family health (the maximalist position).

It is important to note that the minimalist position does not mean that the goal of therapy is <u>free</u> from ethical considerations: "Defining mental health (or 'welfare') as freedom <u>from</u> diagnosable mental disorders or other serious psychological problems entails a relatively limited set of ethical assumptions: as a general rule, it is good to be free from the suffering and other problems associated with psychological problems" (Tjeltveit, 1999, p. 201). Tjeltveit suggested:

Those arguing for concepts of mental health that involve more extensive ethical commitments have, I believe, a greater responsibility to justify their concepts of mental health than those whose concepts of mental health bear a more modest ethical content. The burden of proof is on therapists holding maximalist views. They need to justify why they should venture beyond their training (unless they have relevant education or experience) and the customary societal agreement regarding therapy. (pp. 203–204)

Tjeltveit concluded with the importance of psychological goals: "Psychotherapists should undoubtedly emphasize psychological goals, since we are trained to address psychological issues and most clients assume therapy will focus on them" (p. 197). Johnson (2001) similarly suggested a relatively modest (but realistic) goal for family therapy as a profession: "Family therapy cannot succeed as all things to everyone, the earth's New Jerusalem . . . what must matter in the end—at least for us as a discipline—is how well our ideas improve human relationships" (p. 10).

While there are diverse views on this matter (e.g., Hardy, 2001; McGoldrick, 2001; Sluzki, 2001), the position in this chapter agrees with Tjeltveit (1999), Johnson (2001), and others, who maintain that the "welfare" of clients should be related to the relational or psychological goals that clients present with and which can be addressed through the usual skills learned by family therapists during the course of training. Principle III of the AAMFT ethics code states: "Marriage and family therapists maintain high standards of professional competence and integrity." Maintaining this high standard of professional competence requires that marriage and family therapists practice within the scope of their professional training.

The varied problems that Kay and Ben's family face are certainly in interaction with each other, and their therapist needs to be aware of and sensitive to all of these issues. At the same time, the therapist's professional skills will be primarily in intervening in the relational and psychological problems the family is struggling with. Thus, the therapist might establish goals with the family of changing Jennifer's behavior or even improving the marital relationship; however, intervening in the transfer of manufacturing jobs offshore would seemingly be outside the scope of the therapist's training. If the therapist attempted to intervene professionally in this latter problem, Subprinciple 3.7 would apply: "Marriage and family therapists practice in specialty areas new to them only after appropriate education, training, or supervised experience."

Narrowing the focus of therapy to psychological or relational goals still leaves the therapist with a multiplicity of decisions. Which of the myriad of models of family therapy with their varied interventions should she draw from to try to advance the welfare of the family she is consulting with? Since this question involves "should" it is a decision with ethical implications.

SOURCES OF INFORMATION FOR CLINICAL DECISION MAKING

There are many sources a clinician may rely on for clinical decision making (Zarin, Seigle, Pincus, & McIntyre, 1997). First, a theory about the cause of a problem may be used to derive an intervention. If, for example, one assumes that diffuse boundaries are associated with the development of family problems, then it would be logical to assume that the goal of helping a family develop firmer boundaries should be associated with improvement in the presenting problem. A second source for clinical decision making can be tradition: "this is how we have always done it here." A third factor in decision making is skill that a clinician has or the availability of services. Therapists without skills in couple therapy, for example, may recommend individual psychotherapy for clients who present with relationship complaints. Cost can be a fourth factor in clinical decision making. Perhaps a client cannot afford to attend individual psychotherapy but would be able to afford group psychotherapy. A fifth factor relevant to information that bears on clinical decision making is unsystematic observation derived from one's clinical practice (Evidence-Based Medicine Working Group, 1992). In other words, in the clinician's experience, it "seems" that a certain approach has worked with a certain type of problem. A final factor, the opinion of a noted authority, might be used in the decision of selecting an intervention to use.

The field of family therapy has been especially vulnerable to having therapists' draw on the role of authorities in clinical decision making. Sprenkle and Ball (1996) have noted, "Our field remains too often dominated by charismatic clinician/teachers whose ideas have rarely been empirically tested with anything approaching scientific rigor""(p. 392). The models of such clinician/teachers are often accepted without sound evidence of their efficacy other than the testimony of their originator. It then seems that the authority commanded by the models declines, again often without sound evidence that they are not effective. When therapists do not consciously process the sources of information that drive clinical decisions, the client may not benefit from the therapy.

    Case Example: Leslie and Her Mother. Leslie and her mother were seeing a therapist in a metropolitan family service agency. The therapist was primarily trained in solution-oriented therapy in her graduate program. The entire staff in the family service agency where the therapist also did her internship had recently received training in narrative therapy and was shifting their practice in that theoretical direction. In the initial session, the therapist began with the intervention of encouraging the mother and daughter together to tell their story; however, the mother did all of the talking, was very expressive and emotional, while Leslie remained silent.

Leslie, a 9-year old girl, lived with her mother, Sara, age 32, and Leslie's brother Ross, age 7. The family lived in a modest three-bedroom home in a middle class neighborhood. Sara and her husband Dave, a junior high school teacher, had divorced nine months earlier, and he had moved to Minneapolis. He paid regular child support and the children lived with him during the summer when he was off from teaching and able to work flexible hours at a second job.

Two months after school started the previous fall, in November, Sara learned from Leslie that a neighbor boy, age 13, had been sexually molesting her. The abuse had begun shortly after school started in September. Sara had been desperate to find a child care arrangement for the children to cover them between the time they got home from school at 3:30 until she got home from work at 5:30. Because the elementary school was only a block away, the children were able to walk to and from school; and in the past, their dad had either picked them up or was at home by the time they got home. When a neighbor four houses down the street offered to have her son Jason watch the children for the two hours a day for $10 a week, Sara thought it was a good deal. The cost would not strain her budget, and she felt good about knowing that the kids would be in their own home.

In November, when Leslie told her mother about the abuse, Sara was overwhelmed with guilt and shock. Sara said she expressed her exasperation at that time with Leslie, asking why the child did not tell her mother as soon as the boy had touched her. She raised the same question to Leslie again in the session, but the child remained silent. Sara said that she became even more worried when she told Dave about the abuse and he blamed Sara and made threats about trying to get full custody of the children. He went to the city during the time of the adjudication of the boy, who was in an outpatient treatment program for young sex offenders at the time. The boy still lived with his mother in the same neighborhood.

Sara reported that she was then worried about Leslie because the child was behaving so differently: "Leslie has changed and is now very difficult to manage. It is a struggle to get her ready for school every morning. She refuses to wear a lot of her clothes. I offer her three or four outfits and she throws them on the floor. The other thing is that she won't do her school homework. She also used to go outdoors and play in the yard or play with a couple of other girls her age who live close by. She just says she doesn't want to play with them. Bedtime is another hassle. She argues and whines about going to sleep in her room. After a while, I just couldn't deal with it anymore; so I let her fall asleep in my bed and then carry her to her room later."

The session was nearly over before the therapist could focus on the fact that Leslie had been mostly silent. Sara had begun to tell her story, but it included a litany of problems she saw in her daughter, her own emotional expressions of anxiety, guilt, and worry associated with Leslie's sexual abuse, and her frustration with Leslie's current behaviors. When the therapist scheduled to see them both again for the second appointment, she wondered if that was the best decision. On discussing her approach with a colleague, without taking the case to her supervisory group, the therapist decided she would continue to see Leslie and Sara together and proceed with her understanding of the narrative method. On the day of the next scheduled session, Sara called to cancel, saying Leslie had refused to attend and had thrown a tantrum.

This case example points to the need for therapists to have a great deal of knowledge about human behavior and specific problems as well as knowledge and skills relevant to interventions. It raises the important question of knowledge that should go into clinical decisions, perhaps even before the first session, such as whom to see, and in what kind of format, and how best to use referral information. Another question to consider, at least tentatively, is the nature of presenting problems and how various theories might explain their onset and continuance. Additional issues center on professional training in new or specialty areas of practice, evaluation of the new methods for specific client problems, and the need for close supervision while learning and implementing new methods. The extent and nature of Leslie's behavioral problems and their likely association with the recent sexual abuse, as well as the impact of this event and its aftermath on the child's symptoms and family relationship all point to the need for immediate case consultation, supervision, and consideration of various intervention methods and their established effectiveness for dealing with this type of problem.

THE "ETHICS OF EVIDENCE"

Miké (1999) proposed the use of scientific evidence as an ethical imperative to protect the public from useless or even harmful interventions. Proper statistical design is even implied in Rules 2 and 3 of the Nuremberg Code (1949). Miké further stated, "It is unethical to use powerful medical procedures without careful evaluation of their safety and effectiveness" (p. 11). An imperative resulting from this ethics of evidence is "to create, disseminate, and use the best possible scientific evidence as a basis for every phase of medical decision making" (p. 18).

As noted earlier, the AAMFT ethics code states that marriage and family therapists are to advance the welfare of their clients and to do so in a way that allows for monitoring the benefits to clients (Principle I: Subprinciple 1.9). A logical corollary to this position would be to say that marriage and family therapists should seek to use interventions that will best advance the welfare of their clients. This position also finds support from the ethical guideline to "maintain high standards of professional competence and integrity" (Principle III) and "pursue knowledge of new developments" (Subprinciple 3.1). An even stronger guideline in support of the ethical responsibility to stay abreast of "scientific" knowledge appears in the Code of Ethics of the American Counseling Association: "Counselors recognize the need for continuing education to maintain a reasonable level of awareness of current scientific and professional information in their fields of activity" [emphasis added] (American Counseling Association, 1995,

C.2.f.). Thus, professional ethics suggest that identifying what the best treatments are should be part of one's ethical responsibility to maintain competence and to advance the welfare of clients.

Family therapy is not alone in utilizing sources for clinical decision making that are of questionable utility. All of the health care professions have begun to ask difficult questions about the efficacy of their interventions and are increasingly attempting to use rules of evidence to evaluate their clinical practices. For example, the Code of Ethics of the American Counseling Association deals with standards for counselor educators and trainers: "Varied Theoretical Positions. Counselors present varied theoretical positions so that students and supervisees may make comparisons and have opportunities to develop their own positions. Counselors provide information concerning the scientific bases of professional practice." [emphasis added] (American Counseling Association, 1995, F.1.f.). The evidence-based movement consists of an attempt to identify what is variably referred to as empirically validated treatment, empirically supported treatment, empirically evaluated treatment (e.g., Kendall, 1998) or evidence-based treatment (e.g., Evidence-Based Medicine Working Group, 1992). These terms are used interchangeably here.

THE EVIDENCE-BASED TREATMENT MOVEMENT

The evidence-based treatment movement is ". . . the formalization of the aim to promote health care based on evidence, by making more effective use of the medical literature in everyday practice" (Miké, 1999, p. 17). While the primary reason to identify the most effective interventions is to serve clients in the highest ethical manner, additional forces have also propelled professions towards identifying evidence-based treatments. The methodology to evaluate clinical interventions has increased in sophistication over the past 30 years. Prior to the 1960s, "the randomized clinical trial was an oddity" (Evidence-Based Medicine Working Group, 1992). Today, it is an accepted minimum for research on nearly all types of clinical interventions. As research methodology has become more sophisticated, the questions investigators ask have become more complex. Similarly, continual advances in computer technology have made accessing the clinical research literature increasingly easier to accomplish. Access to appropriate information is essential to evidence-based practice. Access makes it possible to keep up with the new developments in research methodology and research findings—both of which are part of the ethical responsibility to maintain a high level of competence.

Another factor in the move towards evidence-based practice is the new emphasis on accountability and quality assurance. Toward the end of the last century, those paying for clinical services, whether clients or third parties, increasingly demanded evidence that services being provided were both effective and cost-effective (Waehler, Kalodner, Wampold, & Lichtenberg, 2000). The services of psychotherapists are now increasingly in competition with psychotropic medications. In the United States, pharmaceutical companies are required to provide evidence of the efficacy of new agents to meet the requirements of the Food and Drug Administration. Another goal of the evidence-based practice movement in psychotherapy has been an effort to provide payors and public policy makers with the type of evidence that is available for psychotropic medications.

Evidence-based practice is becoming more prevalent in a variety of health care professions, including medicine (e.g., Zarin et al., 1997); psychology (DeRubeis & Crits-Christoph, 1998; Kazdin & Weisz, 1998); social work (Sheldon, 1998); and occupational therapy (Seale & Barnard, 1999). Marriage and family therapists must be knowledgeable about practices and standards within all of the mental health professions and maintain a high level of competence in their services that clients and third party payors will value. The position here agrees with that of Miké (1999) and others (e.g., Pellegrino, 1999) that the use of evidence is primarily an ethical imperative. Thus, to best advance the welfare of individuals and families, marriage and family therapists have an ethical obligation to begin moving towards a standard of evidence-based practice.

CHARACTERISTICS OF EVIDENCE-BASED PRACTICE

Evidence-based practice refers to the selection and use of treatments for which there is some evidence of efficacy. Definitions have included: "decision making based on an evaluation of available data regarding the likely impact of different treatments on patient outcomes" (Zarin et al., 1997, p. 641); and the use of "treatments shown to be efficacious in controlled research with a delineated population" (Chambless & Hollon, 1998, p. 7). Evidence-based practice "requires . . . efficient literature searching and the application of formal rules of evidence evaluating the clinical literature" (Evidence-Based Medicine Working Group, 1992, p. 2420).

An important question in evidence-based treatment is deciding what criteria will be used to evaluate the research literature. For example, Chambless and Hollon (1998) presented criteria that can be utilized in evaluating whether a treatment has obtained empirical support. Their criteria, in summary, include (1) the treatment in question has been shown to be superior to no-treatment or placebo groups or at least equivalent to an established treatment in well-designed studies; (2) these studies have been conducted with a treatment manual, a delineated population, reliable and valid outcome measures, and with appropriate data analysis; (3) for a designation of efficacious the treatment must have been shown superior to a wait-list control in at least two independent research settings; (4) for a designation of possibly efficacious, the treatment must have been shown superior in one study; and (5) for a designation of efficacious and specific the treatment must have been shown to be superior to a nonspecific (placebo) intervention or to an alternative treatment by two independent research teams.

Although the full implementation of evidence-based practice requires a critique of original research articles, one tool that has been used to help clinicians is the development of treatment guidelines. Treatment guidelines have been distinguished from treatment standards and treatment options. Standards are recommendations that apply more than 95% of the time, guidelines apply approximately 75% of the time, while options apply approximately 50% of the time (Eddy, 1990). For example, the former Agency for Health Care Policy and Research (now the Agency for Health Care Research and Quality) of the United States Department of Health and Human Services published a guideline for the treatment of depression in primary care (Rush, Golden, Hall, Herrera, Houston, & Kathol, 1993). The American Psychiatric Association published a number of treatment guidelines including one for the treatment of major depressive disorder in adults (American Psychiatric Association, 2000) and the treatment of bipolar disorder (American Psychiatric Association, 1994b). The American Psychological Association Division of Clinical Psychology's Task Force on Promotion and Dissemination of Psychological Procedures published a report listing psychotherapies that are considered qualified to be labeled as efficacious (Task Force on Promotion and Dissemination of Psychological Procedures, 1995). In a related area, algorithms have been developed for the use of psychotropic medications based on available evidence (Crismon et al., 1999; Rush et al., 1999). There is now some empirical evidence that following treatment guidelines is associated with improvement in care, at least for people suffering with depression (Fortney, Rost, Zhang, & Pyne, 2001).

EVIDENCE-BASED PRACTICE AND FAMILY THERAPY

It is beyond the scope of this chapter to provide a thorough analysis of evidence-based treatments in marriage and family therapy. Additionally, the results of such an analysis will be changing with the continual emergence of new research literature. While evidence-based practice should be focused ultimately on the review of original research articles, recent reviews survey the current status of evidence-based couple therapy in the treatment of relationship distress and adult mental health problems (e.g., Baucom, Shoham, Mueser, Daiuto, & Stickle, 1998; Carr, 2000b) and of family interventions for child-focused problems (Carr, 2000a).

ARGUMENTS AGAINST EVIDENCE-BASED PRACTICE

There are both pragmatic and philosophical tensions resulting from the application of evidence-based practice to psychotherapy. These tensions may exist most noticeably between practitioners and researchers, researchers and managed care, and practitioners and managed care. The result is to impede the advancement of marriage and family therapy as an independent profession. However, productivity can evolve from the discomfort arising from these tensions and can be used in ways that will promote the science and practice of the profession. For instance, marriage and family therapists can learn from the fields of clinical psychology and medicine about the struggles and obstacles related to evidence-based practice. As has been stated elsewhere

Psychotherapy researchers have tried to align themselves with practicing clinicians by offering evidence-based treatments as demonstrated efficacious interventions, and as a hopeful response to managed care's demand for accountability, as well as the perceived hegemonic threat of pharmacological interventions. Yet these treatments continue to meet with much debate, controversy, and suspicion. (Addis, Wade, & Hatgis, 1999, p. 430)

Now, more than ever before, therapists have to provide justifications for how they work with clients, their treatment and intervention choices, and how these choices impact client outcomes (Addis et al., 1999). Practitioners have described their concerns about the implementation of manual-based treatments (Addis; Wolfe, 1999). These concerns include how evidence-based practice (1) affects the therapeutic relationship; (2) affects job satisfaction; (3) restricts clinical innovation and creativity; (4) serves the needs of clients; (5) affects feasibility; and (6) impacts the credibility of treatment. In addition, some practitioners have stated that research findings are not helpful in making clinical decisions, are often difficult to understand and apply to their work with clients, and often do not relate to their clinical concerns (Reynolds, 2000). Clinicians have also complained that they do not have enough time to keep up with new clinical research developments (Reynolds, 2000).

There have been other ethical arguments against the use of evidence-based practice in psychotherapy. One argument is that conclusions based on current effectiveness research are premature and have flaws in their current research designs (Waehler et al., 2000). In addition, it has been stated that current outcome studies offer limited findings because they do not generalize to the therapy that is conducted in "the real world" (Goldfried & Wolfe, 1998; Havik & VandenBos, 1996). Another argument is that, since outcome studies typically assess disorder-specific interventions, evidence-based practice might promote the dehumanization of clients based on diagnoses from the Diagnostic and Statistical Manual of Mental Disorders (American Psychiatric Association, 1994a). A final argument is that evidence-based practice inhibits clinician creativity and innovation, a limitation that may then hinder the effectiveness of treatment (Waehler et al., 2000). While these arguments all have validity at the present time, it is likely that advances in psychotherapy research will increasingly make research more relevant to clinicians and weaken arguments against evidence-based practice.

EVIDENCE-BASED PRACTICE AND THE POSTMODERN PARADIGM

At first glance, the evidence-based practice movement appears to be embedded in modernism. This is because it seems to incorporate a belief that psychotherapy treatment and intervention can be reduced to one way of operating to provide a treatment that is "rational," "measurable," and "observable" (Laugharne, 1999, p. 642). This modernistic appearance clearly has implications for the role of the therapist and the client-therapist relationship. For instance, some scholars have described the therapist's role as "a technician" in the context of evidence-based practice (Waehler et al., 2000, p. 661), a role that threatens the autonomy and creativity of therapists (Reynolds, 2000). In another drastic description from a sociopolitical perspective, evidence-based practice has been referred to as a recent form of "authoritarianism" in psychotherapy (Reynolds, 2000). In reality, however, the knowledgeable user of statistics understands that statistical results always contain an element of uncertainty (e.g., Miké, 1999).

At the same time, others have argued that one can operate from a postmodern paradigm and still support evidence-based practice. For example

A commitment to social constructionism as an overarching framework for practice does not preclude a commitment to quantitative-based research generally and evidence-based practice in particular. Diagnostic criteria, scores on individual and family based assessment instruments, statistical formulae, rules concerning statistical and clinical significance of results are all social constructions. (Carr, 2000a, p. 51)

While this reflection has an inclusive flair of neutrality, the "reality" of the current climate in psychotherapy is one of controversy and fear that stems from the pressure to produce and implement evidence-based treatments so the profession does not become obsolete. One advantage of the relative youthfulness of the marriage and family therapy profession is that its members can learn from attempts other disciplines have made, including medicine and clinical psychology, in bridging the gap between research and practice.

CHALLENGES OF MOVING TOWARDS EVIDENCE-BASED PRACTICE

The movement towards evidence-based practice has created numerous challenges within several professional disciplines. The profession of marriage and family therapy should prepare to address similar questions and new ethical challenges. These are bound to impact educators, researchers, and clinicians.

Marriage and Family Therapy Educators

Most models of marriage and family therapy are based on theory rather than empirical evidence. Marriage and family therapy programs provide training to students in various schools of family therapy including structural, strategic, and narrative, to name a few. While marriage and family therapy theory courses touch on the various schools of family therapy, trainees often adopt models according to their personal worldviews, beliefs, and interests. In addition, the preferences of supervisors for certain models influence the modalities used in marriage and family therapy training clinics, practica, and internships.

Much like physicians, marriage and family therapists are often guided by theory and tradition (Zarin et al., 1997) in their practices. While theory and tradition connect current practitioners to the founding roots of marriage and family therapy, many of these theories and traditions have not been empirically tested in accordance with the evidence-based practice guidelines mentioned earlier. The Standards of Accreditation, Version 10.0 of the Commission on Accreditation for Marriage and Family Therapy Education (COAMFTE) address evidence-based practice in standard 310.02, which states that coursework ". . . will address the historical development, theoretical and empirical foundations, and contemporary conceptual directions of the field of marriage and family therapy [emphasis added]."

While this standard is a step toward evidence-based practice, restructuring the training of marriage and family therapists would be a daring leap forward. To take this leap forward, the faculty who train marriage and family therapists will need to be familiar with evidence-based practice guidelines and research. Perhaps, more importantly, for this shift to be successful, marriage and family therapy educators will need to believe in the concept of evidence-based practice as an ethical basis of practice. Further, marriage and family therapy faculty will need to draw on these evidence-based models in their supervision of trainees.

Shifting toward an ethics of evidence requires a working knowledge of statistical design and methods. One reason, noted earlier, is to be able to evaluate the scientific evidence in clinical decision making. This is Miké's first imperative of the ethics of evidence (1999). The second imperative of the ethics of evidence is "to increase awareness of, and come to terms with, the extent and ultimately the irreducible nature of uncertainty" (Miké, 1999, p. 24). That is, it is inherent in statistical methodology that uncertainty can never be eliminated. Thus, students must learn both the value and the limitations of scientific evidence so that they neither irrationally endorse nor irrationally reject research findings. This ability is equally important for practitioners prepared at the master's level. Making the relevance of statistical methodology clear to students will be one of the challenges for educators in successfully moving towards evidence-based practice.

Marriage and Family Therapy Researchers

With regard to research, the AAMFT ethics code states: "Marriage and family therapists make efforts to prevent the distortion or misuse of their clinical and research findings" (Subprinciple 3.12). This subprinciple requires that marriage and family therapists seek and obtain evidence beyond their own unsystematic clinical observations before advocating widespread adoption of their therapeutic interventions. This guideline provides further ethical support for moving marriage and family therapy towards a standard of evidence-based practice.

Evidence-based practice requires research data that allow readers to evaluate the efficacy and effectiveness of interventions in question. This type of data has been lacking in much of the marriage and family therapy research literature. Wampler (2001) called for more research on the effectiveness and efficacy of marriage and family therapy:

Our weak research base has potentially disastrous consequences in terms of development as a profession and acceptability as a practice. Solid research on process and outcome of marriage, family, and couple therapy must be made available for use by practitioners and by policy-makers. This research needs to be focused on the value of systemic therapies in the areas of greatest need. (p. 2)

This type of research is also what is needed for evidence-based practice. Areas of need cited include research on the provision of services to underserved populations, enhancing health service delivery, family interventions for serious mental illness, mitigating the effects of divorce, reducing domestic and community violence, and the family treatment of substance abuse (Wampler, 2001).

To provide evidence of efficacy and effectiveness, research studies should follow currently accepted standards of psychotherapy research. Onken, Blaine, and Battjes (1997) proposed a stage model of behavioral therapies research that describes three stages in the taking of a new idea through initial development to efficacy research and, finally, to effectiveness studies. This model of psychotherapy development has now become a standard in psychotherapy research: Stage I consists of treatment development and feasibility testing; Stage II consists of randomized clinical trials to evaluate the efficacy of the new treatment; and Stage III consists of effectiveness studies testing the ability of the treatment to be transported into a variety of clinical settings.

Rounsaville, Carroll, and Onken (2001) have compiled the results of a series of workshops conducted by the National Institute on Drug Abuse (NIDA) Treatment Research Branch on guidelines for Stage I psychotherapy research. They recommend dividing Stage I into substages of Ia and Ib. The primary tasks of Stage Ia consist of therapy development and manual writing. Other tasks in this substage include (1) the development of training materials such as videotaped sessions to demonstrate successful or unsuccessful attempts to apply key therapeutic techniques; and (2) the drafting of adherence and competence measures and their initial reliability testing on videotapes of these early cases. Stage Ib consists of the pilot testing of a final, or nearly final, version of the therapy to demonstrate the feasibility of the new treatment. This pilot test usually consists of a randomized clinical trial.

Miklowitz and Hooley (1998) have described essential questions that treatment manuals for family interventions need to answer. These include

> *What are the core interventions that comprise the treatment? How does one address resistances to the treatment approach? If patients get off track from the agenda, how does one get them back on? How is the treatment terminated? What referrals are made? (p. 425)*

Other sources (e.g., Carroll & Nuro, 1997; Rounsaville et al., 2001) also provide guidelines for the areas that a treatment manual needs to address. These include "specification of unique and common elements of the therapy, decision rules for choice among alternative interventions, description of interventions excluded from the new approach and specification of key treatment parameters such as frequency and duration of treatment" (Rounsaville et al., 2001, p. 136).

Standards of psychotherapy research continue to evolve and must continually be monitored by family therapy researchers. Whereas it has been considered state-of-the-art to assess fidelity to a psychotherapy treatment manual, Waltz, Addis, Koerner, and Jacobson (1993) have pointed out that it is possible to employ interventions prescribed by a treatment manual without necessarily employing them skillfully. They distinguished between adherence and competence in implementing a psychotherapy treatment manual. Adherence is "the extent to which a therapist used interventions and approaches prescribed by the treatment manual and avoided the use of intervention procedures proscribed by the manual" (p. 620), whereas competence is "the level of skill shown by the therapist in delivering the treatment" (p. 620). In assessing competence, they recommend consideration of other variables that will affect the outcome of psychotherapy, such as (1) severity of the problem being treated; and (2) the stage of therapy. For example, interventions appropriate to the assessment stage might not be appropriate at the termination stage.

Producing the type of research data necessary for ethical evidence-based practice requires raising the overall standard of research in marriage and family therapy. AAMFT has sponsored a series of research conferences toward this end. Conducting clinical trials of the type described above cannot be accomplished in a single study and requires systematic programs of research. This type of research will be beyond what graduate students can accomplish in a dissertation. Other fields of science, including clinical psychology, usually mandate a postdoctoral research fellowship to learn the advanced research methods required for a specific area of research. At the present time, there are not enough marriage and family therapy researchers conducting this type of research who can offer this type of postdoctoral training. Without such postdoctoral research training, new investigators will not emerge. To meet this serious challenge, the profession of marriage and family therapy may need to have students pursue postdoctoral research fellowships in other areas so they can then apply the methods to couple and family interventions. Again, the AAMFT-sponsored research conferences are a worthy attempt to "jump-start" marriage and family therapy research to this new level of sophistication.

MARRIAGE AND FAMILY THERAPY CLINICIANS

The AAMFT ethics code states, " Marriage and family therapists pursue knowledge of new developments and maintain competence in marriage and family therapy through education, training, or supervised experience" (Subprinciple 3.1). Practicing clinicians will face several challenges in moving towards ethical evidence-based practices. To implement evidence-based practices, clinicians must be able to evaluate original research literature to answer the following questions:

Is this study of interest to the clinical situation I am facing?

Who were the subjects in the study and how were they recruited?

How accurate were the data collected?

Were the measures used valid and reliable?

Were the statistical methods used appropriate and properly executed?

What did the study find?

What are the implications of the study? (Churchill, 1998)

If practitioners have not been trained in these appraisal skills, they may find analyzing the research literature a daunting experience.

Scientific journals have begun publishing guides to aid clinicians, e.g., guides to help clinicians appraise clinical guidelines (e.g., Warner & Blizard, 1998). The Journal of the American Medical Association (JAMA) has published papers to help clinicians evaluate medical literature in a series entitled "User's Guides to the Medical Literature" (e.g., Guyatt et al., 2000). The British Medical Journal has published a similar series entitled "How to Read a Paper" (e.g., Greenhalgh, 1997; Greenhalgh & Taylor, 1997). Similarly, family therapy journals (e.g., the Journal of Marital and Family Therapy) could publish papers to help marriage and family therapists evaluate the family therapy research literature.

While the profession of marriage and family therapy is probably not ready for treatment guidelines at this point, family therapy journals could feature special articles on evidence-based treatments similar to the series of articles published by journals such as Psychiatric Services and The Clinical Psychologist.

Another challenge facing practicing clinicians who are no longer in school or training is learning new evidence-based treatments. Research has found that education alone does not have a strong impact on the practices of health care providers (e.g., Davis, Thomson, Oxman, & Haynes, 1995; Lin et al., 1997; Oxman, Thomson, Davis, & Haynes, 1995). To discover what factors would motivate clinicians to learn and implement new evidence-based treatments, "how they learn a new practice, and what they perceive as barriers to change," Torrey et al. (2001) conducted a series of focus groups with clinicians:

Clinicians indicated that, first, they must be convinced that the practice is worth learning; second, they need to learn a practice through observation, training, and reading; and, third, they benefit from efforts to reinforce the practice over time, such as regular supervision and feedback on activities. (p. 47)

The participants in these focus groups endorsed either traveling to a training site, having a trainer come to their site, or watching instructional videotapes. Written materials in the form of practical workbooks, supervision, posters, and Internet resources were also mentioned as aids to learning the new practice.

Another avenue for marriage and family therapists to learn new evidence-based treatments is through traditional continuing education offerings, such as the annual conferences of the AAMFT (and its divisions). Learning new skills, however, may require more "hands-on experience in the form of practice or role play with the new material" that may need to occur over several days (Calhoun, Moras, Pilkonis, & Rehm, 1998, p. 158). It would be desirable to "certify" practitioners in the new treatment, but the ability to assess competency is challenging. Although competency scales are often developed for research studies evaluating new interventions, the use of these scales is time consuming and expensive. At the least, continuing education programs can provide updates of evidence-based practices to keep practitioners current on the latest research developments.

Finally, practice ". . . based on evidence can still be no better than the quality of the available evidence" (Miké, 1999, p. 18). In marriage and family therapy, there are many areas of clinical practice for which there is no scientific evidence to guide the clinician in treatment planning. To be ethical, the marriage and family therapist will have to await further research developments to fully engage in evidence-based practice. In the meantime, clinicians will have to rely on alternative sources of information for decision making as described earlier.

CONCLUSION

This chapter has proposed that marriage and family therapists have an ethical obligation to begin moving toward the use of treatments that have some evidence supporting their efficacy. This ethical obligation cuts across several major guidelines from the AAMFT ethics code, including principles relating to responsibility to clients, professional competence and integrity, and responsibility to the profession.

Calling on marriage and family therapists to employ an "ethics of evidence" (Miké, 1999) in clinical decision making, the discussion here noted that many of the treatments commonly employed in marriage and family therapy have little or no evidence supporting their use—other than the testimony of practitioners. Consequently, moving toward a standard of evidence-based practice will have to be phased in over time. This entire process will undoubtedly present challenges for educators, researchers, and clinicians; but the profession can prepare for these and learn from the similar struggles of other disciplines with the new developments in evidence-based practice.

It has been over 30 years since Paul (1967) raised the question, "What treatment, by whom, is most effective for this individual with that specific problem under which set of circumstances?" (p. 111). While marriage and family therapists and other psychotherapists still cannot answer that question in many cases, new evidence is appearing regularly in the scientific literature which allows us to draw closer to such an answer. The therapists in the case examples above (Kay, Ben and their family and Leslie and her mother) may or may not find that the scientific literature is of much help in determining which interventions to employ at present with these client families. If research provides little guidance, they may need to rely on older, traditional sources of information for clinical decision making. In the future, however, family therapy research will no doubt make strides in identifying efficacious family interventions. Thus marriage and family therapists will need to stay current with scientific developments in order to maintain ethical practice as they seek to advance the welfare of their clients.

REFERENCES

Addis, M. E., Wade, W. A., & Hatgis, C. (1999). Barriers to dissemination of evidence based practices: Addressing practitioners' concerns about manual based psychotherapies. Clinical Psychology: Science and Practice, 6, 430–441.

American Association for Marriage and Family Therapy. (2001). COAMFTE standards revision. (Version 10). [Electronic data file]. Retrieved from http://www.aamft.org/COAMFTE/StandardsV10.htm.

American Counseling Association. (1995). Code of ethics and standards of practice. Alexandria, VA: Author.

American Psychiatric Association. (1994a). Diagnostic and statistical manual of mental disorders (4th ed.). Washington, DC: Author.

American Psychiatric Association. (1994b). Practice guideline for the treatment of patients with bipolar disorder. American Journal of Psychiatry, 151(December Suppl.), 1–36.

American Psychiatric Association. (2000). Practice guideline for the treatment of patients with major depressive disorder (revision). American Journal of Psychiatry, 157(April Suppl.), 1–45.

Baucom, D. H., Shoham, V., Mueser, K. T., Daiuto, A. D., & Stickle, T. R. (1998). Empirically supported couple and family interventions for marital distress and adult mental health problems. Journal of Consulting and Clinical Psychology, 66, 53–88.

Bowen, M. (1978). Family therapy in clinical practice. Northvale, NJ: Jason Aronson.

Calhoun, K. S., Moras, K., Pilkonis, P. A., & Rehm, L. P. (1998). Empirically supported treatments: Implications for training. Journal of Consulting and Clinical Psychology, 66, 151–162.

Carr, A. (2000a). Evidence-based practice in family therapy and systemic consultation. I. Child-focused problems. Journal of Family Therapy, 22, 29–60.

Carr, A. (2000b). Evidence-based practice in family therapy and systemic consultation. II. Adult-focused problems. Journal of Family Therapy, 22, 273–295.

Carroll, K., & Nuro, K. (1997). The use and development of treatment manuals. In K. Carroll (Ed.), Improving compliance with alcoholism treatment (pp. 53–72). Bethesda, MD: National Institute on Alcohol Abuse and Alcoholism.

Chambless, D.L., & Hollon, S.D. (1998). Defining empirically supported therapies. Journal of Consulting and Clinical Psychology, 66, 7–18.

Churchill, R. (1998). Critical appraisal and evidence-based psychiatry. International Review of Psychiatry, 10, 344–352.

Crismon, M. L., Trivedi, M. H., Pigott, T. A., Rush, A. J., Hirschfeld, R. M., Kahn, D. A., et al. (1999). The Texas Medication Algorithm Project: Report of the Texas consensus conference panel on medication treatment of major depressive disorder. Journal of Clinical Psychiatry, 60, 142–156.

Davis, D. A., Thomson, M. A., Oxman, A. D., & Haynes, R. B. (1995). Changing physician performance: A systematic review of the effect of continuing medical education strategies. Journal of the American Medical Association, 274, 700–705.

DeRubeis, R. J., & Crits-Christoph, P. (1998). Empirically supported individual and group psychological treatments for adult mental disorders. Journal of Consulting and Clinical Psychology, 66, 37–52.

Eddy, D. (1990). Practice policies–what are they? Journal of the American Medical Association, 263, 877–880.

Evidence-Based Medicine Working Group. (1992). Evidence-based medicine: A new approach to teaching the practice of medicine. Journal of the American Medical Association, 268, 2420–2425.

Fortney, J., Rost, K., Zhang, M., & Pyne, J. (2001). The relationship between quality and outcomes in routine depression care. Psychiatric Services, 52, 56–62.

Goldfried, M. R., & Wolfe, B. E. (1998). Toward a more clinically valid approach to therapy research. Journal of Consulting and Clinical Psychology, 66, 143–150.

Greenhalgh, T. (1997). How to read a paper: Papers that tell you what things cost (economic analyses). British Medical Journal, 315, 596–599.

Greenhalgh, T., & Taylor, R. (1997). How to read a paper: Papers that go beyond numbers (qualitative research). British Medical Journal, 315, 740–743.

Guyatt, G. H., Haynes, R. B., Jaeschke, R. Z., Cook, D. J., Green, L., Naylor, C., et al. (2000). User's guides to the medical literature XXV: Evidence-based medicine: Principles for applying the User's Guides to patient care. Journal of the American Medical Association, 284, 1290–1296.

Hardy, K. V. (2001). Healing the world in fifty-minute intervals: A response to "Family therapy saves the planet." Journal of Marital and Family Therapy, 27, 19–22.

Havik, O. E., & VandenBos, G. R. (1996). Limitations of manualized psychotherapy for everyday clinical practice. Clinical Psychology: Science and Practice, 3, 264–267.

Johnson, S. (2001). Family therapy saves the planet: Messianic tendencies in the family systems literature. Journal of Marital and Family Therapy, 27, 3–11.

Kazdin, A. E., & Weisz, J. R. (1998). Identifying and developing empirically supported child and adolescent treatments. Journal of Consulting and Clinical Psychology, 66, 19–36.

Kendall, P. C. (1998). Empirically supported psychological therapies. Journal of Consulting and Clinical Psychology, 66, 3–6.

Laugharne, R. (1999). Evidence-based medicine, user involvement and the post-modern paradigm. Psychiatric Bulletin, 23, 641–643.

Lin, E. H., Katon, W. J., Simon, G. E., Von Korff, M., Bush, T. M., Rutter, C. M., et al. (1997). Achieving guidelines for the treatment of depression in primary care: Is physician education enough? Medical Care, 35, 831–842.

McGoldrick, M. (2001). Response to "Family therapy saves the planet." Journal of Marital and Family Therapy, 27, 17–18.

Miké, V. (1999). Outcomes research and the quality of health care. Evaluation & the Health Professions, 22, 3–32.

Miklowitz, D. J., & Hooley, J. M. (1998). Developing family psychoeducational treatments for patients with bipolar and other severe psychiatric disorders: A pathway from basic research to clinical trials. Journal of Marital and Family Therapy, 24, 419–435.

Minuchin, S. (1974). Families and family therapy. Cambridge, MA: Harvard University Press.

Nuremberg Code. (1949). Trials of war criminals before the Nuremberg Military Tribunals under Control Council law no. 10 (Vol. 2, pp. 181–182). Washington, DC: U.S. Government Printing Office.

Onken, L. S., Blaine, J. D., & Battjes, R. (1997). Behavioral therapy research: A conceptualization of a process. In S. W. Henngler & R. Amentos (Eds.), Innovative approaches from difficult to treat populations (pp. 477–485). Washington, DC: American Psychiatric Press.

Oxman, A. D., Thomson, M. A., Davis, D. A., & Haynes, R. B. (1995). No magic bullets: A systematic review of 102 trials of interventions to improve professional practice. Canadian Medical Association Journal, 153, 1423–1431.

Paul, G. A. (1967). Outcome research in psychotherapy. Journal of Consulting and Clinical Psychology, 31, 109–118.

Pellegrino, E. D. (1999). The ethical use of evidence in biomedicine. Evaluation & the Health Professions, 22, 33–43.

Reynolds, S. (2000). Evidence based practice and psychotherapy research. Journal of Mental Health, 9, 257–266.

Rounsaville, B. J., Carroll, K. M., & Onken, L. S. (2001). A stage model of behavioral therapies research: Getting started and moving on from Stage I. Clinical Psychology, 8, 133–142.

Rush, A. J., Golden, W. E., Hall, G. W., Herrera, M., Houston, A., & Kathol, R. G. (1993). Depression in Primary Care: Volume 2. Treatment of Major Depression. Clinical Practice Guideline No. 5. AHCPR Publication No. 93-0551. Rockville, MD: U.S. Department of Health and Human Services, Public Health Service, Agency for Health Care Policy and Research.

Rush, A. J., Rago, W. V., Crismon, M. L., Toprac, M. G., Shon, S. P., Suppes, T., et al. (1999). Medication treatment for the severely and persistently mentally ill: The Texas Medication Algorithm Project. Journal of Clinical Psychiatry, 60, 284–291.

Seale, J. K., & Barnard, S. (1999). Ethical considerations in therapy research. British Journal of Occupational Therapy, 62, 371–375.

Sheldon, B. (1998). Social work practice in the 21st century. Research on Social Work Practice, 8, 577–588.

Sluzki, C. (2001). All those in favor of saving the planet, please raise your hand: A comment about "Family therapy saves the planet." Journal of Marital and Family Therapy, 27, 13–15.

Sprenkle, D. H., & Ball, D. (1996). Research in family therapy. In F. P. Piercy, D. H. Sprenkle, & J. L. Wetchler (Eds.), Family therapy sourcebook (pp. 392–421). New York: Guilford.

Task Force on Promotion and Dissemination of Psychological Procedures. (1995). Training in and dissemination of empirically-validated treatments: Report and recommendations. Clinical Psychologist, 48, 2–23.

Tjeltveit, A. C. (1999). Ethics and values in psychotherapy. London: Routledge.

Torrey, W. C., Drake, R .E., Dixon, L., Burns, B. J., Flynn, L., Rush, A J., et al. (2001). Implementing evidence-based practices for persons with severe mental illnesses. Psychiatric Services, 52, 45–50.

Waehler, C. A., Kalodner, C. R., Wampold, B. E., & Lichtenberg, J. W. (2000). Empirically supported treatments (ESTs) in perspective: Implications for counseling psychology training. Counseling Psychologist, 28, 657–671.

Waltz, J., Addis, M. E., Koerner, K., & Jacobson, N. S. (1993). Testing the integrity of a psychotherapy protocol: Assessment of adherence and competence. Journal of Consulting & Clinical Psychology, 61, 620–630.

Wampler, K. S. (2001). Incoming editorial: Both–and. Journal of Marital and Family Therapy, 27, 2.

Warner, J. P., & Blizard, R. (1998). How to appraise clinical guidelines. Psychiatric Bulletin, 22, 759–761.

White, M. (1995). Re-authoring lives: Interviews and essays. Adelaide, South Australia: Dulwich Centre Publications.

Wolfe, J. (1999). Overcoming barriers to evidence-based practice: Lessons from medical practitioners. Clinical Psychology: Science and Practice, 6, 445–448.

Zarin, D. A., Seigle, L., Pincus, H. A., & McIntyre, J. S. (1997). Evidence-based practice guidelines. Psychopharmacology Bulletin, 33, 641–647.

CHILDREN IN FAMILY THERAPY

Jane DiVita Woody and Robert Henley Woody

6

This chapter is intended to prevent ethical lapses and violations, assist in resolving ethical dilemmas, and enhance the effectiveness of family therapy with children. The discussion explains: how increased attention to ethics in services to children has evolved from the context of family therapy and changing professional and social conditions; the unique ethical issues within family therapy models that focus on children; ethical considerations implied in two innovative therapy approaches to children's problems within the family; and child custody issues as a basis for analysis of numerous ethical issues and their interface with the law.

CONTENTS

The topic of children in family therapy raises numerous ethical issues, and the potential complications can seem overwhelming. Among the most common ethical concerns are

(1) how to meet the needs and welfare of both the child and the parent(s), especially when these seem in conflict;

(2) how to help parents with major life decisions that affect the welfare of the child, in cases of conflicting child and adult needs;

(3) whether a child or adolescent should give formal consent to treatment; and whether the duty of confidentiality applies to a child in family therapy;

(4) how to be professionally competent, given the array of severe and normative problems that children and families present;

(5) how to function ethically in collaborative roles with diverse service providers, including the legal system, that impact on many child and family problems; and

(6) how to approach the many value-laden issues of family life in the context of therapy, given that the therapist's personal values and needs can subtly or blatantly inappropriately influence all aspects of treatment.

As will be revealed, these are not simple issues, and the prudent practitioner must rely on several sources: (1) behavioral science (e.g., research on child development); (2) therapeutic theories and techniques (e.g., constructing an intervention rationale and selecting techniques according to the needs of the particular clients); (3) professional ethics (e.g., the AAMFT ethics code); and (4) law (e.g., pertaining to mental health practice, confidentiality and privileged communications, parental rights, and child protection). Without substantial knowledge of each of these four areas, the marriage and family therapist will be walking through an ethical and legal quagmire.

For several reasons, ethical issues involving children and youth are much more in the minds of both clients and therapists today than in the past. First, although parents have long been the initiators in bringing their children to therapy, there is now much more focus on children's rights than in the past. Second, the context of family therapy with children is a complex format, yet little specific guidance on children comes from professional ethics codes (Koocher & Keith-Speigel, 1990). Third, the evolution within the profession of marriage and family therapy has expanded the ethical burden of therapists. Fourth, the rapid shifts in the sociocultural climate have highlighted the diverse and often polarized values, especially about family life, that exist in society; and the different ideologies are often linked with or blamed for the problems among children, youth, and adults.

This chapter focuses on the important ethical concerns that arise when marriage and family therapists work with children in family therapy. Specifically, it discusses the following:

(1) the increased attention to ethics in services to children that has evolved from the context of family therapy and changing professional and social conditions;

(2) the unique ethical issues that are inherent in family therapy models that focus on children;

(3) the ethical issues implied in two innovative therapy approaches to the inter-related problems of children and parents; and

(4) child custody issues as a basis for analysis of numerous ethical issues noted in the list above and their interface with the law.

The discussion draws on the AAMFT ethics code as a valuable resource for negotiating routine intervention procedures, as well as for avoiding the hazards of therapy that emerge in the interlocking problems of children and the family. Like the overall objective of this book, this chapter is intended to prevent ethical lapses and violations, assist in resolving ethical dilemmas, and enhance the effectiveness of treatment.

THE ATTENTION ON ETHICS IN SERVICES INVOLVING CHILDREN

By its nature, the situation in which children come to therapy under their parents' authority raises ethical concerns. Because of linear thinking about the development of problem behaviors and also because of personal defensiveness, parents commonly believe that a child has the problem and that treatment should focus primarily on the child.

On the contrary, contemporary marriage and family therapists conceptualize childhood problems as having circular causation and prefer to assess and influence, if not actually treat directly, the whole family. The difference in perception about causation requires that the marriage and family therapist be vigilant in spotting problematic conditions in the treatment plan and case management and have acute ethical awareness.

Ethical Issues Related to the Family Context

The following example shows how conceptualizations of linear and circular causation may differ, Mark and Mary had a son with a severe neurological birth injury and a daughter who was intellectually gifted. In seeking treatment, the parents united in their request for help in dividing up the duties of caring for the child with the disability. In their minds, their marital discord was due solely to the difficulties associated with caring, night and day, for the birth-injured child. After a few therapy sessions, they realized that their marital problems were really due to incompatibilities and a lack of love and commitment to each other. Mark and Mary decided that they should divorce, and were able to fashion custody and visitation arrangements that would allow for shared responsibility for both of the children.

The AAMFT ethics code gives no specific guidance with regard to children per se. At the most, there is an implied reference to children in Subprinciple 1.2, which states

Marriage and family therapists obtain appropriate informed consent to therapy or related procedures and use language that is reasonably understandable to clients. The content of informed consent may vary depending upon the client and treatment plan; however, informed consent generally necessitates that the client: (a) has the capacity to consent; (b) has been adequately informed of significant information concerning treatment processes, procedures, risks and benefits; (c) has been adequately informed of potential risks and benefits of treatments for which generally recognized standards do not yet exist; (d) has freely and without undue influence expressed consent; and (e) has provided consent that is appropriately documented. When persons, due to age or mental status, are legally incapable of giving informed consent, marriage and family therapists obtain informed permission from a legally authorized person, if such substitute consent is legally permissible.

In Subprinciple 1.2, the critical sentence is: "When persons, due to age or mental status, are legally incapable of giving informed consent, marriage and family therapists obtain informed permission from a legally authorized person, if such substitute consent is legally permissible. This means that children who have not reached the legal age of majority (which may vary by jurisdiction), or have not been emancipated legally, are deemed, because of age, "legally incapable of giving informed consent." Therefore, a parent or guardian would have the legal capability to authorize treatment or, among other things, release confidential information about the child. As an example of a dilemma due to a child's refusal to consent to treatment, consider the following case.

Jannine. When Jannine's disruptive behavior and belligerence toward teachers led to her dismissal from school, her parents, Jerry and Janet, agreed that, if the school would allow her back into classes, they would seek family therapy. From the outset, the last place that Jannine wanted to be was in the office of the marriage and family therapist. Stated simply, Jerry and Janet forced Jannine to attend the sessions. The marriage and family therapist was perplexed, because clearly Jannine had not consented to the treatment; she could not decide whether to basically ignore Jannine's presence or persistently attempt to elicit her cooperation and involvement.

It should be noted that, in some jurisdictions, licensing boards (and other governmental agencies) have statutes or rules that pertain to the rights of children. Therefore, the prudent therapist will readily consult with an attorney knowledgeable about these matters for the jurisdiction in which the professional services are provided.

Since there will likely be situations in which the child does not agree with the parent or guardian about treatment matters or the release of confidential information, the therapist must wrestle with reconciling divergent preferences. Principle I of the AAMFT ethics code, Responsibility to Clients, advises the marriage and family therapist to "advance the welfare of families and individuals." The unique context of family therapy means that the therapist must presumably give simultaneous consideration to the needs and preferences of the parents (or guardian) and of the child as individuals, even though the child may lack legal competency per se.

The following case exemplifies how a youth's refusal to allow parents access to her confidential information can create a nightmare of clinical, ethical, and legal considerations. As will be evident, there may be no simple solution, and complicated clinical and legal ramifications will have to be weighed and accommodated.

Suzanne. A highly intelligent 17-year old, Suzanne was failing her first year of college classes. Her family's wealth, along with an ethnic background that elevates the importance of daughters, led to their catering to Suzanne's whims and fancies. A year ago, Suzanne dropped out of high school and went off to Germany, supposedly to study (which never happened). After a few aimless weeks, Suzanne became pregnant from a casual sexual contact, and had a faulty abortion that led to her being hospitalized for both mental and physical reasons. For several years, she had been frequently using all sorts of street drugs, "but only for recreational purposes," and for the past few months she had been consuming a considerable amount of alcohol every day. Although she seldom saw her family physician, he kept her supplied with an ongoing prescription for antidepressant medication.

Suzanne and her parents went to the therapist for the stated purpose of helping Suzanne become better adjusted. In a recent individual session, Suzanne expressed suicidal ideation, along with a plan for accomplishing suicide. She insisted that the therapist not tell her parents about the suicide ideas or about her long-term use of street drugs and her heavy current consumption of alcohol.

Without mentioning the suicide, drugs, or alcohol, the therapist spent the next few family sessions recommending and reinforcing the idea of inpatient treatment for Suzanne. The parents did not believe that hospitalization was necessary and Suzanne opposed it mightily. The whole family agreed that a weekly individual session with Suzanne and an occasional family session was what they needed; they would not agree to any other treatment options.

Knowing the gravity of the problem but believing that she was constrained from releasing information about Suzanne to the parents, the therapist felt stymied. After consulting with a senior colleague, she recognized that, in addition to the informed consent and authorization issues, she must provide services that are in the clinical interests of the client, and she did not believe sporadic outpatient services were adequate (see Subprinciple 1.9: "Marriage and family therapists continue therapeutic relationships only so long as it is reasonably clear that clients are benefiting from the relationship").

With the help of an attorney knowledgeable about mental health practices, the therapist began fashioning a new plan: Unless Suzanne and her parents would cooperate adequately with the preferred treatment plan and authorize an open exchange of clinical information between family members, the therapist would cease to provide them with services. The therapist was, however, careful to be sure that the termination plan would include appropriate referrals (see Subprinciple 1.10: "Marriage and family therapists assist persons in obtaining other therapeutic services if the therapist is unable or unwilling, for appropriate reasons, to provide professional help") and avoid abandonment of the family (see Subprinciple 1.11: "Marriage and family therapists do not abandon or neglect clients in treatment without making reasonable arrangements for the continuation of such treatment"). This part of the plan reflected attention to ethics as well as the need to manage potential legal risks.

The nature and extent of children's rights continue to be debated in society and within the law. As mentioned earlier, laws relevant to minors vary among jurisdictions, such as a child's right to keep information about therapy from the parents, as opposed to the parents' right to know therapeutic information about their child. Even in situations where the child is instrumental in initiating treatment, the child's rights or best interests may not be or remain primary. For example, treatment planning may compromise the rights of a child who independently consults a school counselor or pastor or one who is in the custody of the state or lives in a residential treatment facility. Although Principle I of the AAMFT ethics code directs the marriage and family therapist to advance the welfare of families and individuals, the reality is that the law sets limits on children's rights in some situations and limits on parents' rights in other situations. Consequently, many ethical issues can arise in treating a minor child, especially in the context of individual sessions and personal concerns, such as sexuality.

Ethical Issues Related to Changing Professional and Social Conditions

The evolution of the profession of family therapy has given rise to increased attention to ethical issues, including those involving children and youth (more will be said about adolescents later on). From its beginnings, the innovation of family therapy and subsequently the emergence of the profession of marriage and family therapy was curiously intertwined with ethical concerns. Proponents touted early theories of family therapy as a needed corrective for the existing individual models of treatment. Treating the whole family as a system was supposed to be the best remedy for children's problems.

Today the models and methods of family therapy continue to reflect innovation as well as integration; and these, to varying degrees, continue to give rise to unacknowledged ethical questions. In addition, therapists, as part of the mental health industry, have expanded their practices to many types of service settings, another change that complicates the treatment of children's problems.

Other professional developments have called attention to children in therapy. Both the child advocacy and the feminist therapy movements pointed to children's relative powerlessness, lack of guaranteed rights, the role of social context in their lives, and to the lack of appreciation for diversity and difference (Conoley & Larson, 1995; Koocher, 1995).

Larger societal and cultural "revolutions" occurring at the same time that family therapy made its appearance have raised questions about what constitutes ethical practice with children in family therapy. The consumer movement eventually shifted mental health practice beyond the primary control of professionals. Other cultural upheavals also continue to impact on family therapy: the widespread prevalence of divorce, greater openness about sexuality and sexual problems, the feminist movement, changing family structures, the knowledge explosion, and the ever-present influence of the communication media on children and families.

Among the general public and professionals alike, questions arise as to what is and what should be the nature of family life, the "right" family structure and organization, good child care, good discipline, and so on. Today people are often highly polarized on the values surrounding these emotionally loaded aspects of family life. Many of these issues have resulted in litigation that have left the courts to rule on aspects of family life, with outcomes being quite diverse and complex. For example, in the situation of abortion, both the teenager and her parents have some limited but not absolute rights (again, these rights vary with the jurisdiction).

Given the ongoing vociferous political and social debate about "family values," therapists must be especially cognizant of their own personal values versus the professional values essential to ethical practice. The risk is that the therapist's own strong personal values and beliefs about family life, while not obviously expressed in therapy, may permeate his or her assessment practices, selection of models and methods, and intervention. One ethical issue is whether the therapist's values operate in a blatant or subtle manner to persuade or dictate personal decisions that belong to the client. In other words, there must be no violation of Subprinciple 1.8 of the AAMFT ethics code, which states

Marriage and family therapists respect the rights of clients to make decisions and help them to understand the consequences of these decisions. Therapists clearly advise the clients that they have the responsibility to make decisions regarding relationships such as cohabitation, marriage, divorce, separation, reconciliation, custody, and visitation.

For the client to truly exercise decision making, the therapist must be cognizant of and be able to control subtle (unspoken) influences. In discussions of clients' life decisions, therapists should be thoughtful of how they frame their interventions and responses to assure that a decision comes from the client's needs and values rather than from attempts to please the therapist. In the context of the therapeutic relationship, some clients may reenact established but maladaptive relationship patterns, such as placating or pleasing others. (Recall that Chapter Two differentiates between the therapist's giving direct advice on a life decision and empowering the client to evaluate options and reach his or her own decision.)

Many problems experienced by children today, which will be specified shortly, seem more severe and extreme than in the past. Contemporary societal problems involving children place great demands on therapists for continual refinement and expansion of their competence and skills. As Principle III, Professional Competence and Integrity, of the AAMFT ethics code states, "Marriage and family therapists maintain high standards of professional competence and integrity." Also, Subprinciple 3.1 says, "Marriage and family therapists pursue knowledge of new developments and maintain competence in marriage and family therapy through education, training, or supervised experience."

Among the more severe disturbances impacting on today's children are juvenile violence and offenses, child sexual abuse, child and adolescent sexual misconduct, substance abuse, adolescent depression and suicide, severe developmental disabilities, children with HIV, and so on. Other childhood adjustment problems may connect to family conditions, such as parents' hostile divorce and custody/visitation conditions, sexual disorders, sexual offenses, addictions, and severe mental disorders. In addition to working with the most severe of children's problems, marriage and family therapists also see the range of what might be called "normative" difficulties: learning, behavioral, and emotional problems; poor school performance, adjustment, failure, or drop-out; parent-child conflicts and discipline issues; teenage rebelliousness; and risk-taking behavior.

The range and severity of children's problems create ethical challenges. Most important, therapists need to maintain professional competence and not practice beyond their level of competence; and they should consistently self-monitor for countertransference reactions that may lead to overidentification with certain individuals in the family.

The nature and variety of children's problems today also suggest the diversity of service settings/facilities in which marriage and family therapists work: psychiatric, medical, rehabilitation, residential, educational, community and governmental agencies (including home-based intervention) as well as employee assistance and private practice groups. Much of the expanded therapeutic endeavor by marriage and family therapists involves collaboration with other professionals or service agencies, including attorneys and the courts. This aspect of practice also creates new demands to understand the function of other providers and to meet the ethical standards involved in collaboration. (On this latter point, recall the discussion in Chapter Two on strict adherence to protecting confidentiality and the need for a signed release to share information.)

It is likely that the recent innovative and integrative models in family therapy have evolved as part of the search for more effective treatment for children's problems. It appears that various problems, contrary to early high hopes, have not responded consistently to the original system-based models, such as structural family therapy, intergenerational family therapy, communication/interactional models, and their numerous derivatives. Consequently, the newer generation of marriage and family therapists has offered integrated or refined models. The integrative movement within psychotherapy and marriage and family therapy has been called "the quiet revolution" (Blow & Sprenkle, 2001, p. 400). Some of these innovations imply, even if they do not directly address, various ethical complexities of working with the child in the context of the family and other systems.

CHILDREN IN FAMILY THERAPY: UNIQUE ETHICAL ISSUES

Numerous factors have given rise to the ethical issues associated with therapy that involves children. Perhaps because of these reasons some marriage and family practitioners prefer to not work with children's problems at all. With the current marketplace, however, most marriage and family therapists want to expand, not to restrict, their practices. Yet ethical and legal risks inevitably come with the focus on children in family therapy.

Children and Families in the Treatment System

The way in which children enter and participate in family therapy raises several ethical challenges for the therapist. These include attending to the welfare of individuals and the family; respecting adults' right to make important family decisions; understanding the intricacies of consent and confidentiality when minors are involved; assuring that professional competence and integrity guide practice; and monitoring for the inappropriate influence of the therapist's personal values and needs.

As mentioned earlier, the AAMFT ethics code announces the marriage and family therapist's responsibility to attend to the welfare of families and individuals, but beyond this rather general guideline, the code does not give specific directions for achieving this directive. When a therapist sees several members of a family, including a child presented as "the problem," the challenge is to provide therapy that benefits each individual and the whole family. The respective psychological needs of the family members may, of course, sometimes be in actual or apparent conflict; and the needs of one or more individuals may not serve the needs of the family as a whole. For example, not all parents are nurturing and knowledgeable about the kind of care, supervision, or communication that will foster the child's development. Some parents neglect or abuse their children. In other cases, out-of-control adolescents may attempt to control, even terrorize, parents to assert full autonomy for their lives, without family restrictions.

In such situations, the therapist has several options, such as:

(1) finding a common ground that might allow for meeting needs of both the individuals and the family system;

(2) moving toward advocacy for an individual (if warranted by legal mandate); or

(3) using some combination of both strategies.

Selecting the option must, of course, be based on the needs of the particular family treatment regime.

Evaluating the clinical factors and deciding about the treatment options depend most clearly on the ethical principle of professional competence and integrity. In other words, the therapist needs a high level of expertise and skill to build an alliance with the whole family. Effective assessment and intervention strategies flow from an extensive knowledge base that would include family systems; child, adult, and family developmental needs; personality; serious mental disorders; and a range of effective individual and family change strategies.

The therapist must be sensitive to the ethical demands of such a complex treatment format. The task is to negotiate exactly who is the client (i.e., individuals or the family as a whole). If the client is the whole family, the child deserves the safeguards of confidentiality and informed consent, because these are not clear rights but depend on the good will of parents (Koocher & Keith-Speigel, 1990).

With regard to the ethical subtleties involved in therapy with children, therapists need to show sensitivity to the relative vulnerabilities of all parties and approach each family with awareness that ethical issues could arise. The following guidelines, based on the work of Koocher (1995), may help with this challenge:

(1) Negotiate constructive therapy goals, involving all the relevant parties and considering the child's needs and wishes.

(2) When contemplating hospitalization or other treatments that would require due process or formal consent procedures by adults, give preference to the least restrictive ones consistent with the needs and best interests of the child.

(3) Seek to foster mutual understanding while respecting the possible different personal values of the child and the parents.

(4) Be aware of potential dual-role relationships, especially in small towns or rural locales, and avoid these as much as possible.

(5) Monitor for countertransference reactions toward the child or parents and maintain appropriate boundaries.

(6) Avoid aversive therapeutic strategies and use only with proper consent from parents or guardian, only if less negative or forceful methods have failed, and only where the problems threaten harm for the child.

(7) Be familiar with legal standards in the jurisdiction and remain aware of the limits of your knowledge in this area.

These guidelines highlight the several processes in therapy with children in which the practitioner should be alert to "red flags" that could produce an ethical dilemma.

The Dynamics and Analysis of an Ethical Dilemma

The following case exemplifies a therapy situation that contains all of the dynamics discussed above. The demands of this sort of case are many, and require keen clinical acumen to respond to the many ethical issues.

Ashley. A 15-year old Caucasian female, Ashley, was referred to a therapist who provides, under contract with the state Department of Social Services (DSS), therapy to children in foster care. Ashley had been placed with the Smith family. She was not returned to her biological family because they had been deemed neglectful of Ashley's mental health needs, particularly her depression, and suicide attempts; her mental condition eventually resulted in her being placed for inpatient hospitalization in a mental health facility. She continued on medication for major depression.

The Smiths had two biological children, a 14-year old son and an 8-year old daughter. The family, strongly religious in a very conservative faith, invited Ashley to participate in church activities, and she willingly did so. The foster father was employed in a white-collar position, and the foster mother was looking for full-time employment.

Ashley had been with the family less than a week when she and the 14-year old son engaged in intercourse. Ashley had already been given the Norplant contraceptive by the Department of Social Services before the foster placement because she had been sexually active when the DSS became involved.

To deal with this problem, the DSS worker and the parents arrived at a plan to structure the physical home environment so that the two teens were never together at home without an adult present. The only time the youths would be alone was when they were in their rooms located on separate floors. Ashley's room was near the foster parents' room while the 14-year old son's room was on a lower floor.

Through notes, the foster parents subsequently discovered that the two youths had engaged in intercourse on two more occasions; thus, the referral for therapy was made. In the meantime, the foster parents invested in alarms for the doors of both teens' rooms and implemented the rule that the two teens would not ever be allowed on the same floor of the home without an adult present. The foster parents were extremely upset, their son was angry and defiant, and Ashley was crying and saying that she only wanted to feel loved.

The Smiths stated they were committed to working through these problems within the family and with Ashley, but did not want their other children involved in the therapy. Ashley expressed a strong desire to remain in the home as she was responding well to the medication for her depression, liked the family a lot, and was doing well in school. She also said she was sorry about the sexual behavior and was worried about losing the placement.

This example raises all of the ethical issues noted above and more, and leads to the following questions:

Is it possible to meet the needs of both the individual primary client, Ashley (who is the state's primary concern), and the foster parents and their children (as the state's secondary concern)?

Should the therapist advocate the best interests of Ashley, and her several needs, such as for stability, nurturing from a caring family, succeeding in school, and achieving her normal developmental tasks, including understanding and managing her sexuality?

Are these various needs likely to be obtainable within the context of this particular family?

Can the therapist also advocate the overall welfare of this foster family that includes not only Ashley, but also the parents and their son and daughter?

What are the barriers that might prevent the therapist from developing goals and interventions that would benefit Ashley within this family and the whole family system?

What is the role of the therapist in regard to the referring agency, collaboration efforts, and recommendations?

How might the values about sexuality held by the DSS worker, the marriage and family therapist, and the foster family affect the course of therapy?

Certainly there are no simple answers to these questions.

The decision a professional makes to resolve an ethical dilemma needs to be ethically defensible, both to the practitioner making it and to others who might judge it. It is possible that more than one resolution of a given dilemma could meet this criterion. In the case of Ashley, the therapist, in consultation with the caseworker, arrived at a defensible resolution. The analysis that resulted in the decision generally followed the models of ethical analysis and decision making presented in Chapter One. The decision about Ashley's situation and its rationale follow.

1. The therapist considered all of the options and paths that Ashley's treatment might take.

2. The caseworker and therapist jointly decided that the best interests of Ashley, who was in the custody of the state, must remain primary.

3. Ashley's vulnerability in this situation and this family was judged to be greater than the vulnerability of the foster family and individuals in that unit.

4. Alternatives for carrying out the state's and the therapist's primary responsibility to Ashley were considered and weighed for their potential consequences and values.

5. The decision was to remove Ashley from the family and develop a new treatment plan based on the following:

(a) The environmental solutions within the family placement were not working to reduce the sexual behavior and the risks it posed. Addressing this issue in therapy, such as by engaging the family and the two young people in a rational approach to sex education and decision making, which both young people needed, had very little chance of success, or timely success, to prevent further harm to Ashley.

(b) Changing Ashley's placement was seen as less of a detriment to her welfare than having her remain in a family where the sexual situation could not be quickly resolved and which threatened her overall welfare.

(c) Although no setting is ideal for a child in Ashley's situation, the decision was made to obtain a new placement for her in a residential treatment center for children, and not with another foster family. The professionals involved believed that this placement was the best option for meeting Ashley's several developmental needs in a setting that could remain stable over a long period of time.

(d) Although the residential center could not provide the family setting and atmosphere, it offered nurturing caregivers, a school program with educational guidance, and ongoing individual and group therapy and social skills educational programs. The latter could focus on assisting Ashley with all adolescent developmental tasks, including understanding and managing her sexuality.

COMPLEX CHILD-FAMILY PROBLEMS AND CONTEMPORARY THERAPEUTIC INNOVATIONS

Therapists have long been aware that certain child and family problems demand high levels of therapeutic competence and professional integrity. Because certain problems typically include conflicting needs and interests of the child and the parents, ethical concerns are common. As family therapy has continued to develop, innovative approaches have evolved to address specific family problems. These may also elaborate on the nature of the problem in an effort to clarify whether the approach advocates for the child, for the parents, or for both. Rather than being addressed directly, ethical considerations are often implied and remain unattended.

Often it seems that new therapy approaches carry implications for ethics, but those who develop theories rarely attend to or address these directly. In fact, the well-established models of family therapy are typically silent on the whole issue of ethics in their conceptualizations and strategies. As mentioned in Chapter One, a quick review by the authors of eleven textbooks that present models of family therapy revealed that only six of these even indexed the term "ethics." And the coverage in these six was typically limited to a few sentences, or at most a couple of pages. This lack of integration of ethical issues within theoretical models points to the need for a book such as this—with the goal of raising awareness of ethical problems that are common to family therapy.

The following discussion reviews two innovative strategies for two quite different child-family problems: the effects of a "difficult divorce" on children, and the effects of dominating, threatening youths on themselves and their families.

The Difficult Divorce

The difficult divorce is one in which the parents and the child are not coping with the stress that divorce brings to family life. In addition, instead of protecting the child from their out-of-control disputes, parents may lose confidence in their parenting abilities, abdicate their care taking, push the child to take sides, or all of the above.

In almost any difficult divorce, it seems appropriate for the therapist to attempt to assure that the interests of children are served. Issacs, Montalvo, and Abelson (1986) offer an approach that acknowledges children as the priority, but argue that parents themselves make the best adjustment to separation and divorce when they are successful with their children. Once the assessment reveals that children are at risk from the parents' activities surrounding their divorce, the goal of therapy is to focus on and emphasize the child's welfare. However, the parents are enlisted in the therapeutic process, and carefully designed strategies are used to help them make the changes that will benefit the child (and most likely themselves as well). Different formats are used: children may be seen individually and/or with siblings; and parents may be seen individually, together, and/or with their child on occasion and as the course of therapy requires.

An array of strategies may be used, with the strategic selection depending on the unique family situation. The therapist should seek to engage the parents therapeutically, which calls for all family members' honoring controlled conditions that respect boundaries. For example, parents are not seen together if they are already living separately. Partners are encouraged to contact and deal directly with their lawyers without the therapist's involvement.

To engage the parents, the therapist might use persuasion, influence, or even guilt, to move the parents toward whatever position will allow them to better meet the child's needs. Individual sessions prepare each parent for the joint encounter in therapy, where together they agree to the goal of doing their separation and divorce differently. The therapist builds trust with each parent individually, and becomes his or her advocate. Each parent receives coaching and preparation to monitor and control his or her self in the planned joint encounter, such as during any heated exchanges between the dissonant (ex)spouses.

The therapist evaluates the success of the encounter and determines the strategies needed to address the outcome. These strategies would differ for parents who continue to battle with each other, for those who are indirect versus direct fighters, and for situations calling for violence prevention. A range of therapeutic techniques might be used. These include assessing the level of stagnation of their conflict; crisis making through magnifying the consequences of their stagnation; taking a skeptical bias by bringing all current and past unfinished business to the surface; sponsoring a final "failed" parental encounter; seizing the opportunity of their continued failure to reorient them to cooperation; moving them toward resolution rituals; and helping them accept reasonable goals such as containing negative feelings and displaying only what is required for a workable relationship for the task at hand.

This approach, which was developed over 15 years ago (Issacs et al., 1986), has obvious ethical implications, such as informed consent, but does not specify or define them as such. For example, the parents know and accept that the goals of therapy center on primary concern for the children; parents are also informed of the need and rationale for the different therapy stages and formats. The implication is that parents, by virtue of their participation in this type of therapy, are implicitly giving informed consent for themselves and also for their children. Strategic or confrontational strategies are used cautiously and only after an assessment supports that more direct, educative techniques have not reduced the risks to the child. Also, the therapist respects the importance of the need for legal consultation apart from this kind of therapy. This approach openly advocates for all children who are subjected to hurt by their parents' difficult separation or divorce. It is important to note that the advocacy is not an afterthought or due to countertransference on the part of the therapist.

To employ this approach today and to conform to the AAMFT ethics code, the therapist would need to give careful attention to several ethical issues implied in the model. Because the general procedures and process of the treatment are made clear early on, documenting the consent for parents and children in writing should be simple. Although not mentioned as such in the model, problems around confidentiality could easily arise. Thus confidentiality and its limits should be openly discussed; and family members should give written permission for what constitutes "confidences" that may be shared with others in the treatment unit.

Therapist competence and integrity need to be of the highest quality for this type of therapy. The reason is that influence, persuasion, and strategic interventions elevate the risk that the therapist may inject personal values or subtly influence parents' decisions. The only discussion of ethics in the book presenting this model (Issacs et al., 1986) centers on whether strict neutrality should apply in the case of a particular couple who were considering dissolution of their marriage. Specifically, was neutrality the only defensible ethical stance for the therapist? Issacs et al. (1986) determined that a strict "conservative stance of neutrality" in this case would have been "clinically incorrect and unethical" because of the couple's long history of escalating violence and the wife's strong stance of wanting out of the marriage. Consequently, these data justified the use of a strategic intervention called the "confrontation parade," in which the couple's children tell parents "what they have already told the therapist: that they are suffering more from the parents' staying together than they would if the parents separated" (Issacs et al., 1986, pp. 146–147).

It seems that the therapist drew on both behavioral science knowledge and the ethical/legal obligations around dangerousness and violence in resolving the ethical question. However, the nature of this therapy approach could potentially lead to ethical problems around the blurring of therapist's professional and personal values.

Dominating or Threatening Adolescents and Their Families

Families characterized by intense parent-child conflict typically experience severe behavioral and emotional upheaval for both the parents and the child. Therapy for this kind of problem can give rise to many ethical issues.

In working with the tough adolescent and family, Price (1996) drew on structural and strategic concepts to offer treatment that would provide both power and compassion. The teenager who is dominating, threatening, and attempting to control parents and other family members may be prematurely asserting or striving for total control over his or her life. This model appears to advocate for the parents but also assumes that the adolescent with problems of this kind will fare best when the parents become able to provide parental leadership and needed care.

Various methods and formats may be used, but the initial goal is to engage both the parents and the young person in therapy. Usually, the parents willingly come with the complaint whereas the teenager comes involuntarily or not at all. With a youth who refuses to come to treatment, the therapist coaches parents on things to say to the child that will usually bring him or her into the treatment system. For example, "We will be talking about you behind your back," or, "This is a new rule that we decided on for you in therapy" (Price & Margerum, 2000). The two-fold assumption is that (1) the youth's age-appropriate needs call for and deserve parental support, caring, and leadership; and (2) the therapy focuses on enabling parents to provide these behaviors. Once therapy is underway, the preceding goals become clear to and usually (if not always) acceptable to the parents and youth alike.

Ethical issues are implied in this model, although they are not defined as such; and the validity of the model is defended, not the ethics per se. Both the parents and the teenager apparently receive a clear message about the nature of the treatment and its goals. This explanation could be seen as an early and understandable account of therapy procedures and a treatment plan to which clients apparently give informed consent verbally. According to the AAMFT ethics code, however, the therapist should document appropriately that the clients have expressed consent (such as by noting this in the family's file).

Another ethical issue that is made clear to all of the family members is that confidentiality is not promised to a teenager. The justification is that, with angry and explosive youths, a power struggle is underway between parent and child; and appropriate power needs to be restored to parents. Thus, "Confidentiality in families is held within the family and not by individual members. Therefore, the therapist has latitude to share whatever needs to be shared" (Price & Margerum, 2000, p. 53). The point is that the therapist and parents need to be able to deal with such issues as a youth's drug use, sexual activities, smoking, and dangerous friends in order to find solutions. Price and Margerum do not describe how the therapist should present this approach or how to proceed if highly personal information is to be revealed to the parents.

A strict interpretation of the AAMFT ethics code suggests that the marriage and family therapist using this approach should obtain the youth's written permission for this flexibility with confidentiality; see Subprinciple 2.2, which states

When providing couple, family or group treatment, the therapist does not disclose information outside the treatment context without a written authorization from each individual competent to execute a waiver. In the context of couple, family or group treatment, the therapist may not reveal any individual's confidences to others in the client unit without the prior written permission of that individual.

As discussed earlier, the AAMFT ethics code allows for the fact that a child or youth may lack competence to consent. Nonetheless, it seems that the ethical intent is to accord informed consent and permission rights to every member of the family; and note that these matters should be documented in writing.

Other components in this model enable the parents to regain appropriate authority. The parents learn how to set needed rules or consequences without defending or arguing about them; to keep an aura of privacy around their own lives; and to gain, but not to share with the child, knowledge that they gather about their child's life outside the family (rather than simply giving up if the child tries to hide or lie about this sort of information).

Finally, this approach focuses on solutions, which might involve other systems, such as the school or the criminal or judicial system, and suitable parental allies. The latter could include family friends, relatives, or the parents of the child's peers. The assumption is that the solutions will have the potential to yield a win-win result in families with severely conflicting parental and child needs. The model draws on selected concepts from strategic therapy, family systems, and developmental psychology. As with all therapeutic methods, ethical practice demands careful assessment of the unique client and family situation. This model focuses on "abusive" youth who, according to Price (1996), have likely had too big a dose of parental permissiveness. This parental stance, however, may not be a primary factor in the more typical, normative efforts of teens to assert autonomy or begin to separate from the family.

This model merits further empirical evaluation, beyond anecdotal case examples, of its ethical implications and its effectiveness. As discussed in several chapters in this book, the field of family therapy, like all of the mental health professions, faces the challenge of accountability for its interventions from many sources. Assessing the quality of the evidence for the effectiveness of a therapeutic approach is a starting point. Evaluation can counteract the potential tendency to embrace a therapeutic model simply because it fits the therapist's personal values or personality. That is, a model should be chosen on the basis of efficacy, not unconsciously selected as a vehicle for the therapist to rework his or her own history with adolescence or parenthood. (See Chapter Five for extensive discussion of professional competence and how ethics interface with the new focus on evidence-based therapy models.) In other words, professional competence and integrity demand not only continually updating knowledge and skills but also continual self-awareness and scrutiny by the practitioner.

These two examples of contemporary integrative models that deal with complex child-family problems address some of the issues that arise from conflicting parent and child needs, but the ethical issues are more implied and incidental than conscious. The value of the AAMFT ethics code is that it enables therapists to examine more consciously the ethical ramifications of the treatment models that are part of family therapy's history and future.

CHILD CUSTODY ISSUES AND ETHICS

In the United States, the divorce rate is approaching 66% (Tiesel & Olsen, 1992). With divorce involving over one million children per year (Butler, Mellon, Stroh, & Stern, 1995), therapists have an integral role to play in helping clients with family crises associated with divorce, child custody, visitation, and parenting children after divorce.

Many of the ethical and legal dilemmas associated with child custody (and there are many) can arise inadvertently if a therapist is not attuned adequately to the risks. Child custody, visitation, and abuse cases spawn more complaints to licensing boards and ethics committees than any other type of case. Except in rare instances and a few jurisdictions, only the judge has immunity from legal actions.

Part of the problem comes from the expanded roles that professionals play in treating family problems. Before a couple decides to divorce, a marriage and family therapist may have been treating them, or one (or all) of their children; subsequently, that same therapist may treat individuals or family members with adjustment to separation, divorce status, and problems associated with custody and visitation. These are difficult issues within the context of therapy, but if parents begin legal actions regarding custody and visitation, these issues can create ethical and legal minefields. Therapists must be wary when a client moves in this direction and seeks the therapist's involvement.

With a view to the risks to therapists involved with custody cases, the AAMFT ethics code newly addresses the issue of multiple professional roles in custody and visitation actions, under Principle III, Professional Competence and Integrity. Specifically, Subprinciple 3.14 states

To avoid a conflict of interest, marriage and family therapists who treat minors or adults involved in custody or visitation actions may not also perform forensic evaluations for custody, residence, or visitation of the minor. The marriage and family therapist who treats the minor may provide the court or mental health professional performing the evaluation with information about the minor from the marriage and family therapist's perspective as a treating marriage and family therapist, so long as the marriage and family therapist does not violate confidentiality.

Although it might seem logical and pragmatic (e.g., cost saving) to have the therapist take on a multiple-role assignment, the problems usually arise simply from wearing too many professional hats. In fact, contemporary public policy and laws now place restrictions, with some variations between jurisdictions, on the role that any mental health professional can play in child custody legal proceedings.

The detailed AAMFT ethics code's subprinciple cited above offers guidance to prevent ethical and legal problems arising from assuming multiple roles in a client's case. Prior to the evolution of standards intended to prevent conflict of interest and dual professional roles by the therapist, it was possible for the parents' attorneys to stipulate to the court that, if a therapist had provided pre-divorce counseling to the parents or child, the same therapist should be allowed to be the court-appointed evaluator for custody and visitation, guardian for the children, or mediator of disputes. Most inappropriately, the therapist was sometimes called on to act like a quasi-judge, being asked by attorneys or even by the judge to give a "professional opinion," in definite terms, about which parent should have custody and what should be the terms for visitation.

As an aside, it is ill advised for any therapist to address an ultimate legal question, such as which parent should have custody and what should be the visitation schedule. There is not substantial behavioral science research to allow a mental health practitioner of any ilk to make distinctions of that ultimate nature. Without adequate behavioral science research, the therapist is precluded from issuing an opinion that is truly "professional." In addition, only the trier of fact (the judge) has the endorsement of public policy and the legal authority (by statute) to make those ultimate decisions.

Besides the ethical guideline above, other aspects of the AAMFT ethics code also offer guidance for these situations. Even if the parents, the attorneys, or the judge may want the therapist to fulfill multiple professional roles, the practitioner should respectfully object (e.g., the marriage and family therapist should cite Subprinciple 3.14 that proscribes his or her being in multiple professional roles). In addition, consider the statement made in Subprinciple

3.4: "Marriage and family therapists do not provide services that create a conflict of interest that may impair work performance or clinical judgment." And Subprinciple 3.12 states, "Marriage and family therapists make efforts to prevent the distortion or misuse of their clinical and research findings."

Adherence to these and other guidelines derived from the AAMFT ethics code should help prevent the most difficult ethical and legal dilemmas; however, dealing with child custody issues in any professional role is demanding and requires a high level of clinical acumen and ethical awareness. One reason, aside from the legal ramifications, is that this whole area of family life is filled with values that often elicit high emotion from clients and therapists alike; and emotion can impair professional judgment.

Consider the possible professional services that a therapist may provide that could involve child custody issues to a greater or lesser extent:

(1) Before or after the divorce, the therapist may provide therapy to children experiencing distress about the separation of the parents; adjustment to problems associated with living, custody, and visitation arrangements; and confusion over the parents' new love interests, new work schedules, and new financial status.

(2) Upon remarriage, the therapist may help the adults and child deal with the challenge of achieving a success-fully blended family.

(3) With specialized assessment skills, the therapist may provide professional information, through expert testi-mony, to assist the trier of fact (i.e., the judge) to recognize the unique needs of the child and make judicial determinations that are in the best interests of the child, such as for residential custody, visitation, or modifi-cations of previous determinations about these matters. (This third role, according to the AAMFT ethics code, should not be assumed if the therapist has been involved in the first two roles above, or others, in serving the client family. The obvious rationale is that these prior therapeutic roles may limit the objectivity needed for these types of services.)

It is assumed, of course, that the therapist has the specialized competencies to perform these services, which do, in fact, require more advanced knowledge and skills than are provided by the traditional entry-level training program. While it is beyond the scope of this chapter to cover the details of the specialized knowledge, skills, and supervision that are appropriate for custody issues, the discussion below suggests several directions for boosting professional competence.

Basically, two major areas of knowledge come into play: the behavioral sciences and the law. Although both of these areas interface at times, they derive from different assumptions. While therapists should be informed in general about legal aspects of custody issues for all cases, they should rely on legal advice from attorneys if they are in the role of providing professional information through expert testimony.

The Best Interests of the Child

The best interests of the child is a concept that has become part of the law but derives in part from concepts based on behavioral science. An understanding of this concept can point to the theoretical and practice knowledge that therapists should possess to practice competently with divorce and custody issues.

Over the past 30 years, the prevailing notion in legal proceedings has been that determinations of custody and visitation should be based on the best interests of the child: "Currently, the best interests of the child is the governing standard in virtually all child custody disputes between natural parents arising within the fifty states" (Rohman, Sales, & Lou, 1987, p. 62).

Although aligned with the best interests of the child, statutory definition of the term varies among jurisdictions. Some scholars cite as a prototype of the best interests of the child, the criteria for evaluation that are set forth in the child custody statute from the State of Michigan:

(a) The love, affection, and other emotional ties existing between the parties involved with the child.

(b) The capacity and disposition of the parties involved to give the child love, affection, and guidance and to continue the education and raising of the child in his or her religion or creed, if any.

(c) The capacity and disposition of the parties involved to provide the child with food, clothing, medical care or other remedial care recognized and permitted under the laws of this state in place of medical care, and other material needs.

(d) The length of time the child has lived in a stable, satisfactory environment, and the desirability of maintaining continuity.

(e) The permanence, as a family unit, of the existing or proposed custodial home or homes.

(f) The moral fitness of the parties involved.

(g) The mental and physical health of the parties involved.

(h) The home, school, and community record of the child.

(i) The reasonable preference of the child, if the court deems the child to be of sufficient age to express preference.

(j) The willingness and ability of each of the parties to facilitate and encourage a close and continuing parent-child relationship between the child and the other parent or the child and the parents.

(k) Domestic violence, regardless of whether the violence was directed against or witnessed by the child.

(l) Any other factor considered by the court to be relevant to a particular child custody dispute. (Michigan Child Custody Act, MCLA 722.23)

Clearly, these criteria for determining the best interests of the child require psychological, social, health, and educational information about the child, as well as about the parents who are contenders for meeting the needs of the child. A fundamental problem, however, is that, while professional opinions are wanted, these criteria are ill defined:

The vagueness of the best interests of the child standard affords broad discretion to trial courts and limits appellate review. The heavily factual nature of the standard requires case-by-case determination and allows little purely legal precedent to develop. Thus prospective litigants cannot easily predict what courts will decide. This lack of predictability has been criticized as the cause for an increase in custody litigation. (Wyer, Gaylord, & Grove, 1987, p. 14)

The vagueness of the elements within the best interests of the child concept means that the therapist must draw upon specialized knowledge and skills to appropriately address the criteria and evaluate how they apply to the specifics of any case.

A great deal of behavioral science theoretical and research-based knowledge is essential to the ethical practice of the therapist in any of the roles involving child custody and visitation and for interpreting the best interests criteria. The following areas of knowledge, to name but a few, could apply: the broad field of child development; psychodynamic theories of family and child development, such as object relations theory that emphasizes the role of caregiving and personality development; learning theory that encompasses all aspects of the child's intellectual, emotional, and social learning; systems theory, especially as it applies to the family within the social environment and the internal structure and dynamics of the family; and specific theories of child abuse and family violence.

Given the complexity of child custody actions, the AAMFT ethics code makes clear the ethical responsibility to gain specialized training for practice with these issues. Subprinciple 3.12 states, "Marriage and family therapists do not diagnose, treat, or advise on problems outside the recognized boundaries of their competence." Also, Subprinciple 3.7 sets forth, "Marriage and family therapists practice in specialty areas new to them only after appropriate education, training, or supervised experience." Other ethical principles clearly place the responsibility for competence on the practitioner. The AAMFT ethics code indicates that marriage and family therapists must "pursue knowledge of new developments" (Subprinciple 3.1); and "maintain adequate knowledge of and adhere to applicable laws . . ." (Subprinciple 3.2).

Knowledge of Legal Processes and Concepts

With public policy and the law pertaining to the field of child custody changing so often, the therapist must exercise diligence to know what society and the law expect and require from professionals' providing evaluations and testimony to the legal proceedings. Tthe AAMFT ethics code offers the reminder, "While developing new skills in specialty areas, marriage and family therapists take steps to ensure the competence of their work and to protect clients from possible harm" (Subprinciple 3.7).

Many of the ethical and legal difficulties therapists face in custody cases arise from their lack of knowledge about the law or their failure to seek legal advice (see Woody, 2000, 2001). The following scenarios are brief examples that point out the importance of recognizing the role of the law custody-related situations.

1. <u>When Ethics and Law Are in Conflict</u>. Of particular concern, the highly complex nature of child custody and visitation issues may result in ethics and the law not always being in accord. The Preamble for the AAMFT ethics code addresses this problem area, noting

> Both law and ethics govern the practice of marriage and family therapy. When making decisions regarding professional behavior, marriage and family therapists must consider the AAMFT Code of Ethics and applicable laws and regulations. If the AAMFT Code of Ethics prescribes a higher standard than that required by law, marriage and family therapists must meet the higher standard of the AAMFT Code of Ethics. Marriage and family therapists comply with the mandates of law, but make known their commitment to the AAMFT Code of Ethics and take steps to resolve the conflict in a responsible manner.

This means that a marriage and family therapist cannot stay out of a difference between ethics and law; action must be taken.

As a case example, a therapist received a court order that directed her to release a teenager's treatment records to each of the divorcing parents. The therapist believed deeply that certain comments made by the teenager would infuriate one or both of the parents, and would jeopardize the family relations for years to come.

In the therapist's particular practice jurisdiction, there was no statute or licensing board rule that would allow her to argue against the court's directive. Mindful of a statement in the Preamble of the AAMFT ethics code that "Marriage and family therapists who are uncertain about the ethics of a particular course of action are encouraged to seek counsel from consultants, attorneys, supervisors, colleagues, or other appropriate authorities," the therapist consulted with and retained an attorney to file a Motion for a Rehearing.

At the hearing, the therapist appeared before the judge, explained her concern about harmful effects resulting from the release of certain information, and requested an "in camera" review of the records (i.e., for the judge to personally review the records before ordering that the records be released to others). The outcome was that the judge ordered the therapist to redact (remove) certain information from the teenager's records, and limited the scope of testimony by the therapist accordingly. That is, in her testimony at the child custody proceedings, the therapist did not have to reveal the redacted information that could have a deleterious effect on family relations.

     2. <u>Having an Opinion About Visitation.</u> It is common for attorneys and judges to ask a therapist to issue an opinion about visitation.

In any kind of professional services, the AAMFT ethics code specifies that "Marriage and family therapists maintain high standards of professional competence and integrity" (Principle III). Also, even though requested by attorneys or judges, "Marriage and family therapists, because of their ability to influence and alter the lives of others, exercise special care when making public their professional recommendations and opinions through testimony or other public statements" (Subprinciple 3.13).

When asked for a view or opinion on visitation, the therapist should attempt to identify a scholarly or research basis for such an opinion. In point of fact, there is little high-quality research about alternative visitation schedules upon which a marriage and family therapist could fashion a truly professional opinion. Without such a behavioral science foundation, the opinion is, in fact, no different than what might be offered by a layperson.

The foregoing does not mean that the therapist cannot give information that will aid the trier of fact (i.e., a judge or jury) in making a determination or judgment. But any informative statement should be based on behavioral science theory or knowledge. For the issue of visitation, as one example, Goldstein, Freud, and Solnit (1973) offered the following:

Placement decisions should safeguard the child's need for continuity of relationships. (p. 31)

Placement decisions should reflect the child's, not the adult's, sense of time. (p. 40)

Child placement decisions must take into account the law's incapacity to supervise interpersonal relationships and the limits of knowledge to make long-range predictions. (p. 49)

As mentioned before, since the determinations about custody and visitation can only be properly made by the trier of fact, the role of the marriage and family therapist is to give testimonial information that will assist that decision making.

3. <u>Understanding Legal Terms Relating to Custody.</u> Using terms such as "joint custody" and "shared parental responsibility," legislators and judges have promoted the standard that both parents should have a continuing role in the decision making for their child. For example, consider the Florida statute that defines shared parental responsibility:

For purposes of shared responsibility and primary residence, the best interests of the child shall include an evaluation of all factors affecting the welfare and interests of the child, including, but not limited to:

(a) The parent who is most likely to allow the child frequent and continuing contact with the nonresidential parent.

(b) The love, affection, and other emotional ties existing between the parents and the child.

(c) The capacity and disposition of the parents to provide the child with food, clothing, medical care or other remedial care recognized and permitted under the laws of this state in lieu of medical care, and other material needs.

(d) The length of time the child has lived in a stable, satisfactory environment and the desirability of maintaining continuity.

(e) The permanence, as a family unit, of the existing or proposed custodial home.

(f) The moral fitness of the parents.

(g) The mental and physical health of the parents.

(h) The home, school, and community record of the child.

(i) The reasonable preference of the child, if the court deems the child to be of sufficient intelligence, understanding, and experience to express a preference.

(j) The willingness and ability of each parent to facilitate and encourage a close and continuing parent-child relationship between the child and the other parent.

(k) Evidence that any party has knowingly provided false information to the court regarding a domestic violation proceeding . . . .

(l) Evidence of domestic violence or child abuse.

(m) Any other fact considered by the court to be relevant. (Florida Statute 61.13 (3))

This statute weights parental cooperation for facilitating parent-child relations, as well as false information and actual conduct relevant to domestic violence and child abuse (this latter topic is discussed in Chapter Seven). In addition, some current statutes, depending on the jurisdiction, disavow a presumption that the gender of the parent per se will determine the best interests of the child.

4. <u>Relocating the Child.</u> Florida law also honors the best interests of the child when a primary residential

parent wishes to relocate the child. Even though the move may materially affect the visitation schedule and access of the secondary parent, the court <u>must</u> consider the following factors:

1. Whether the move would be likely to improve the general quality of life for both the residential parent and the child.

2. Whether and the extent to which visitation rights have been allowed and exercised.

3. Whether the primary residential parent, once out of the jurisdiction, will be likely to comply with any substitute visitation arrangements.

4. Whether the substitute visitation will be adequate to foster a continuing meaningful relationship between the child and the secondary residential parent.

5. Whether the cost of transportation is financially affordable by one or both parties.

6. Whether the move is in the best interests of the child. (Florida Statute 61.13 (3) (d)).

For a mental health professional to have an adequate behavioral science basis for an opinion about any or all of these six criteria, extensive information gathering and evaluation would be necessary.

Every therapist should be fully versed in the child custody laws for his or her jurisdiction. For an overview of practice standards, ethical issues, and legal safeguards (set forth as specific guidelines) pertaining to child custody, see Woody (2000). Also, for a compilation of family law legislation, see Wadlington (1995). Finally, a scholarly overview of child custody in divorce proceedings is available in Chapter Sixteen of Melton, Petrila, Poythress, and Slobogin (1997).

When properly prepared, the therapist can provide valuable evaluation and treatment services and expert testimony to the legal system. In any event and as mentioned earlier, the services provided must be within the confines of one legitimate professional role and must allow for a conflict of interest or services beyond the scope of competence.

CONCLUSION

As evidenced throughout this chapter, family therapy involving children creates challenges to provide interventions that are both effective and ethically sound. Treatment models, custody issues, certain types of children's problems, all of which have been discussed in previous sections, can alert therapists to the need to anticipate and address common ethical problems. The AAMFT ethics code offers guidelines for preventing dilemmas around professional competence and integrity; promoting the welfare of both the child and the family; dealing with informed consent, confidentiality, and multiple roles; and meeting the ethical standards involved in collaborating with other service providers, including the law and the courts.

REFERENCES

Blow, A. J., & Sprenkle. D. H. (2001). Common factors across theories of marriage and family therapy: A modified Delphi study. <u>Journal of Marital and Family Therapy, 27,</u> (3) 385–402.

Butler, B. O., Mellon, M. W., Stroh, S. E., & Stern, H. P. (1995). A therapeutic model to enhance children's adjustment to divorce: A case example. Journal of Divorce & Remarriage, 22 (3/4), 77–90.

Conoley, J. C., & Larson, P. (1995). Conflicts in care: Early years of the lifespan. In E. J. Rave & C. C. Larson (Eds.), Ethical decision making in therapy: Feminist perspectives (pp.202–222). New York: Guilford.

Goldstein, J., Freud, A., & Solnit, A. J. (1973). Beyond the best interests of the child. New York: The Free Press (Simon & Schuster).

Issacs, M. B., Montalvo, B., & Abelson, D. (1986). The difficult divorce: Therapy for children and families. New York: Basic Books.

Koocher, G. P. (1995). Ethics in child psychotherapy. Child and Adolescent Psychiatric Clinics of North America, 4 (4), 779–791.

Koocher, G. P., & Keith-Speigel, P. C. (1990). Children, ethics, and the law. Lincoln, NE: University of Nebraska Press.

Melton, G. B., Petrila, J., Poythress, N. G., & Slobogin, C. (1997). Psychological evaluations for the court: A handbook for mental health professionals and lawyers (2nd ed.). New York: Guilford.

Price, J. A. (1996). Power and compassion: Working with difficult adolescents and abused parents. New York: Guilford.

Price, J. A., & Margerum, J. (2000). The four most common mistakes in treating teens. Family Therapy Networker, 24 (4), 52–55.

Rohman, L. W., Sales, S. B., & Lou, M. (1987). The best interests of the child in custody disputes. In L. A. Weithorn (Ed.), Psychology and child custody determinations (pp. 59–105). Lincoln, NE: University of Nebraska Press.

Tiesel, J. W., & Olsen, D. H. (1992). Preventing family problems: Troubling trends and promising opportunities. Family Relations, 2 (3), 208–215.

Wadlington, W. (Ed.). (1995). Family law statutes, treaties and legislative models. Westbury, NY: Foundation Press.

Woody, R. H. (2000). Child custody: Practice standards, ethical issues, and legal safeguards for mental health practitioners. Sarasota, FL: Professional Resource Press.

Woody, R. H. (2001). Psychological information: Protecting the right of privacy. Madison, CT: Psychosocial Press (International Universities Press).

Wyer, M. M., Gaylord, S. J., & Grove, E. T. (1987). The legal context of child custody evaluations. In L. A. Weithorn (Ed.), Psychology and child custody determinations (pp. 3–22). Lincoln, NE: University of Nebraska Press.

VIOLENCE, DANGEROUSNESS, ABUSE, AND NEGLECT

7

Brian Jory

This chapter discusses a complex issue that challenges even the most skilled and seasoned clinician: the forms of violence, dangerousness, and abuse and neglect that may appear in the context of marriage and family therapy. These behaviors demand the ethic of responsibility to and care for the client or client system but may also demand care for others outside of therapy who are at risk. Both ethical and legal duties coalesce in such situations and impact the obligation to maintain confidentiality and point to instances in which a breach of confidentiality may be permitted or mandated. Three major topics are covered: mandatory child abuse reporting laws; the duty to warn and protect; and self-destructive and suicidal clients. Providing detailed case examples, the discussion expands both theoretical and practical knowledge in addressing the following: definitions of important terms; public policy and the therapist's responsibility to know and implement relevant laws; emerging trends in both ethics and clinical management to deal appropriately with these issues; and the importance of such practice skills as observation, risk factor analysis, obtaining outside consultation, clinical decision-making, and documentation.

CONTENTS

By one estimate, 18,000 people are violently victimized on an average day in the United States, with 65 being victims of homicide (Dobrin, Wiersema, Loftin, & McDowal, 1996). While violence rates have been decreasing over the past decade, the methods of violence have become more lethal, with the number of gunshot and stab wounds increasing (Brady, 1996). Traditional notions that violence occurs primarily in alleys, perpetrated mostly by strangers, gave way in the 1990s to a recognition that most violence occurs in intimate forums like family and dating relationships (Maguire & Pastore, 1998). This recognition has expanded scientific awareness in the 21st Century to previously ignored victims like women, children, and the elderly (Fineman & Mykitiuk, 1994), and also to emerging forms of violence and victimization like stalking (Meloy, 1998), animal cruelty (Ascione & Arkow, 1999), and self mutilation (Levenkron, 1998).

(1) In 1996, there were 970,000 confirmed victims of child abuse: 229,332 of these were victims of physical abuse, 500,032 victims of neglect, and 119,397 victims of sexual abuse (National Center on Child Abuse and Neglect, 1998). The number of children who die every year at the hands of their parents or other caretakers is estimated between 1,215 (Daro, 1996) and 2,000 (U.S. Advisory Board on Child Abuse and Neglect, 1995).

(2) The National Violence against Women Survey, conducted between November, 1995, and May, 1996, found that 56% of 8,000 women interviewed had been a victim of some form of violence during their lifetime. Based on an analysis of these data, Tjaden and Thoennes (1998) estimate that 1,309,061 women are victims of physical assault at the hands of an intimate partner on an annual basis, and this number increases to 1,812,546 when any form of victimization such as stalking or sexual assault is considered. About 680 men are killed by wives or girlfriends each year, and more than 1,400 women are slain by husbands or boyfriends (U.S. Department of Justice, 1994).

(3) The National Elder Abuse Incidence Survey found that approximately 450,000 elderly persons living in domestic settings were abused and/or neglected in 1996 (National Center on Elder Abuse, 1998).

Most therapists believe that their clients will not harm themselves or others, and most of the time this is true (Slovic & Monahan, 1995). However, this fact is overshadowed by the reality that mental health professionals provide treatment for groups that are at slightly higher risk than the general population for committing violence against others, and at substantially higher risk for violence directed against themselves (Monahan, 1995). For example, 10% to 15% of patients with major psychiatric disorders (i.e., affective disorder, substance use disorders, and schizophrenia) will die by suicide (Brent, Kupfer, Bromet, & Dew, 1988), and somewhere between 32% and 69% of suicidal clients visited their primary therapist in the week preceding the suicide (Diekstra & Van Egmond, 1989). Many suicidal clients view the therapist as a last hope, and when therapeutic interventions fail or results are slow, clients can experience a sense of hopelessness that can trigger violence towards themselves (Slaby, 1998) or others (Milner & Campbell, 1995).

This chapter will pursue two objectives. First, the ethical and legal duties of therapists to warn and/or protect potential victims of violence, abuse, and dangerousness will be clarified. Second, general concerns for therapy practice will be discussed in light of the duties to warn and protect, keeping in mind the confusing, sometimes conflicting, ethical and legal issues faced by practitioners. Throughout, specific forms of dangerousness typically encountered in the practice of therapy will be highlighted, and specific actions for therapeutic management will be suggested.

The chapter is primarily for clinicians, and is intended as a contribution to the ongoing discussion about professional standards of care for violent, dangerous, and abusive clients. It should not be considered the final word on any issue.

A professional standard of care for clients who are potentially violent or suicidal involves more than a simple referral or habitually scheduling weekly appointments. Rather, a standard on this matter involves systematically and repeatedly assessing the potential for violence, thoughtfully selecting reasonable steps of intervention, and implementing these steps in a professional manner (Appelbaum, 1985). By diligently following professional standards of care, therapists are most likely to practice ethically and legally.

At one point in his career, the author was employed as a social worker in a metropolitan police department doing victim and witness assistance, child abuse investigations, and domestic violence interventions. In law enforcement, it is routine to observe the terrible trauma and, in some cases, the finality of violence. The role of police social worker required professional involvement in a number of cases of violence by mental health patients, and opened the door for the author to review court records, police reports, and to interview victims, perpetrators, and the mental health professionals who were treating them. In this chapter, three of these cases are discussed, although identifying features have been changed to protect the confidentiality of all individuals involved. The purpose of examining these cases is not to blame the therapists who were involved, but to learn from them. In the real world, therapists do not have the advantage of hindsight, and predictions of future violence are always made with less knowledge than the clinician would like (Meloy, 2000).

Definitions

The following definitions are essential for understanding the concepts developed in this chapter.

Violence is an act characterized by the application or overt threat of force which is likely to result in injury to oneself or others (Monahan, 1995). Violence can be intentional or random, and includes threatening behavior, like holding a gun on someone or like shooting a gun at someone, even though the person does not actually hit the other person. Violence is always dangerous, but not every dangerous behavior is violent.

Abuse refers to acts committed on vulnerable and dependent persons that results in, or has the potential to result in, physical or severe psychological trauma. For the purposes of this chapter, abuse includes serious neglect or maltreatment, inflicting physical pain or trauma, sexual exploitation, emotional tormenting, and in some cases, financial exploitation. In general, abuse is an ongoing series of acts, typically occurring in relationships where power and dependency are unbalanced (Jory, Anderson, & Greer, 1997). Victims are typically children, battered women, the dependent elderly, and persons with physical, psychiatric, or developmental disabilities.

Dangerousness refers to behavior, repeated or singular, which has the potential to result in death, bodily injury, or the severe destruction of property either in the immediate or long-term. Examples of dangerous behavior include HIV-infected clients' engaging in unprotected sex or sharing needles (Appelbaum & Appelbaum, 1990), client self-mutilation (Levenkron, 1998), a client with advanced anorexia who is starving herself to death (Miller, 2000), or a client who is out-of-control and who is allowed to drive a car or operate machinery (Godard & Bloom, 1990). In general, a dangerous client is one whose current mental condition or propensity for violence promises to lead to serious physical harm to self or others.

A duty to warn is the ethical and/or legal obligation to notify an identified, potential victim, or group of victims, of possible danger. In some situations, the duty to warn may also involve a duty to report potential dangerousness to law enforcement authorities or a government agency. In a recent case, the Canadian Supreme Court may have expanded the obligation into a "duty to inform" by requiring mental health professionals to testify about dangerous clients when the public interest is at stake (Glancy, Regehr, Bryant, & Schneider, 1999).

A duty to protect is the ethical and/or legal obligation to implement "a reasonable plan of intervention" to avert or de-escalate client behavior that may harm self or others (Tarasoff vs. Regents of the University of California, 1976, p. 20). In essence, the duty to protect is a two-edged sword because, in the face of impending danger, the principle simultaneously permits therapists to take appropriate professional actions, and in some situations the principle may also require therapists to take steps to protect potential victims.

CLIENT CONFIDENTIALITY AND PUBLIC POLICY OBLIGATIONS

Confidentiality is the ethical and legal protection afforded to clients in therapy that certain information cannot be revealed without the client's consent. Through the belief that their intimate and personal self-disclosures will be held private, clients establish trust in the therapist and feel free to divulge self-revealing information essential in their treatment, without fear of social recrimination (Gustafson & McNamara, 1987).

Confidentiality of service means that the therapist will not disclose that an individual is seeking mental health services. Confidentiality of substance means that the therapist will not reveal a client's concerns, diagnoses, treatment plan, or other facts about the client or the treatment. This kind of protection dates back over 2,500 years to the Hippocratic oath: "Whatsoever I see or hear in the course of my profession in my intercourse with men, if it be what should not be published abroad, I will never divulge, holding such things to be holy secrets" (Plueckhahn & Cordner, 1991, p. 2).

Virtually all professional associations for mental health practitioners require members to adhere to a standard of confidentiality in the belief that therapist breaches of client confidences not only harm the individual whose privacy is betrayed, but also harm all clients by breaking down public trust in mental health experts. Subprinciple 2.2 of the AAMFT ethics code states

Marriage and family therapists do not disclose client confidences except by written authorization or waiver, or where mandated or permitted by law. Verbal authorization will not be sufficient except in emergency situations, unless prohibited by law. When providing couple, family or group treatment, the therapist does not disclose information outside the treatment context without a written authorization from each individual competent to execute a waiver. In the context of couple, family or group treatment, the therapist may not reveal any individual's confidence to others in the client unit without the prior written permission of that individual.

All members of the AAMFT ascribe to this level of confidentiality, and although the AAMFT ethics code does not carry weight of law (unless adopted, for instance, by a state legislature for a particular jurisdiction), members who violate confidentiality may be subject to sanctions. In jurisdictions that license marriage and family therapists, practitioners who violate confidentiality are subject to sanctions or license revocation. Furthermore, any mental health practitioner who harms a client by breaching confidentiality can be held liable in civil proceedings for invasion of privacy (Ahia & Martin, 1993).

Woody and Woody (1988) have described governmental regulations of the methods and practices of mental health professionals as "public policy obligations." Public policy obligations emanate from legislative or judicial desires to sway professional practices in the direction of serving the public good, or the belief that there is a need to police professionals whose practices are a threat to public welfare. In the case of potential violence, abuse, and dangerousness, public policy obligations permit, and in some cases, require therapists to break client confidentiality in order to warn and/or protect the client or potential victims. These public policy obligations emerge from three sources: (1) statutory law requiring therapists to report child abuse and neglect; (2) common and statutory law requiring therapists to protect the public from violent clients (i.e., the so-called duties to warn and/or protect); and (3) standards of care requiring therapists to protect suicidal and self-injuring clients. Each of these public policy and legal obligations has its own unique history and requirements. Therefore, each is discussed in turn, following a discussion of attitudes regarding confidentiality in mental health practice.

Confidentiality has never been absolute in medicine, since the Hippocratic phrase, "if it be what should not be published abroad" (Plueckhahn & Cordner, 1991, p. 2), has permitted physicians to use their own discretion as to what should and should not be divulged. For example, it has been suggested that some of Freud's case histories were so poorly disguised (e.g., Little Hans or the Wolfman) that they might lead to lawsuits in today's litigious environment (Karpf, 1996). Also, in the interest of public good, physicians have long been required to report persons with epilepsy who operate dangerous machinery, persons with dangerous or contagious diseases, and victims of gunshot and stab wounds (Beck, 1990).

Ormrod and Ambrose (1999) reviewed several studies and concluded that it is a widely held belief by the public at large, by therapists, and by mental health clients that confidentiality is essential to effective therapy. These researchers also concluded that the general public expects a high level of confidentiality from therapists, and that actual clients, especially those entering therapy for the first time, expect absolute confidentiality from their therapist, similar to that expected from priests. However, in their own study, Ormrod and Ambrose found that when the non-client public was presented with real-life scenarios about client violence, abuse, and dangerousness, the majority supported therapist disclosure of client confidences and were surprised to find that there was a question as to whether therapists would break confidentiality to avert violence and dangerousness. It is important to keep these public attitudes in mind with regard to the three public policy and legal obligations that permit or require breaches of client confidentiality.

MANDATORY CHILD ABUSE REPORTING LAWS

Current statutes regarding mandatory reporting of child abuse date back to 1965, when model legislation was designed to require physicians to contact authorities when they had evidence that the severe injury of a child had occurred at the hands of a parent or other adult caretaker (Kalichman, 1999). This provided the impetus for the proliferation of mandatory reporting laws in every state of the United States, except Hawaii, by 1966. In the ensuing decade, public awareness of child abuse skyrocketed as child victims were graphically exhibited on television programs and in print media. One particular impetus was the 1974 Child Abuse Prevention and Treatment Act, which stipulated that "only states that provide for the reporting of known or suspected instances of child abuse and neglect" would qualify for federal child abuse prevention and intervention grants (45 Code of Federal Regulations, section 1340.3(2)(i)). With federal funds at stake, and in an effort to close holes in the net of child protection, laws were expanded to include a wider range of professionals mandated to report and more patterns of abuse to be reported. Soon mandatory reporting laws were fairly uniform in all 50 states and the territories of Guam, the Philippines, and Puerto Rico, and in Canada, England, Australia, and New Zealand.

The Importance of Knowing the Law and Reporting Procedures

Many therapists work with parents and children, and have service contracts with schools, Head Start programs, and government agencies, where they come into daily contact with children. For this reason, therapists who learn about reporting laws in the jurisdictions where they practice demonstrate both clinical prudence and ethical responsibility. Subprinciple 3.2 of the AAMFT ethics code states: "Marriage and family therapists maintain adequate knowledge of and adhere to applicable laws, ethics, and professional standards."

Therapists cannot be expected to be lawyers, but they should know the law relevant to their professional services. Awareness of child abuse can arise unexpectedly in many clinical settings, and in some cases, protecting a child who is at risk can constitute an emergency. Waiting to learn about reporting laws and procedures until the need arises might lead to an unnecessary trauma for a child. Furthermore, delay may make statutory compliance impossible and can put the therapist at risk of sanctions or litigation.

Mandatory reporting laws are now fairly uniform across North America, although there are differences in the jurisdictional procedures. Because the procedures for reporting can affect substantial differences in outcomes, it is important for therapists to know the law, and be prepared to act on it. Essentially, the jurisdictional differences are in the following:

(1) <u>Who must report</u>. In every U.S. state and territory, and every Canadian province, therapists who have reason to suspect that a child is being neglected or mistreated are mandated to report, as are physicians, teachers, nurses, day care workers, dentists, chiropractors, and other professionals. At the present time, about half of the states require any citizen who witnesses or suspects child abuse to report to authorities. In half of the states, the reporter is not required to reveal his or her identity, although the validity of the report is often bolstered if the reporter is willing to disclose his or her relationship to the child victim or the perpetrator. In every state, individuals who make a report in good faith, including therapists, are immune from civil litigation for violation of privacy.

(2) <u>What must be reported</u>. In all jurisdictions, professionals are required to report suspected neglect, physical abuse, and sexual abuse of a child under the age of 18. In about half of all jurisdictions, professionals must also report emotional abuse. Also in about half of all jurisdictions, abuse of the elderly and other vulnerable adults must be reported to adult protective services. Most jurisdictional statutes detail the kinds of behavior that qualify as abuse. All jurisdictions require the reporting of past abuse, as a way of assessing current dangerousness based on perpetrator history, for tracking perpetrators who move from jurisdiction to jurisdiction (a common pattern), to aid in identification and prosecution, and to maintain statistical databases for epidemiological studies.

(3) <u>How the report must be made</u>. In some jurisdictions a phone call is required; in others a letter or written complaint can be made. It is wise for professionals to follow up their phone calls with a letter for documentation. In some jurisdictions, therapists must report to the police; in others, reports must be made to the department of child protection. In many situations, it would be wise to contact both law enforcement and child protective services, depending on the impending danger to the child. In some jurisdictions, statutes specifically allow professionals who are employed by schools, hospitals, or social service agencies to make a report to a supervisor, who in turn must report to appropriate authorities. In some jurisdictions, an immediate report must be filed; in other jurisdictions, the report can be delayed up to 48 hours, except in emergencies.

According to Conte, Plutchik, Picard, and Karasu (1989), most mental health professionals, along with their professional associations, embrace mandated reporting. The supportive professional associations include the National Association of Social Workers, the American Psychiatric Association, the American Psychological Association, the

American Counseling Association, and the American Association for Marriage and Family Therapy. It is worth noting that "family systems counselors," as they were called at that time, were instrumental in the passage and proliferation of some child abuse reporting statutes, particularly getting sexual abuse included as a crime that must be reported (Weisberg, 1984).

According to Bollas and Sundelson (1995), none of the major mental health professional associations were invited to offer input at the inception of mandatory reporting laws. They argue that mandatory reporting undermines client trust in therapists and impedes client self-disclosure, therefore undermining the effectiveness of therapy for all clients. To be candid, the arguments offered by Bollas and Sundelson appear insensitive to the plight of child victims and probably exaggerate the sanctity of client-therapist confidentiality. These arguments are more likely to persuade the unconvinced of the necessity for mandatory reporting rather than vice versa (e.g., Karpf, 1996).

More to the point, from the inception of legislative debates about mandatory reporting in 1963, lawmakers gave complete consideration to the ramifications that mandatory reporting would have on the mental health professions, particularly in the area of client confidentiality. The underlying rationale of mandatory reporting is that protecting vulnerable children serves a greater good than maintaining the confidences of a single individual, particularly if that individual is harming children. By mandating reports of possible abuse and neglect, legislators hoped to release professionals from the shackles of confidentiality, and open up an opportunity to help abused and neglected children in a way that would be prohibited if the therapist was required to maintain absolute confidentiality. In this way, legislators intended to accomplish the most good for the most individuals—by protecting children and giving an umbrella of protection to professionals who report.

To be sure, in every jurisdiction, the failure to report suspected child abuse or neglect is a misdemeanor, which can be punished by fines, imprisonment, or other legal sanctions such as loss of license. Since legislators saw mandatory reporting more in the light of opening up an opportunity for therapists, and less as imposing a requirement, the sanctions are largely symbolic and few therapists in the United States have been prosecuted for failing to report child abuse (Adler, 1995).

Emerging Patterns in Identification and Treatment of Child Abuse and Neglect

Throughout the 1990s, driven by an avalanche of funding for research programs, knowledge about the ways that children and vulnerable adults can be mistreated continued to expand. Beyond what has long been known about beating, bruising, burning, and broken bones, researchers have increased knowledge about malicious biting (Monteleone & Broder, 1996), imposed hypothermia (Gustavson & Levitt, 1996), shaken baby syndrome (Mehl, 1990), Munchausen syndrome by proxy (Mercer & Perdue, 1993), hand-mashing (Johnson, Kaufman, & Callendar, 1990), sexual abuse and exploitation (Haverkamp & Daniluk, 1993), drowning and suffocation (Monteleone & Broder, 1996), and other emerging patterns of abuse (Berkowitz, 1995).

The most frequent type of child protection case involves child neglect and/or endangerment. While the impact of neglect can be disastrous, such as when unattended children die in house fires, it is important that therapists recognize the differences between intentional neglect, neglect caused by ignorance about safety, neglect caused by caretaker drug abuse, and poverty. Poverty is not neglect, but might involve a child who has no shoes, or who wears dirty clothes because there is no laundry detergent. Poverty might best be handled by a referral to a social welfare agency, rather than to child protective services.

Two thirds of physical abuse cases involve infants and toddlers under the age of 3, and these children are most vulnerable to severe injury or death (Berkowitz, 1995). The most common reason given by parents and other caretakers for the physical maltreatment of children is "discipline" (Doueck, 1995). It is not only unethical, but it is a sign of poor clinical judgment for a therapist to accept "discipline" as a rationalization for severe and inappropriate punishment of children. Once the therapist has reported an incident, protective services workers can investigate and make a determination about parental practices and motives. Most protective agencies can distinguish between parents who mean well, but are misguided, and those who willfully intend to injure their child. Often well-intentioned parents are allowed to continue therapy with the understanding that they learn humane discipline strategies, or they are sometimes referred to parent education groups. Meanwhile, their children are under the watch of the child protection agency.

THE CASE OF MICHAEL

One weekend morning, shoppers alerted police to noises coming from the trunk of a car parked at a shopping center. Inside the trunk, officers found an 8-year old boy named Michael. Duct tape had been placed tight over his mouth to keep him quiet, and it was thickly wrapped around his arms and legs to keep him still. Officers easily located Michael's mother shopping inside a store. It was difficult separating Michael from his mother, who kept shouting, "I love you" to him across the parking lot. A sobbing Michael pleaded, "Please let me stay with my mommy."

Michael was first transported to the emergency room and then to a shelter. That afternoon, his mother defended her treatment of Michael, explaining that she was "disciplining him." She explained that Michael was a troubled boy who was being counseled for behavior problems by a therapist who was paid by his school.

It was confirmed that Michael was in therapy with a therapist who was under a contract to provide services for families referred by the school. The therapist was shocked to learn about Michael, but admitted suspecting abuse. For example, the therapist knew that the mother had been making Michael sleep in the bathtub, naked and without blankets, to teach him about bed-wetting. After confronting the mother about this action, the therapist "thought that mom was doing better . . . until last Friday." Michael and his mother had visited the therapist's office on Friday afternoon. When they were leaving, Michael's mother "jokingly" told the therapist, "I'm going to kill this kid this weekend."

The therapist felt uneasy, and phoned the school principal to report concern about child abuse, but failed to report the mother's exact statement, thinking that this might be a violation of the mother's confidentiality. Based on this conversation, the school principal and therapist agreed that they would file a report with child protective services on Monday. According to the therapist, "It was Friday afternoon. The school principal and I both thought the report could wait until Monday."

Skills and Attitudes in Identifying Child Abuse

The case of Michael raises the question of whether and when a reasonable therapist would have suspected and reported child abuse. Many individuals joke about violence towards others—wanting to kill someone, choke them, break their legs, poke their eyes out, and so on. A joke may not be a reason to make a report.

In this case, however, the therapist had knowledge that the mother had previously exercised harsh discipline by making Michael sleep unclothed in a bathtub. Excessive or inappropriate discipline is the most common form of physical abuse to children, and the fact that the therapist spoke with the mother about this suggests that the therapist believed it was inappropriate.

Abuse usually occurs as a series of acts, and it is most likely to occur in close relationships with power differentials, such as between a parent and child. Would not a prudent therapist have been suspicious about what other kinds of harsh discipline Michael was being subject to? In this case, the therapist was suspicious, but was "withholding judgment."

Michael, in this particular case, had been exhibiting aggressive behavior towards his peers and, on more than one occasion, towards the teacher. A therapist who works with children on school problems should be aware of the correlation between aggressive behavior and child abuse (Milner, 1995). Was this not further reason for suspicion?

It seems that the therapist might have reasonably made a report earlier in treatment. However, let us consider one possible explanation for the therapist's failure to contact child protective services sooner.

In a survey of various types of mental health professionals, 87% indicated that they would not report every case of suspected child abuse, even knowing they are obligated to do so (Department of Health and Human Services Publication, 1988). As discussed previously, some therapists refuse to report out of "principle," albeit faulty in logic. One study found that 26% of psychiatrists who were surveyed claim to maintain absolute confidentiality, even when a child is being abused (Brosig & Kalichman, 1992). The majority of therapists surveyed, however, indicated that they might avoid reporting child abuse out of a fear of parental reprisal against the child, i.e., making it worse for the child because of the report.

In the case of Michael, the therapist intervened by talking with Michael's mother and delayed making a report to protective services. If the therapist's intervention did, in fact, stop the mother from making him sleep unclothed in the bathtub (which is doubtful), the therapist averted some abuse directed towards Michael. On the other hand, consider the logic of this. If a therapist suspects that a parent would unfairly punish a child because someone made a report to protective services, should the therapist not consider this as further indication that the child is at risk of abuse? If so, child protective service intervention should be involved.

There are many mental health disorders where denial is a primary defense, and these individuals often have negative reactions to interventions initiated by others (e.g., substance abuse disorders, eating disorders, depression). With all these disorders, therapists plan interventions that upset the client, such as hospitalization, referral for specialized treatment, etc. In the case of child abuse, does it make sense to abandon a child to an abusive parent because effectively confronting the parent might upset them?

Whatever steps are taken by a therapist to directly intervene in cases of abuse or neglect, direct intervention is not a legal or ethical substitute for the duty to report. This is particularly salient when there are other children in the home, when the therapist may be unaware of other harsh discipline in the home, of other abusers in the home, or of the abuser's prior history of child maltreatment. These are concerns that protective services can investigate more thoroughly, and often with information about previous reports not available to the therapist.

In Michael's situation, the therapist's intervention with the mother might have been more effective if complemented with a report to child protective services, offering the mother counseling or referring her for it, enrolling her in a parenting class, and warning her that the therapist would continue to monitor the abuse.

The Duty to Appropriately Implement the Law

Let us consider whether the therapist fulfilled the legal obligation to report suspected abuse by calling the school principal. In about half of all jurisdictions, a report to a school principal fulfills the obligation if the reporter is an employee of the school.

In the case of Michael, the therapist was paid for services under a contract with the school board; however, the therapist also maintained an independent private practice. Michael and his mother met with the therapist in the private office, not at the school. From the standpoint of reporting laws in almost every jurisdiction, a report to only the principal was misdirected, as the therapist was required to contact the police, child protective services, or both. Since the report was misdirected, though perhaps well intentioned, the therapist might have lost immunity from civil litigation if the mother filed suit for breaching confidentiality.

A reasonable conclusion seems to be that the therapist lacked adequate knowledge about reporting laws and practices in her jurisdiction. The therapist believed that by calling the school principal, the duty to report had been fulfilled.

If the therapist followed the law by making a telephone report directly to the police department or to child protective services on Friday afternoon, a police officer or social worker might have visited the home on Friday evening or Saturday for a "safety check." For police officers and child protection workers, a safety check is a routine procedure. This would likely have irritated Michael's mother, and potentially have made it more difficult to work with her in therapy. But it would have brought Michael's case into the child protection system, and might have averted the traumatic incident where he was bound, gagged, and left in an automobile trunk.

THE DUTY TO WARN AND PROTECT

In 1969, Prosenjit Poddar, a graduate student at the University of California, began psychotherapy with Dr. Moore, a psychologist on staff in the university counseling center. Poddar was distraught over Tatiana Tarasoff, a student whom he had dated months earlier. Tarasoff had broken off the relationship, and Poddar was still disturbed. Poddar made a number of threats towards Tarasoff, and when he purchased a gun, Dr. Moore took the threats seriously. Dr. Moore contacted campus police, both by telephone and in a letter, seeking assistance in having Poddar hospitalized. After interviewing him, campus police found Poddar to be mentally stable; they extracted a promise from him that he would leave Tarasoff alone, and they released him. Subsequently, the Director of Psychiatry requested that campus police return Dr. Moore's letter. The letter and therapy notes were destroyed, and no action was taken to hospitalize Poddar. Two months later Poddar went to Tarasoff's home and brutally killed her.

Tarasoff's parents alleged that the university counseling center was negligent for not notifying either them or Tatiana about Tatiana's being in danger.

The trial court found in favor of the university. Upon appeal, the California Supreme Court found that a psychologist has "a duty to warn a potential victim, when in the exercise of [his or her] professional skill and knowledge, [he or she] determines, or should determine, that a warning is essential to avert danger arising from the medical or psychological condition of [his or her] client" (Tarasoff v. Regents of the University of California, 1976, p. 131). Subsequently, the Court modified its opinion, heralding the so-called duty to protect.

As for a duty to warn, the Court stated that a therapist has "an obligation to use reasonable care to protect the intended victim against such danger. The discharge of this duty may require the therapist to take one or more of various steps, depending upon the case. Thus it may call for [him or her] to warn the intended victim or others likely to apprise the victim of the danger, to notify the police, or to take whatever other steps are reasonably necessary under the circumstances" (p. 20). The Court stated specifically that unnecessary warnings are "a reasonable price to pay for the lives of possible victims that may be saved" (p. 20).

In the last two decades plus, dozens of cases have alleged that a mental health practitioner failed to warn or protect an identified victim, and in essentially every case, Tarasoff has been the benchmark against which the case was assessed (Perlin, 1997). While only 14 jurisdictions have adopted statutes requiring therapists to contact authorities, the symbolic power of Tarasoff is such that mental health practitioners should presume that the duty to warn and protect potential victims of client dangerousness is the law (Beck, 1990; Perlin, 1997; VandeCreek & Knapp, 1993; Woody & Woody, 1988).

Principles for Clinical Practice

Most therapists work with individuals who are in close, but troubled, relationships, such as problematic marital, parent/child, and dating relationships. When close relationships are strained, feelings of betrayal, rage, jealousy, rejection, and control have the potential for becoming unmanageable. These negative conditions create a challenge for the therapist to make a learned decision about whether or not to issue a warning of dangerousness.

When therapists are called upon to make decisions about the duty to warn and protect in clinical practice, four principles deserve special consideration.

(1) A reasonable plan of intervention. In general, the courts have recognized that therapists cannot be held responsible for the behavior of another, such as a therapy client. This means that therapists are obligated to conduct a reasonable plan of intervention with potentially violent clients, but they do not need to accurately predict client violence. In every court case involving a violent client's harming a third party, the therapist's responsibility has been evaluated on whether the plan of intervention was reasonable. Did the therapist conduct a thorough evaluation? Was there adequate record-keeping? Were records of the client's previous therapy sought and considered? Had the therapist consulted with colleagues? In every finding against therapists, it seems that the court found that the practitioner had been negligent in some factor other than the failure to accurately predict violence (e.g. failure to consult records, failure to conduct an assessment).

(2) A special relationship. The duty to warn and protect emanates from the special relationship that a mental health practitioner has with a therapy client. A special relationship is defined by the control that the therapist is expected to have over the client. For example, therapists ostensibly have more control over inpatients than outpatients, and there have been more lawsuits involving inpatients than outpatients, particularly when a patient harms others following a decision to discharge the patient or to allow a patient to leave the facility on a pass. On an inpatient unit, the duty to warn and protect is presumed to apply to all staff on the unit.

(3) Clear and imminent danger. The duty to warn and protect should be invoked when there is an immediate risk to others. While past violence is usually considered a predictor of future dangerousness, it alone is not a sufficient reason to violate client confidentiality to warn possible victims. For example, if a 40-year old man reveals that, at age 10, he shot his cousin, or if a woman reveals that she gave her terminally ill mother a lethal dose of pain medication five years ago, the therapist would be acting outside the bounds of the duty to warn

by alerting authorities—unless there was reason to believe that the client was likely to repeat these acts in the foreseeable future. On the other hand, if a teenager reveals that she has been stabbing vegetables with a knife as practice for stabbing her mother, it could be construed that the mother is in clear and imminent danger.

(4) An identifiable victim. Generally, the duty to warn is applicable when there is a victim, or group of victims, that can be predicted with a fair amount of certainty. In the case of an overt threat towards a spouse, a work supervisor, or a parent, the identifiable victim is probably certain. However, in some situations, identification might call for a judgment by the therapist. For example, Prosenjitt Poddar never specifically threatened Tatiana Tarasoff by name, but the court found that the intended victim was easily identifiable, proof being that Dr. Moore knew her name and details about her. When multiple victims are potentially involved (such as a threat "to blow up the entire neighborhood"), the best course of action, considering that the therapist believes the threat should be taken seriously, may be to hospitalize the client, warn the police, block the client's access to weapons or explosives (if feasible), or warn the client's family rather than alert every person in the neighborhood.

In most situations, the decision to breach confidentiality in order to warn potential victims has serious implications for both the client and the therapist. This is particularly true when a warning might bring about recrimination against the client, such as being terminated from employment, being dismissed from school, or souring family or peer relationships. In these situations, the therapist must consider both the well being of his or her client along with the safety of others. Still, in no situation is it legal or ethical to allow the safety of others to be endangered solely for the well being of one's client.

It is important to realize that warning and protecting may be independent activities, but they are not mutually exclusive. In some situations, the greatest good may emerge from considering the duty to warn as a last resort which should be undertaken only after reasonable steps to protect a victim have failed. Any intervention to protect potential victims does not preclude also warning them either before or after one has implemented protective interventions. In choosing to protect others without directly warning them, the therapist has the legal and ethical obligation to conduct frequent follow-up assessments to ascertain whether the interventions are effectively protecting potential victims.

A number of reasonable treatment interventions have been suggested that have the potential to protect victims without directly warning them, depending on the situation (Meloy, Haroun, & Schiller, 1990; Simon, 1990). For example, the therapist could hospitalize the client for treatment or evaluation; alert others who have control over the client (e.g., parents, school security, corporate security, police); change the mode of therapy; increase the number of therapy sessions; adjust the client's medication; seek psychiatric consultation; or provide the client with an emergency phone number. From these or other possible intervention strategies, therapists can decide for themselves the kinds of reasonable interventions that might be effective in a given case.

Human Immunodeficiency Virus (HIV) and the Duty to Warn

In general, the duty to warn and protect has been applied to violent acts rather than dangerous conditions or situations. In many dangerous scenarios, the risks are vague. That is, there is no identifiable victim or group of victims, the danger is not necessarily imminent, and the activities, although seemingly dangerous, are permitted by law.

Throughout the 1990s there was considerable debate among mental health professionals about whether therapists have a duty to warn potential victims of a client who is HIV-positive and who shares needles or practices unprotected sex. Some therapists believe there is an ethical duty to warn and protect potential victims from HIV infection, and at least one professional association adopted an ethical code that permits breaching confidentiality under certain circumstances when a client with HIV infection is endangering others (American Counseling Association, 1995).

Schlossberger and Hecker (1996) present a comprehensive analysis of the legal and ethical complexities of applying the duty to warn to protecting potential victims of HIV. According to Schlossberger and Hecker, the pivotal argument against applying a Tarasoff-type duty to warn in HIV-related cases (i.e., because of the potential to infect others) is that physical violence against others is clearly proscribed by law, whereas unprotected sex, even when one is aware that he or she might transmit HIV, is not illegal in most jurisdictions. In the case of potential violence, the therapist is breaking confidentiality to avert an illegal act; whereas in the case of a sexually irresponsible client who is HIV-positive, the therapist would be depriving the client of a right which is not proscribed by law, simply because the individual is a therapy client. According to Schlossberger and Hecker, "therapists generally are not entitled to deprive clients of their legal rights" (p. 32). In most jurisdictions, violating confidentiality to protect a potential victim of HIV would put the therapist in the position of discriminating against the client, and could result in sanctions or litigation.

Schlossberger and Hecker (1996), however, point out that there are a few jurisdictions where it is illegal to knowingly and wantonly transmit HIV; and in these jurisdictions, the therapist might be permitted, though not necessarily required, to violate client confidentiality to protect potential victims from HIV infection. Even in these jurisdictions, however, there are complexities regarding specific statutes on confidentiality; for example, the particular discipline(s) in which the therapist is licensed may be relevant to the legalities. According to Cohen (1997), breaching client confidentiality regarding the fact that the client is HIV-positive violates public health laws in a number of jurisdictions, and in many jurisdictions that permit releasing such information, only licensed medical doctors may do so.

Subprinciple 2.2 of the AAMFT ethics code states, "Marriage and family therapists do not disclose client confidences except by written authorization or waiver, or where mandated or permitted by law." For this reason, marriage and family therapists should know the laws, or should seek legal consultation, about disclosure of records involving patients with HIV in the jurisdictions where the therapists practice, and they should proceed with caution in considering violating client confidentiality to warn potential victims of HIV infection. According to Schlossberger and Hecker (1996)

In sum, breaking confidentiality may be a requirement in one state and a violation of clients' rights in others. Therapists must consult their own state's laws before acting (preferably by receiving advice from a qualified attorney). There is no substitute for specific and thorough legal research. (p. 31)

At the present time, there is a lack of clarity about the ethical and legal implications of treating clients who are willfully and wantonly transmitting HIV to others through unprotected sex or sharing needles. Therapists who are treating these clients should consider a treatment plan which, in addition to addressing medical, psychological, and relationship concerns, would appeal to the client's moral or ethical reasoning to influence a change of behavior. Treatment objectives might consider the fact that patients who are diagnosed with HIV usually go through periods of denial, when they are angry and resentful, and lowered self-esteem may push them towards illogical actions (e.g., promiscuity), including secrecy and deception in relationships.

By appealing directly to the client's sense of social responsibility, while respecting the client's autonomy and integrity, the therapist would be modeling the kinds of ethical behavior that he or she is seeking to engender in the client.

Although this type of ethical treatment will not be effective with every client, therapists will avoid complicating the situation by illegally violating the client's confidentiality and risking professional sanctions or litigation.

The Case of Anna and Kerry

One afternoon, a man in his 30s ran in the front door of the police station where this author was employed, shouting, "Help me. Somebody shot my wife!" The man, who claimed he had been at work all day, pleaded with police to get him home fast, as he had received a phone call from his 12-year old daughter, Kerry, who had come home from school to find her mother lying on the kitchen floor.

Officers quickly put the man in a cruiser and went speeding towards his house. Officers already on the scene radioed that the woman, Anna, had been dead for hours, shot at close range with a shotgun. At the house, Anna's daughter, Kerry painted a gloomy picture to officers about her father's "temper tantrums." She told the officers that her father had stabbed her mother in the hand two weeks ago. Kerry confided how guilty she felt for not helping her mom. She cried, "My mommy knew daddy was going to kill her, she told me he was going to do something like this." A day later, facing a mountain of physical evidence, the husband admitted that he had shot his wife after Kerry had gone to school and before he left for work that day, after a fight about pepperoni in his lunch bucket.

Anna and her husband had been going to marital therapy, and eventually this author met with the therapist to discuss his knowledge of the case. In an individual session a few days before the murder, Anna's husband had revealed to the therapist that he was having an affair. The husband told the therapist that he was "reaching the end of his rope," that he was "tired of his wife's disrespect," and that he was not "going to take any more of it." The therapist explained, "At first I thought he was talking about a divorce. Eventually, I realized he was out of control. Now I know what he meant."

The therapist believed that the husband had "put me in a bind," because he insisted that the therapist not disclose any information from his individual session with Anna—especially his infidelity. The problem was compounded because the therapist had assured both Anna and her husband at the beginning of therapy that the substance of individual sessions was confidential and would not be divulged by the therapist, even to the other spouse. The therapist believed that maintaining the husband's confidentiality took priority over Anna's right to know about her husband's infidelity, and his escalating rage. In the face of this, the therapist took no action to warn or protect Anna other than to schedule the usual appointment with her for the following week.

Emerging Trends in Confidentiality and Informed Consent with Intimate Violence

With emerging awareness of the high prevalence of violence in marital, family, and couple relationships, the case of Anna should be particularly meaningful to therapists. In recent years, therapists have incurred ethical responsibilities for screening domestic violence and for adopting treatment modalities that protect victims and hold perpetrators accountable (Bograd & Mederos, 1999; Jory, Anderson, & Greer, 1997). For some, these ethical responsibilities challenge traditional systemic thinking that frames the behavior of individuals in neutral-sounding nomenclature like "relational reactions" or "systemic circuitry," and fails to assign responsibility for abuse in the choices and actions of individuals. Goldner (1999) has argued that, in the present state of theoretical development, no single framework, including systems theory, is adequate for assessing and treating intimate violence. Jory & Anderson (2000) have asserted that marriage and family therapists should develop a paradigm for couples work that incorporates accountability for perpetrators along with affirmation of those who have been victimized in intimate relationships.

Under Principle II, Confidentiality, of the AAMFT ethics code, Subprinciple 2.2 states (in part), "In the context of couple, family or group treatment, the therapist may not reveal any individual's confidences to others in the client unit without the prior written permission of that individual." Regarding Subprinciple 2.2, therapists should consider how secrecy can structure power and maintain ongoing abuse and violence in intimate relationships. Studies of couple, family, and other close relationships suggest that secrecy is a form of power in these relationships that benefits individuals differently. For those who abuse others, secrecy works in their favor; for victims of abuse, secrecy helps to maintain the abuse by keeping the victim and others from intervening with it (Fineman & Mykitiuk, 1994). Altering the boundaries of secrecy can alter power structures and deter abuse (Jory & Anderson, 1999). According to one social ethicist, "Secrecy may accompany the most innocent as well as the most lethal acts; it is needed for human survival, yet it enhances every form of abuse" (Bok, 1982, p. xv).

From a theoretical standpoint, emphasizing individual confidentiality within couple, family, or group treatment can be an important deterrent to intimate violence as it affirms the rights of individuals within these treatment groups to establish autonomy and take control of their personal lives. For clients who feel trapped by physical violence and psychological abuse in their intimate relationships, the emphasis on individual confidentiality is an important step in communicating to them that they have a right to personal privacy, and that intrusions on their personal boundaries are wrong and destructive. From a practical standpoint, emphasizing individual confidentiality with abused individuals can be essential for developing the trust necessary for them to share their victimization, for developing a safety plan, for developing resources for a successful exit from the abusive relationship, and for keeping the client's whereabouts safe from further violence.

On the other hand, emphasizing confidentiality can work in favor of an abusive individual, and a therapist who agrees that all individual disclosures will be kept confidential may find herself or himself in the unconscionable position of maintaining secrets that support intimate violence or abuse. For example, consider a mother who reveals that she secretly abuses or neglects the children, but wishes to keep this secret from her husband, who is also in treatment. Or consider an adolescent who admits that he or she steals large amounts of money from a sick or vulnerable grandparent and uses it to purchase drugs.

Since therapists are required, at the beginning of therapy, to inform all clients about the limitations of confidentiality, this dual-edged sword can pose problems. Therapists would do well to inform clients at the beginning of treatment that "healthy" secrets kept for the purpose of respecting privacy (e.g., an adolescent's love interest, a husband's unfulfilled fascination with a coworker, a wife's intent to go back to college) will be respected as confidential by the therapist.

Therapists who misinform clients that all disclosures are confidential might find themselves in the awkward position of either choosing to "keep quiet" about abuse or of violating the individual's confidentiality to warn or protect a victim who is part of the treatment group. It would be better to inform clients that individual disclosures that support or maintain abuse within the treatment group may be disclosed to others within the treatment group, particularly if disclosure is made with the purpose of warning or protecting an individual within the treatment group.

For example, in the case of Anna, the therapist believed that there was an obligation to protect the husband's confidentiality at the expense of protecting Anna from bodily harm. As previously discussed, Subprinciple 2.2 of the AAMFT ethics code states (in part),"Marriage and family therapists do not disclose client confidences except by written authorization or waiver, or where mandated or permitted by law." Embedded in this subprinciple, however, is the public policy obligation to follow the law by warning or otherwise protecting Anna, a potential victim of violence. The therapist was not necessarily obligated to divulge to Anna her husband's infidelity, although some therapists inform clients in advance that disclosures of infidelity will not be kept secret. As distressing as infidelity can be, it is not considered a form of dangerousness, even though it is a critical issue in treatment that must be dealt with in one way or another. From the standpoint of dangerousness, however, Anna did have a right to know that her husband's anger was escalating, and the therapist was obligated to deal with Anna's safety.

The therapist was also obligated to inform Anna's husband of the steps that would be taken in the event that there were threats of violence. Ideally, both Anna and her husband should have been informed about how the therapist would handle "individual confidences that hide abuse" at the beginning of therapy. Subprinciple 2.1 of the AAMFT ethics code states:

Marriage and family therapists disclose to clients and other interested parties, as early as feasible in their professional contacts, the nature of confidentiality and possible limitations of the clients' right to confidentiality. Therapists review with clients the circumstance where confidential information may be requested and where disclosure of confidential information may be legally required. Circumstances may necessitate repeated disclosures.

In Anna's case, the therapist should have clarified the limits of confidentiality at the beginning of therapy, both verbally and in writing.

Informed consent is more than a piece of paper. It is an evolving declaration for patients of what to expect in therapy. This means that, even without declaring the limits of confidentiality at the beginning of therapy in Anna's case, the therapist should have informed the husband about the steps that would be taken to protect Anna. Basically, the first mistake should not have been compounded with a second.

Ormrod and Ambrose (1999) found that many therapists fear that alerting clients to the limits of confidentiality will inhibit their disclosure in therapy, and may influence clients to avoid therapy. In cases of intimate violence, these fears may be unfounded or exaggerated. It is probably true that clients who exhibit psychopathic features probably can hide much criminal intent from clinicians. However, psychopaths tend to avoid therapy anyway.

The more likely scenario of client violence involves a client who is lacking impulse control, is immature, is emotionally distressed, and so on. These clients are generally seeking help for their violent impulses and are not very adept at hiding their potential dangerousness. For them, informed consent may be only slightly problematic.

Clinical Observations, Risk Factor Analyses, and Outside Consultation

The case of Anna raises an important question about appropriate assessment of potential violence. If the client makes a direct threat, Gross, Southard, Lamb, and Weinberger (1987) have suggested a linear model for therapist action based on the threat itself (the following statements are derived from pp. 9–12):

1. Clarify the threat, is it vague or clear?

2. Assess the lethality and intentionality, is there real danger in the threat?

3. Can the client identify a specific, intended victim, or group of victims?

4. Consider whether to warn the specified victim(s).

5. In deciding how to intervene, consider the client's relationship to the victim.

6. Consider whether a family therapy intervention would exacerbate or alleviate the situation.

7. Consider whether civil commitment or involuntary hospitalization might be the best step for client and potential victim(s).

The limitation of this model is that, in most cases, the client has made no direct threat, yet the therapist could reasonably judge that the client intends violence toward an identifiable victim. In Anna's case, the husband did not directly threaten his wife (to the knowledge of the therapist). On the other hand, would a reasonable practitioner have concluded that she was in danger? In considering this, the therapist could have simply asked the husband if he intended to harm his wife. Such an "assessment" would have as much objective validity as an eye exam where the doctor asks the patient if he or she can see all right.

Clinical risk assessments for violence gain validity when they augment clinical observations with structured risk factor analyses and outside consultation (Milner & Campbell, 1995; Monahan, 1995; Regan-Kubinski, 1991). A structured risk factor analysis means that the clinician systematically considers factors that are established correlates in the literature on violence prediction. There is a benefit in combining clinical observations with a structured risk factor analysis. That is, while neither method has strong validity on its own merits, the combination has the power to bring statistical reasoning to clinical hunches and impressions—either for confirmation, rejection, or at the least a clarification of the hunches.

Meloy (2000) has suggested that risk factor analyses for potential dangerousness should be based on a biopsychosocial model, and argues that a biopsychosocial model improves validity. That is, therapists of various professional disciplines gravitate towards their own realm of expertise: psychiatrists consider biological variables; psychologists consider individual variables; family therapists consider systems variables; and social workers consider social variables, like poverty.

According to Meloy (2000), individual factors that are associated with violence towards others include male gender, age 15–25, a history of violence, paranoia, below average intelligence, anger/fear problems, and attachment problems. Social/environmental factors include family of origin violence, violent peer groups, poverty or economic instability, weapons history, a victim pool, use of alcohol or psycho-stimulants, and other cultural factors. Biological factors include central nervous system trauma, central nervous system symptoms, and major mental disorder. Some of these factors are static and some are dynamic. Static variables include factors like intelligence, gender, trauma to the central nervous system, and so on. The most salient of the dynamic factors might be problems involving anger and/or fear, a pool of victims, acts that involved weapons, and so on. Changes in these factors can lead to dramatic changes in the risk assessment, such as when an angry individual purchases a gun.

Depending on the settings in which the therapist practices, risk factor analyses can be refined to fit the particular population the therapist is assessing. A number of excellent resources assess risk factors, such as for domestic violence (Aldarondo & Straus, 1994; Saunders, 1995), physical abuse of children (Kalichman, 1999; Monteleone, 1996; Rittner & Wodarski, 1995; Schellenbach, Trickett, & Sussman, 1991), child sexual abuse (Haverkamp & Daniluk, 1993), elder abuse (Paris, Meier, Goldstein, Weiss, & Fein, 1995), and at-risk adolescents (Berman & Jobes, 1991; Gustafson & McNamara, 1987).

Another way to bolster the validity of risk assessments is through outside consultation with other treatment providers. Outside consultation is a structured, documented review of patient behavior, records, history, and circumstances to determine the likelihood of violence or dangerousness. A consensus by multiple evaluators has high predictive accuracy (Werner, Rose, & Yesavage, 1990). The benefit of multiple independent opinions cannot be overemphasized in dealing with violent and dangerous patients.

Even when combining clinical observation, a structured risk analysis, and outside consultation, the best level of determination that can be reached in most cases is that a client is either high, moderate, or low risk to commit violence. Clients who are high risk require immediate and dramatic intervention, such as voluntary or involuntary hospitalization. Moderate risk clients might require hospitalization, but might also benefit from an increased level of outpatient treatment (Meloy, Haroun, & Schiller, 1990). Low risk clients may require adjustment of treatment and ongoing evaluation to deal with and monitor risk at, perhaps, a secondary level.

Through clinical observation, a structured risk factor analysis, and outside consultation, it is possible that a therapist would have concluded that Anna was in danger from her husband. If so, the therapist might have had a legal and ethical obligation to implement a reasonable plan of intervention to protect her from her husband's violence, even if that meant contacting authorities, warning her, or psychiatric referral for the husband's voluntary or involuntary hospitalization.

SELF-DESTRUCTIVE AND SUICIDAL CLIENTS

In this section, the knowledge gained in previous sections will be enhanced by applying it to clients who are violent towards themselves. When a client is actively threatening to take his or her own life, clinical, legal, and ethical dimensions of therapeutic practice come together as the therapist is called upon to protect human life from impulses of self-destruction (Rosenbluth, Kleinman, & Lowy, 1995). Although therapists often think of the self-destructive client as suicidal, the concept also applies to clients in acute stages of anorexia nervosa, clients who are intentionally self-mutilating, and clients suffering from acute psychotic states, such as compulsive head banging, skin-scratching, and so on, which may lead to violent behavior.

Issues Involving Standard of Care

From a legal standpoint, a standard of care is "that degree of care which a reasonably prudent person or professional should exercise in same or similar circumstances" (Black, 1979, p. 1260). This means that standards of care are established through consensus among therapists about what is standard treatment for a clinical scenario. If the therapeutic care falls below that standard, a therapist may be deemed negligent.

Some researchers have suggested that, with the realities of managed mental health care, standards of care in mental health should be more elaborately defined. For example, Callahan (1996) described a standard of care as "a detailed model of an intervention process—a how-to prototype—that enumerates the goals, objectives, settings, processes, procedures, and interactions of that intervention" (p. 277).

The difficulty with elaborately defined standards is that there are significant regional variations in mental health practice as therapists adapt to local resources, regional training opportunities, variations in treatment facilities, and community customs. For example, the nearest hospital for a depressed client in rural Canada might be 250 miles away, while in New York City there might be four hospitals within walking distance. These regional variations make it difficult to determine what a "reasonably prudent person or professional" would do in all places and at all times. It is prudent for therapists to know local and regional mental health standards, and to work to improve regional practices that are substandard.

Failure to Meet Standards of Care

There is no absolute standard of care for treatment of suicidal clients (Fremouw, de Perczel, & Ellis, 1990). There is, however, consensus in all places and at all times that therapists provide a standard of care that attempts to protect the patient from his or her self-destructive behavior. Ahia and Martin (1993) described three ways that therapists fail to meet the minimum standards of care with suicidal patients: assisting with suicide, negligent diagnosis, and abandonment. The following factors expand on their analysis, and add a fourth way, negligent treatment response to suicidal risk.

(1) Assisting with suicide. There are two ways that this can be accomplished. Assistance can be overt, such as suggesting lethal methods to a suicidal patient or, for physicians, prescribing lethal amounts and combinations of medications. A physician might order that a suicidal patient who is hospitalized be taken off protective watch. More likely, a therapist might covertly assist a patient with suicide by interfering with the treatment of other professionals or by misleading family members about the intentions of the suicidal client. Therapists who work with terminally and chronically ill patients, including the elderly, are most at risk of assisting in suicide. Warning signs that a therapist is at risk of assisting suicide might include strong positive countertransference bonds with clients who wish to die or strong negative countertransference towards draining, manipulative clients who are chronically suicidal.

(2) Negligent diagnosis. Negligent diagnosis occurs when a therapist fails to adequately assess, continuously assess, or properly assess, client risk. Negligent diagnosis does not refer to "a wrong decision," but more importantly to when, how, and how often the assessment was made. As previously discussed, assessment of all biological, individual, and social system variables is essential, including ameliorating factors (Bongar, Maris, Berman, & Litman, 1998). For example, being married ameliorates risk, as does the presence of supportive family and friends.

One important assessment factor is whether the patient is chronically or acutely suicidal. In assessing chronicity, it is essential to request records of previous therapy (Bongar,1991). Sixty to 70% of all patients who complete suicide suffer from either major depression or bipolar illness (Slaby, 1998), particularly if depression is diagnosed along with other major mental disorders (substance abuse, anxiety disorder, or personality disorders, such as borderline). A risk factor related to depression is hopelessness (Beck, Steer, Beck, & Newman, 1993; Slaby, 1998).

(3) Abandonment of the client. Subprinciple 1.11 of the AAMFT ethics code states, "Marriage and family therapists do not abandon or neglect clients in treatment without making reasonable arrangements for the continuation of such treatment." The standard of care to protect suicidal clients calls for the therapist to be reasonably available to the client who is at risk for suicide.

With the suicidal client, it is important that the therapist maintain telephone contact and have adequate back up service. The client with desperate suicidal thoughts is apt to view the therapist as a last hope, and even a misperceived rejection by the therapist can trigger hopelessness which may result in violence towards themselves (Slaby, 1998).

Referrals to another treatment provider can be stressful, as suicidal clients may reject the idea of "starting therapy over." Therapists must insure that referrals of suicidal patients include sufficient time for establishing trust with the new therapist before discontinuing contact. The referring therapist should provide the new therapist with the client's psychosocial history, especially previous suicide ideation or attempts. "Client dumping" of difficult clients can be viewed as abandonment, and if the client were harmed, it could potentially be viewed as negligence in the courts. On the other hand, continuing to treat a client who needs treatment from another source can be problematic; the therapist is supposed to be providing the treatment of choice.

(4) <u>Negligent treatment response to suicidal risk</u>. Once it is decided that a client is at risk, standards of care require therapists to take precautionary steps correlated with the level of risk (i.e., high, moderate, or low). Similar to high risk of violence against others, high risk of suicide usually requires immediate patient hospitalization coupled with a high standard of inpatient care (suicide checks, dangerous object removal, secure storage of medications, etc.). For moderate to low risk clients, the level of intervention should be carefully chosen given the circumstances of the patient.

Some suggestions for managing suicide risk include mandatory inpatient or outpatient treatment, arranging for outside consultations, referral for medication, removal of weapons from the living environment, and suicide checks by family and friends (Meloy et. al. 1990).

The practice of making a "suicide contract" with clients is widespread. Therapists should be aware, however, that there is research that indicates that suicide contracts are not effective with high risk suicidal clients (Davidson, Wagner, & Range, 1995).

THE CASE OF EVAN AND TERRI

Evan and Terri were graduate students in physics. Before coming to the United States, they had been married two years in their country-of-origin. They arrived on education visas and adopted English names.

After Evan failed his comprehensive exams, he was asked to leave the academic department. While Westerners sometimes treat failure casually, in Evan's culture-of-origin, failure meant social disgrace for him, as well as for Terri, his parents, and his siblings.

Facing failure, Evan had become deeply despondent. He stopped sleeping and eating and had begun hearing voices telling him that he deserved to die. With Terri's support, Evan sought therapy from a psychiatrist in private practice. Terri asked to speak with the psychiatrist and gave the information that Evan had recently purchased a handgun and was threatening suicide. Afterwards, while Terri sat in the waiting room, the psychiatrist met with Evan. The psychiatrist prescribed psychotropic medications, including antidepressants for Evan. No follow-up appointment was scheduled, and the couple was assured that Evan would improve if he continued on the medication.

Two weeks later, Evan was decompensating. He was wetting himself, making animal-like noises, had developed a facial tic, and continued to hear voices that were telling him to die. Terri was afraid to leave him alone. She began calling the psychiatrist, leaving desperate messages with the answering service, but the psychiatrist did not return her calls.

After three days with no return phone call from the psychiatrist, Terry left Evan alone and took the bus to the psychiatrist's office. She was told that the psychiatrist was out of the country for three weeks, but that another physician was covering the psychiatrist's patients and would see her if she would wait.

Terri waited six hours before the covering physician was able to meet with her. When she explained that Evan was getting worse, not better, the physician was surprised and told her that the only note in Evan's patient record stated simply, "Patient is depressed." There was no record that Evan was suicidal, no record of prescribed medications, and no record of the psychiatrist's conversation with Evan or Terri.

The covering physician suggested that Terri return home immediately and take her husband to the emergency room. When Terri arrived home, she was stunned to find Evan with the handgun, and making strange noises. She hurried to a neighbor's apartment and called 911. Before police arrived, however, Evan exited the apartment, hid in the bushes outside the apartment complex, and later shot himself in front of police and onlookers. He was pronounced dead at the scene.

Inside Evan's apartment, several bottles of psychotropic medications were lying on the counter. In a note, scribbled in his native language, Evan lamented his shame and hopelessness.

Marriage and Family Therapy with Potentially Suicidal Clients

The case of Evan and Terri raises the question of whether a different type and level of intervention would have saved Evan's life. As therapists move into medical settings, they are increasingly more likely to encounter the challenge of clients with major mental disorders and to see clients who are psychotic and suicidal.

There is no legal duty to work with family members, friends, or others when a client is suicidal or self-destructive. However, when the client has supportive relationships with family or friends it is not only permissible, but it is a desirable treatment option to form collaborative treatment relationships with these individuals (Fremouw et al., 1990; Packman & Harris, 1998). Bongar, et al. (1998) suggested that supportive family therapy be incorporated into treatment whenever it will benefit the patient. By working with client support networks, the therapist communicates that he or she cares about the client (Pope & Vasquez, 1991).

There are some cautions, however. Unlike individual therapy, where the therapist has control over the treatment session, family therapy involves other individuals who may have agendas outside of the therapist's control. Therapists should monitor for hidden abuse by family members, subtle cues from family and friends that might push a client towards suicide, or disappointments that might befall the suicidal client whose hopes are dashed for family reconciliation or resolution of long-standing conflicts.

At times, protecting the client who is self-destructive will involve violating confidentiality to warn the client's support network or to collaborate with others in treatment. Therapists are allowed to breach confidentiality in an attempt to protect clients from inflicting bodily harm on themselves. However, without a written authorization, therapists must limit their contacts to those persons who are in a position—socially or professionally—to help the client.

In the interest of informed consent, Packman and Harris (1998) suggest that therapists not only discuss their approach to treatment with self-destructive clients, but rehearse what will happen if the violence reaches a certain level. Rehearsal focuses on specifics, and includes walking step by step through treatment with the client, talking about what interventions will be taken in response to certain levels of risk, who will be informed if certain actions occur, and what the client is expected to do. For example, the therapist can say, "If you start thinking about cutting yourself, you will tell your mother. If you don't tell your mother, and have begun cutting yourself, you will stop cutting, take the razor blade to the trash can, and call my office."

Family therapy is especially useful with children and adolescents who are self-destructive. Informed consent regarding the limits of confidentiality is critical when working with children and adolescents who may believe that their disclosures are absolutely confidential (Gustafson & McNamara, 1987). If children are not informed that disclosures involving violent or dangerous behavior will not be held in confidence, the therapist can lose the child's trust.

Consider the situation of a 12-year old telling a therapist in confidence: "My friends and I have played Russian roulette after school, but please don't tell my parents, because they won't let me have friends over anymore." A therapist in this situation would be obligated to divulge this information to the parents, and a child who had not been informed about the limits of confidentiality might feel resentful.

Documentation with Potentially Suicidal Clients

Compared with record keeping for clients in general, the need for complete and accurate documentation with potentially suicidal clients takes on an added dimension. In addition to the clinical purposes of therapy records (e.g., to inform subsequent treatment sources about the therapy), the records of suicidal clients serve a risk management purpose. That is, in the event of suicide or injurious self-destructive act, the therapist can use the records to establish that reasonable standards of care were diligently followed. Subprinciple 3.6 of the AAMFT ethics code states, "Marriage and family therapists maintain accurate and adequate clinical and financial records."

For all clients, it is important that the clinical record indicate factors that were considered in every phase of treatment, especially when treatment goals or methods were changed to enhance the quality of treatment. The record should indicate ongoing assessments, including specific clinical observations and risk factor analyses. For example, the record might indicate that "the client reports elevated affect following therapy sessions with his wife." Risk factor analyses should be detailed, such as "the client is happily married, and considers it important to live for his wife and children." (Chapter Nine provides details about what should be in clinical records.)

It is also important to list negative factors that might be leading towards hopelessness and despair. For example, the therapist might write, "the client is Catholic, but reports that he (or she) has lost faith in God and his (or her) religion."

Another important component of adequate records is documentation of outside consultations. Copies of records from colleagues should be kept, and detailed notes of conversations with colleagues are important to show that outside opinions were incorporated into the treatment plan.

Detailed and accurate records not only indicate that the therapist has practiced according to acceptable standards of care, but also that the therapist cares properly about the client. There are few legal cases against therapists for negligence relevant to client suicides, and the vast majority of these are won by clinicians (Gutheil, 1992). However, the cases where courts have made findings against therapists usually hinge on whether the record demonstrates that the therapist actually provided the client with reasonable, adequate, and proper care, and took every reasonable step to avert the suicide.

CONCLUSION

This chapter has examined three conditions under which therapists are permitted or mandated to breach patient confidentiality: to report suspicions of abuse or neglect of a child or vulnerable adult, to warn or protect potential victims of client violence, and to protect a client who may be suicidal or self-destructive. Critical elements of professional and ethical practice have been discussed such as obtaining informed consent from clients, keeping adequate records, conducting structured risk factor analyses, maintaining reasonable contact with clients, seeking outside consultations from colleagues, keeping accurate client records, and knowing the law.

Although the contents of this chapter have focused on standards, laws, duties, and obligations, therapists will find that developing a personal ethic of care is more likely to result in ethical and professional practice than working out of obligation (McConaghy & Cottone, 1998). Principle I, Responsibility to Clients, of the AAMFT ethics code states, "Marriage and family therapists advance the welfare of families and individuals. They respect the rights of those seeking their assistance . . . ."

Work with abuse, dangerousness, violence, and neglect can test even the experienced therapist. Dealing with violent and dangerous clients requires the ability to balance compassionate, perhaps specialized, interventions with limit setting and patience. This extra work can lead to poor judgment with these needy and demanding clients, who often leave little room for error without the potential for catastrophic violence.

Meloy, Haroun, and Schiller (1990) identified a number of countertransference issues that can plague good judgment in therapists who are dealing with violent clients. These include stereotypical judgments that violent individuals cannot be helped, fears of assault, frustration with the level of deception and denial in these patients, and, at times, the therapist's helplessness with violence. Jory (1996) has discussed the fear reactions encountered in young professionals who feel attacked by dangerous clients.

In the face of the strains and challenges encountered, it is understandable that some therapists structure their work with violent and dangerous clients strictly out of a desire to limit their own liability, or out of concern for preserving their practices or their own peace of mind. This is not unethical, and may be wise. Therapists should remember, however, that the best route to a liability-proof career is to practice with high ethical standards, astute consideration of current standards and law pertaining to care, and professional concern for the well being of clients

REFERENCES

Adler, R. (1995). To tell or not to tell: The psychiatrist and child abuse. Australian and New Zealand Journal of Psychiatry, 29, 190–198.

Ahia, C. E., & Martin, D. (1993). The danger-to-self-or-other exception to confidentiality. Alexandria, VA: American Counseling Association.

Aldarondo, E., & Straus, M. (1994). Screening for physical violence in couple therapy: Methodological, practical and ethical considerations. Family Process, 33, 425–439.

American Counseling Association. (1995). Code of ethics and standards of practice. Alexandria, VA: Author.

Appelbaum, P. (1985). Tarasoff and the clinician: Problems in fulfilling the duty to protect. American Journal of Psychiatry, 142, 425–429.

Appelbaum, K., & Appelbaum, P. (1990). The HIV antibody-positive patient. In J. Beck (Ed.), Confidentiality versus the duty to protect: Foreseeable harm in the practice of psychiatry (pp. 121–140). Washington, DC: American Psychiatric Press.

Ascione, F., & Arkow, P. (1999). Child abuse, domestic violence, and animal abuse: Linking the circles of compassion for prevention and intervention. West Lafayette, IN: Purdue University Press.

Beck, J. (Ed.). (1990). Confidentiality versus the duty to protect. Washington, DC: American Psychiatric Press.

Beck, A., Steer, R., Beck, J., & Newman, C. (1993). Hopelessness, depression, suicidal ideation, and clinical diagnosis of depression. Suicide and Life-Threatening Behavior, 23, 139–145.

Berkowitz, C. (1995). Pediatric abuse: New patterns of injury. Emergency Medicine Clinics of North America, 13, 321–341.

Berman, A., & Jobes, D. (1991). Adolescent suicide: Assessment and intervention. Washington, DC: American Psychological Association.

Black, H. (1979). Black's law dictionary. St. Paul, MN: West.

Bograd, M., & Mederos, F. (1999). Battering and couples therapy: Universal screening and selection of treatment modality. Journal of Marital and Family Therapy, 25, 291–312.

Bok, S. (1982). Secrets: On the ethics of concealment and revelation. New York: Pantheon.

Bollas, C., & Sundelson, D. (1995). The new informants: A betrayal of confidentiality in psychoanalysis and psychotherapy. Northvale, NJ: Jason Aronson.

Bongar, B. (1991). The suicidal patient: Clinical and legal standards of care. Washington, DC: American Psychological Association.

Bongar, B., Maris, R., Berman, A., & Litman, L. (1998). Outpatient standards of care and the suicidal patient. In B. Bongar, A. Berman, R. Maris, M. Silverman, E. Harris, & W. Packman (Eds.), Risk management with suicidal patients (pp. 4–33). New York: Guilford.

Brady, T. (1996). Measuring what matters: Measures of crime, fear, and disorder. Research in action. Washington, DC: National Institute of Justice.

Brent, D., Kupfer, D., Bromet, E., & Dew, M. (1988). The assessment and treatment of patients at risk for suicide. In A. Frances & R. Hales (Eds.), American Psychiatric Press review of psychiatry, Vol. 7 (pp. 353–385). Washington, DC: American Psychiatric Press.

Brosig, C., & Kalichman, S. (1992). Clinicians' reporting of suspected child abuse: A review of the empirical literature. Clinical Psychology Review, 12, 155–168.

Callahan, J. (1996). Social work with suicidal clients: Challenges of implementing practice guidelines and standards of care. Health and Social Work, 21, 277–282.

Callahan, J. (1996). Documentation of client dangerousness in a managed care environment. Health and Social Work, 21, 202–208.

Cohen, E. (1997). Ethical standards in counseling sexually active clients with HIV. In The Hatherleigh guide to ethics in therapy (pp. 211–233). New York: Hatherleigh Press.

Conte, H. , Plutchik, R., Picard, S., & Karasu, T. (1989). Ethics in the practice of psychotherapy: A survey. American Journal of Psychotherapy, 43, 32–40.

Daro, D. (1996). Current trends in child abuse reporting and fatalities: NCPCA's 1995 annual fifty-state survey. APSAC Advisor, 9, 21–24.

Davidson, M., Wagner, W., & Range, L. (1995). Clinicians attitudes toward no-suicide agreements. Suicide and Life-Threatening Behavior, 25, 410–414.

Department of Health and Human Services. (1988). Study finding: Study of national incidence and prevalence of child abuse and neglect (DHHS Publication No. ADM-20-01099). Washington, DC: U.S. Government Printing Office.

Diekstra, R., & Van Egmond, M. (1989). Suicide and attempted suicide in general practice, 1979–1986. Acta Psychiatrica Scandinavica, 79, 268–275.

Dobrin, A., Wiersema, B., Loftin, C., & McDowal, D. (1996). Statistical handbook on violence in America. Phoenix, AZ: Oryx Press.

Doueck, H. (1995). Screening for child abuse: problems and possibilities. Applied Nursing Research, 8, 191–198.

Fineman, M., & Mykitiuk, R. (Eds.). (1994). The public nature of private violence. New York: Routledge.

Fremouw, W., de Perczel, M., & Ellis, T. (1990). Suicide risk: Assessment and response guidelines. New York: Pergamon.

Glancy, G., Regehr, C., Bryant, A., & Schneider, R. (1999). Another nail in the coffin of confidentiality. Canadian Journal of Psychiatry, 44, 440–441.

Godard, S., & Bloom, J. (1990). Driving, mental illness, and the duty to protect. In J. Beck (Ed.), Confidentiality versus the duty to protect: Foreseeable harm in the practice of psychiatry (pp.191–204). Washington, DC: American Psychiatric Press.

Goldner, V. (1999). Morality and multiplicity: Perspectives on the treatment of violence in intimate life. Journal of Marital and Family Therapy, 25, 325–336.

Gross, B., Southard, J., Lamb, R., & Weinberger, L. (1987). Assessing dangerousness and responding appropriately: Hedlund expands the clinician's liability established by Tarasoff. Journal of Clinical Psychiatry, 48, 9–12.

Gustavson, E., & Levitt, C. (1996). Physical abuse with severe hypothermia. Archives of Pediatric and Adolescent Medicine, 150, 111–112.

Gustafson, K., & McNamara, R. (1987). Confidentiality with minor clients: Issues and guidelines for therapists. Professional Psychology: Research and Practice, 18, 503–508.

Gutheil, T. (1992). Suicide and suit: Liability after self-destruction. In D. Jacobs (Ed.), Suicide and clinical practice (pp. 147–167). Washington, DC: American Psychiatric Press.

Haverkamp, B., & Daniluk, J. (1993). Child sexual abuse: Ethical issues for the family therapist. Family Relations, 42, 134–139.

Johnson, C., Kaufman, K., & Callendar, C. (1990). The hand as a target organ in child abuse. Clinical Pediatrics, 2, 66–72.

Jory, B. (1996). Special issues in supervision: The abusive man. Supervision Bulletin, 9, 4–5.

Jory, B., & Anderson, D. (1999). Intimate justice II: Fostering mutuality, reciprocity, and accommodation in the treatment of abuse. Journal of Marital and Family Therapy, 25, 349–363.

Jory, B., & Anderson, D. (2000). Intimate justice III: Healing the anguish of abuse and facing the anguish of accountability. Journal of Marital and Family Therapy, 26, 329–340.

Jory, B., Anderson, D., & Greer, C. (1997). Intimate justice: confronting issues of accountability, respect, and freedom in therapy for abuse and violence. Journal of Marital and Family Therapy, 23, 399–419.

Kalichman, S. (1999). Mandated reporting of suspected child abuse: Ethics, law, and policy. Washington, DC: American Psychological Association.

Karpf, R. (1996). A review of The new informants: A betrayal of confidentiality in psychoanalysis and psychotherapy. American Journal of Psychotherapy, 50, 377–378.

Levenkron, S. (1998). Cutting: Understanding and overcoming self-mutilation. New York: Norton.

Maguire, K., & Pastore, A. (1998). Sourcebook of criminal justice statistics. Washington, DC: U.S. Department of Justice.

McConaghy, J., & Cottone, R. (1998). The systemic view of violence: An ethical perspective. Family Process, 37, 51–63.

Mehl, A. (1990). Shaken impact syndrome. Child Abuse and Neglect, 14, 603–604.

Meloy, R. (Ed.). (1998). The psychology of stalking: Clinical and forensic perspectives. San Diego, CA: Academic Press.

Meloy, R. (2000). Violence risk and threat assessment—A practical guide for mental health and criminal justice professionals. San Diego, CA: Specialized Training Services.

Meloy, R., Haroun, A., & Schiller, E. (1990). Clinical guidelines for involuntary outpatient treatment. Sarasota, FL: Professional Resource Exchange.

Mercer, S., & Perdue, J. (1993). Munchausen syndrome by proxy: Social work's role. Social Work, 38, 74–81.

Miller, K. (2000). Practice guidelines for the treatment of patients with eating disorders. American Journal of Orthopsychiatry, 157, 1–39.

Milner, J. (1995). Physical child abuse assessment: Perpetrator evaluation. In J. Campbell (Ed.), Assessing dangerousness—Violence by sexual offenders, batterers, and child abusers (pp. 41–67). Thousand Oaks, CA: Sage.

Milner, J., & Campbell, J. (1995). Prediction issues for practitioners. In J. Campbell (Ed.), Assessing dangerousness—Violence by sexual offenders, batterers, and child abusers, (pp.20–40). Thousand Oaks, CA: Sage.

Monahan, J. (1995). The clinical prediction of violent behavior (New ed.). Northvale, NJ: Jason Aronson.

Monteleone, J. (Ed.). (1996). Recognition of child abuse for the mandated reporter. New York: G.W. Medical Publishing.

Monteleone, J., & Broder, A. (1996). Identifying physical abuse. In J. Monteleone (Ed.), Recognition of child abuse for the mandated reporter (pp. 1–18). New York: G.W. Medical Publishing.

National Center on Child Abuse and Neglect (1998). Child maltreatment 1996: Reports from the states to the National Center on Child Abuse and Neglect. Washington, DC: U.S. Government Printing Office.

National Center on Elder Abuse (1998). The national elder abuse incidence study. Washington, DC: American Public Human Services Association.

Ormrod, J., & Ambrose, L. (1999). Public perceptions about confidentiality in mental health services. Journal of Mental Health, 8, 413–422.

Packman, W., & Harris, E. (1998). Legal issues and risk management in suicidal patients. In B. Bongar, A. Berman, R. Maris, M. Silverman, E. Harris, & W. Packman (Eds.), Risk management with suicidal patients (pp. 150–186). New York: Guilford.

Paris, B., Meier, D., Goldstein, T., Weiss, M., & Fein, E. (1995). Elder abuse and neglect: How to recognize warning signs and intervene. Geriatrics, 50, 47–53.

Perlin, M. (1997). The "duty to protect" others from violence. In The Hatherleigh guide to ethics in therapy (pp. 127–146). New York: Hatherleigh Press.

Plueckhahn, V., & Cordner, S. (1991). Ethics, legal medicine, and forensic pathology (2nd ed.). Melbourne, Australia: Melbourne University Press.

Pope, K., & Vasquez, M. (1991). Ethics in psychotherapy and counseling. San Francisco, CA: Jossey-Bass.

Regan-Kubinski, J. (1991). A model of clinical judgment processes in psychiatric nursing. Archives of Psychiatric Nursing, 5, 262–270.

Rittner, B., & Wodarski, J. (1995). Clinical assessment instruments in the treatment of child abuse and neglect. Early Child Development and Care, 106, 43–58.

Rosenbluth, M., Kleinman, I., & Lowy, E. (1995). Suicide: The interaction of clinical and ethical issues. Psychiatric Services, 46, 919–921.

Saunders, B. (1995). Prediction of wife assault. In J. Campbell (Ed.), Assessing dangerousness: Violence by sexual offenders, batterers, and child abusers (pp. 68–95). Thousand Oaks, CA: Sage.

Schellenbach, C., Trickett, P., & Sussman, E. (1991). A multimethod approach to the assessment of physical abuse. Violence and Victims, 6, 57–73.

Schlossberger, E., & Hecker, L. (1996). HIV and family therapists' duty to warn: A legal and ethical analysis. Journal of Marital and Family Therapy, 22, 27–40.

Simon, R. (1990). The duty to protect in private practice. In J. Beck (Ed.), Confidentiality versus the duty to protect: Foreseeable harm in the practice of psychiatry (pp. 23–42). Washington, DC: American Psychiatric Press.

Slaby, A. (1998). Outpatient management of suicidal patients. In B. Bongar, A. Berman, R. Maris, M. Silverman, E. Harris, & W. Packman (Eds.), Risk management with suicidal patients (pp. 34–64). New York: Guilford.

Slovic, P., & Monahan, J. (1995). Danger and coercion: A study of risk perception and decision making in mental health law. Law and Human Behavior, 19, 49–65.

Tarasoff v. Regents of the University of California, 17 Cal.3d 425, 551 P.2d 334, 131, Cal. Rptr.14 (1976).

Tjaden, P., & Thoennes, N. (1998). Prevalence, incidence, and consequences of violence against women: Findings from the National Violence Against Women Survey. Denver, CO: Center for Policy Research.

U.S. Advisory Board on Child Abuse and Neglect. (1995). A nation's shame: Fatal child abuse and neglect in the United States. Washington, DC: U.S. Department of Health and Human Services.

U.S. Department of Justice. (1994). Uniform crime reports for the United States, 1991. Washington, DC: U.S. Department of Justice, Federal Bureau of Investigation.

VandeCreek, L., & Knapp, S. (1993). Tarasoff and beyond: Legal and clinical considerations in the treatment of life-endangering patients (Rev. ed.). Sarasota, FL: Professional Resource Press.

Weisberg, D. (1984). The discovery of sexual abuse: Experts' roles in legal policy formation. University of California—Davis Law Review, 18, 2–57.

Werner, P., Rose, T., & Yesavage, J. (1990). Aspects of consensus in clinical predictions of imminent violence. Journal of Clinical Psychology, 46, 534–538.

Woody, J., & Woody, R. (1988). Public policy in life-threatening situations: A response to Bobele. Journal of Marital and Family Therapy, 14, 133–137.

MORAL VALUES, SPIRITUALITY, AND SEXUALITY

Dorothy S. Becvar

This chapter considers the impact of moral values, spirituality, and sexuality on the process of marriage and family therapy and the various ethical issues and concerns of which the therapist must be aware relative to these domains. Particular attention is given to the overlap of the domains as well as to their pervasive influence on both clients and therapists. The discussion also includes suggestions that may promote ethical behavior and adherence to the AAMFT Code of Ethics.

CONTENTS
Moral Values
Spirituality
Sexuality
Conclusion: Final Thoughts

To engage in an exploration of ethical issues and the potential for challenges related to moral values, spirituality, and sexuality is to enter a complex realm of concerns comprised of several different levels, many of which overlap. Indeed, there is no aspect of therapy that is not touched by one or more of these dimensions.

First and foremost, at the level of the larger context, family therapy, like all forms of psychotherapy, is inevitably and inherently about moral values (Aponte, 1994; Becvar, 1997a; Dell, 1983). In other words, those phenomena that a society defines as good or bad, right or wrong, health or illness, are symbolic of the values about how that society believes people should or should not behave. When individuals and families come to therapy, it is because they or others believe that they somehow have fallen short of societal norms in this regard. Their so-called problems and pathologies represent a failure to achieve the standards of behavior valued by society. Working within that society, therefore, therapists often find themselves striving to enable clients to meet such standards. This ever-present reality certainly may create ethical concerns and issues requiring our attention.

Secondly, at the level of client-therapist interactions, every aspect of the therapy process is also value-laden. All therapists come equipped with personal beliefs and value systems that form the hub around which discussions revolve. In addition to the inevitable and perhaps unspoken moral assumptions that underlie much of therapy, psychotherapists have been encouraged in recent years to engage actively in discussions of morality and to promote a sense of moral responsibility in their work with clients (Doherty, 1995). However, if therapists proceed in this direction, great sensitivity relative to ethical issues is certainly called for inasmuch as there may be a fine line between therapeutic discussion of values and therapists' imposition of values.

To add a third level of consideration and complexity, for many people, including therapists, spirituality is the foundation, or at least a primary source, of their personal beliefs and value systems. To explain, spirituality has been defined as "a way of being and experiencing that comes about through awareness of a transcendent dimension that is characterized by <u>certain identifiable values in regard to self, other, nature, life, and whatever one considers to be the ultimate</u>" [emphasis added] (Elkins, 1990, p.4). Accordingly, regardless of whether one's spiritual values are imbedded in a specific religious belief system or simply describe a particular way of being in the world outside the realm of institutionalized religion (Becvar, 1997a), spiritual values act as a guide as well as a constraint to both thought and action. Thus, spirituality is likely to influence every therapeutic encounter in some way, either as an unspoken aspect of the larger context and/or as a topic that is specifically addressed.

A fourth level requiring attention is that of discussions focused explicitly on spirituality and religion. The last decade has seen an enormous growth in awareness of and permission to include this topic in the therapeutic conversation (Becvar, 1997a, 1997b; Becvar & Becvar, 2000a; Frame, 2000). Once again, however, ethical issues are likely to emerge as a function of several important considerations. Perhaps most significant is the fact that, at this point in time, few therapists have received training relative to the inclusion of spirituality in therapy as part of their educational programs (Bowman, 1989). Without such training, there may be a lack of awareness of the variety of pitfalls when venturing into this territory (Benningfield, 1997).

Some further overriding ethical concerns relative to spirituality have been described as including respect for the autonomy of clients, safeguarding their welfare, protecting them from harm, and treating them in a just and honest manner (Haug, 1998). Even when therapists are sensitive to issues such as those relative to therapeutic discussions, they are not likely to ever be completely knowledgeable in this area, given the extraordinary range of possible spiritual beliefs. Finally, and particularly relevant to all of these concerns, the realm of sexuality, which is commonly involved in client problems, is greatly influenced by spirituality and the moral values derived therefrom.

Spiritual precepts often speak directly to that which is considered appropriate in the realm of sexuality. For example, sexual orientation, sexual activity outside of marriage, and the roles of women and men are but a few of the aspects of sexuality in which specific behaviors may be valued or proscribed. Depending on his or her spiritual belief system, the therapist may make judgments about, or may have difficulty working with, clients who hold belief systems and who espouse values and behaviors relative to sexuality that differ from those of the therapist.

In addition to the influence of spiritual or religious beliefs on sexual behavior, there are many other aspects of sexuality that are worthy of consideration, and which may also give rise to ethical concerns. For example, the sexuality of both client and therapist are pervasive aspects of therapy (Woody, 1983), and include such dimensions as seduction, power, opportunity, self-interest, and morality (Edelwich & Brodsky, 1991). Also, there is the issue and prohibition of sexual intimacy between therapists and their clients, students, and supervisees. Finally, discussions in therapy focused specifically either on sexual dysfunction or on sexual abuse carry with them the responsibility for ethical awareness and sensitivity, as well as the potential for ethical concerns and dilemmas.

In other words, as this introduction suggests, at both implicit and explicit levels, therapists need to be aware of a variety of challenges relative to moral values, spirituality, and sexuality, as they attempt to practice in a manner that is consistent with and does not violate in any way either the letter or the spirit of the AAMFT ethics code. The following three sections provide analysis and discussion of each of these areas in some depth, including the kinds of situations that clinicians may face, as well as providing case examples relative to specific provisions of the ethics code. The fourth section provides concluding thoughts with regard to the integration and overlap of the three areas and their impact on the ethical practice of marriage and family therapy.

MORAL VALUES

Moral values refer to basic beliefs regarding what an individual, group, or society considers good and right; they represent the standards of appropriate behavior. Some synonyms that further define the word moral include ethical, exemplary, honest, noble, righteous, truthful, and virtuous. And to value means to hold in high esteem or to consider to be of great worth.

In general, two primary ways to think about and discuss moral values have been delineated: moralizing and moral philosophy. It may be important, however, to be aware that the two are often confused in common discourse (Chazan & Soltis, 1973). On the one hand, moralizing describes the process of making judgments about or criticizing specific behaviors, principles, and values characteristic of a society or other group. Recognized as a vital operation,

Moralizing is an indispensable aspect of social life, for it is a means of evaluating adherence to accepted principles, of preventing too dangerous deviation from accepted principles, and of enabling periodic modifications of accepted principles . . . . Indeed, a tradition of thoughtful moralizing is the crucial mechanism a creative society utilizes for the prevention of either moral anarchy or moral totalitarianism. (Chazan & Soltis, 1973, p. 3)

When therapists make determinations about the degree to which certain behaviors do or do not meet various values and related expectations, they are moralizing. For example, throughout history, there has been a great deal of moralizing related to the family and the extent to which it is perceived to be in chaos or is breaking down (Becvar, 1983, 1997b).

Moral philosophy, on the other hand, is concerned with "the more general and rational study of the nature of moral concepts, problems, and issues" (Chazan & Soltis, 1973, p. 4). It may involve the analysis of ideas and dilemmas central to the moral domain, as well as the definition of the latter. It may also include the specification of prescriptions regarding either what is to be considered good and/or the context of justification for moral decisions. In either case, however, the focus is broad, moving well beyond the local and the specific. For example, assuming general agreement with the idea that everyone should act in a manner that is good and right, moral philosophers face such perplexing questions as, "How do we know or prove what is good or right?" (Chazan & Soltis, 1973, p. 51).

As noted in the introduction, therapy is inherently about moral values. Indeed, there would be no necessity for therapy if certain behaviors and states of being were not valued. A dilemma arises when there is a conflict between the moral values of clients and those of the society and its agents, of which therapists represent a significant group. Although therapists inevitably moralize, whether spoken or unspoken, they must also engage in moral philosophy, asking themselves how they know or can prove what is good or right for their clients.

It seems appropriate to consider the first principle of the ethics code, which reads as follows:

> *Principle I: Responsibility to Clients - Marriage and family therapists advance the welfare of families and individuals. They respect the rights of those persons seeking their assistance, and make reasonable efforts to ensure that their services are used appropriately.*

While few, if any, marriage and family therapists would argue with the importance of such a responsibility to clients, the issue at hand concerns who it is who has the right to decide what is in the best interests, or advances the welfare of families and individuals. Do marriage and family therapists allow clients to specify their goals for therapy, or are the goals specified by therapists as a function of the models or theories according to which they choose to operate? If the latter option is selected, how can marriage and family therapists be sure that this is what is best for their clients?

A significant issue is the degree to which therapists respect the rights of those persons seeking their assistance when they presume to know, based on their theoretical orientation, how clients should act or be. As one therapist notes,

> *. . . disposing of our fellow man against his will, even when this appears to us as the only proper course, can be highly problematical. We can never know wherein lies the real meaning of an individual human life. The goal of individual and collective actions is always seen somewhat differently by other people at other times. Our present values are not the only or final ones. (Guggenbuhl-Craig, 1999, p. 6)*

Two additional subprinciples of the ethics code also seem relevant in this regard and lead to further discussion regarding concerns both about that which advances the welfare of clients and about value imposition: Subprinciple 3.12 states, "Marriage and family therapists make efforts to prevent the distortion or misuse of their clinical and research findings"; and Subprinciple 3.13 states, "Marriage and family therapists, because of their ability to influence and alter the lives of others, exercise special care when making public their professional recommendations and opinions through testimony or other public statements."

Relevant to the preceding two subprinciples, one of the major ethical issues raised in recent years, particularly by those espousing a postmodern perspective in marriage and family therapy, relates to the tendency of modernist theorists and therapists to presume to know, and thus to prescribe, appropriate standards of behavior for individuals and families. For example, Michel Foucault is often cited by postmodernists for having pointed out that what the human science disciplines generally do is to "characterize, classify, specialize; they distribute along a scale, around a norm, hierarchize individuals in relation to one another, and if necessary disqualify and invalidate" (White & Epston, 1990, p. 74). A related critique is that social scientists, having engaged in research according to which such judgments and classifications are made, often then proceed to offer their findings as representing the truth about human behavior (Gergen, 1985, 1991).

The problem is that both therapists and clients become the consumers of such "truths" and ultimately may find themselves defining health or dysfunction accordingly. However, given the inevitable subjectivity that characterizes the human experience (Bronowski, 1978), a postmodern perspective recognizes that one cannot ever know that what one knows is truth in any absolute sense. A postmodern, social constructionist approach advocates acknowledgment that an unbiased, objective view of the world and of what is or is not true is not possible (Longino, 1990). Therefore, therapists are advised to hold on to their theories lightly and to allow clients to participate in a collaborative process in which their expertise, as well as that of the therapist, is recognized and considered (Anderson, 1997). What is more, the nature of therapy is redefined. From such a stance there is an awareness that "the entire therapeutic venture is fundamentally an exercise in ethics; it involves the inventing, shaping, and reformulating of codes for living together" (Efran, Lukens, & Lukens, 1988, p. 27). The following fictional scenario illustrates some potential ethical issues therapists may encounter when they pay more attention to their theory than to their clients.

Sam is an experienced therapist with a long history of training and supervision in Bowenian (Bowen, 1978) family therapy. He has had many successes over the years and is well known for his work, which typically includes constructing a genogram as well as sending his clients "home" to explore and confront family-of-origin issues. The goal of these activities is to help clients achieve differentiation relative both to their family emotional system and in terms of their personal ability to regulate their own reactivity (Friedman, 1991).

Not long ago, a young couple went to Sam seeking help. The wife was experiencing physical symptoms related to the stress involved with attempting to create a relationship with her new husband while at the same time dealing with intrusive behaviors on the part of her father. There was a resulting increase in the emotional reactivity between the husband and the wife. Sam worked long and hard with the couple, focusing particularly on enabling the wife to achieve the ability to respond differently to her father and to be able to succeed in differentiating from her family of origin in healthy ways. He also attempted to help the couple behave with each other in a calmer and more rational manner. However, while the couple was able to understand what was going on, not only was the young woman unable to violate the norms of her family of origin by responding to her father in new ways, but her physical symptoms became increasingly more severe. Ultimately, the couple dropped out of therapy.

It is not likely that charges would ever be made against Sam for violating the ethics code. Nevertheless, it is reasonable to ask whether his therapeutic behavior was as ethical as it might have been. That is, if they truly are to be able to advance the welfare of their clients, therapists who work with one or more models that generally have served them well must also be sensitive to the need for theoretical flexibility. They must be cautious about presuming either to know what is best for their clients or to believe that their models and theories are always true just because they sometimes work (Longino, 1990).

Therapists also must recognize that they hold influence with clients simply by virtue of their professional role and status. Therefore, they must offer their ideas and suggestions tentatively and carefully rather than as statements of fact or truth. Even when therapists appropriately and ethically draw on such professional values as promoting health and rejecting violence and abuse in their work with clients, they attempt to engage clients to collaborate with them on the selection of healthful goals, rather than simply prescribing their own goals. Therapeutic discussions of moral responsibility are certainly appropriate from time to time, but imposing values on clients is not appropriate, unless this is the only means available to protect a client from doing grave harm to self or others. (See Chapter Five on the ethical issues involved in client dangerousness, violence, and abuse.)

Therapists certainly may discuss the pros and cons of various decisions that their clients may make. But they do not choose for or tell clients what the right choice is, except, as noted above, when ethical or legal mandates render a particular choice unacceptable. Therefore, regardless of the topic, therapists can best adhere to the letter and spirit of the AAMFT ethics code by respecting clients' right to self-determination relative to personal values and beliefs and by realizing that theories and models of therapy carry certain value assumptions about life. Certainly this is also the case when conversations move into the realm of spirituality.

SPIRITUALITY

Spirituality refers to a way of being and believing that is derived from one's perspective on things immaterial. It often refers to the realm of the soul and assumes recognition of a transcendent dimension. It also generally carries with it a connotation of that which is sacred, holy, and pure. Given the importance attributed to spirituality and religion, it is little wonder that folk wisdom traditionally has advised against discussions in this area for fear of the potential for conflict.

The emergence of spirituality as an important and discussible dimension in therapy presents some interesting challenges for marriage and family therapists. On the one hand, it now becomes possible to make the covert overt, to recognize, acknowledge, and consider the origin of many of the cherished values of both clients and therapists, as well as the role that spirituality and religion plays in their lives. On the other hand, the potential for value imposition and discrimination is increased by virtue of the more public nature of this topic, the fact that both therapists and clients are more likely to reveal and discuss their spiritual orientations and related beliefs.

At the most basic and obvious level, therapists are constrained from behaving in an inappropriately biased manner as a function of this knowledge about a client's religion, which would include spirituality. According to Subprinciple 1.1 of the AAMFT ethics code, "Marriage and family therapists provide professional assistance to persons without discrimination on the basis of race, age, ethnicity, socioeconomic status, disability, gender, health status, religion, national origin, or sexual orientation."

There are certainly instances in which therapists may believe that they cannot work effectively with clients because of differences in religious or spiritual orientation and related values. Indeed, in some cases, attempting to do so would violate the ethics code. For example, in the case of a young woman who is exploring options for effective contraception, the welfare of the client may not be best served if the therapist, because of personal religious or spiritual values, permits only a discussion of abstinence from sexual intercourse as a contraceptive method. Therapists have an ethical duty to bring relevant behavioral science knowledge and research to bear on their clinical work. Thus, whether recognition of a potential serious values conflict occurs early or later in the course of therapy, therapists also have the ethical responsibility to seek supervision regarding their conflicting beliefs in order to attempt to work effectively with the clients. If after supervision this still does not seem to be possible, therapists must make sure that clients are referred appropriately and are helped to find alternative professional help that is suitable for them.

Consider in this regard the following two subprinciples: Subprinciple 1.10 states, "Marriage and family therapists assist persons in obtaining other therapeutic services if the therapist is unable or unwilling, for appropriate reasons, to provide professional help"; and Subprinciple 1.11 states, "Marriage and family therapists do not abandon or neglect clients in treatment without making reasonable arrangements for the continuation of such treatment."

By contrast, in instances in which there is sufficient compatibility of belief systems, or at least lack of conflict relative to spirituality, therapists must be aware of several other potential ethical issues. For example, various religious and spiritual belief systems are very specific about behaviors considered to be unacceptable. Behaviors such as sex before marriage, cohabitation, and divorce are all proscribed in some traditions.

It is highly likely that therapists and clients will, from time to time, experience differences of opinion or value conflicts relative to behaviors such as these. However, according to Subprinciple 1.8 of the AAMFT ethics code,

> *Marriage and family therapists respect the rights of clients to make decisions and help them to understand the consequences of these decisions. Therapists clearly advise the clients that they have the responsibility to make decisions regarding relationships such as cohabitation, marriage, divorce, separation, reconciliation, custody, and visitation.*

For example, although a therapist may be opposed to divorce because of the tenets of his or her religious belief system, he or she does not have the right to prevent couples from moving in this direction if that is their desire. The therapist may enable clients to consider the impact of divorce upon children and the separating partners, and even the various long-term ramifications of such a choice. Nevertheless, the decision to divorce, or not, ultimately belongs to the clients.

Perhaps the most important challenge relative to spirituality arises from the fact that therapists may have had little instruction or experience regarding the handling of this topic with clients. As indicated elsewhere,

. . . outside of seminary-based programs, preparation in this area is rarely part of the training of mental health professionals. Whatever knowledge we have acquired probably has derived from personal pursuits and in all likelihood does not provide us with in-depth understanding of traditions other than our own or those in which we have a special interest. (Becvar, 1997a, pp. 55-56)

Stated differently, without the appropriate training and preparation, the marriage and family therapist is likely to be prone to rely on personalized notions.

Given the growing acceptance of the topic of spirituality in therapy, therapists may wish to be inclusive and to permit or even encourage discussions of spirituality. If they do so, however, they must assure themselves and others of their competence by obtaining the appropriate knowledge and skills. Indeed, the AAMFT ethics code addresses this issue in several subprinciples that are relevant to the newly emerging realm of spirituality in therapy:

Subprinciple 3.1: Marriage and family therapists pursue knowledge of new developments and maintain competence in marriage and family therapy through education, training, or supervised experience.

Subprinciple 3.7: While developing new skills in specialty areas, marriage and family therapists take steps to ensure the competence of their work and to protect clients from possible harm. Marriage and family therapists practice in specialty areas new to them only after appropriate education, training, or supervised experience.

Subprinciple 3.11: Marriage and family therapists do not diagnose, treat, or advise on problems outside the recognized boundaries of their competencies.

Subprinciple 4.4: Marriage and family therapists do not permit students or supervisees to perform or to hold themselves out as competent to perform professional services beyond their training, level of experience, and competence.

Subprinciple 8.8: Marriage and family therapists do not represent themselves as providing specialized services unless they have the appropriate education, training, or supervised experience.

Without training relative to spirituality and therapy, marriage and family therapists may be vulnerable to violation of the AAMFT ethics code. Such training, acquired through workshops, certificate programs, postgraduate work and supervision, will enable marriage and family therapists to avoid the pitfalls due to either a lack of appropriate sensitivity or a tendency to be too zealous regarding the role of spirituality in clients' lives (Benningfield, 1997). What is called for is a balance that also recognizes that a neutral or value-free position is never possible. In other words, therapists all have values that bias their reactions in one direction or another. Therefore, an honest admission of one's biases may be most appropriate and may help to foster a trusting relationship and prevent implicit value imposition.

For example, when grief following the death of a significant person brings clients to therapy, discussions are likely to arise regarding the meaning of life and beliefs about what happens after a person dies (Becvar, 2001). Clients may find themselves bereft not only as a function of the loss of a loved one but also because their former belief systems may no longer be adequate. They thus may find themselves exploring spiritual realms far outside the mainstream and what they often seek is validation for such explorations. Therapists who operate from more traditional or just different perspectives must avoid making judgments or telling clients how they should think or what they should believe. Therapists may do well to acknowledge their different beliefs even as they support clients in their spiritual search and work together to achieve some resolution for the grief.

Additional concerns relate to the need to prevent the therapist's personal issues about spirituality from intruding on the therapeutic process. Indeed, education and training in this area, as described previously, may enable therapists to remain sensitive to the influence and importance of the client's spiritual values, while also avoiding the potential to get "hooked" inappropriately by these. With proper training, marriage and family therapists may acquire a perspective that is broad enough to accommodate a wide range of spiritual beliefs (Prest & Keller, 1993), thus fostering an ability to work with clients who represent a variety of spiritual orientations.

A final consideration deals with the possibility that a marriage and family therapist also may be an ordained clergy person. In some cases, the therapist and client may be members of the same denomination or the same church. In either case, while therapy is not precluded (Ryder & Hepworth, 1990), care must be taken to avoid the potential for danger inherent in multiple relationships (Frame, 2000). As stated in the AAMFT ethics code,

Subprinciple 1.3: Marriage and family therapists are aware of their influential positions with respect to clients, and they avoid exploiting the trust and dependency of such persons. Therapists, therefore, make every effort to avoid conditions and multiple relationships with clients that could impair professional judgment or increase the risk of exploitation. Such relationships include, but are not limited to, business or close personal relationships with a client or the client's immediate family. When the risk of impairment or exploitation exists due to conditions or multiple roles, therapists take appropriate precautions.

This subprinciple creates a strong mandate for careful and constant scrutiny and monitoring of one's values and needs. In order to achieve such a stance, help may be needed from another source, such as a colleague or supervisor.

For members of the clergy who are also marriage and family therapists, the issue of professional influence is compounded. A client may hold the therapist/clergy person in high esteem because of his or her membership in the same church or denomination, thus potentially expanding the therapist's power and influence. For example, clients may be reluctant to disclose their true feelings or reveal certain behaviors. Also, they may be unwilling even to express differences of opinion let alone disagree with the therapist. For therapists and clients who are both lay members of the same church, similar issues and concerns may be worthy of recognition and consideration if the clients' best interests are to be served. The following fictional vignette describes a situation in which the therapist failed to handle appropriately the issue of spirituality in therapy.

Sue is a deeply religious woman who is very involved in her church and has derived great comfort and support from her spiritual tradition. While she has been a marriage and family therapist for many years, until very recently she has studiously avoided any mention of religious or spiritual issues in the context of therapy. However, because professional seminars and literature have recently begun to recognize the importance of a spiritual dimension in the lives of many people, she now feels she has permission to discuss this once-taboo subject with her clients. She has found it very meaningful to be able to pray with and for her clients, which she now does at the beginning and end of every session.

While many people come to her because they are aware of her attention to spirituality, Sue sometimes focuses on this realm to the exclusion of other issues that are also important or have a bearing on what is going on with her clients. What is more, in her enthusiasm for prayer time, she may cut short discussions deemed important by her clients, who go away feeling frustrated and dissatisfied with the session. Sue is thus treading on ethical thin ice to the extent that she follows her own agenda rather than that of her clients. She also risks imposing her values as she sometimes encourages clients to attribute to spirituality the same importance it has for her.

Therapy that acknowledges and includes spirituality requires skills and sensitivity in several areas. The initial assessment might include questions regarding the role of religion and/or spirituality in the lives of clients. An awareness of the degree to which this may or may not be an important dimension can suggest whether clients wish to address this issue or whether it is relevant to their specific issues and goals. When deemed appropriate and for the benefit of the client, the therapist may also share personal religious or spiritual beliefs or experiences that have been helpful in her or his life.

To include, in an ethical manner, client's spiritual issues within the context of therapy, therapists must ensure that they have adequate education and training to handle issues in this realm. They must also be able either to work with differing value systems and related beliefs and behaviors, or to make appropriate referrals. And they must also recognize the degree to which their own spiritual values may pervade and influence the therapeutic enterprise. Of particular relevance in this regard is the influence of spirituality on issues related to sexuality in therapy.

SEXUALITY

Sexuality in this discussion is inclusive both of the gender of marriage and family therapists, clients, students, and supervisees and of the expression or exercise of sexual functions on the part of therapists and those with whom they interact in a professional context. Accordingly, therapists once again find themselves considering a dimension that is all pervasive inasmuch as each person has a gender and is a sexual being. Sexuality is inevitably an implicit element in therapy and its presence must be considered and dealt with in an ethical manner. Sexuality is also often an explicit dimension requiring appropriate attention and handling.

With regard to sexuality, it is important to recognize first that the same constraints and guidelines noted above apply as well to sexual orientation. That is, therapists may not discriminate against or fail to provide appropriate services, they must seek supervision in the case of conflicts between personal and professional values, and they may need to make referrals when necessary on the basis of religious issues (Subprinciples 1.1, 1.10, and 1.11 of the AAMFT ethics code). Second, it is important to be aware that this is one of the areas in which spiritual influences may also come into play. For example, homosexuality is considered to be sinful behavior in some religious traditions. Therefore, a therapist who subscribes exclusively to the tenets of this type of religious tradition and applies them to clients is unlikely to be able to work effectively with homosexual clients. Nevertheless, an ethical responsibility is to first seek supervision, and should this not resolve the issues, then to help clients who are homosexual make arrangements for the continuation of therapy elsewhere. Should a client be struggling to come to terms with his or her sexual identity, the therapist is precluded from influencing the outcome of such struggles in one direction or another (Subprinciple 1.8), since decisions about relationships belong to the client. Further, therapists must also be aware of the potential for undue subtle influence relative to such decisions (Subprinciples 1.3 and 3.13).

Values and beliefs about the appropriate roles of men and women in families also may derive from one's spiritual belief system. In some religious traditions men may be considered the head of the household, or even may hold the status of a priest, whereas women may be relegated to a secondary or sometimes subservient role. Although this issue may not arise when the clients and therapist are members of the same religious or spiritual tradition, different values on this matter have the potential for value conflict and inappropriate imposition of values.

Regardless of spiritual orientation, therapists must be sensitive to many other subtle and not so subtle factors relative to the role of sexuality in clients' lives. Indeed, it has been noted, "Family therapists deal constantly with sex in one form or another" (Woody, 1983, p. 154). For example, clients often describe relationship difficulties or dysfunction in the sexual arena as presenting problems. When this is the case, once again therapists must be sure that they are operating within the limits of their competence before proceeding (Subprinciples 3.1, 3.7, 3.11, 4.4, and 8.8). Do they have a broad-based knowledge of the range of normal sexuality and of sexual disorders and dysfunctions? And have they developed the clinical skills for intervening effectively with clients' specific sexual concerns? In addition, therapists must also be sensitive to the need for referral or consultation with physicians as appropriate, because many sexual problems involve medical and illness factors.

Ethical issues regarding sexuality and intimacy may also arise as a function of the therapist's gender or values about gender. For example, a female therapist who espouses a feminist perspective may seek to facilitate a balance between male and female marriage partners as part of a commitment to focus on and attempt to ameliorate the gender-based power differentials inherent in our society. Conversely, a male therapist who operates in a manner consistent with the traditional values of our society may, either covertly or overtly, work to prevent a wife from gaining greater independence and power in her relationship with her husband. Depending upon the belief systems of the clients, such therapists risk value imposition when pursuing either course (Subprinciples 1.3 and 1.8).

Another area of potential risk that requires ethical sensitivity is the manner in which therapists explore the client's sexual issues, and especially the issue of sexual abuse or assault. If the therapist acts inappropriately, he or she may violate the standard of care prevailing in the profession. Standard of care refers to the generally accepted norms for appropriate therapist behaviors:

That is, if a client has special vulnerabilities, be they psychological or physical, and the family therapist knows or should have known about them, a failure to properly accommodate these unique needs can result in a breach of the standard of care. For example, leading the client into an affective exploration of a highly charged sexual area, say incest, knowing (or supposedly knowing) that the client has weak ego controls and has the potential of suffering emotional devastation, and then not handling the evoked affect to the benefit of the client, could result in the family therapist's failing to meet the standard of care. (Woody, 1983, pp. 160-161)

Violation of such standards of care may be cause for discipline in ethical or licensing complaint proceedings, or an adverse judgment in a civil action, or even a criminal conviction.

Inappropriate explorations of sexuality may also result in marriage and family therapists' finding themselves immersed in the quagmire known as the repressed memory syndrome (Knapp & VandeCreek, 1997). Accordingly, legal charges may be brought against professionals in response to memories recovered in therapy and subsequent allegations of sexual abuse by clients against family members. Therapists are advised to tread very lightly and carefully when entering this arena.

The issue of sexuality in marriage and family therapy also has several other dimensions that may or may not overlap with spirituality. For example, nowhere is the AAMFT ethics code more explicit than in its prohibition of sexual intimacy between marriage and family therapists and clients, supervisees, and students, or in its delineation of appropriate behavior with former clients, supervisees and students. The following four subprinciples speak specifically to such behaviors in a variety of contexts.

Subprinciple 1.4: Sexual intimacy with clients is prohibited.

Subprinciple 1.5: Sexual intimacy with former clients is likely to be harmful and is therefore prohibited for two years following the termination of therapy or last professional contact. In an effort to avoid exploiting the trust and dependency of clients, marriage and family therapists should not engage in sexual intimacy with former clients after the two years following termination or last professional contact. Should therapists engage in sexual intimacy with former clients following two years after termination or last professional contact, the burden shifts to the therapist to demonstrate that there has been no exploitation or injury to the former client or to the client's immediate family.

Subprinciple 4.3: Marriage and family therapists do not engage in sexual intimacy with students or supervisees during the evaluative or training relationship between the therapist and student or supervisee. Should a supervisor engage in sexual activity with a former supervisee, the burden of proof shifts to the supervisor to demonstrate that there has been no exploitation or injury to the supervisee.

Subprinciple 4.6: Marriage and family therapists avoid accepting as supervisees or students those individuals with whom a prior or existing relationship could compromise the therapist's objectivity. When such situations cannot be avoided, therapists take appropriate precautions to maintain objectivity. Examples of such relationships include, but are not limited to, those individuals with whom the therapist has a current or prior sexual, close personal, immediate familial, or therapeutic relationship.

The prudent marriage and family therapist accepts that romantic and sexual intimacies should not occur, regardless of circumstances, with clients, students, or supervisees. There also seems to be a current trend for this proscription to apply to the close family members and associates of clients, students, and supervisees.

Strean (1993) has noted, "Ever since the formal inception of psychotherapy as a profession, psychotherapists have had major difficulties in monitoring their sexual wishes toward patients" (p. 1). Indeed, sexual exploitation of a client represents one of the most common violations of codes of ethics, regardless of therapeutic orientation or professional affiliation. Nevertheless, the harmful impact on clients of sexual intimacy with therapists has been well documented (Bates & Brodsky, 1989; Rutter, 1989). Clearly, therapists should seek supervision immediately if they are at any kind of risk for violation of ethical behavior in this area.

Finally, therapists are also constrained from behaviors that would make them liable to charges of sexual harassment. According to the Subprinciple 3.8 of the AAMFT ethics code, "Marriage and family therapists do not engage in sexual or other forms of harassment of clients, students, trainees, supervisees, employees, colleagues, or research subjects."

Sexual harassment, a type of sex discrimination, has been defined and explained by the U.S. Equal Employment Opportunity Commission (1997) as follows:

> *Unwelcome sexual advances, requests for sexual favors, and other verbal or physical conduct of a sexual nature constitutes sexual harassment when submission to or rejection of this conduct explicitly or implicitly affects an individual's employment, unreasonably interferes with an individual's work performance or creates an intimidating, hostile or offensive work environment. (p. 1)*

Further considerations include the fact that both men and women can perpetrate sexual harassment. It can occur between members of the same sex. It may also be that the victim has not been directly harassed but has been affected by conduct directed at another but considered to be offensive by the victim.

Several important issues may be inferred from such delineation. For example, therapists are prohibited from making inappropriate sexual remarks, or innuendoes of a sexual nature, to clients, students, or supervisees. Jokes with a sexual bias or orientation would thus be considered unacceptable. Even if such remarks or jokes were acceptable to those to whom they were directed, if overheard by another client, student, or supervisee who considered them offensive, sexual harassment charges might be valid. Sexual advances or the request for sexual favors of any kind would also constitute clear violations of the ethics code. To conclude this section, the following fictional situation is offered as an illustration of ethical issues relative to sexuality.

Marilyn is a marriage and family therapist in private practice, who, as an adjunct instructor, also teaches a course that is part of the practicum experience in marriage and family therapy at a university in her area. Her qualifications are excellent, and trainees, aware of her reputation as a marriage and family therapist, are excited to be able to take this course from her. In addition to a vast store of knowledge and a wealth of information, she has lots of personal stories to share and a great sense of humor. She also, however, has some biases that become more and more noticeable with time and ultimately influence the experience for most, if not all, of her students.

Part of her personal history is relevant. At one time Marilyn desired to become a nun; but for reasons that are unclear, she was not permitted to take her final vows and eventually left the convent. As a function of this difficult period in her life, Marilyn has very negative views about women in general and those in religious life in particular. Although many of her students find her stories about life in the convent funny, those with a religious vocation are frequently offended. In addition, her female students often learn that they are not as privileged as are their male counterparts, and they receive much less attention and generally lower grades.

The fact that Marilyn is in a position of power is intimidating for her students. Worried that formal complaints about her might hurt their grades, the students often choose to suffer in silence or at least in private. They also worry about having sufficient proof to support a charge against Marilyn.

Therapists must be sensitive to ethical dilemmas and violations, no matter what the context and regardless of their subtlety. Given the fact that all human beings have biases, beliefs, and feelings that may connect to their gender and sexuality, therapists must exercise extreme caution in the realm of sexuality. Further, the ethical practitioner will recognize that the sexual dimension of life is always part of the therapeutic process as are moral values and spirituality.

CONCLUSION: FINAL THOUGHTS

As has been discussed, to enter the realm of marriage and family therapy is to be engaged in an enterprise that inevitably includes moral values, spirituality, and sexuality. Unlike many of the other topics discussed in this book, there is no time when these dimensions, whether separately or as they interface in some way, are not present in marriage and family therapy. Like an intricate tapestry, the stories of marriage and family therapists and those of their clients, students, and supervisees are always interwoven with threads emanating from all three of the domains considered in this chapter—moral values, spirituality, and sexuality. And the colors of these threads take on different shades and hues by virtue of those that are chosen for inclusion or rejection in these co-created stories, the way in which they overlap, and/or their proximity to one another.

It is not surprising that several of the principles and many of the subprinciples of the AAMFT ethics code have relevance to moral values, spirituality, and sexuality. In fact, the ethics code as a whole represents a statement about the moral values considered acceptable by and for the members of the profession of marriage and family therapy.

Conversely, therapy may be understood as a process based on moral values, those that a society and the professional representatives of that society choose as worthy of promoting and attaining.

Regardless of context, therapists and their referral and other collateral sources convey their personal values. The personal values of all participants are both derived from and consistent with their belief systems, which are strongly influenced by their spiritual orientation. Such a spiritual orientation, defined as a way of being and behaving in the world, may involve either the acceptance or rejection of a specific religious tradition. It may be addressed explicitly or remain implicit. Nevertheless, it is part and parcel of each individual's unique self and is always present.

Each person brings with him or her both a gender identity and a sexual orientation. Each person's experience has been and always will be influenced as a function of her or his sexuality. Any interaction between two people is influenced by their sexuality. There are norms of behavior and role expectations that are different for men and women. In our society, there is differential treatment by gender; and the world is perceived differently as a function of the gender lens through which one is looking. In each society there are socially sanctioned values relative to sexual orientation. Finally, given the nature of therapy, it is highly likely that sexual issues will arise from time to time, and often may become the focus of assessment, conversations, and interventions.

Accordingly, to adhere to the letter and spirit of the AAMFT ethics code, therapists need a high degree of awareness relative to the interlocking values that relate to morality, spirituality, and sexuality. When questions or concerns arise, therapists are advised to seek out and consult with someone who is qualified to act as a supervisor. Supervisors engaged in the training of therapists are also encouraged to highlight constantly both ethics in general and ethical issues relative to moral values, spirituality, and sexuality. To illustrate these final thoughts, as well as to conclude this chapter, the following fictional scenario is presented.

Mark is an AAMFT Approved Supervisor who works part-time in a post-degree training institute. The institute is respected for its preparation of highly competent marriage and family therapists, many of who go on to succeed in a variety of contexts. Mark often has responsibility for supervision and he is well known for being both rigorous and fair in his dealings with students, other faculty members, and clients. Indeed, his approach has a great deal to do with the success of the training program.

Participants both in Mark's supervision groups and in individual supervision are expected to come prepared to present and discuss their cases. They must bring videotape of a therapy session that has been reviewed and with areas of discussion ready to be highlighted. If readings have been assigned, the expectation is that they will have been read. Supervisees know that a discussion of ethical issues and implications will always be part of the process. In addition to providing basic information about the client system, developmental considerations, identified problems, desired solutions, and attempted interventions, supervisees are required to respond to the following considerations relative to each case presented:

A. Describe the impact of your field of practice and setting.

B. Describe the impact of time.

C. Describe the impact of practice modality/approach selected.

D. Describe the impact of therapist/client characteristics relative to class, ethnicity, gender, age, sexual orientation, physical challenges.

E. Describe the impact of value and ethical issues.

F. Provide a brief summary/story about case as a whole. (Becvar & Becvar, 2000b, p. 97)

Supervision necessitates the collection of a considerable amount of information, the ability to describe and analyze, and a willingness to learn and make adaptations in professional functioning. Therapists and supervisors, such as Mark, are effective because of their integrity and because they attend to ethics as an ongoing part of the therapy, training, and supervision processes. They are aware that they must not only have familiarity with the ethics code and be able to talk about ethics, but they must also be ethical in all of their dealings. They recognize the influence of all contextual dimensions. Finally, they are particularly sensitive to issues related to moral values, spirituality, and sexuality.

REFERENCES

Anderson, H. (1997). Conversation, language and possibilities: A postmodern approach to therapy. New York: Basic Books.

Aponte, H. J. (1994). Bread and spirit: Therapy with the new poor. New York: Norton.

Bates, C., & Brodsky, A. (1989). Sex in the therapy hour: A case of professional incest. New York: Guilford.

Becvar, D. S. (1983). The relationship between the family and the society in the context of American ideology: A systems theoretical perspective. St. Louis University, St. Louis, MO. (Unpublished Doctoral Dissertation).

Becvar, D. S. (1997a). Soul healing: A spiritual orientation in counseling and therapy. New York: Basic Books.

Becvar, D. S. (Ed.). (1997b). The family, spirituality and social work. New York: Haworth.

Becvar, D. S. (2001). In the presence of grief: Helping family members resolve death, dying and bereavement issues. NY: Guilford.

Becvar, D. S., & Becvar, R. J. (2000a). Family therapy: A systemic integration (4th ed.). Boston: Allyn & Bacon.

Becvar, D. S., & Becvar, R. J. (2000b). Instructor's manual for family therapy: A systemic integration (4th ed.). Boston: Allyn & Bacon.

Benningfield, M. (1997). Addressing spiritual/religious issues in therapy: Potential problems and complication. In D. S. Becvar (Ed.), The family, spirituality and social work (pp. 25–42). New York: Haworth.

Bowen, M. (1978). Family therapy in clinical practice. New York: Jason Aronson.

Bowman, E. S. (1989). Understanding and responding to religious material in the therapy of multiple personality disorder. Dissociation, 2 (4), 231–238.

Bronowski, J. (1978). The origins of knowledge and imagination. New Haven, CT: Yale University Press.

Chazan, B. I., & Soltis, J. F. (Eds.). (1973). Moral education. New York: Teachers College Press.

Dell, P. F. (1983). From pathology to ethics. Family Therapy Networker, 1 (6), 29–64.

Doherty, W. F. (1995). Soul searching: Why psychotherapy must promote moral responsibility. New York: Basic Books.

Edelwich, J., & Brodsky, A. (1991). Sexual dilemmas for the helping professional. New York: Brunner/Mazel.

Efran, J. A., Lukens, R. J., & Lukens, M. D. (1988). Constructivism: What's in it for you? Family Therapy Networker, 12 (5), 27–35.

Elkins, D. (1990, June). On being spiritual without necessarily being religious. Association for Humanistic Psychology Perspective, 4–5.

Frame, M. W. (2000). Spiritual and religious issues in counseling: Ethical considerations. Family Journal: Counseling & Therapy for Couples and Families, 81 (1), 72–74.

Friedman, E. (1991). Bowen theory and therapy. In A. Gurman & D. Kniskern (Eds.), The handbook of family therapy (pp. 134–170). New York: Brunner/Mazel.

Gergen, K. I. (1985). Social constructivist movement in psychology. American Psychologist, 40, 266–275.

Gergen, K. I. (1991.) The saturated self. New York: Basic Books.

Guggenbuhl-Craig, A. (1999). Power in the helping professions. Myron Grubitz, trans. Woodstock, CT: Spring Publications.

Haug. I. (1998). Including a spiritual dimension in family therapy: Ethical considerations. Contemporary Family Therapy, 20 (2), 181–194.

Knapp, S. J., & VandeCreek, L. (1997). Treating patients with memories of abuse: Legal risk management. Washington, DC: American Psychological Association.

Longino, H. (1990). Science as social knowledge. Princeton, NJ: Princeton University Press.

Prest, L., & Keller, J. (1993). Spirituality and family therapy: Spirituality, myths and metaphors. Journal of Marital and Family Therapy, 19, 137–148.

Rutter, P. (1989). Sex in the forbidden zone. New York: Fawcett Crest.

Ryder, R., & Hepworth, J. (1990). AAMFT ethical code: "Dual relationships." Journal of Marital and Family Therapy, 16 (2), 127–132.

Strean, H. S. (1993). Therapists who have sex with their patients: Treatment and recovery. New York: Brunner/Mazel.

U.S. Equal Employment Opportunity Commission. (1997). Facts about sexual harassment. Internet: http://www.eeoc.gov/facts/fs-sex.html.

White, M., & Epston, D. (1990). <u>Narrative means to therapeutic ends</u>. New York: Norton.

Woody, R. H. (1983). Ethical and legal aspects of sexual issues. In J. D. Woody & R. H. Woody (Eds.), <u>Sexual issues in family therapy</u> (pp. 153–167). Rockville, MD: Aspen Systems.

PRACTICE MANAGEMENT: INTEGRATING ETHICS INTO BUSINESS

9

O. Brandt Caudill

This chapter explains that ethical principles and obligations must not remain merely at the theoretical or clinical level. Instead, ethics interface with the day-to-day conduct of the practice of therapy and must be integrated into the operations and procedures of the therapy practice. This chapter, in demonstrating how to accomplish this, serves as a review of many ethical principles covered throughout this book. Incorporating relevant legal issues as well, the discussion offers practical guidelines to assure that ethical principles are put into practice and that practitioners manage the risks associated with providing mental health services. When ethical issues become part of routine business and clinical procedures, therapists are more likely to fulfill major ethical responsibilities, such as those relating to informed consent, confidentiality, protecting clients from exploitation and multiple relationships, record keeping, risks of technology, contracts with employees and other professionals, and overall financial management of the practice. Having ethically sound business procedures and operations can reduce ethical dilemmas and complaints.

CONTENTS

While the practice of therapy has often been seen as more of an art than a science, it has also not been treated as a business, when it should have been. Some ethical and legal problems often arise because many therapists do not thoughtfully integrate their professional responsibilities into the business aspects of a professional practice.

It is easy to offer theoretical analyses about ethics and guidelines as if each decision resides solely with the individual practitioner. Nothing could be further from the truth. The ethical obligations of therapists are numerous; these are best met when they are integrated into the routine business operations of the practice. To make this point clear and to offer practical guidelines for practice management, this chapter covers the following major topics that carry both business and ethical implications: business operation issues; personnel issues; liability insurance; technology issues; advertising issues; subpoenas and confidentiality; contracts with clients; informed consent; note taking and records; and financial issues.

Therapists need to be aware of these issues. They directly bear on ethical complaints, employment litigation, malpractice litigation, and other problems due to poor practice management that can impact on the professionals in charge of the practice, its employees, its clients, and its financial stability and continuing existence. The goal here is to offer concrete advice to enable therapists to avoid potential ethical and legal dilemmas by taking a proactive stance in the management of their practices.

BUSINESS OPERATION ISSUES

A first issue to consider is whether the practice is actually being conducted in a businesslike manner. Historically, many psychotherapists, including marriage and family therapists, have been reluctant to treat the practice of psychotherapy as a business and to take steps to operate in a businesslike and legal fashion. In practices involving more than one practitioner, a first issue is to determine the precise relationship between the business associates.

PARTNERSHIP AND PROFESSIONAL STATUS ISSUES

While the most common form of practice is the sole proprietorship, it is not that uncommon to have unincorporated associations of therapists or to have partnerships. In many jurisdictions, if the operating situation is sufficiently ambiguous, a court may elect to treat several therapists as partners, even though they do not consider themselves as such. The key risk here is that partners are vicariously liable for each other's acts. This means that if one partner engages in an unethical or negligent act, all of the other partners can be just as liable as if they had done the act themselves, assuming it to be an act within the course and scope of the partnership business. For example, if a client receives negligent care leading to suicide and the dead client's family files a lawsuit, all of the partners may be equally liable if the business is a partnership.

A court may find that a partnership exists for the purpose of litigation, even where none was intended, if the actual ownership of the business is so ambiguous or uncertain that the public may have a reasonable basis for believing that independent practitioners are actually partners. This type of ambiguity relates to the AAMFT ethics code, which states that marriage and family therapists are to avoid using professional names that could mislead the public (Subprinciple 8.3). In addition, the use of misleading professional names may lead a court to treat the group as a de facto partnership.

If the clients, upon arriving at the office, see the names of the various therapists but do not see anything identifying them as independent practitioners, they may erroneously assume that the practitioners are partners. Thus it is important for a therapist in a multiple-professional practice to have the precise relationships clearly spelled out so that the client sees this upon entering the waiting room. Frequently, therapists share office space and share costs, but have no arrangement for profit sharing, which is the standard determiner of whether a partnership exists. In such instances it may be helpful to have language in client contracts and in the waiting room noting that the practitioners are all independent, or that the office is an association of independent practitioners, or some similar language that gives public notice that there is no partnership in operation. Joint advertising under a center name of independent practitioners also poses some risk of creating misperceptions on the part of the public.

There are several areas that often give rise to ethical or legal disputes. The first is using interns who are not properly identified as such or creating circumstances in which the intern may be misperceived as a licensed person. The second circumstance is that in which a licensed therapist wants to leave the practice and take clients with him or her. Generally, therapists would be well advised to have contracts with all professional employees stating the terms of employment, the grounds for which termination could occur, and what happens in the event of termination.

If the therapist is an intern, in the eyes of the law, the patient is legally the client of the supervisor of the intern. Under Subprinciple 8.7 of the AAMFT ethics code (and most licensing laws), the supervisor will have an obligation to take steps to ensure that the intern does not misrepresent his or her status and to assess that the intern is an appropriate person for the client to see. A necessary protection for a therapist who employs interns or other licensed therapists is the use of a written contract. Unfortunately, it appears that many therapists do not use written contracts with professional employees. One reason that such a contract is important is that it is a vehicle for identifying areas that are outside the scope of the employee's function and, consequently, acts for which the therapist as employer should not be legally responsible. This can become particularly important when a therapist's intern or employee-therapist is sued, such as for acts of sexual misconduct and/or engaging in multiple relationships.

Vicarious Liability

Vicarious liability refers to the liability that one has for the professional behavior of business partners, employees, staff, and interns. This concept means that the therapist must pay close attention to how these business relationships are defined, entered into, and monitored, since the ethical and legal implications can be serious. Consider the example regarding sexual intimacy with a client.

The AAMFT ethics code prohibits sexual intimacy with clients (Subprinciple 1.4). As discussed more fully below, the case law is divided on the extent to which an employer can be vicariously liable for acts of sexual misconduct by an employee therapist. The jurisdictions that allow such claims to be asserted against the employer also generally look to three issues regarding the employer's potential liability: (1) what the employee's duties were, (2) whether the employee's acts violated any policy of the employer, and (3) whether the employer had any actual knowledge of the employee's potential propensity to engage in such acts. The following discussion explains these issues and offer guidelines for the therapist-employer.

The first issue can be taken care of by having in place a written contract that identifies the employer's policy and the scope of the employee's duties.

The second issue points to another theory on which a therapist may be sued for, say, sexual misconduct by professional employees; namely, the employee was either negligently hired, negligently trained, or negligently retained.

These three aspects of negligence on the part of the employer, although sounding similar, are quite different. The theory that an employee was negligently hired centers on the adequacy of the investigation conducted by the employer of a potential employee. The theory of negligent training indicates that the employee was not properly instructed or given the skills necessary to carry out the job and/or to understand what conduct was acceptable on the job. The theory of negligent retention goes to a situation where the employer has some actual or constructive knowledge that the employee has a propensity to engage in acts of the type currently accused of engaging in.

LIABILITY RELATED TO HIRING EMPLOYEES

The issue of negligent hiring is one that can generally be dealt with only at the inception of the relationship—by doing at least a minimal investigation of the employee's background and qualifications for the position. A therapist seeking to hire an intern or a licensed therapist should explore a series of questions. It would be better to have questions in written form with the answers filled out by the job applicant, so that if the applicant misleads the employer or makes false statements, the record is clear as to the employer's having been misled. Some typical questions to ask of a potential intern or employee are the following:

(1) Where did you obtain your professional degree?

(2) Are there any professors whom you have had that you believe would be good source of professional and personal information about you? May I contact them?

(3) Did you have any specific training in [insert the specific theoretical orientation of the supervising therapists].

(4) What are your professional interests?

(5) Have you ever been a party in any litigation? What type? What was the result?

(6) Have you had any prior supervisors? When? How would you describe that relationship and its termination?

(7) Have you read the AAMFT ethics code?

(8) Will you agree to abide by the AAMFT ethics code in the services you provide to our clients?

(9) Have you ever been convicted of a crime? (Note, it is improper to ask if an applicant has been "arrested," but not "convicted.")

(10) What are your current professional and personal goals?

(11) What do you believe makes you a good candidate for this position?

(12) What do you think your former supervisor would say are your strengths and weaknesses?

(13) What would you say are your strengths and weaknesses as a therapist?

(14) Are there any types of patients or disorders with whom you would be uncomfortable working?

(15) To your knowledge, have you had any licensing board complaints?

(16) Can you describe for me, without revealing confidential information, the most difficult clinical situation you have faced as a therapist?

This list does not exhaust the types of questions to ask.

Therapists should be conscious that, as potential employers, certain areas of inquiry are foreclosed by state or federal law, particularly areas that could lead to a charge of some type of discrimination. For example, it would be impermissible to question a female job applicant about whether she plans on having children or whether she is pregnant. Similarly, inquiring into the religious beliefs of a potential employee could be seen as potentially discriminatory. For a good discussion on what not to ask applicants, see Riemersma (1992). If the person is either licensed or registered with a state licensing agency, it is important to contact that agency for publicly available information about the applicant.

In addition to obtaining the written job application, the therapist should, as part of the application process, require a résumé, a transcript of graduate education and undergraduate education (if possible), a copy of any current registration as an intern, and one or two references to check. It is not uncommon for therapists and other employers to hire people quickly to meet job needs, and then to face difficulties that a proper but minimal investigation could have revealed. In a survey of AAMFT clinical members, Brock and Coufal (1998) found that 31.6% of the respondents indicated that they never, rarely, or only sometimes verified résumés of their employees. Failure to conduct a thorough investigation of potential interns or employees is legally risky and a poor business practice.

Because of fear of litigation, many former employers will no longer discuss a job applicant's performance on prior jobs, especially if the performance was poor. In fact, some labor law firms recommend that, when a potential employer contacts the former employer of a job applicant, the only thing the former employer should provide is verification that the applicant did work there and the dates of employment.

The preceding viewpoint recognizes that disgruntled job applicants have sued former employers for giving negative references. In addition, some courts have held that, if a former employer seeks to give a reference for a job applicant, the former employer must provide an accurate picture and cannot provide only positive information to the prospective new employer.

An example of the endorser being potentially liable for not revealing both the positives and the negatives occurred in California where a school vice-principal had been accused of sexual improprieties with a student and applied for a job in a different school district. The applicant's former employer gave the prospective employer a detailed positive recommendation and made no mention of the alleged misconduct with students. The vice-principal was hired by the new school district and then was accused of engaging in similar sexual misconduct at the new place of employment.

The California Supreme Court held that the former employer could be sued, as well as the teacher, for failing to fully disclose information that would have guided the new school district on whether or not to hire him as vice-principal. This rule could be stated succinctly as, "If you're going to say anything about a job applicant, you have to speak accurately and fully" (Randi W. v. Muroc Joint Unified School District, 1997). Some jurisdictions have refused to recognize a cause of action for negligent referral, such as Illinois (Neptuno Treuhand Und Verwal Tungesellschaft, MBH. v. Arbor, 1998). Obviously these issues apply to therapists who are asked about former employees, as well as to therapists seeking to employ people.

LIABILITY RELATED TO TRAINING EMPLOYEES

Once a professional employee has been hired, then the question concerns the training provided, both as to technical competency and as to ethical guidelines. In this regard, it is important to have a contract that spells out the following as terms of employment:

(1) The employee-therapist understands that sexual misconduct is unacceptable and is grounds for immediate termination.

(2) The employee-therapist is precluded from providing services to clients off the employer's premises (to avoid compromising situations) without the employer's advance written consent.

(3) Business dealings and socialization with present or former clients are prohibited and grounds for immediate termination.

(4) The employee-therapist has read, understands, and will comply with the AAMFT ethics code (a copy should be provided to the employee at the time the contract is signed); this can be a condition even if the employee is not an AAMFT member.

(5) Interns are required to have every client pay all fees directly to the supervisor, and no cash should be given to the intern directly, nor should checks be made out in the intern's name (to avoid possible misrepresentation).

(6) The intern or therapist-employee will take session notes sufficient to allow the supervisor to track the course of therapy if he or she reviews the file.

(7) The therapist-employee will advise the employer within five business days of the receipt of any ethics complaint, licensing board complaint, civil suit, or threat to sue.

(8) For independently licensed professional-employees, the employer can require their maintaining malpractice insurance in certain dollar amounts, which should be reflected in the employment contracts.

(9) The employment contract should state that it is the entirety of the agreement, that no changes can be made without the written consent of both sides, and that all prior negotiations have been merged into the contract (this prevents the employee from alleging that the terms of employment were actually different than the written contract).

(10) The agreement should also specify with clarity the employee's rate of compensation, and the facilities and services that will be provided by the employer.

LIABILITY RELATED TO RETENTION OF EMPLOYEES

Once the professional employees have been hired, put under contract, and trained, an issue is whether their actions create any notice to the employer of any propensity to act in an unethical manner. For example, if a client complains that a professional employee used sexually inappropriate language, then the therapist-employer has an obligation to investigate the claim and determine whether some disciplinary action is appropriate.

The failure to make such an investigation would be grounds for a claim of negligent retention. Generally, the type of investigation conducted when a complaint of some impropriety occurs involves the employer's discussing the matter directly with the complaining client, then talking to the accused employee, and determining whether some type of discipline is appropriate. This assumes, of course, that no lawsuit has been filed and that the client continues to receive treatment at the employer's facility. In some instances the situation may be a simple misunderstanding or distortion, which can be cured by an apology or a meeting to clear the air. In more serious situations (e.g., alleged sexual misconduct or improper multiple relationships), the employer has other decisions to make. These include whether to direct that the employee have no contact with the client; whether the employee may meet with the client only with third persons present; or whether to direct that the therapy be terminated or provided by another therapist.

Another way of avoiding a claim of negligent retention is for the therapist-employer to have clear records of what supervision was provided to interns and employees, and what specific guidance was given with regard to the handling of particular clients. For example, in the eyes of the law, the clients of the intern are the clients of the supervisor. It is, therefore, not correct for a supervisor to believe that he or she cannot talk directly with a client because the client is the intern's patient. By definition, if the intern cannot independently see the client without supervision (e.g., because of licensure restrictions), then the supervisor can talk to the client without the consent of the supervisee. Depending on the jurisdiction, an employer of an independently licensed employee may or may not be able to talk directly to the client served by the latter.

Because issues of sexual misconduct might arise, which may prove to be true or false, the employer should be aware of what is legally required by the particular jurisdiction. This is important information to know under any circumstance, but if a client alleges sexual misconduct by an employee or intern, knowledge of the law becomes essential.

Therapists are required to comply with applicable laws that require reporting alleged unethical conduct (Subprinciple 1.6), and this would apply to their professional employees. A California statute provides that all marriage and family therapists and other therapists are required to have in their offices a booklet, prepared by the state, that explains that sexual intimacy is a violation of law and is unethical (California Business and Professions Code §728). When a client reports to a therapist that he or she has been the subject of sexual misconduct, the therapist is required to provide the client with the brochure, but the therapist cannot report the matter to licensing boards or other authorities without the client's consent.

DIFFERENTIATING BETWEEN EMPLOYEES AND INDEPENDENT CONTRACTORS

A common issue in litigation is whether a person accused of negligence or misconduct was an employee, for whose acts the employer may be liable, or an independent contractor. The U.S. District Court discussed the issue of independent contractor status under Connecticut law in Garamella v. New York Medical College (1988). That case involved a suit by a man claiming that as a boy he had been sexually molested by a psychiatric resident at New York Medical College, and that the college and the psychiatrist (with whom the alleged abuser underwent personal analysis as a requirement of training) were liable. The hospital's defense, in part, was that the psychiatrist who was conducting the personal analysis of the alleged molester was an independent contractor.

The court noted that, under Connecticut law (1) an independent contractor is one who contracts to do a piece of work according to his or her own method and without being subject to the control of the employer except as to the result of the work; and (2) that a fundamental distinction exists between an employee and an independent contractor regarding the right to control the means and method of the work (supra, at 23 F.2d 162). The court reviewed the relationship between the psychiatrist who provided personal analysis and the college. The court concluded that the psychiatrist was not an independent contractor based on the requirement that he report back to the college about how the resident was progressing in personal psychoanalysis, and whether he was a good candidate to be certified as a psychoanalyst.

A Wisconsin court used the requirement of supervision to hold that therapists working in a clinic were employees for the purposes of unemployment fund contributions (Goldberg v. Department of Industry Labor and Human Relations, 1992).

As a general rule, it would be inappropriate to call an employee an independent contractor if the employee is required by law or licensing board regulation to be supervised. The designation of independent contractor is intended to apply to an individual who is retained to provide a service in which the manner and method of providing the contracted services are up to the independent contractor. A therapist can employ another licensed person as an independent contractor, but not anyone to whom a statutory duty of supervision applies.

Therapists should also be aware that the Internal Revenue Service (IRS), for tax purposes, may question the extent to which an intern can be categorized as an independent contractor. The IRS view on how to determine whether a person is an employee or an independent contractor can be found in IRS Publication 15-A "Employers Supplemental Tax Guide" page 5 (January 2001). That publication indicates that where no statute applies, the IRS looks to a common law test that has three primary questions:

(1) Who has behavioral control?

(2) Who has financial control?

(3) What is the nature of relationship between the parties?

Behavioral control is defined as the right to direct or control how a person does the work. The person is an employee if the employer can direct or control how the work is done. The person is an independent contractor if the employer cannot dictate how the work is done. Financial control means the right to direct or control the business part of the work. A person with a significant monetary investment is not likely to be seen as an independent contractor. If a person receives no reimbursement for expenses and does not share in profits or losses, this indicates the status of independent contractor. The relationship of the parties can be established by how payments and benefits are made and/or by a written contract (which the IRS will take into consideration).

Attempting to categorize an intern as an independent contractor for tax purposes may also create problems for the supervisor-employer with regard to the state or federal labor laws. An intern is more likely to be treated as an hourly employee who is subject to various wage and hour limitations and overtime requirements. Failure to comply with state or federal law in this regard could subject the employer to civil suit. The same requirements generally do not apply to an independent contractor.

There is a split in case authority as to whether an employer of therapists may be vicariously liable for their sexual misconduct with clients. Jurisdictions holding that supervisors may be vicariously liable include Alaska (Doe v. Samaritan Counseling Center, 1990); Virginia (Doe v. U.S., 1995; Plummer v. Center Psychiatrists Ltd., 1996); Minnesota (Marston v. Minneapolis Clinic of Psychiatry & Neurology Ltd., 1982); Nevada (Ray v. Value Behavior Health, Inc.,1997); and Washington (Simmons v. U.S., 1986).

Jurisdictions that have held that the employer cannot be liable for the sexual misconduct of an employee psychotherapist include Utah (Birkner v. Salt Lake County, 1989); Wisconsin (Block v. Gomez, 1996); Ohio (Bunce v. Parkside Lodge of Columbus, 1991); New York (Noto v. St. Vincent's Hospital & Medical Center of New York, 1990); and Alabama (Swift v. Doe, 1990).

An example of a legal case that held that the employer could be vicariously liable for sexual misconduct by a therapist is Simmons v. United States (1986, supra). A social worker, Mr. Kammers, was counseling Ms. Simmons through the Indian Health Service. Ms. Simmons alleged that she had had sexual intercourse with Mr. Kammers that began on an out of town trip and continued throughout the treatment. Mr. Kammers' supervisor was allegedly apprised of the existence of the relationship and took no action to either correct the improper counseling or relieve the social worker of his duties. The client suffered a series of emotional problems culminating with a suicide attempt. When suit was brought, the federal government, as the employer, contended that no claim could be asserted against them because it was outside the scope of the social worker's employment to have engaged in sexual misconduct.

The Ninth Circuit Court of Appeal held against the government, finding that the essence of the social worker's malpractice was the mishandling of transference, and handling transference was within the scope of his employment. The court also found that there was supervisory negligence that arose from the failure of Mr. Kammers' supervisor to act upon being apprised of the situation. The court's decision is particularly interesting because at least some of the alleged sexual misconduct occurred on out of town trips, off the employer's premises, and outside of business hours.

The jurisdictions that have held that employers may be vicariously liable have generally focused on the foreseeability of sexual misconduct between therapists and clients, and have suggested that it is important that employers have official policies that sexual misconduct is impermissible in their business. The best means of dealing with this ethical and risk management issue is to put in both client contracts and employee contracts that sexual misconduct is unethical and grounds for termination of employment.

For the therapist who employs interns, the better practice is to have the intern covered by the employer/supervisor's malpractice insurance to be sure that both supervisor and supervisee are covered. Independent contractors, on the other hand, would be expected to provide their own malpractice coverage.

PERSONNEL ISSUES

The therapist who employs clerical or administrative employees (e.g., secretaries, receptionists, or on-site billing personnel) should be aware of the requirements of state law for having workers' compensation insurance and to be sure that he or she has an adequate amount of such insurance in place.

Once the employment contract is in place, then the question to address is the training and education that is provided regarding the employee's professional duties. For example, with regard to interns, under the AAMFT ethics code, the employer has the direct responsibility for ensuring that the employee does not act beyond the scope of his or her competency and does not misrepresent his or her intern status (Subprinciple 8.7). Training can consist of in-house seminars, reading assignments, and/or presentations. The training could also involve having the intern attend continuing education workshops. Topics that would be important to cover are, to name but a few, the jurisdiction's laws on confidentiality; child abuse and elder abuse reporting requirements; the duty to warn, and threats of violence; the circumstances to consider in referring a client for medication evaluation; and general ethical issues (e.g., the potential impropriety of multiple relationships).

TRAINING FOR CONFIDENTIALITY ISSUES

It is particularly important for clerical and administrative employees (e.g., secretaries, receptionists, transcriptionists, and billing persons) to be made aware of the legal requirements of confidentiality. The employer has the responsibility for maintaining confidentiality of client records, and thus must prepare staff for their part in this ethical and legal obligation. The simple act of sending a bill with a diagnosis on it to a person's place of employment may inadvertently trigger an alleged breach of confidentiality. By the same token, clerical and administrative employees should be aware that they cannot release records simply on a verbal request from someone other than the client; and in some states, such as California, a written release is required to release the records to the client.

The issue of confidentiality, as noted above, also involves the duty of training nonprofessional employees to be aware of the limits of confidentiality, and to not discuss clients outside the office. Some employees may understandably find the information that they receive interesting to discuss with their significant others or friends, but such conduct would be a breach of confidentiality that could be asserted against the employer. In addition, clerical and nonprofessional employees should be cautioned about acknowledging clients as such outside the office, for example if they run into them in public. Nonprofessional employees should also be counseled about the necessity of maintaining clear boundaries and avoiding sexual, social, or business relationships with present or former clients of the therapist-employer. A good practice is to have clerical or nonprofessional employees sign a statement acknowledging that they understand the importance and requirements of confidentiality, that they will abide by them, and that a breach of confidentiality can be grounds for discipline, including termination.

Other issues can arise with regard to the use of nonprofessional staff. Because of the nature of a therapy practice, it is particularly important that secretarial-level employees who may be involved in the preparation of reports or notes be conscious of confidentiality requirements. It is a good practice to educate all employees about confidentiality and about not identifying clients as such in a public setting. The therapist-employer should also educate the staff on the legal requirements for release of client records. Generally, jurisdictional laws impose on the professional the duty to maintain confidentiality; and if records are inadvertently produced or produced based on incorrect understanding of the law, the therapist may be at risk. Woody (2001) provides details about record keeping and releasing records.

These types of problems can easily occur if staff employees do not understand either the requirements of confidentiality, or what precisely is needed to produce records. The therapist-employer should educate all staff members about local requirements for compliance with confidentiality statutes. If subpoenas are received, the therapist-employer must be immediately notified, and no records should be produced without the knowledge of the therapist-employer.

The AAMFT ethics code clearly provides for the client's confidentiality, and the code and the law ultimately impose the duty to be sure that such records are treated confidentially by the therapist-employer. The AAMFT ethics code also specifically provides for how confidential records should be stored and disposed of (Subprinciple 2.4). It is important to share ethical and legal requirements about confidentiality and record keeping with those employees who actually work with the records to be sure that they handle them in compliance with both ethics and the law.

A particularly difficult area can arise when clients are in litigation, especially in family law matters, and a nonprofessional employee is contacted and requested to produce records. Similarly, both professional and nonprofessional employees must be educated on what to do when subpoenas are received for records, because subpoenas can be erroneously perceived as an automatic authorization or requirement that records be disclosed. Training employees on these issues will prevent potential ethics disputes. Specific procedures for dealing with subpoenas are discussed below in the section Subpoenas and Confidentiality.

SUPERVISION RESPONSIBILITIES

The different states' criteria regarding supervision of therapists or interns that one employs are reflected in each state's licensing board statutes or regulations and may be either extremely detailed, (such as in California, 16 CCR §1833) or not detailed at all. For example, California law specifies, in part, that an applicant for licensure must have at least one hour of individual face-to-face supervision or two hours of group supervision (with not more than eight persons), that not more than five hours of supervision can be credited during any single week, and that experience gained under the supervision of a spouse, relative, or domestic partner cannot be counted toward licensure.

As a general rule, if an intern is to provide services to a client, the client should be notified in writing at the inception of the therapy, as part of documenting an informed consent, of the intern's status. This precludes the matter becoming an issue at a later date. In addition, the intern should be required to provide the services on-site and should be advised that he or she is not allowed to receive direct payment from clients (since to do so creates a potential for misrepresentation and also for the supervisor to not be paid, as required). The author knows of numerous instances where interns have either purposefully or inadvertently been allowed to function in a manner that leads clients to think that they are independently licensed.

Failure to supervise an intern properly can subject the supervisor to discipline by the licensing board for the jurisdiction(s) in which the therapist practices (Steckler v. Ohio State Board of Psychology, 1992) and/or civil liability (Montoya v. Bebensee, 1988).

A continuing issue has been the extent to which the supervision provided to supervisees can be seen as the functional equivalent of psychotherapy. For example, a supervisor discussed sexual topics with a supervisee, who was left feeling uncomfortable. The question raised was whether this focus was, in effect, the supervisor's providing counseling in lieu of supervision. To help resolve such a concern and identify whether the supervision is appropriate, three factors are relevant: (1) the goals, (2) the primary focus, and (3) the structure of the supervision (Brock, 1998).

A more practical problem is that supervision that becomes too similar to psychotherapy can create the potential for a supervisee to claim malpractice against the supervisor. While such claims are rare, the author has defended two such cases involving psychologists and psychological assistants who alleged that the supervision was the equivalent of psychotherapy and became overly focused on sexual issues. Those cases also involved alleged sexual interactions between the psychologists and their supervisees.

The supervisor has the responsibility to provide competent supervision. The trend seems to be one of shifting away from allowing supervisees to dictate the content of supervision and toward requiring that the supervisor conduct focused inquiries regarding the cases with which the supervisee is working. In addition, there seems to be support for supervisors to take notes of supervision in order to be able to document which cases and concepts were discussed.

A particularly difficult scenario can arise when a supervisor works with a supervisee for a lengthy period of time, develops sufficient confidence in that supervisee, and begins to disregard the technical requirements of supervision, such as the required amount of time for supervisor sessions, providing case materials, etc. This situation can pose serious potential problems. As long as supervision is taking place, all of the standard requirements of supervision should be met. (Chapter Four provides details of the responsibilities, procedures, and ethical obligations associated with supervision.)

LIABILITY INSURANCE

A problem area of operations is the failure to obtain insurance coverage that is adequate for protection of the therapist regarding business-related liability. While many therapists have obtained malpractice insurance, some practitioners believe mistakenly that the absence of insurance protects them from litigation. The author's position is that the failure to maintain adequate levels of insurance of the right type does not protect against litigation; instead, it "protects" against being solvent after litigation.

The important question is what type of insurance do therapists need. Obviously, it is necessary to carry "errors and omissions" insurance or malpractice insurance. There are a variety of programs available to nonmedical therapists, and most of the premiums are substantially less than those charged for similar insurance for attorneys or physicians. Where possible, therapists should obtain administrative hearing coverage (e.g., for defending against a licensing complaint) at the highest level that is available and can be afforded. At this point in time, the most that is offered by any carrier, to the author's knowledge, is $50,000. Some insurance policies will offer coverage up to $2,500 or $5,000 for having legal counsel present at depositions given by the insured. Once the requisite malpractice insurance has been obtained, it must be faithfully maintained.

The therapist must also be conscious of whether the insurance is "occurrence" or "claims-made" coverage. "Occurrence" insurance is the easier and better choice from the perspective that, if it is in effect "at the time the services are provided to the client, it is in effect forever." "Claims-made" insurance is slightly different because it requires that the therapist be insured both at the time the services are provided to the client, and at the time that the litigation occurs. This becomes a particular problem if the therapist switches policies from one insurance company to another, and there is a change in the type of policy. Although details are not necessary here, additional coverage can be purchased for claims-made policies referred to as nose or tail coverage. "Nose coverage" extends the policy retroactively to cover acts prior to the inception of the policy, while "tail coverage" extends the policy into the distant future. For example, if a therapist was in the process of retiring and had a claims-made policy, he or she would want to obtain some type of tail coverage to extend that protection into the future.

In addition to malpractice coverage, therapists must be conscious of the increasing risk of litigation from general claims, such as those under the Americans with Disabilities Act of 1990 (ADA). Such claims will generally not be covered by malpractice insurance and would come under a more general type of insurance, if at all. Thus, when a therapist is establishing the practice or wants to be sure of maximal protection, it is important to have coverage for any type of general liability claims, such as slips and falls, injuries due to defective equipment or premises, claims under ADA, and so forth.

As a potential successful business owner, a therapist must also be careful to have adequate levels of automobile insurance coverage. A good practice is to have some type of umbrella personal liability policy. Such policy acts to some extent as an excess policy and comes into play if other policies do not, or if the coverage under another policy is exhausted. For example, if a therapist had very low automobile insurance coverage and was in a bad accident in which the other party was seriously hurt, an umbrella policy could provide up to a million dollars in additional coverage from a possibly ruinous claim. Typical umbrella policies do not provide in excess of a million dollars per claim, although there may be an aggregate amount for multiple claims up to three million dollars.

TECHNOLOGY ISSUES

With the advent of managed care, technology has seemed to be a benefit in minimizing the costs of a therapy practice. Recent cases, however, at the trial court level have demonstrated that technology can have some unforeseen and negative consequences. For example, a voice-mail system may take the place of a receptionist, but it leaves the therapist with no means of establishing that particular communications were received. In general, voice-mail systems keep the messages only 10 to 14 days. This presents a problem if the therapist needs to document receiving a phone call on a certain date. In the author's experience, this issue has arisen several times with regard to potential suicide cases, such as to what was communicated to the therapist at a key point in time about the mental status of a client.

Regarding the documentation of key voice mails, the simplest solution is to maintain a hand-held dictation machine and tape messages that contain significant content, such as reports of child abuse, elder abuse, homicidal thoughts, suicidal thoughts, and sexual interest in the therapist. Taping live conversations without the consent of the other party is illegal; however, this is not the case with the taping of messages that are left.

The therapist and his or her employees need to recognize that, if a voice-mail system is being used, others may be able to access its code. The author has seen two cases in which clients were able to ascertain the voice-mail code of the therapist and were thereby able to access the voice-mail of the therapist! Since confidentiality is a critically important principle in psychotherapy, as reflected by Principle II, Confidentiality, of the AAMFT ethics code, utilizing a voice-mail system may create risks to confidentiality. Consequently, no voice-mail system should be used unless the therapist uses a non-predictable code. Preferably whatever code is used should not be readily associated with the therapist and should not be a predictable numeric sequence.

E-mail presents somewhat unusual problems that are only now being recognized. In a litigation circumstance, a client who had a therapist's e-mail address created e-mail in the name of the therapist purporting to come from the therapist. In another situation, a therapist unintentionally e-mailed a sexually explicit joke to a client by accident, when the joke was intended to be sent to only personal friends.

Except in extraordinary circumstances, it is generally a bad idea to have e-mail communications with clients. E-mail may be accessed by skilled hackers and may also be the subject of a subpoena. Many therapists may not realize that, although an e-mail is deleted from a computer system, it is still maintained in a backup mode and may be accessed at a later date. Several concerns also arise about the use of e-mail to provide therapy across state lines, which may be deemed to be unlicensed practice in another state.

Fax machines in therapists' offices pose a possible risk of inadvertent breaches of confidentiality. Most law firms utilize cautionary statements on the cover sheet of faxes, stating that the documents contain confidential communication intended only for the stated recipients, and that any person inadvertently receiving it should not read the contents. However, there is not anything that precludes an unintended recipient of a fax from reading it. The author is unaware of any specific case where a fax communication has been the basis for a claim of breach of confidentiality, but it is easy to hypothesize circumstances where that would occur.

As a general rule, the more sensitive the information, the less appropriate it is to fax the information, as opposed to using overnight mail or express mail. By the same token, cell phones are subject to interception and create potential risk of breach of confidentiality if an unintended recipient receives the cell phone call.

Teletherapy, sometimes termed telehealth, although becoming somewhat more prevalent, is also under close scrutiny by some licensing boards and ethics committees. For example, those issuing cautionary statements and guidelines about electronic communications with clients include the California Board of Psychology, the American Psychological Association, and the American Medical Association (American Medical Association, 2001; American Psychological Association, 1997; Dudder & Roth, 1997; Nagy, 1992). (Chapter Ten further elaborates on telehealth services and their ethical implications.)

The use of e-mail, fax machines, and teletherapy can often coincide with the use of home offices. While home offices, particularly as an adjunct to another office, are not prohibited, they do present certain problems with regard to confidentiality. A therapist utilizing a home office must be particularly sure that there is a system of protecting the confidentiality of records and notes from inadvertent disclosure to family members. Another consideration is that, if the therapist receives phone calls from clients at a home office, it is possible to have family members or significant others overhear confidential communications. Any message machine that is being used in a home office should clearly specify that it is a home office, so that the client leaving a message is aware of that fact and may elect not to leave a message on that particular machine. The fact that an office is in a home setting does not make any less stringent the ethical requirements of storing the records appropriately.

Although a home office may not violate the ethical standard, in a number of cases that the author has defended, the use of home offices has seemed to trigger transference issues and has raised potential issues with regard to multiple relationships. In addition, by having a client in one's home, even in an area that is designated as an office, the therapist is giving the client potential access to personal information. For example, a client can observe the therapist's family and/or personal pictures and portraits. The therapist is also giving the client the ability to describe the interior of the house, which could be a factor in the event of a false claim of sexual misconduct. For some clients with borderline personality disorder, being allowed into the therapist's home, even into a designated office setting, may fuel unrealistic expectations of social and/or personal relationships. Woody (1999) has provided numerous examples of violations occurring due to the therapist's not adequately separating personal and professional activities.

ADVERTISING ISSUES

Principle VIII, Advertising, of the AAMFT ethics code provides as follows: "Marriage and family therapists engage in appropriate informational activities, including those that enable the public, referral sources, or others to choose professional services on an informed basis." The eight subprinciples deal with the obligation to have accurate advertising, and to not have marriage and family therapists or their employees or supervisees misrepresent their qualifications.

Generally, licensing board actions and civil suits do not arise solely because of advertising issues. It is not uncommon, however, for a licensing board, as part of an action or civil suit, to also allege that a therapist engaged in fraudulent advertising. The most common claim for false advertising relates to exaggeration of qualifications or advertising in a manner that suggests that the therapist is a psychologist or a psychiatrist, when he or she is actually from another (or no) mental health discipline.

In California, the Board of Behavioral Sciences has had several cases that focus on marriage and family therapists who have Ph.D. degrees from questionable or unaccredited institutions. The problem can arise from using the title "Doctor" in letterhead, business cards, or advertising, particularly if the marriage and family therapist does not identify his or her license status on the letterhead, card, or advertising. Subprinciple 8.5 of the AAMFT ethics code addresses this issue. It specifies that a marriage and family therapist should list and claim only those degrees that are earned from institutions accredited by regional accreditation sources recognized by the United States Department of Education, or from institutions recognized by states or provinces that license or certify marriage and family therapists, or from equivalent foreign institutions. A marriage and family therapist with a Ph.D. degree would have no legal or ethical problem referring to himself or herself by the title "Doctor." To avoid potential confusion and/or claims of impropriety, the marriage and family therapist should list the title and the license number on letterhead, business cards, and advertising.

The author has seen several instances in which marriage and family therapists have gotten into difficulty because their advertisements have been incorrectly placed in the psychologists' section of Yellow Page telephone book advertising. Although such placement of advertising may be due to misunderstanding on the part of the telephone advertising service, the responsibility for ensuring that the qualifications are accurately represented is with the marriage and family therapist. Typically, this becomes an issue in a licensing board complaint or a civil suit when a patient alleges that he or she saw an advertisement that implied or led the client to reasonably assume that the marriage and family therapist was a psychologist or psychiatrist.

In some states, the intention to mislead the public is not an essential ingredient to claims of false or misleading advertising. In California, for example, under Business and Professions Code 17500, an action can be brought against the marriage and family therapist simply if the advertising is misleading to the public.

The claim of false or misleading advertising against a therapist often focuses on the claim to have specialization in areas such as eating disorders, addiction, sexual abuse, dissociative disorders, and so forth. As the Supreme Court of New Hampshire has noted in Hungerford v. Jones (1998), merely taking a workshop or two does not qualify someone as a specialist or expert; and holding oneself out in that fashion after a brief training will most likely lead to some type of difficulty. Under the AAMFT ethics code, marriage and family therapists can practice in new specialty areas only after receiving appropriate education, training, or supervised experience (Subprinciple 3.7).

Because incorrect advertising can lead to licensing board action up to and including injunctions against the use of particular advertising, the therapist must be sure that his or her supervisees are extremely careful in their advertising and marketing. Whatever advertising or promotional literature the supervisee uses should state that he or she is a supervisee and state the name of the supervisor. Of course, the supervisor should review and approve all promotional materials set forth by the supervisee.

SUBPOENAS AND CONFIDENTIALITY

The AAMFT ethics code, Principle II, Confidentiality, has six subprinciples, with the four subsections that are most pertinent to this chapter being:

Subprinciple 2.1: Marriage and family therapists disclose to clients and other interested parties, as early as feasible in their professional contacts, the nature of confidentiality, and possible limitation of the client's right to confidentiality. Therapists review with clients the circumstances where confidential information may be requested, and where disclosure of confidential information may be legally required. Circumstances may necessitate repeated disclosures.

Subprinciple 2.2: Marriage and family therapists do not disclose client confidences except by written authorization or waiver, or where mandated, or permitted by law. Verbal authorization will not be sufficient except in emergency situations, unless prohibited by law. When providing couple, family or group treatment, the therapist does not disclose information outside the treatment context without a written authorization from each individual competent to execute a waiver. In the context of couple, family or group treatment, the therapist may not reveal any individual's confidences to others in the client unit without the prior written permission of that individual.

Subprinciple 2.4: Marriage and family therapists store, safeguard, and dispose of client records in ways that maintain confidentiality and in accord with applicable laws and professional standards.

Subprinciple 2.5: Subsequent to the therapist moving from the area, closing the practice, or upon the death of the therapist, a marriage and family therapist arranges for the storage, transfer, or disposal of client records in ways that maintain confidentiality and safeguard the welfare of clients.

As noted above, both ethics and the law of the particular jurisdiction impose on therapists an obligation to maintain the confidentiality of clients. A common scenario where confidentiality can be breached due to a mistaken understanding of law is that in which a subpoena is served for the client's records by an adverse party. Subpoenas call for the production of either persons or documents, both for either depositions or testimony at a trial or hearing. Subpoenas can seek the production of live testimony or documents in civil suits, criminal proceedings, licensing board actions and other administrative proceedings.

Each jurisdiction has different requirements for what is a valid subpoena. For example, in some jurisdictions, failure to attach a witness fee or payment for documents invalidates the subpoena. Jurisdictions also differ in whether there are details provided about what steps, if any, must be taken to advise the client whose records are being sought by the subpoena.

As a general rule, subpoenas are supposed to be served on opposing parties. Therefore, if the therapist receives a subpoena for a client's record and the client is a party to a proceeding, one would normally suppose that he or she knew of the subpoena. It is not uncommon, however, for subpoenas to be improperly served and to have a situation where a client does not know that his or her records have been subpoenaed. Under the AAMFT ethics code, a client's written consent is required for the disclosure of confidential information. Laws in a given jurisdiction may set different requirements, such as requiring that the person who sends a subpoena for therapy records must send a written notice to the consumer whose records are being sought (California Code of Civil Procedure, 1985).

If the notice is provided to the client, in theory the therapist who receives the subpoena can produce the records and be immune from complaint or from being sued by the client, because the notice imposes on the client the obligation to take steps to obtain an order preventing the disclosure of the records pursuant to the subpoena. Inabnit v. Berkson (1988) held that a physician could not be sued by his patients for turning over records pursuant to a subpoena where a proper notice to consumer was served on the patients and they did nothing about it.

Attorneys who advise therapists generally take the position that even where the requirement of a notice to client has been met, the therapist should have the client's written consent to produce the information requested. A fairly common problem with subpoenas occurs when a subpoena has been served on the therapist, and an attorney adverse to the client asserts that the claims that the client made, in whatever proceeding is pending, constitute a waiver of the psychotherapist-patient privilege. If the client and his or her attorney agree, then there should be no problem with providing the therapist with a written statement authorizing release of the records or information. If, as is not uncommon, the client and his or her attorney disagree about whether the institution of the action has waived the psychotherapist-patient privilege, the therapist will be caught between attorneys who take inconsistent positions on whether the records should be disclosed. In such cases, the courts have ruled in favor of clients' claims for breach of confidentiality (Rost v. State Board of Psychology, 1995; Kennestone Hospital v. Hopson, 2000).

This is not the type of issue that the therapist can resolve alone. If the client does not agree that the privilege has been waived, then the therapist's only protection is to have a court resolve the matter on a motion. Generally, the motion would take the form of either a motion to compel production by the therapist brought by the attorney seeking the records, or a motion for protective order brought by the client's attorney seeking to quash the subpoena. Thus, on receiving a subpoena, if the client is not willing to provide a written release for the records to be disclosed, then the therapist should consult competent legal counsel to determine what process to follow to minimize risk and ensure that the client's confidentiality is protected.

The confidentiality issues become more complex if the therapist was providing conjoint therapy, and one party to the conjoint therapy signs a release for the records, and the other party objects. In a situation in which more than one client is involved in the therapy, the therapist should consult an attorney, but consent of all parties is generally required for the documents to be disclosed.

Under the AAMFT ethics code, Subprinciple 2.2 states that the written consent of all parties participating in the therapy is required for the records to be disclosed. This is a sound principle for general guidance.

Particularly difficult problems arise when the therapist provides therapy to a couple who later become involved in divorce or custody litigation. Even though both were involved in the same treatment sessions, if only one wants the records released and the other objects, it is likely a matter than can best be resolved by the court, not by the therapist.

Several appellate decisions around the country involve circumstances where one party to conjoint sessions requested a therapist to provide a declaration or testimony in a custody or divorce action adverse to the other party. The general standard seems to be: if two clients were involved in treatment and the therapist takes a position adverse to one of them by releasing information at the request of the other party, the therapist may be liable for breach of confidentiality. For example, in Cutter v. Brownbridge (1986), a licensed clinical social worker provided a declaration making negative statements about the husband for a wife in a custody dispute.

It is easier to defend a therapist who produces records under the mistaken impression that a subpoena is legally sufficient to compel disclosure than it is to defend a therapist who voluntarily provides a declaration or testimony adverse to a client at the request of another client with adverse interests to the first one. While both types of conduct may result in breaches of confidentiality, with the former, there may be ways to justify the mistaken disclosure pursuant to a subpoena, or there may be protection under an immunity from litigation that would not apply to a voluntary disclosure of confidential information.

This is an era when litigation involving therapy clients is common. By virtue of needing therapeutic help, it might be postulated that therapy clients are often lacking effective judgment and decision making, with a potential byproduct being litigation. Therefore, the therapist must have a thorough understanding of the ethical and legal implications of confidentiality and releasing client records and information, since problems with these can lead to ethical, licensing, and legal (malpractice) complaints. Woody (2001) offers an authoritative text on these matters.

CONTRACTS WITH CLIENTS

It is somewhat surprising that many therapists still do not utilize written contracts with clients, an omission that creates several types of ethical and legal vulnerability. One risk is that the client may dispute the amount of the agreed upon fee. The best evidence of the fee arrangement is to have a contract signed by the client reflecting the fee. In addition, it is extremely difficult to show that the client gave the requisite informed consent without some type of written form reflecting the informed consent discussion. Therefore, at the inception of the therapeutic relationship, the therapist should have clients sign a written contract and an informed consent form (note that informed consent may have to be obtained on multiple occasions, not just at the outset of services).

Minimum Topics for a Contract with the Client

At a minimum, the contract with the client should address the following three matters. As will be discussed, there are certain other issues that can and perhaps should be included in a contract with the client.

(1) What the applicable state's legal prescriptions and proscriptions are on confidentiality with regard to child abuse, elder abuse reporting, and the duty to warn (if any).

(2) That the therapist does not guarantee any particular result or that the client will be happier when the therapy is over. This provision is necessary because clients often come to therapy with unrealistic expectations anticipating some magical healing process. In addition, the author has witnessed a number of circumstances in which therapy, which was effective to break through a client's denial and reach difficult issues, actually created resentment rather than appreciation.

(3) The fee agreed upon, and whether the therapist is agreeing to accept insurance. With regard to this issue, marriage and family therapists must carefully review Principle VII, Financial Arrangements, of the AAMFT ethics code, which imposes a responsibility to make financial arrangements with clients and third-party payers that are reasonably understandable and which conform to accepted professional practices. Subprinciple 7.2 states,

Prior to entering into the therapeutic or supervisory relationship, marriage and family therapists clearly disclose and explain to clients and supervisees: (a) all financial arrangements and fees related to professional services, including charges for cancelled or missed appointments; (b) the use of collection agencies as legal measures for nonpayment; and (c) the procedure for obtaining payment from the client, to the extent allowed by law, if payment is denied by the third-party payer. Once services have begun, therapists provide reasonable notice of any changes in fees or other charges.

Subprinciple 7.4 imposes a responsibility to truthfully represent facts to clients and third-party payers (as well as supervisees) regarding services rendered.

Additional Possible Topics for a Contract with the Client

In addition to discussing the financial terms, the contract with the client should mention conduct that is or is not appropriate. For example, due to the severity of the consequences for the therapist and client alike, the contract should contain an express statement that sexual misconduct is unethical and will not be condoned. This notice is helpful in attempting to limit the vicarious liability of an employer if this type of situation arises, involving an employee and a client.

If the jurisdiction in which the therapist practices allows arbitration clauses, then such a clause should be considered for inclusion in the therapist-client contract. For example, California has a very specific statute governing medical malpractice arbitration, which applies to marriage and family therapists as well. If the statutory language is used in the statutory format and with the statutorily specified type size and color, then any claims arising from the therapy would have to be arbitrated (California Code of Civil Procedure §1295).

There are two schools of thought on whether including an arbitration clause is a benefit or detriment to the therapist. One view is that the inclusion of an arbitration clause is likely to persuade clients to litigate, because it suggests a fairly easy avenue of pursuing a claim. The second view is that the inclusion of an arbitration clause discourages litigation; the reasoning is that most attorneys do not like to pursue claims in arbitration and would prefer to have claims that can be taken before a jury, which is likely to be more generous than arbitrators.

Given today's generally litigious climate, it is unrealistic to think that the inclusion of an arbitration clause encourages litigation. The reality is that arbitration is significantly less costly than other types of litigation. Further, the courts generally have a strong policy favoring arbitration because it leads to resolution of cases outside the court process, and thereby lightens the court's load. There are, however, some types of claims that may not be subject to arbitration, such as claims of racial or sexual discrimination of employees where the employee has disproportionate bargaining power (Broughton v. Cigna Health Plan, 1999).

Where arbitration clauses are used, the therapist must consider whether to include a clause for attorneys' fees as well. Generally, for an attorneys' fees clause to be enforceable, it must provide that the prevailing party would be awarded attorneys' fees, not just that the therapist could get reimbursement for his or her attorney's fees. The inclusion of attorneys' fees clause may well encourage litigation because it would enhance the attractiveness of pursuing the claim. Consequently, the inclusion of an attorneys' fees clause is not recommended, particularly because most therapists will have some form of insurance available, and therefore will not be paying the costs of litigation themselves.

In addition to the inclusion of the various terms set forth above, a contract with clients should provide that it cannot be modified orally and can only be modified by a writing signed by both parties. This is called an "equal dignities" clause, and the purpose is to avoid a situation where a client contends that a therapist verbally modified the contract or said that a particular term did not require compliance. Stating that any changes or modifications must be in writing ensures that this type of argument cannot be successful. For the same reason, the contract should specify that there are no other agreements between the parties other than the ones in the contract, and that all negotiations have been merged into the contract. Finally, the contract should specify the therapist's policy on charges for sessions cancelled within 24 hours.

A common failing of therapists who do use written contracts with clients is to put in language which either exaggerates the nature of the services to be provided or unintentionally raises the standard of care that the therapist is to provide. The standard of care is the standard of the average practitioner in a therapist's jurisdiction. It is a "C" student standard. However, clients may assume a higher standard if the therapist puts language into the contract stating that the therapist will provide the best or highest or first-rate services. The contract should specify that the therapist will provide therapy, and not qualify the services or inflate the client's expectations by the use of superlatives.

INFORMED CONSENT

Subprinciple 1.2 of the AAMFT ethics code requires a marriage and family therapist to obtain the client's informed consent, which should be appropriately documented, at the inception of the therapeutic relationship (and perhaps later as well). Informed consent is a doctrine that originated in medical malpractice cases and has been applied to psychotherapy with mixed success (Cobbs v. Grant, 1972; Truman v. Thomas, 1980).

In approaching the documentation that therapists should prepare at the inception of the therapeutic relationship, informed consent is an important consideration. Generally, informed consent is defined as a risk-benefit analysis that gives the client an adequate amount of information to make a meaningful decision as to whether to proceed with a particular course of therapy or not. (The topic is also discussed in Chapter Two of this book.)

What constitutes informed consent has been the subject of some controversy. One definition is that of Ebert (1997), former chair of the California Board of Psychology. He identified the following elements of informed consent: (1) the limits of confidentiality such as elder abuse reporting, child abuse reporting, and threats to third parties, (2) the nature and extent of the therapist's record keeping system, (3) the therapist's title, training, experience, and expertise, (4) the therapist's estimate of the probable length of therapy, (5) the risk of any of the therapy, (6) alternative approaches to the therapy, (7) the fees and billing practices, (8) the right not to use the sessions, and (9) who the patient can contact in an emergency.

The author believes that informed consent is adequate if it contains the limits of confidentiality, the theoretical orientation of the therapist, the estimate of the probable length of therapy, the risks of any of the therapy, alternative approaches to the therapy, and the fees and billing practices. Although informed consent is necessary under the AAMFT ethics code and various state laws, informed consent cannot authorize acts that are illegal or contrary to ethical standards, such as beating patients (Rains v. Superior Court, 1984) or unlicensed practice where a statute requires a license for the services to be provided.

The AAMFT ethics code states that the client's consent should be "appropriately documented" (Subprinciple 1.2.e); this could imply some type of written documentation placed in the client's file without specifying a formal signed consent form. This author believes that a written consent form is advisable, with the form tailored to reflect the therapist's theoretical orientation. Once the form has been prepared, to be valid, it must be signed by the therapist, each client, and each participant in couples or group therapy.

If the therapist is using an experimental treatment or one that is controversial, then a special consent will be required disclosing the nature of the controversy. The AAMFT ethics code requires informing clients of "potential risks and benefits of treatments for which generally recognized standards do not exist" (Subprinciple 1.2.c). There is no clear-cut standard of what is considered to be controversial, although the more unusual the technique, the more likely it will be seen as controversial. The newer the technique, the more likely it will be seen as experimental. The less empirical research on a given technique, the more likely it will be seen as experimental.

Special consent forms may be necessary for the use of such methods as eye movement desensitization reprocessing (EMDR), thought field therapy, breath work, or any of a number of transpersonal and other techniques that may not be readily accepted by more conventional therapists. In addition, hypnosis probably requires a separate informed consent that addresses the issues of confabulation and possible false memories. There is a very good form prepared by the American Society for Clinical Hypnosis that therapists can obtain from that organization. For a case discussing the issue of informed consent in the context of entity depossession techniques, see <u>Modi v. West Virginia/Board of Medicine</u> (1995).

Two other issues relevant to consent should be mentioned. First, if therapists intend to utilize videotaping, audio recording, or having the sessions observed by a third party, then Subprinciple 1.2 of the AAMFT ethics code requires a written consent. To assure that the consent is truly informed, it should state clearly and specifically the purposes and uses of the recorded materials or observation (Brock, 1998). Second, an excellent practice, which is required in some states (e.g., California), is to have the informed consent specifically disclose, when relevant, that an intern is providing the services. This aspect of consent can prevent questions at a later date as to the person's licensure status (California Board of Psychology Regulation 16 C.C.R. §1391.6; Board of Behavioral Sciences Regulation 16 C.C.R. §1833.1).

NOTE TAKING AND RECORDS

Historically, the decision of whether notes would be taken has been left to the discretion of the individual therapist. In a survey, first published in 1989, conducted of clinical members of AAMFT, Brock and Coufal (1998) found that approximately 47% of those responding indicated that they, at least rarely, limited their notes to name, date, and fee. Subprinciple 3.6 of the AAMFT 2001 ethics code states that marriage and family therapists will maintain accurate and adequate clinical and financial records.

The AAMFT ethics code guideline now requires what the realities of modern practice mandate, namely that clinical notes be taken. Once the duty to take such notes is recognized, however, the issues are what content to put in notes and how to maintain them.

As a general rule, the notes must present an accurate picture of what is happening in the therapy. Drawing on this guideline, the author, who has defended numerous legal cases involving this issue, recommends that the following should be in the notes:

(1) Diagnosis and treatment plan.

(2) The date and general content of the informed consent discussion, and any subsequent consent discussions.

(3) Any expression of suicidal thought, and how it was handled by the therapist.

(4) Any expression of homicidal thought and what the therapist did about it. If the jurisdiction that the therapist practices in is one that requires a warning in the event of a serious threat to harm a third party, then the steps that are taken to comply with state law should be noted.

(5) Any discussion by the client of ongoing, contemplated, or past litigation.

(6) The prior therapists that the client has seen, and the reasons for the termination of the therapy. The therapist

should also request that the patient provide a release for obtaining the prior therapy records. If the client refuses to do so, the refusal should be noted.

(7) Any statements indicating delusional thinking and/or ideas of reference.

(8) Any expressions of romantic or sexual interest in or fantasies or dreams about the therapist. It is not adequate to simply use the term "transference" because that is too vague a term to indicate what was actually said. Where some expression of romantic or sexual interest occurs, the client's words should be recorded as accurately as possible.

(9) Any expression of hostility towards the therapist (whether or not it is an expression of transference). Here the client's words should be recorded as precisely as possible.

(10) Any consideration that the therapist gives to the idea of referring the client for a medication evaluation and/or psychological testing.

(11) Whether the client's affect is consistent or inconsistent with the statements being made.

(12) With any documents including poetry or journal entries coming from the client, the therapist should maintain a copy in the file, including the date on which the therapist received the document and what, if anything, was discussed about it.

(13) All letters, greeting cards, photographs, and other items received from a patient should be maintained in the file.

(14) Comments by the patient about the progress or lack of progress in the therapy, and what specific techniques have been helpful or not helpful.

(15) The homework assignments given, if any, and what the patient does as far as complying or not complying with these assignments.

Again, these fifteen recommendations are those of the author; other cautionary actions may also be appropriate.

Because Subprinciple 2.5 specifically requires provisions for how records are stored, transferred, and disposed of in the event of the therapist's moving, closing a practice, or death, it is important to have a written plan for the disposal and transfer of the records. The plan should be disclosed to the clerical or nonprofessional employees who would be arranging for the transfer or disposal of the records, and also to the professional employees who may be affected by it. In one case, a former therapy client filed a malpractice action against the estate of a deceased marriage and family therapist. The therapist's records were critically important in the defense. The availability and accessibility of those records proved to be a significant factor whereby the estate prevailed in the malpractice action.

While some therapists might have the view that they need not worry about what occurs after their death, this is not true. The therapist's family, an estate, or partners could be subject to litigation following the therapist's death. The plan that provides for the storage, transfer, and disposal of records should also provide for the disposition of records in the event the therapist becomes either mentally incompetent or disabled.

ETHICAL ISSUES REGARDING FINANCES

Principle VII of the AAMFT ethics code deals with financial arrangements. Among the most important are Subprinciple 7.1 which states that marriage and family therapists do not offer or accept payment for referrals; Subprinciple 7.2 which states that marriage and family therapists clearly, at the beginning of services, disclose and explain all financial arrangements to clients and supervisees; and Subprinciple 7.4 which states that marriage and family therapists represent facts truthfully to the clients, third-party payers, and supervisees regarding the services rendered.

The issue of payment for referrals is important because in some jurisdictions (e.g., California), referral fees can also be a basis for criminal prosecution and/or loss of licensure. The issue of whether a particular therapist's fees are excessive is somewhat rare. The area where most ethics disputes seem to arise lies with Subprinciple 7.2, which deals with the disclosure of fees at the inception of the services, and Subprinciple 7.4, which requires representing facts truthfully to clients and third-party payers. At this point, it is clear that the concept of informed consent inherently incorporates the idea that a client is given some indication of how long the therapy may last and what the therapy may cost over time.

A common argument by plaintiffs' attorneys in malpractice litigation is that, if a client had known how long a therapy would take, he or she would not have agreed to undergo the therapy. Such an argument can be successful, particularly in an instance where a client has incurred a substantial bill.

The major arena in which finances and insurance collide, to the therapist's detriment, is in billing the client's carrier for payment. The following are practices that can lead to problems and allegations of fraud: (1) using a deliberately false diagnosis that is less pejorative than the actual diagnosis, with the assumption being that if the insurance company knew the correct diagnosis it would not pay for services; (2) billing for sessions that did not occur (e.g., billing the insurance company for missed sessions); (3) using the insurance of a family member as if that person were part of or the only person in the sessions, because insurance would not cover the actual client(s) (e.g., providing family therapy, but billing it as individual therapy); (4) falsely stating the date and the conditions for which treatment was provided in order to gain insurance coverage; (5) routinely waiving a client's co-payment; and (6) falsely representing that the services were provided by the licensed therapist, when services were actually provided by an intern, whom the insurance company would not pay if the true facts were known (Steckler v. Ohio State Board of Psychology, 1992, supra).

These are just a few of the varieties of possible insurance fraud that the author has seen in different cases. Over the years, insurance carriers have become more aggressive about pursuing reimbursement of monies fraudulently paid, and licensing boards have also become more aggressive about pursuing discipline over professionals' providing false statements to insurance carriers. In addition, in some instances making false claims under federal programs may create a potential for criminal liability. For example, in United States v. Monick (1984), a psychiatrist was convicted of Medicaid fraud for allegedly billing for services not provided, and her staff was allowed to testify to billing practices that were found to be objectionable.

There tends to be a subjective perception that making false statements to insurance companies is not bad if it is intended to help the client by funding therapy. In the survey conducted of AAMFT clinical members mentioned earlier, Brock and Coufal (1998) asked specifically whether respondents tailored a diagnosis to meet insurance criteria. Only 27 percent of the respondents said they never did, and only 26 percent of the respondents said that tailoring a diagnosis to meet insurance criteria was absolutely unethical. Such actions, however, are likely seen by both insurance companies and state licensing boards as fraud. Hopefully, since the Brock and Coufal survey, therapists have become more aware of the ethical aspects of billing insurance companies. Therapists should realize that submitting false statements to an insurance company can irreparably damage their credibility as a professional service provider.

It is important, therefore, that the notes of sessions with clients be consistent with the insurance billing, both as to the diagnosis and as to dates on which treatment was provided. A problem with the use of off-site billing services is that frequently the dates of the billing and the dates of the session notes do not coincide. While typographical errors are not particularly problematic, a significant lack of correlation between the billing dates and the session notes raises questions as to whether the notes have been fabricated, or prepared after the fact of a dispute arising.

Potential ethical issues also arise with regard to the attempts by a therapist to collect on outstanding bills (Geis v. Landau, 1983). The practitioner should never allow a client's bill to get to a level where it creates an issue of dependency on the therapist. Feelings of dependency can arise when a bill is so large that the client believes that he or she can never pay it. The client may also come to have unrealistic expectations of the therapist who allows continued attendance at sessions in spite of not paying for the therapy.

While there is no ethical proscription against using a collection agency, therapists should be aware that a likely response to an attempt to use a collection agency is for the client to threaten or initiate a counteraction (Kennestone Hospital v. Hopson, 2000). In one case that the author handled, a female client owed a bill of approximately $100; she had been in therapy and had been shot by her boyfriend, who had attended conjoint treatment sessions with the same therapist. When the female client received a bill for the unpaid $100, she suddenly became willing to pursue litigation against the therapist. This action led to a legal claim being filed against the therapist, based on a failure to warn the female client of the male's dangerousness. Obviously, the exposure due to this claim far exceeded the unpaid bill.

Although there are few cases that deal with the methods used by therapists to collect bills, the case law that does exist suggests that a therapist may not hold a client's records hostage until bills are paid, or may not withhold a report on condition of full payment, or of a lien being signed (Parsons v. Farmer's Insurance Group of Companies, 1997). This same point is made very clear in the AAMFT ethics code; that is, marriage and family therapists "may not withhold records under their immediate control that are requested and needed for a client's treatment solely because payment has not been received for past services, except as otherwise provided by law" (Subprinciple 7.6). By statute or regulation, some jurisdictions prohibit conditioning release of clinical records on paying for past-due professional services (e.g., Florida Statute §456.057(4)).

A final point with regard to finances and managed care contracts is that most managed care contracts contain a provision not to charge clients in excess of the agreed-upon rate. There have been instances where therapists have tried to charge the client more than that allowed by the managed care contract. This is seen as a form of fraud.

It is not uncommon for therapists to have sliding scale fees. According to the AAMFT ethics code, under Principle VII, Financial Arrangements, and the subprinciples contained therein, as long as the sliding scale fees are not excessive and are accurately disclosed, there is no inherent ethical problem. Issues can arise where a therapist has a sliding fee structure and a client wants to have the fees reimbursed by an insurance carrier. The insurance carrier may take the position that the lower end of the fee scale should apply, not the higher end. A sliding fee scale must be a true sliding scale. This means that the client's financial condition should be a factor in determining whether the low end or the high end of the scale applies. It is improper to have an artificially high fee for clients with insurance and a lower fee for the same services for clients who do not have insurance, but do have the assets with which to pay a regular fee. The use of such fees for therapy has been implied in some decisions by courts where parties have agreed to use a therapist who provided a sliding scale fee (In re Joshua, 1990).

CONCLUSION

Marriage and family therapists need to see that ethical principles and obligations are not simply theoretical issues. Ethics interface with the day-to-day conduct of the therapy practice. Considerations relevant to both ethics and the law must be thoughtfully integrated into the routine business operations and procedures of the therapy practice.

Although the various business issues and recommended procedures and guidelines discussed above may seem complex, by carefully becoming aware of these and the associated ethical principles, therapists can avoid unnecessary legal or ethical problems. The proper management of ethical responsibilities does not just happen, and it should not just happen on a case-by-case basis. Instead, therapists are more likely to fulfill their major ethical responsibilities and avoid ethical dilemmas and violations when they carefully put in place ethically sound and legally safe business and clinical procedures and operations.

REFERENCES

American Medical Association. (2001, July 19). Guidelines for physician-patient electronic communications. Washington, DC: Author.

American Psychological Association. (1997, November 15). Position paper: Services by telephone, teleconferencing, and internet. Washington, DC: Author.

Americans With Disabilities Act of 1990, 42 U.S.C. 12101, et seq.

Birkner v. Salt Lake County, 771 P.2d 1053 (1989 Utah).

Block v. Gomez, 201 Wis 2d 795, 549 NW 2d 783 (1996).

Brock, G. W. (Ed.). (1998). Ethics casebook. Washington, DC: American Association for Marriage and Family Therapy.

Brock, G. W., & Coufal, G. (1998). A national survey of the ethical practices and attitudes of marriage and family therapists. In G. W. Brock (Ed.), Ethics casebook (pp. 175–201). Washington, DC: American Association for Marriage and Family Therapy.

Broughton v. Cigna Health Plan, 21 Cal.4th 1066 (1999).

Bunce v. Parkside Lodge of Columbus, 62 Oh St.3d 1425, 577 NE2d 1107 (1991).

California Board of Psychology Regulation 16 C.C.R. §1391.6; Board of Behavioral Sciences Regulation 16 C.C.R. §1833.1.

California Code of Civil Procedure § 1985.3.

California Code of Civil Procedure §1295 on arbitration.

Cobbs v. Grant, 8 Cal.3d 229 (1972).

Cutter v. Brownbridge, 183 Cal.App.3d 830 (1986).

Doe v. Samaritan Counseling Center, 791 P.2d 344 (Alaska 1990).

Doe v. U.S., 912 F.Supp. 913 (Ed. VA 1995).

Dudder, P., & Roth, J. A. (1997, May/June). Report on the Board of Psychology. California Psychologist, 30 (6), 13.

Ebert, B. (1997, January). Informed consent. California Board of Psychology Update, 3, 3, 13.

Florida Statute §456.057(4), Ownership and control of patient records; report or copies to be furnished.

Garamella v. New York Medical College, 23 F.Supp.2d 153 (D. Conn 1988).

Geis v. Landau, 117 Misc.2d 396, 458 NYS 2d 1000 (Civil Court NY 1983).

Goldberg v. Department of Industry Labor and Human Relations, 484 NW 2d 568 (Wis. App. 1992).

Hungerford v. Jones, 722 A.2d 478 (1998).

Inabnit v. Berkson, 199 Cal.App.3d. 1230 (1988).

In re Joshua Z., Conn. super. Lexis 1779 (not officially reported) (1990).

Kennestone Hospital v. Hopson, 538 SE2d 742 (Ga 2000).

Marston v. Minneapolis Clinic of Psychiatry & Neurology Ltd., 329 NW2d 306 (Minn. 1982).

Modi v. West Virginia/Board of Medicine, 468 S.E.2d 230 (W.Va 1995).

Montoya v. Bebensee, 731 P.2d 285 (Col. 1988).

Noto v. St. Vincent's Hospital & Medical Center of New York, 142 Misc.2d. (1990).

Nagy, T. (1992, Winter). The benefits and hazards of teletherapy. Stanford Medical Group, Stanford University Clinic Primary Care Group, p. 23.

Neptuno Treuhand Und Verwal Tungesellschaft, MBH. v. Arbor, 295 Ill. App. 3d 567, 692 N.E. 2d 812 (1998).

Parsons v. Farmer's Insurance Group of Companies, 52 Cal.App. 4th 813 (1997).

Plummer v. Center Psychiatrists Ltd., 476 SE2d 172 (1996 VA).

Rains v. Superior Court, 198 Cal.App.3d 249 (1984).

Randi W. v. Muroc Joint Unified School District, 14 Cal.4th 1066 (1997).

Ray v. Value Behavior Health, Inc., 967 F.Supp. 4117 (NV 1997).

Riemersma, M. (1992, May/June). The dos and don'ts of interviewing interns and trainees. California Thera-pist, 4 (3), 13.

Rost v. State Board of Psychology, 659 A2d 626 (Pa Commw. 1995).

Simmons v. U.S. 805 F.2d 1363 (Ninth Cir. 1986).

Steckler v. Ohio State Board of Psychology, 613 NE 2d 1070 (Ohio App. 1992).

Swift v. Doe, 570 S.2d 1209 (Ala S.Ct. 1990).

Truman v. Thomas, 27 Cal.3d 285 (1980).

United States v. Monick, 753 F.2d 1085 (9th Cir. 1984).

Woody, R. H. (1999). Domestic violations of confidentiality. Professional Psychology: Research and Practice, 30 (6), 607–610.

Woody, R. H. (2001). Psychological information: Protecting the right of privacy. Madison, CT: Psychosocial Press (International Universities Press).

THE FUTURE OF MARRIAGE AND FAMILY THERAPY

Robert Henley Woody and Jane DiVita Woody

This chapter discusses four assumptions and salient issues that are impacting professional ethics currently and will do so in the future as well. (1) Science and technology have moved everyone into a global context that downplays parochial concerns, and the therapist must integrate global and international considerations into practices. (2) Social justice supports that the therapist honor ethnic, social class, and cultural factors; and adaptations in underlying theoretical assumptions and practice techniques will be necessary to accommodate cultural diversity. (3) In this age of managed care organizations that emphasize cost control versus quality care, ethics must support that quality care, as determined by a professional therapist (as opposed to an accountant) is preferred. (4) Because behavioral science must undergird marriage and family therapy, professional ethics must support the importance of further research on therapeutic processes and services. This chapter discusses these assumptions and further explores three special issues: societal conflict, abuse, and violence; gay and lesbian relationships; and telehealth services.

CONTENTS

When a therapist meets with clients, there is always an ethical umbrella over the interactions. Every event and communication, verbal or non-verbal, must be in accord with the professional ethics that are prevailing at the time. Although ethics are continually evolving, certain core dimensions will always merit primary consideration. The core dimensions are evidenced, for example, by the principles in the AAMFT ethics code, although the substance of a principle might change, with the differences being reflected in the subprinciples.

In keeping with the ever-changing nature of professional ethics, the practitioner should be mindful that what appears to be the "total story" at one point in time will surely be somewhat different later on. For example, ethics used to preclude bold print in advertisements for mental health services. Consumerism and marketplace competition led to elimination of this restraint; the law now is the controlling source, and it provides that any type of advertisement may be used, as long as it is truthful and neither misleading nor deceptive. This example illustrates that ethics change and that the law may, in some instances, take over ethical functions.

To prepare for what may be on the horizon, the marriage and family therapist should monitor current trends in and the intertwining of societal and professional values and views of mental health services. This awareness will enable the practitioner to identify matters and issues that call for action in day-to-day practice and that may require adaptations in the foreseeable future.

Whether at present or at some point in the future, every event or communication within the therapeutic context has the potential for ethical implications. Given the increasing complexity of mental health services in society, therapists should get used to the idea of relying extensively on professional ethics.

An ethics code is a signal from the profession that alerts each marriage and family therapist to be prepared to encounter, analyze, and deal effectively with current practice issues as well as problems that are likely to arise in the future. Chapter One explained that professions, by definition, must continually advance their scholarly base and develop innovative strategies for improving services to consumers. As the AAMFT ethics code states in Subprinciple 3.1, "Marriage and family therapists pursue knowledge of new developments and maintain competence in marriage and family therapy through education, training, or supervised experience." In accord with this subprinciple, the preceding chapters have attempted to advance practitioners' knowledge and competence. The focus was on the ways in which critical aspects of practice affect ethics and are, in turn, affected by ethics and how both need to draw on behavioral science research.

This chapter similarly aims to expand professional knowledge, competence, and ethical awareness. The discussion here will pinpoint specific issues that have emerged from the overall analysis, and other issues that are likely to bring future challenges to the profession in general and the individual therapist in particular.

GLOBAL MARRIAGE AND FAMILY THERAPY

In the future, the interconnections and interdependence between all countries will be strengthened. The condition of the family will be an index of each nation's health and potential for making a positive contribution to civilization and peace. International interdependence is certainly consonant with the general systems theory that underlies much of marriage and family therapy, which has long been recognized by family system theorists (e.g., Bateson, 1972).

An inevitable product of globalism will be an increase in ethnic and racial diversity among the consumers of mental health services. Although many industrialized countries, such as Canada and the United States, assume the presence of a culturally diverse citizenry and of pluralism as part of democracy, there will always be a challenge to live up to these espoused ideals.

For the individual therapist, ethnicity may become more important than ever in effectively serving diverse clients. On the other hand, the overwhelming presence of ethnic diversity will potentially lessen the impact of ethnicity as a controlling factor in therapeutic processes. Being sensitive to cultural factors will, of course, extend to the therapist's self understanding, as well as to appreciating and accepting the varied characteristics of clients.

In the future, therapists will need knowledge of how family issues are handled in various nationalities and awareness of the increasing international influence on American life. Integrating global and international considerations into day-to-day practices will not be easy and will necessitate going beyond a parochial stance. Therapists may experience stress on a personal level as they attempt to process and understand diverse values in relation to their own personal and professional values. Clearly, education and supervision will be essential in the training and development of marriage and family therapists for intercultural matters.

In addition to a personal challenge to the individual therapist, globalism means that the profession will need to guard against inappropriate or ill-advised pilgrimages toward or away from ethnic accommodations. Even now, the therapist must not impose theories of family theories that were created for and are applicable to Western industrialized values and family forms.

An analysis of "planet" concerns by Johnson (2001) mentioned the risk of "messianic strains" in the related family systems literature. Johnson seems to believe that, in the writing of some proponents of family systems theories, there are certain assumptions that these theories have the most value for or relevance to developing a healthy family (saving sick societies), without giving credence to qualities unique to other cultures. In keeping with ethics, the prudent therapist should exercise safeguards against allowing messianic tendencies to occur. Without this awareness, there is the risk of bias, or as the senior author of this chapter has termed it in the past, "pious bias." One result might be the imposition of the therapist's national viewpoint about, say, family constitution, rather than honoring a client's national viewpoint on the subject. In other words, rigid pursuit of a particular definition or set of preferred conditions for the family can potentially turn a well-meaning professional into a zealot.

Marriage and family therapy will continue to promote positive societal conditions through, for example, legislative actions in conjunction with a state chapter of AAMFT. There will also be a commitment to helping service users resolve family dilemmas that have their roots in society (for example, substance abuse, domestic violence). Intervening in societal conditions and family dilemmas may become increasingly complex as a result of internationalism and cultural diversity. On a practical level, there will be no easy solutions. In day-to-day practice, therapists will, as in the past, need to understand the immediate dynamics of clients' relationships, as well as how their problems connect to broader sociopolitical and physical environments in which clients live, including the ethnic composition of the family and community.

When serving a family or working in a community, practitioners must respect other cultures and their concomitant values. Indeed, Johnson (2001) recognized how certain family systems theorists reveal bias and exaggeration in their "wholly unwarranted elevation of what they call the wisdom of the East over the 'epistemological errors' of 'Occidental thinking'" (p. 9). Johnson does not dispute the dangers facing our global society, such as the "terrible dangers of ecological contamination and military conflict" (p. 10). But he wisely endorses professional humility and staving off any messianic tendency, to "better the lives of families and couples before that hopefully distant Armageddon" and to "make a world most might agree was worth having lived in" (p. 11). Among the numerous controversial family issues that have already emerged for practitioners, consider the different cultural views of gender roles in marriage, the age at which families may arrange marriages for young girls, the practice of clitoridectomy, and the mores and values about sexuality (such as for Hassidic Jewish couples or for Muslin couples).

Social Justice

In practical terms, the therapist in the future will face a greater number of and more complex intercultural issues.

For example, the AAMFT ethics code indicates that, regardless of circumstance, Subprinciple 1.1 is applicable, namely, "Marriage and family therapists provide professional assistance to persons without discrimination on the basis of race, age, ethnicity, socioeconomic status, disability, gender, health status, religion, national origin, or sexual orientation." Although it is not stated expressly in the ethics code, the issue goes beyond discrimination. It is fundamental that the marriage and family therapist respects, adequately and fully, the cultural qualities brought to treatment by the clients, which would include, but would not be limited to, the conditions for family values and interactions provided by the clients' cultural identity.

Psychotherapy in general has long been criticized as serving the needs of the educated and affluent. Therapists, almost regardless of personal background or effort, are destined to think and behave like middle-class persons during their therapeutic services to clients.

Most clinicians have been trained to voice, but not necessarily practice, acceptance of clients' unique cultural factors. Theoretically, it is questionable whether the therapist can serve clients free from his or her own cultural characteristics. As Goldenberg and Goldenberg (2000) have said, "Constructionists believe objectivity is impossible, and that the therapist, presumably an outside observer of a family, in actuality participates in constructing what is observed" (p. 105). They added a suggestion:

> . . . *each therapist's values are inevitably embedded in that person's gender, ethnic, and social class experiences and current circumstances. Since therapists inevitably expose these perspectives (biases?) in their interactions with their clients, they need to be aware of their own values and beliefs as they help client families to sort out theirs. (p. 55)*

They also pointed out that training programs today are helping trainees achieve "a raised consciousness regarding the role played by ethnic, social class, and cultural factors in influencing outlooks and behavior in order to better differentiate among universal, transcultural, culture-specific, or idiosyncratic family behaviors" (pp. 380–381). Speaking from the point of view of trainers, Hardy (2001) reported that "the skills that we endeavor to teach, as well as the wisdom we hopefully impart, is never divorced from the larger sociocultural context" (p. 21); and he favors "raising the social justice bar for family therapists" (p. 19).

Training in marriage and family therapy will have to prepare practitioners for the changing sociocultural context. Many of the underlying theoretical assumptions and practice techniques must be examined to assure that they accommodate changing ethnic or racial situations; for example, something as straightforward as a genogram must be adjusted to various definitions of what constitutes a family (Milewski-Hertlein, 2001).

One of the difficult future challenges for therapists will be working with ethnic issues that are intertwined. Negy and Snyder (2000) offered valuable insights into interethnic couples' relationship experiences, and indicated, "The racial and ethnic demographics of the United States have changed dramatically over the last three decades . . . as more individuals are marrying outside their own ethnic or racial group" (p. 293). Killian (2001) noted that these changes create the need for additional competence by therapists as they must deal with the conflicts faced by an interracial couple: "Crossing the borders of race, ethnicity, and culture carries social and psychological implications for couples, raising questions about group and family loyalties and partner and couple identities" (p. 40).

To help therapists achieve "multicultural competence," training in the future should emphasize ". . . therapists' awareness of their own culture, therapists' knowledge of the worldview of the culturally different client, and therapists' behaviors or use of culturally appropriate treatment strategies and interventions" (Bean, Perry, & Bedell, 2001, p. 43).

The emerging attention to social justice in the field of marriage and family therapy must become central in training programs as students need preparation to deal effectively with changes in clients' sociocultural environments. Although there are noteworthy efforts, much remains to be done. McGoldrick et al. (1999) set forth the dilemma for trainers:

Obviously we cannot settle for simple minded ideas such as that all women understand women's experience better than any man, or that all people of color understand racial oppression better than any white person, or that gay and lesbian perspectives about homosexuality should always be privileged over those of any heterosexual. At the same time the dominant group member's opinion does tend in almost all contexts to be privileged over that of members of oppressed groups. (p. 207)

Solving this training dilemma is complex but essential. Social justice is so critical to the overall profession that, immediately and in the future, trainers of all therapists, including marriage and family therapists, will need to integrate it into all aspects of curriculum and supervision.

On a positive note, the profession is certainly reflecting an increase in sensitivity to cultural issues, broadly defined. For example, professional conferences and publications, such as those offered by the AAMFT, have given increasing attention to cultural diversity and to the impact of societal conditions and institutions on the problems and lives of clients.

MANAGED CARE ORGANIZATIONS AND POLITICAL FORCES

Closely related to globalization and the link between culturally diverse consumers and funding their health care and human services needs, there is a powerful economic force operating within mental health services, including marriage and family therapy. It is worthwhile, but sobering, to remember that mental health professionals sought to be part of the health care industry. Whether right or wrong, their motive was for financial gain to practitioners as much or more than it was to assure quality health care for consumers.

As with any industry, expenditures and revenues influence what is made available to consumers. Stated bluntly, but accurately, economics often dictate and control mental health services. Although this is already true, the prevailing economic attitudes of consumers and their governmental representatives support that the same will be true, or more so, in the future.

Finances and the Health Care Industry

Many mental health practitioners have been surprised that joining the ranks of the health care industry has lessened or diluted professional decision making and increased economically based determinations about treatment services. While therapists may propose a treatment plan believed to be in the best interest of the client, approval depends upon a fiscal source, such as a case manager employed by an insurance or managed care company. This review source is employed to give primary importance to controlling costs, with the well being of the client being, at best, secondary.

As a typical concomitant of managed care, therapists have also found that their incomes have not increased, as they may have hoped in the effort to become part of the health care industry. The reason for this economic effect is twofold.

First, managed care is predicated on cost control. Consequently, policies and practices are committed to reducing expenses, such as the fee paid to a therapist. This stance may result in giving priority to services from less expensive treatment providers. The result can be assignment of a client to a therapist who has less than adequate training to meet the clinical needs of the particular client.

Second, it is a matter of fact that training programs have produced an abundance of mental health practitioners, which has resulted in a simply supply and demand effect. That is, there are more therapists available to whom a managed care organization can refer a potential client. To receive referrals, the practitioner must have a competitive fee. The bottom line is that many therapists report a significant degrease in income or earning potential from what was true, say, in a previous era.

It is not self-serving for any mental health profession, including marriage and family therapy, to be concerned about how the emphasis on cost control affects both the quality of care provided to clients and professional incomes. To assure the best quality for all health-related services, including therapy, it is in society's best interest for practitioners to be satisfied with the remuneration they receive for their professional services. The old adage comes to mind, "You get what you pay for."

The following example shows how the emphasis on cost control can affect both professional incomes and the quality of care provided to clients. A marriage and family therapist had an initial session with a family, during which the teenage son admitted openly that he was planning to commit suicide. The parents did not take the matter seriously. With the goal of providing the young man with an immediate and comprehensive treatment program to safeguard against the possibility of suicide, the therapist spent two additional hours with the family, the managed care organization, and referral sources. The managed care organization, however, would approve payment for only one hour of time, and this doctoral level therapist received $40!

Society should also be concerned about managed care policies that promote the use of practitioners with less training rather than drawing on the total pool of therapists. Although master's level practitioners can and do fulfill an important need, there are certain competencies that necessitate more advanced training and experience. Over-reliance on master's level therapists because they will accept lower fees than, say, doctoral level therapists is ill advised for clients, the mental professions, and society. A result of this business practice is that some doctoral level therapists have ceased to offer services to clients whose payment comes from a managed care organization.

Certainly doctoral level therapists can properly fulfill supervisory and consulting roles for master's level therapists, but their clinical services are also needed for certain purposes. Assuming that advanced training yields higher levels of competency, the mental health professions and clients may lose benefits if doctoral level practitioners are by-passed by managed care organizations. There should be room and remuneration for both doctoral level and master's level therapists; drawing on the skills and services of both could presumably preserve quality services for the consumer and cost control as well.

There is reason to doubt that cost savings are passed on to the service users, as opposed to reaping profits for the managed care organizations. Sluzki (2001) stated, "What we assumed were healing professions have become a set of practices that are managed at a distance by third parties" (p. 13). This view points to a decline of professional authority in favor of nonprofessional management. He further stated,

The extraordinary expansion of what has been called the 'health care industry,' namely, for-profit hospital conglomerates, the move of the massive private insurance companies and of other for-profit intermediaries into the business of regulating access to health care—a blatant conflict of interests—has changed the way we practice our trade—anonymous purse-string holders instruct us to follow guidelines dictated by for-profit criteria: The fewer the services that are provided, the more the money for the stockholders. (p. 13)

Negative consequences for mental health are evident: "Spending on mental health benefits has declined more than 54% over the past decade . . . [and] reimbursement for mental health services has decreased far more than any other area in health care" (Reed, Levant, Stout, Murphy, & Phelps, 2001, p. 67). Nonetheless, health care costs continued to "explode" (p. 66).

Issues in Quality of Care

Ethics are of particular importance when it comes to assuring quality care for the service user. One of the most troubling outcomes of the expansion of managed care organizations and their role in determining health care practices is the professional's loss of control of the substance of services. Managed care organizations commonly monitor services, require extensive documentation from the therapist to justify reimbursement for services, and have the discretion to deny coverage (i.e., reimbursement). The latter reaches the core issue of who determines the substance of therapy, which clearly connects to quality control. Although the managed care organizations purport to be assuring quality care for their insured, there is no doubt that preserving their financial objective (i.e., generating a profit) guides their decision making. Consequently, many therapists, to assure that quality care is primary, are opting out of managed care organizations, and emphasize services to consumers who will make personal payments for treatment. This decision may restore to a professional, duly recognized by society as a licensed health care practitioner (not a fiscal accountant), the responsibility to decide on the preferred treatment approach, but it may not bring a clientele sufficient for a living income.

Despite its obvious limitations and shortcomings, managed care, with the support of political forces, has expanded tremendously during the last two decades. The political-commercial union is evidenced by the trend in the current market towards "the rapid privatization of public programs through government contracts with managed care companies" (Reed et al., 2001, p. 67).

There is an incipient distrust between the mental health professions and managed care sources. As mentioned earlier, the former believes that quality control and clinical decision making will be diminished for crass financial reasons, whereas the latter believes that clients will overutilize services, thereby unnecessarily elevating costs to the insurer. No doubt, an argument could be made for both sides in this dispute. Howard and Bassos (2000) addressed this issue:

Insurers, through their benefits structure, set requirements for the reimbursement of mental health treatment. Insurers must either rely on the integrity of therapists to give a good-faith effort to accurately diagnose their patients or, if insurers do not trust therapists to do this, control the decision regarding medical necessity themselves. Conversely, psychologists who serve as gatekeepers for insurers must provide unbiased assessment of patients' conditions and treatment needs. When therapists are in doubt, the decision regarding authorization should favor the patient. (p. 530)

As with many areas of contemporary practice, the lawmakers, licensing boards, and ethics committees seem to have shied away from providing authoritative definitions and guidelines that would potentially solve this issue of clinical control.

As stated earlier, financial factors can influence the quality of care. For the therapist, the fee can influence motivation to provide the best possible treatment; and for the client, confusion about or dissatisfaction with financial responsibility can potentially have a negative effect on the client's commitment to therapy and thus to its outcome.

These issues highlight the importance of the ethical responsibility to deal realistically with financial matters—with both clients and third-party payment sources. Failure to deal properly with financial issues has ethical implications. Honesty and integrity with regard to financial matters are part of the AAMFT ethics code. Principle VII, Financial Arrangements, states, "Marriage and family therapists make financial arrangements with clients, third-party payors, and supervisees that are reasonably understandable and conform to accepted professional practices." In addition, Subprinciple 7.4 states, "Marriage and family therapists represent facts truthfully to clients, third-party payors, and supervisees regarding services rendered."

Recently a marriage and family therapist told the senior author of this chapter about the success and client satisfaction from her conducting multiple-family group therapy for families that had a senior family member in a nursing home (e.g., she helped them with their grief over the diminished mental and physical capacity of the senior family member). Despite all of the positive effects, the insurer had declined coverage, saying in effect that the services were not primarily for the benefit of the senior who was covered but were for the benefit of family members who were not covered. Obviously, a family therapist could offer a theoretical rationale that supported that healthier family members would contribute substantially to the welfare of the senior family member, but this type of professional knowledge and competence was not recognized or accepted by the insurance source.

From the point of view of professional ethics, therapists must not blindly relegate the standards and substance of their professional services to any nonprofessional source. Most certainly they must not allow nonclinical and nonprofessional sources, like the managed care organizations that are concerned primarily with fiscal issues, to usurp, denigrate, or alter unjustly the principles within a professional code of ethics that aim to benefit consumers of the professional services. Unfortunately, it may be easier to voice this position than to carry it out, as the following situation reveals.

A therapist treated a husband and wife for about five years. The therapy was primarily for the husband's psychiatric problems and to help the wife cope with the situation. At times, members of their family were also included in the treatment sessions. The health insurance company alleged that the husband was "overutilizing" services. With an attorney on the payroll to pursue legal actions, the health insurance company demanded that the therapist refund over 30 thousand dollars for past treatment services that the health insurance company had decided, years after the services had been provided, were unjustified.

The therapist was frightened at the prospect of a legal action, but believed that the past services were justifiable, that the client and his family still needed treatment, and that, because of the strong therapeutic relationship, he was in the best position to provide it to them. The health insurance company apparently did not disagree with the need for further treatment, since, in fairly short order, it offered the therapist an alternative to legal action. If the therapist would quit treating the husband and wife, the health insurance company would provide the couple with the names of three other therapists from whom they could choose a subsequent provider of services, and the insurance company would cancel the demand for the refund of 30 thousand dollars. The intention of this offer was clearly to channel the husband and wife, by fiscal mandate, to a therapist who would likely dance to the tune of the managed care piper.

Although the therapist truly believed that the existing strong therapeutic relationship would yield the best benefits to the husband and wife, he felt forced to withdraw, and he explained to the clients that he could not financially afford to do legal battle with the health insurance company. He accepted the agreement to cease providing treatment to the client and his family.

Professional Challenges

Health care is, of course, a high priority for virtually any government, but economic interests can influence governmental actions. Advocates for managed care have invested considerable resources to gain governmental support and accommodation. It is naïve for therapists to believe that public policies and law are free from influences dedicated to commercial interests over quality care for service recipients. Indeed, many mental health professionals believe that, in the case of health care policies, the government has sometimes supported managed care organizations at the expense of consumers and health care professionals. For example, Sluzki (2001) stated,

Political and economic forces are always present, but their impact on this era is massive, and they are moving us implacably toward the erosion of the social entitlements and the progressive replacement of governmental commitments to provide accessible, affordable health care to all, by a philosophy of "health care as a commodity." (p. 13)

He also nicely clarified the challenge facing the profession of marriage and family therapy:

> *Now more than ever—when our trade and our professions are being industrialized, dehumanized, decontextualized, and we are being treated by the health care industry and by the political conservatism of the health policies as pawns without voice, without agency—now more than ever we have to keep a contextual eye and an inclusive view, fight against the seductive language of this brave new world, keep our critical voice in good shape, and exercise our right, if not our duty, to make ourselves heard. (p. 15)*

Without constant vigilance and powerful resistance to the efforts of managed care organizations and political forces to control professional services, grave consequences lie ahead for the future of marriage and family therapy. Most basically, the AAMFT ethics code captures the "call to arms" in Principle VI, Responsibility to the Profession, which states, "Marriage and family therapists respect the rights and responsibilities of professional colleagues and participate in activities that advance the goals of the profession." Also relevant, Subprinciple 6.6 states, "Marriage and family therapists participate in activities that contribute to a better community and society . . . ." Subprinciple 6.7 adds, "Marriage and family therapists are concerned with developing laws and regulations pertaining to marriage and family therapy that serve the public interest, and with altering such laws and regulations that are not in the public interest."

RESEARCH

To offer services that are truly professional, marriage and family therapists must constantly attempt to enhance the scholarly basis for the services provided to clients. This section examines the adequacy of the current state of research in marriage and family therapy and identifies certain goals for the future.

Systems concepts and the context of multiple clients make research about marriage and family therapy uniquely difficult. For example, Booth and Cottone (2000) pointed out that predicting the treatment paradigm for marriage and family therapy is not very successful. In other words, it may be that marriage and family therapists do not "practice what they preach." Of course, the same may be said for other therapeutic modalities or other professionals as well.

Notwithstanding the methodological problems, it is possible to identify core aspects of behavior change due to therapeutic interventions. Woolley, Butler, and Wampler (2000) put it this way, "There is growing recognition in individual and relationship therapies of the significant proportion of outcome variance accounted for by 'common factors' unrelated to the model being used" (p. 325). They recommend use of process methodology to uncover the interactional sequence between the therapist and the clients, and concomitant change events.

Marriage and family therapy has been amassing impressive efficacy studies, although far more and continuing research on the subject is needed. Summaries of demonstrated efficacy of models of marriage and family therapy have been provided by Gurman, Kniskern, and Pinsof (1986); Miller, Johnson, Sandberg, Stringer-Seibold, and Gfeller-Strouts (2000); and Sandberg, et al. (1997).

One of the positive contributions of the bumbling attempts at health care reform and the onerous presence of managed care has been the demand that therapists document the efficacy of their therapeutic interventions. Since ethics require that professional services should, with a degree of surety, provide benefits to the consumer, it is a reasonable expectation that the therapist should monitor, measure, and document the effectiveness and efficacy of therapeutic interventions. Although managed care has provided some impetus for this expectation, it is also part of the practitioner's ethical responsibility to advance the welfare of clients. This goal implies the importance of knowing which elements of therapy actually benefit the client.

A review of the professional literature reveals that there have been precious few studies of the comparative effects of individual, group, couple, and family therapy. Often the results of a study intended to examine efficacy are shrouded in ambiguity, such as being void of clear specification of the conditions present in the therapeutic intervention.

After a useful review of efficacy studies, Law and Crane (2000) examined medical records of clients who had received marital and family therapy, and concluded that they experienced a significant reduction in the need for subsequent medical services. That is, those clients receiving marriage and family therapy had a 10% reduction in utilizing health care services, as compared to subjects from the same pool of patients in a health maintenance organization. This finding suggests a mechanism by which therapy may create overall health benefits. Although only speculation, it may be that marriage and family therapy, for example, reduces stress, which leads to a reduction in other stress-related illnesses. Law and Crane wisely recognized the limitations due to the research methodology, and called for additional research of this nature with other types of subjects and levels of health/illness, and means for cost analysis/reductions. They also noted that the effects of marriage and family therapy likely extend beyond medical conditions alone. This study illustrates one type of efficacy research that needs to be pursued in the future. This sort of study also supports the view that integrated health care, involving marriage and family therapy, may become more prevalent in the future (Simon, 2001).

Unfortunately, marriage and family therapy, like certain other clinical services, has often relied more on the apparent soundness of the theoretical rationale than on empirical outcome studies. Sprenkle and Bailey (1995) argued, "if our discipline is to remain a viable 'player' in the health care system, it will be necessary to demonstrate our effectiveness both clinically and financially" (p. 339). In the future, efficacy studies relevant to marriage and family therapy will be central to sustaining the profession. (Chapter Five in this book discusses in detail the challenges of linking the ethic of professional competence and the ethic of care for the client with the movement toward evidence-based treatment.)

It would be tempting to allege that any dearth of research in marriage and family therapy is due to a lack of emphasis on research in training programs. According to research by Johnson, Sandberg, and Miller (1999), "the mere quantity of research training a family therapist receives in graduate school has a limited influence on his or her future research practices" (p. 248). Although they warn that the reasons for failure to engage in research remain to be determined, they identify a lack of collaboration between practitioners and researchers and a lack of understanding of research methods and statistics.

Beyond the aforementioned issues of collaboration and methodology/statistics, for the typical practitioner, the nature of marriage and family therapy restricts involvement in research. There are many issues that complicate research with clients, and the clinician may not be able to manage these:

(1) The clinical information (i.e., the data) must be guarded for confidentiality and is difficult, if not impossible, to quantify at the level of precision required for scholarly research;

(2) The practitioner may be hesitant to "impose" on clients for time and information that will not offer benefits directly to the clients (that is, if the clients receive only indirect benefits through contributing to research to advance the profession);

(3) Even seeking research subjects as volunteers from among clients receiving clinical services may create unacceptable pressure for a client to participate and possibly be a violation of a research subject's rights; and

(4) The practitioner may be reluctant to relinquish income-generating time to data collection and analysis, which yield no personal/financial benefits for the practitioner or assurance of respect or acceptance by other members of the profession (indeed, the nature of scholarship means that any research must be subjected to critique).

Although the foregoing barriers exist, the marriage and family therapist should be willing and able to circumvent them. As a reminder, behavioral science is essential to formulating appropriate interventions and services.

Even though conducting independent research in the context of practice is difficult, marriage and family therapists can and should collaborate with well-designed research that is directed by academic-based professional training programs. In other words, there are ways for practitioners to help further the development of knowledge that will benefit the profession and society.

In summary, empirical research as a foundation for the practice of marriage and family therapy is essential for survival of the profession. AAMFT deserves accolades for its efforts to promote research through conferences, education, standards, and publications. Nevertheless, in a content analysis of research in family therapy journals, Hawley, Bailey, and Pennick (2000) recognized the advances and the positive efforts (such as those of AAMFT), but also concluded, "the MFT field still has significant room for improvement in order to establish a credible research base that will justify its practices" (p. 16).

In terms of ethics, the rights of persons who are research subjects (i.e., provide the data used for analysis) must be safeguarded. The AAMFT ethics code addresses the responsibility to research participants, such as in Principle V,

Responsibility to Research Participants: "Investigators respect the dignity and protect the welfare of research participants, and are aware of applicable laws and regulations and professional standards governing the conduct of research." Four subprinciples elaborate on Principle V. (Chapter Four in this book further discusses relationships with research subjects.)

Practitioners need to be aware of the extensive rights of research subjects. One doctoral student had a zealous academic advisor who, due to seeking tenure, insisted on co-authorship of all student research publications. He encouraged the student to surreptitiously obtain data from the clinic in which the student worked. The academic advisor and the student totally ignored the potential ethical and legal ramifications of the student's providing the data from identifiable clients to an outsider and publishing data that belonged to the employer.

SPECIAL ISSUES

In the future, and as the profession of marriage and family therapy gains continued acceptance in society, practitioners will be called upon to address new and varied problems and conditions that impact families and society. Here, the cultural and political forces discussed earlier often come together to define the public policy that prescribes and proscribes what will or will not be done by mental health professionals. In the future, there will surely be untold and unforeseen problems or conditions with which families and their therapists will have to cope. At this point in time, three issues deserve special consideration in this discussion about the future of marriage and family therapy: contemporary societal conflict, abuse, and violence; gay and lesbian relationships; and telehealth services.

Societal Conflict, Abuse, and Violence

Even now, the most culturally and economically enfranchised countries, such as Canada and the United States, are in a state of crisis. There is an unprecedented degree of concern—in fact, profound alarm—at the increasing incidence of youth violence (e.g., school shootings, bullying, gangs), senseless crimes, the epidemic of substance abuse, unwanted pregnancies, domestic and child abuse, and a host of other devastating problems. Marriage and family therapists have a definite and critical role to play in finding effective interventions to address these problems that affect youth and families.

Incidents of abuse and violence toward family members and others have escalated. There is no denying that violence has become a prominent dimension of society's constitution, as witnessed by the popularity of violent depictions in the news and entertainment media. Anderson and Cramer-Benjamin (1999) have concluded that the "problem of family violence is systemic and embedded in multiple levels of contemporary society" (p. 14), and that "violence affects not only every level of society but every member of the family system, whether they have been directly abused or not" (p. 15). (Chapter Seven in this book provides a detailed discussion of the many ethical issues involved in therapy that deals with violence, dangerousness, and abuse.)

Abuse and violence are particularly problematic for young people: "Intentional interpersonal violence accounts for one third of all injury-related deaths in the United States, and it disproportionately involves young people as both perpetrators and victims" (Peterson & Newman, 2000, p. 509). Of special concern, "research data clearly support the view that children are affected adversely by the violent and conflictual interactions that occur within their families" (Anderson & Cramer-Benjamin, 1999, p. 14); yet "family therapists and other mental-health professionals are not sufficiently aware of the impact of witnessing violence on children" (p. 1).

Given the prominence of young people in this problem and the belief that the family is crucial to curbing youth violence, family conflicts should be a priority for the profession of marriage and family therapy. Citing research sources, Stern (1999) asserted that family conflicts increase when a child reaches adolescence, that most families with an adolescent can cope reasonably well with the youngster's quest for independence, but that the family with poor communication and problem-solving skills can experience delinquency, substance abuse, and other problems. She found that conflict management training for parents and their adolescents led to "acquisition of communication and problem-solving skills and a decrease in conflict at home" (p. 191).

If conflict reaches an abusive or violent level, the direct effects on children who simply witness abuse or violence are profound, leading to both mental and physical problems. For example, they may experience a range of internalizing reactions (sadness, crying, fear, anxiety, withdrawal, attachment problems, depression, somatic complaints); externalizing behavior problems (aggression, defiance, destruction of property, disobedience); social-skills problems (getting along with others, poor conflict resolution skills, difficulty making or keeping friends); and low academic achievement (Anderson & Cramer-Benjamin, 1999).

Since familial conflict can be a precursor to anger, abuse, and violent conduct, marriage and family therapy seems well suited for providing conflict-reduction services. In the future, society's concern about abuse and violence will likely call for greater emphasis on preventive intervention for conflict situations.

Beyond conflict resolution, marriage and family therapists must be prepared to manage the violent patient, including for self-protection. Woody (1996) summarizes the risks to and measures taken by mental health practitioners to avoid danger from clients. Tishler, Gordon, and Landry-Meyer (2000) also acknowledge the danger that some patients pose to their therapists and offer insightful guidelines for creating safeguards. At the same time, they believe in the power of the therapeutic relationship to modulate violence "if the clinician understands the nature of the therapeutic alliance and the management of violent and potentially violent patients" (p. 39).

At present, marriage and family therapists often provide services to clients who are threatened by or experiencing abusive and violent behavior. An important issue to face, hopefully sooner than later, is that some current common interventions lack a cohesive, research-based theoretical framework. Bograd and Mederos (1999) state: "There is little consensus among marriage and family therapists about how to conceptualize and treat domestic violence cases, as demonstrated by the polarized controversy about whether couples or conjoint therapy for battered women and their partners is or is not dangerous, unethical, or ineffective" (p. 291). All mental health professionals need to address problems of abuse and violence and make a stronger effort to design evidence-based services for clients suffering the consequence of abuse and violence, including proactive, preventive interventions (e.g., psycho-educational programs).

Gay and Lesbian Relationships

Gay and lesbian issues have achieved recognition by the mental health professions and are now being included in training curricula, including for marriage and family therapy (recall that Subprinciple 1.2 in the AAMFT ethics code proscribes discrimination based on sexual orientation). Regardless, there remain unsettled and controversial concerns about same-sex orientation. Therapists must become competent to deal personally and therapeutically with these issues now and as they may further evolve.

In the future, society must give further public policy and legal consideration to the possibility of gay and lesbian couples' being married under law. Whether public policy and law will support gay/lesbian marriages remains for conjecture, but the outcome of the debate will impact professional practice and training.

At this time, prior to any widespread acceptance of gay/lesbian marriages per se, there can be no professional dispute about the gay/lesbian couple's right to receive services from a marriage and family therapist: "When seeking therapy, lesbian and gay couples have the right to expect that their coupleness will be affirmed by the therapist as being equally valid and significant as heterosexual marriage" (Bepko & Johnson, 2000, p. 409). Special therapeutic issues may arise when the therapist does not share the client's sexual orientation, because "there is an initial sense of 'otherness' that must be bridged in building a therapeutic relationship" (Bernstein, 2000, p. 443).

Consciously and unconsciously, therapists must monitor whether their own values, beliefs, or attitudes create a mindset toward pathologizing a person who has a gay or lesbian sexual orientation. Sexual orientation per se justifies neither a unique therapeutic framework nor clinical diagnosis. Whether the service user espouses a heterosexual or a homosexual orientation, the therapist is ethically obliged to respond to the person's unique characteristics and history, free from stereotyping. A person with a gay or lesbian sexual orientation is neither more nor less vulnerable to human frailties as a person with a heterosexual orientation. In formative training and ongoing professional development, the therapist must be prepared to offer effective services that respect each person's sexual orientation. Now and in the future, sexual orientation should be but one aspect of identity, among many, that influence the treatment plan and interventions.

Telehealth Services

All over the world, communication technology is the rage. The result is a rapid escalation of health-related communications, especially with video capability. Nickelson (1998) defined telehealth as "the use of telecommunications and information technology to provide access to health assessment, diagnosis, intervention, consultation, supervision, education, and information across distance" (p. 527). This discussion uses the term telehealth services although the term teletherapy also appears in the literature. (Chapter Nine in this book deals with the ethical and legal risks associated with common electronic-based communications such as voice-mail, fax machines, e-mail, cell phones, etc.)

Every marriage and family therapist has experienced telephone calls from clients in distress, and has offered supportive or therapeutic communications. In other words, the telephone "is an essential communications tool in professional practice today . . ." and "is nearly universal" (VandenBos & Williams, 2000, p. 491).

The Need for Standards and Guidelines. Interestingly, professional monitoring sources, such as licensing boards and ethics committees, have been reluctant to address the propriety of offering therapeutic services by telephone or on-line via the Internet. The escalation of use of electronic means for communication between therapist and service user merits both ethical and legal attention.

When considering a petition for a declaratory statement that would define the parameters of acceptable and unacceptable on-line counseling, one licensing board indicated that it would prefer that a particular national professional association set forth guidelines on the subject. The national professional association (not AAMFT) to which the licensing board wanted to show deference had a comparable discussion, and indicated that it would prefer that state licensing boards establish legal standards from which the association could derive and formulate ethics.

In the preceding example, the similar positions of "passing the buck" likely stemmed from the same motive, namely a wish to avoid the anticipated political and professional controversy. Being without precedent, any movement into such uncharted waters would likely make waves.

There still remains a noticeable absence of guidelines and standards for providing therapeutic services by telephone or other electronic media. Recognizing this absence, VandenBos and Williams (2000) have underscored the need for action: "Efforts around standards and guidelines, as well as inclusion of such services' reimbursement plans, should begin now, before such service delivery is widespread" (p. 492). Although the ethical implications of this matter have not been addressed, in the near future professional associations will most certainly face the issues and provide practitioners with ethical guidelines.

To create a framework for practice, the therapist should be mindful of the rapid refinement and expansion of today's technological innovations. The commonplace telephone is being replaced by the video telephone, which allows the communicants to see each other on a video screen. Focusing on interactive televideo (IATV), Jerome and Zayler (2000) have described behavioral telehealth innovations, recognizing how these increase access to psychological services, and deeming it "imperative that the complexity of this new medium is thoroughly researched . . . for therapeutic endeavors" (p. 482).

Even more profound in potential usefulness for therapeutic services, the Internet allows the dissemination of rapid, economical, and mass communications from a health care provider to consumers. Maheu and Gordon (2000) reported, "There is a growing number of people using the Internet to provide counseling and therapy to the public, despite the absence of empirical evidence supporting such activities" (p. 484). It is noteworthy that research by Jacobs, Christensen, Snibbe, Dolezal-Wood, Huber, and Polterok (2001), which compared short-term traditional individual therapy with a computer-based intervention overseen by a therapist, supported that "electronic therapy packages have potential value" (p. 95), although their findings suggested that therapist involvement was important for enhanced outcomes.

The regulators, such as licensing boards and ethics committees, cannot remain silent on the issue of telehealth, broadly defined. As Maheu and Gordon (2000) put it: "Legislative issues surrounding the Internet require immediate attention from behavioral health care professionals" (p. 486). But that is not likely to happen. Koocher and Morray (2000) have argued that ethical guidelines "tend to lag substantially behind technological innovations and there currently are no generally accepted professional standards on these emerging technologies" (p. 503).

Therapists' Responsibility and Evolving Standards. Until there are both ethical principles and legal standards that determine proper and improper use of telehealth modalities, therapists must, by necessity, rely on self-determinations. Guidelines for ethical decision making offered previously (particularly in Chapter One) can be applied to analysis of telehealth scenarios, but caution is advised. When there is a void in ethical and legal views, the practitioner who moves into experimental treatment is at risk. Having peer review of innovations is advisable, but does not assuredly protect the practitioner against allegations of impropriety or misconduct. Telehealth methods would come under the AAMFT ethical subprinciple that deals with clients' informed consent (Subprinciple 1.2). Namely, the client must be "adequately informed of potential risks and benefits of treatments for which generally recognized standards do not yet exist."

The preceding caveat acts, to some extent, against advancing or creating services that could potentially benefit service users. Part of professionalism does involve practitioners' seeking improved theories, methods, and techniques for providing services; and certainly telehealth modalities seem to have much potential. Nonetheless, it remains for telehealth services to be defined and authorized by appropriate monitoring sources, such as licensing boards and professional associations. Collaboration with these monitoring sources should promote professionalism in general and quality care for service users and risk management for therapists in specific.

An advance toward standards is evident in the ten principles for telehealth practice offered by Reed, McLaughlin, and Milholland (2000):

> Principle 1: The basic standards of professional conduct governing each health care profession are not altered by the use of telehealth technologies to deliver health care, conduct research, or provide education. Developed by each profession, these standards focus in part on the practitioner's responsibility to provide ethical and high-quality care. (p. 172)

> Principle 2: Confidentiality of client visits, client health records, and the integrity of information in the health care information system is essential. (p. 173)

> Principle 3: All clients directly involved in a telehealth encounter must be informed about the process, the attendant risks and benefits, and their own rights and responsibilities, and must provide adequate informed consent. (p. 173)

> Principle 4: Services provided via telehealth must adhere to the basic assurance of quality and professional health care in accordance with each health care discipline's clinical standards. (p. 173)

> Principle 5: Each health care discipline must examine how its patterns of care delivery are affected by telehealth and is responsible for developing its own processes for assuring competence in the delivery of health care via telehealth technologies. (p. 174)

> Principle 6: Documentation requirements for telehealth services must be developed that assure documentation of each client encounter with recommendations and treatments, communication with other health care providers as appropriate, and adequate protections for client confidentiality. (p. 175)

> Principle 7: Clinical guidelines in the area of telehealth should be based on empirical evidence, when available, and professional consensus among involved health care disciplines. (p. 175)

> Principle 8: The integrity and therapeutic value of the relationship between client and health care practitioner should be maintained and not diminished by the use of telehealth technology. (p. 176)

> Principle 9: Health care professionals do not need additional licensing to provide services via telehealth technologies. At the same time, telehealth technologies cannot be used as a vehicle for providing services that otherwise are not legally or professionally authorized. (p. 176)

> Principle 10: The safety of clients and practitioners must be ensured. Safe hardware and software, combined with demonstrated user competence, are essential components of safe telehealth practice. (p. 177)

These guidelines apparently do not have legal authority, but reportedly are being endorsed by certain professional associations (see footnote in Reed et al., 2000, p. 170). Guidelines of this type seem to offer reasoned and professionally sound ideas that could lead to standards.

As health care practitioners, marriage and family therapists will surely become more reliant on technologically-assisted communications in the future, but without additional empirical research, such usage could create the risk of both ethical and legal violations (Humphreys, Winzelberg, & Klaw, 2000). Without definite standards, such as might be derived from professional ethics or licensing laws, and without empirical research to justify particular professional interventions, the marriage and family therapist using telehealth technologies faces considerable risk of legal or ethical violations.

Conclusion: On to the Future

As history supports, the profession of marriage and family therapy has matured masterfully, and offers society incomparable benefits. As a professional association, AAMFT has demonstrated peerless commitment to professionalism and practice excellence, and its ethics code aims to ensure highly professional services that will benefit service users and society.

Rather than rest on the laurels of AAMFT or the profession, every marriage and family therapist should personally support applying a behavioral science foundation for practice (e.g., through conducting or using research on process and efficacy), enhancing professional competencies (e.g., through rigorous training programs and continuing education), and focusing on benefits for clients (e.g., through empirically-based interventions).

Ethics must be part of the practitioner's professional and personal identity, not merely an afterthought once an ethical dilemma appears. Although admittedly simplistic, the therapist who consciously adopts and maintains a positive attitude toward ethics can prevent many ethical dilemmas. Said in plain language, the therapist should get friendly with ethical principles and make them a part of everyday practice.

Each practitioner should examine ethical principles for applications that will enhance therapeutic interventions. For example, because of the practical benefits of informed consent, the therapist should be cognizant of keeping clients fully informed and accepting of the service. Jensen, Josephson, and Frey (1989) support this approach and argue that informed consent strengthens the engagement of the client and increases collaboration and compliance.

Another positive framework is to see and use ethical awareness as a safeguard against overstepping and taking too much control, power, and responsibility; this pro-active stance can prevent the therapist from getting caught in emotion-laden countertransference reactions (Kuyken, 1999). Professionals need to remain positive about the following basic ethical assumptions. Therapy is for the benefit of the service user(s). The quid pro quo for the therapist is the client's making financial payment, cooperating with the policies of the practice, and collaborating in the development of the treatment plan. The client can be self-determining, while also collaborating with the therapist, who provides a therapeutic relationship, information, reinforcement, and clarification, as would facilitate psychological growth for the client.

Another practical way to integrate ethics into one's professional identity is to incorporate ethical guidelines into the routines of office management, record keeping, and all the stages of treatment, from initial contacts through termination and evaluation. Of course, all persons in the practice, including secretaries and other support staff members, should function in accord with the ethics maintained by the therapist; the outcome will be both quality service for the client and effective risk management for the therapist. (Chapter Nine offers details about bringing practice management into accord with both ethics and risk management.)

Marriage and family therapy is second to no other mental health profession for reasonably anticipating a bright tomorrow. Professional ethics, such as contained in the AAMFT ethics code, provide the drum beat for the practitioner's confident and competent march into the future.

It is important to remember that the basic principles of an ethics code will remain stable even while the code evolves, as influenced by the needs and preferences of society and the profession. Since every aspect of an ethics code is subject to further examination, expansion, and revision, debate among professionals is an expectable and desirable outcome. This book has encompassed numerous theoretical and philosophical assumptions that impact ethics and that should be explored in greater depth (such as post-modern, modern, and pragmatic perspectives of ethics).

On the issue of informed consent, which is of critical importance to all therapeutic services, further dialogue about the current ethics code in future professional conferences and forums will enable the membership to air concerns and gain clarity. To date, questions have arisen as to exactly when the client must give informed consent and whether this is necessary for what might be called ordinary and routine treatment. For example, R. S. Leslie (personal communication, March 8, 2001) questions obtaining informed consent at the outset of services for treatment procedures. He reports that the law in the state of California gives leeway to marriage and family therapists to disclose at "an appropriate time during the therapy of his/her theoretical orientation, education, experience, specialties and such other information as the therapist deems appropriate."

To some extent, the contents of this book will be almost timeless. For example, ethical principles pertaining to responsibilities to the client, competence, and confidentiality will always be essential to the practice of mental health, and much of what is relevant today will be applicable tomorrow. A review of the professional literature on ethics reveals that the fundamental ethical principles date back decades, with far more similarities than differences over the years.

For any mental health practitioner, the study of professional ethics should be a continuing commitment. With comprehensive knowledge, appreciation, acceptance, and implementation of ethics into practice, the marriage and family therapist will achieve the ideals of the profession.

REFERENCES

Anderson, S. A., & Cramer-Benjamin, D. B. (1999). The impact of couple violence on parenting and children: An overview and clinical implications. American Journal of Family Therapy, 27 (1), 1–19.

Bateson, G. (1972). Steps to an ecology of mind. New York: Chandler.

Bean, R. A., Perry, B. J., & Bedell, T. M. (2001). Developing culturally competent marriage and family therapists: Guidelines for working with Hispanic families. Journal of Marital and Family Therapy, 27 (1), 43–54.

Bepko, C., & Johnson, T. (2000). Gay and lesbian couples in therapy: Perspectives for the contemporary family therapist. Journal of Marital and Family Therapy, 26 (4), 409–419.

Bernstein, A. C. (2000). Straight therapists working with lesbians and gays in family therapy. Journal of Marital and Family Therapy, 26 (4), 443–454.

Bograd, M., & Mederos, F. (1999). Battering and couples therapy: Universal screening and selection of treatment modality. Journal of Marital and Family Therapy, 25 (3), 291–312.

Booth, T. J., & Cottone, R. R. (2000). Measurement, classification, and prediction of paradigm adherence of marriage and family therapists. American Journal of Family Therapy, 28 (4), 329–346.

Goldenberg, I., & Goldenberg, H. (2000). Family therapy: An overview (5th ed.). Belmont, CA: Brooks/Cole.

Gurman, A. S., Kniskern, D. P., & Pinsof, W. M. (1986). Research on the process and outcome of marital and family therapy. In S. L. Garfield & A. E. Bergin (Eds.), Handbook of psychotherapy and behavior change (3rd ed., pp. 565–624). New York: John Wiley.

Hardy, K. V. (2001). Healing the world in fifty-minute intervals: A response to "Family therapy saves the planet." Journal of Marital and Family Therapy, 27 (1), 19–22.

Hawley, D. R., Bailey, C. E., & Pennick, K. A. (2000). A content analysis of research in family therapy journals. Journal of Marital and Family Therapy, 26 (1), 9–16.

Howard, R. C., & Bassos, C. A. (2000). The effect of screening versus nonscreening on treatment authorization in a managed care setting. Professional Psychology: Research and Practice, 31 (5), 526–530.

Humphreys, K., Winzelberg, A., & Klaw, E. (2000). Psychologists' ethical responsibilities in Internet-based groups: Issues, strategies, and a call for dialogue. Professional Psychology: Research and Practice, 31 (5), 493–496.

Jacobs, M. K., Christensen, A., Snibbe, J. R., Dolezal-Wood, S., Huber, A., & Polterok, A. (2001). A comparison of computer-based versus traditional individual therapy. Professional Psychology: Research and Practice, 32 (1), 92–96.

Jensen, P. S., Josephson, A. M., & Frey, J. (1989). Informed consent as a framework for treatment: Ethical and therapeutic considerations. American Journal of Psychotherapy, 43 (3), 378–386.

Jerome, L. W., & Zaylor, C. (2000). Cyberspace: Creating a therapeutic environment for telehealth applications. Professional Psychology: Research and Practice, 31 (5), 478–483.

Johnson, S. (2001). Family therapy saves the planet: Messianic tendencies in the family systems literature. Journal of Marital and Family Therapy, 27 (1), 3–11.

Johnson, L. N., Sandberg, J. G., & Miller, R. B. (1999). Research practices of marriage and family therapists. American Journal of Family Therapy, 27 (3), 239–249.

Killian, K. D. (2001). Reconstituting racial histories and identities: The narratives of interracial couples. Journal of Marital and Family Therapy, 27 (1), 27–42.

Koocher, G. P., & Morray, E. (2000). Regulation of telepsychology: A survey of state attorneys general. Professional Psychology: Research and Practice, 31 (5), 503–308.

Kuyken, W. (1999). Power and clinical psychology: A model for resolving power-related ethical dilemmas. Ethics & Behavior, 9 (1), 21–37.

Law, D. D., & Crane, D. R. (2000). The influence of marital and family therapy on health care utilization in a health-maintenance organization. Journal of Marital and Family Therapy, 26 (3), 281–291.

Maheu, M. M., & Gordon, B. L. (2000). Counseling and therapy on the Internet. Professional Psychology: Research and Practice, 31 (5), 484–489.

McGoldrick, M., Almeida, R., Preto, N. G., Bibb, A., Sutton, C. E., Hudak, J., et al. (1999). Efforts to incorporate social justice perspectives into a family training program. Journal of Marital and Family Therapy, 25 (2), 191–209.

Milewski-Hertlein, K. A. (2001). The use of the socially constructed genogram in clinical practice. American Journal of Family Therapy, 29 (1), 23–38.

Miller, R. B., Johnson, L. N., Sandberg, J. G., Stringer-Seibold, T. A., & Gfeller-Strouts, L. (2000). An addendum to the 1997 outcome research chart. American Journal of Family Therapy, 28 (4), 347–354.

Negy, C., & Snyder, D. K. (2000). Relationship satisfaction of Mexican American and Non-Hispanic white American interethnic couples: Issues of acculturation and clinical intervention. Journal of Marital and Family Therapy, 26 (3) 293–304.

Nickelson, D. (1998). Telehealth and the evolving health care system: Strategic opportunities for professional psychology. Professional Psychology: Research and Practice, 29 (6), 527–535.

Peterson, J. L., & Newman, R. (2000). Helping to curb youth violence: The APA-MTV "warning signs" initiative. Professional Psychology: Research and Practice, 31 (5), 509–514.

Reed, G. M., Levant, R. F., Stout, C. E., Murphy, M. J., Phelps, R. (2001). Psychology in the current mental health marketplace. Professional Psychology: Research and Practice, 32 (1), 65–70.

Reed, G. M., McLaughlin, C. J., & Milholland, K. (2000). Ten interdisciplinary principles for professional practice in telehealth: Implications for psychology. Professional Psychology: Research and Practice, 31 (2), 170–178.

Sandberg, J. G., Johnson, L. N., Dermer, S. B., Gfeller-Strouts, L. L., Seibold, J. M., Stringer-Seibold, T. A., et al. (1997). Demonstrated efficacy of models of marriage and family therapy: An update on Gurman, Kniskern, and Pinsof's chart. American Journal of Family Therapy, 25 (2), 121–137

Simon, R. (2001). Psychotherapy's soothsayer. Psychotherapy Networker, 25 (4), 34–39 & 62.

Sluzki, C. E. (2001). All those in favor of saving the planet, please raise your hand: A comment about "Family therapy saves the planet." Journal of Marital and Family Therapy, 27 (1), 13–15.

Sprenkle, D. W., & Bailey, C. E. (1995). Editor's introduction. Journal of Marital and Family Therapy, 21 (4), 339–340.

Stern, S. B. (1999). Anger management in parent-adolescent conflict. <u>American Journal of Family Therapy,</u> <u>27</u> (2), 181–193.

Tishler, C. L., Gordon, L. B., & Landry-Meyer, L. (2000). Managing the violent patient: A guide for psychologists and other mental health professionals. <u>Professional Psychology: Research and Practice, 31</u> (1), 34–41.

VandenBos, G. R., & Williams, S. (2000). The Internet versus the telephone: What is telehealth anyway? <u>Professional Psychology: Research and Practice, 31</u> (5), 490–492.

Woody, R. H. (1996). Dangerous patients: The therapist as "weaponless policeman." <u>Journal of Psychohistory,</u> <u>23</u> (4), 438–446.

Woolley, S. R., Butler, M. H., & Wampler, K. S. (2000). Unraveling change in therapy: Three different process research methodologies. <u>American Journal of Family Therapy, 28</u> (4), 311–327.

APPENDIX A - AAMFT CODE OF ETHICS - EFFECTIVE JULY 1, 2001

PREAMBLE

The Board of Directors of the American Association for Marriage and Family Therapy (AAMFT) hereby promulgates, pursuant to Article 2, Section 2.013 of the Association's Bylaws, the Revised AAMFT Code of Ethics, effective July 1, 2001.

The AAMFT strives to honor the public trust in marriage and family therapists by setting standards for ethical practice as described in this Code. The ethical standards define professional expectations and are enforced by the AAMFT Ethics Committee. The absence of an explicit reference to a specific behavior or situation in the Code does not mean that the behavior is ethical or unethical. The standards are not exhaustive. Marriage and family therapists who are uncertain about the ethics of a particular course of action are encouraged to seek counsel from consultants, attorneys, supervisors, colleagues, or other appropriate authorities.

Both law and ethics govern the practice of marriage and family therapy. When making decisions regarding professional behavior, marriage and family therapists must consider the AAMFT Code of Ethics and applicable laws and regulations. If the AAMFT Code of Ethics prescribes a standard higher than that required by law, marriage and family therapists must meet the higher standard of the AAMFT Code of Ethics. Marriage and family therapists comply with the mandates of law, but make known their commitment to the AAMFT Code of Ethics and take steps to resolve the conflict in a responsible manner. The AAMFT supports legal mandates for reporting of alleged unethical conduct.

The AAMFT Code of Ethics is binding on Members of AAMFT in all membership categories, AAMFT-Approved Supervisors, and applicants for membership and the Approved Supervisor designation (hereafter, AAMFT Member). AAMFT members have an obligation to be familiar with the AAMFT Code of Ethics and its application to their professional services. Lack of awareness or misunderstanding of an ethical standard is not a defense to a charge of unethical conduct.

The process for filing, investigating, and resolving complaints of unethical conduct is described in the current Procedures for Handling Ethical Matters of the AAMFT Ethics Committee. Persons accused are considered innocent by the Ethics Committee until proven guilty, except as otherwise provided, and are entitled to due process. If an AAMFT Member resigns in anticipation of, or during the course of, an ethics investigation, the Ethics Committee will complete its investigation. Any publication of action taken by the Association will include the fact that the Member attempted to resign during the investigation.

PRINCIPLE I – RESPONSIBILITY TO CLIENTS

Marriage and family therapists advance the welfare of families and individuals. They respect the rights of those persons seeking their assistance, and make reasonable efforts to ensure that their services are used appropriately.

1.1. Marriage and family therapists provide professional assistance to persons without discrimination on the basis of race, age, ethnicity, socioeconomic status, disability, gender, health status, religion, national origin, or sexual orientation.

1.2 Marriage and family therapists obtain appropriate informed consent to therapy or related procedures as early as feasible in the therapeutic relationship, and use language that is reasonably understandable to clients. The content of informed consent may vary depending upon the client and treatment plan; however, informed consent generally necessitates that the client: (a) has the capacity to consent; (b) has been adequately informed of significant information concerning treatment processes and procedures; (c) has been adequately informed of potential risks and benefits of treatments for which generally recognized standards do not yet exist; (d) has freely and without undue influence expressed consent; and (e) has provided consent that is appropriately documented. When persons, due to age or mental status, are legally incapable of giving informed consent, marriage and family therapists obtain informed permission from a legally authorized person, if such substitute consent is legally permissible.

1.3 Marriage and family therapists are aware of their influential positions with respect to clients, and they avoid exploiting the trust and dependency of such persons. Therapists, therefore, make every effort to avoid conditions and multiple relationships with clients that could impair professional judgment or increase the risk of exploitation. Such relationships include, but are not limited to, business or close personal relationships with a client or the client's immediate family. When the risk of impairment or exploitation exists due to conditions or multiple roles, therapists take appropriate precautions.

1.4 Sexual intimacy with clients is prohibited.

1.5 Sexual intimacy with former clients is likely to be harmful and is therefore prohibited for two years following the termination of therapy or last professional contact. In an effort to avoid exploiting the trust and dependency of clients, marriage and family therapists should not engage in sexual intimacy with former clients after the two years following termination or last professional contact. Should therapists engage in sexual intimacy with former clients following two years after termination or last professional contact, the burden shifts to the therapist to demonstrate that there has been no exploitation or injury to the former client or to the client's immediate family.

1.6 Marriage and family therapists comply with applicable laws regarding the reporting of alleged unethical conduct.

1.7 Marriage and family therapists do not use their professional relationships with clients to further their own interests.

1.8 Marriage and family therapists respect the rights of clients to make decisions and help them to understand the consequences of these decisions. Therapists clearly advise the clients that they have the responsibility to make decisions regarding relationships such as cohabitation, marriage, divorce, separation, reconciliation, custody, and visitation.

1.9 Marriage and family therapists continue therapeutic relationships only so long as it is reasonably clear that clients are benefiting from the relationship.

1.10 Marriage and family therapists assist persons in obtaining other therapeutic services if the therapist is unable or unwilling, for appropriate reasons, to provide professional help.

1.11 Marriage and family therapists do not abandon or neglect clients in treatment without making reasonable arrangements for the continuation of such treatment.

1.12 Marriage and family therapists obtain written informed consent from clients before videotaping, audio recording, or permitting third-party observation.

1.13 Marriage and family therapists, upon agreeing to provide services to a person or entity at the request of a third party, clarify, to the extent feasible and at the outset of the service, the nature of the relationship with each party and the limits of confidentiality.

PRINCIPLE II - CONFIDENTIALITY

Marriage and family therapists have unique confidentiality concerns because the client in a therapeutic relationship may be more than one person. Therapists respect and guard the confidences of each individual client.

2.1 Marriage and family therapists disclose to clients and other interested parties, as early as feasible in their professional contacts, the nature of confidentiality and possible limitations of the clients' right to confidentiality. Therapists review with clients the circumstances where confidential information may be requested and where disclosure of confidential information may be legally required. Circumstances may necessitate repeated disclosures.

2.2 Marriage and family therapists do not disclose client confidences except by written authorization or waiver, or where mandated or permitted by law. Verbal authorization will not be sufficient except in emergency situations, unless prohibited by law. When providing couple, family or group treatment, the therapist does not disclose information outside the treatment context without a written authorization from each individual competent to execute a waiver. In the context of couple, family or group treatment, the therapist may not reveal any individual's confidences to others in the client unit without the prior written permission of that individual.

2.3 Marriage and family therapists use client and/or clinical materials in teaching, writing, consulting, research, and public presentations only if a written waiver has been obtained in accordance with Subprinciple 2.2, or when appropriate steps have been taken to protect client identity and confidentiality.

2.4 Marriage and family therapists store, safeguard, and dispose of client records in ways that maintain confidentiality and in accord with applicable laws and professional standards.

2.5 Subsequent to the therapist moving from the area, closing the practice, or upon the death of the therapist, a marriage and family therapist arranges for the storage, transfer, or disposal of client records in ways that maintain confidentiality and safeguard the welfare of clients.

2.6 Marriage and family therapists, when consulting with colleagues or referral sources, do not share confidential information that could reasonably lead to the identification of a client, research participant, supervisee, or other person with whom they have a confidential relationship unless they have obtained the prior written consent of the client, research participant, supervisee, or other person with whom they have a confidential relationship. Information may be shared only to the extent necessary to achieve the purposes of the consultation.

Principle III – Professional Competence and Integrity

Marriage and family therapists maintain high standards of professional competence and integrity.

3.1 Marriage and family therapists pursue knowledge of new developments and maintain competence in marriage and family therapy through education, training, or supervised experience.

3.2 Marriage and family therapists maintain adequate knowledge of and adhere to applicable laws, ethics, and professional standards.

3.3 Marriage and family therapists seek appropriate professional assistance for their personal problems or conflicts that may impair work performance or clinical judgment.

3.4 Marriage and family therapists do not provide services that create a conflict of interest that may impair work performance or clinical judgment.

3.5 Marriage and family therapists, as presenters, teachers, supervisors, consultants and researchers, are dedicated to high standards of scholarship, present accurate information, and disclose potential conflicts of interest.

3.6 Marriage and family therapists maintain accurate and adequate clinical and financial records.

3.7 While developing new skills in specialty areas, marriage and family therapists take steps to ensure the competence of their work and to protect clients from possible harm. Marriage and family therapists practice in specialty areas new to them only after appropriate education, training, or supervised experience.

3.8 Marriage and family therapists do not engage in sexual or other forms of harassment of clients, students, trainees, supervisees, employees, colleagues, or research subjects.

3.9 Marriage and family therapists do not engage in the exploitation of clients, students, trainees, supervisees, employees, colleagues, or research subjects.

3.10 Marriage and family therapists do not give to or receive from clients (a) gifts of substantial value or (b) gifts that impair the integrity or efficacy of the therapeutic relationship.

3.11 Marriage and family therapists do not diagnose, treat, or advise on problems outside the recognized boundaries of their competencies.

3.12 Marriage and family therapists make efforts to prevent the distortion or misuse of their clinical and research findings.

3.13 Marriage and family therapists, because of their ability to influence and alter the lives of others, exercise special care when making public their professional recommendations and opinions through testimony or other public statements.

3.14 To avoid a conflict of interests, marriage and family therapists who treat minors or adults involved in custody or visitation actions may not also perform forensic evaluations for custody, residence, or visitation of the minor. The marriage and family therapist who treats the minor may provide the court or mental health professional performing the evaluation with information about the minor from the marriage and family therapist's perspective as a treating marriage and family therapist, so long as the marriage and family therapist does not violate confidentiality.

3.15 Marriage and family therapists are in violation of this Code and subject to termination of membership or other appropriate action if they: (a) are convicted of any felony; (b) are convicted of a misdemeanor related to their qualifications or functions; (c) engage in conduct which could lead to conviction of a felony, or a misdemeanor related to their qualifications or functions; (d) are expelled from or disciplined by other professional organizations; (e) have their licenses or certificates suspended or revoked or are otherwise disciplined by regulatory bodies; (f) continue to practice marriage and family therapy while no longer competent to do so because they are impaired by physical or mental causes or the abuse of alcohol or other substances; or (g) fail to cooperate with the Association at any point from the inception of an ethical complaint through the completion of all proceedings regarding that complaint.

PRINCIPLE IV - RESPONSIBILITY TO STUDENTS AND SUPERVISEES

Marriage and family therapists do not exploit the trust and dependency of students and supervisees.

4.1 Marriage and family therapists are aware of their influential positions with respect to students and supervisees, and they avoid exploiting the trust and dependency of such persons. Therapists, therefore, make every effort to avoid conditions and multiple relationships that could impair professional objectivity or increase the risk of exploitation. When the risk of impairment or exploitation exists due to conditions or multiple roles, therapists take appropriate precautions.

4.2 Marriage and family therapists do not provide therapy to current students or supervisees.

4.3 Marriage and family therapists do not engage in sexual intimacy with students or supervisees during the evaluative or training relationship between the therapist and student or supervisee. Should a supervisor engage in sexual activity with a former supervisee, the burden of proof shifts to the supervisor to demonstrate that there has been no exploitation or injury to the supervisee.

4.4 Marriage and family therapists do not permit students or supervisees to perform or to hold themselves out as competent to perform professional services beyond their training, level of experience, and competence.

4.5 Marriage and family therapists take reasonable measures to ensure that services provided by supervisees are professional.

4.6 Marriage and family therapists avoid accepting as supervisees or students those individuals with whom a prior or existing relationship could compromise the therapist's objectivity. When such situations cannot be avoided, therapists take appropriate precautions to maintain objectivity. Examples of such relationships include, but are not limited to, those individuals with whom the therapist has a current or prior sexual, close personal, immediate familial, or therapeutic relationship.

4.7 Marriage and family therapists do not disclose supervisee confidences except by written authorization or waiver, or when mandated or permitted by law. In educational or training settings where there are multiple supervisors, disclosures are permitted only to other professional colleagues, administrators, or employers who share responsibility for training of the supervisee. Verbal authorization will not be sufficient except in emergency situations, unless prohibited by law.

PRINCIPLE V - RESPONSIBILITY TO RESEARCH PARTICIPANTS

Investigators respect the dignity and protect the welfare of research participants, and are aware of applicable laws and regulations and professional standards governing the conduct of research.

5. 1 Investigators are responsible for making careful examinations of ethical acceptability in planning studies. To the extent that services to research participants may be compromised by participation in research, investigators seek the ethical advice of qualified professionals not directly involved in the investigation and observe safeguards to protect the rights of research participants.

5. 2 Investigators requesting participant involvement in research inform participants of the aspects of the research that might reasonably be expected to influence willingness to participate. Investigators are especially sensitive to the possibility of diminished consent when participants are also receiving clinical services, or have impairments which limit understanding and/or communication, or when participants are children.

5.3 Investigators respect each participant's freedom to decline participation in or to withdraw from a research study at any time. This obligation requires special thought and consideration when investigators or other members of the research team are in positions of authority or influence over participants. Marriage and family therapists, therefore, make every effort to avoid multiple relationships with research participants that could impair professional judgment or increase the risk of exploitation.

5.4 Information obtained about a research participant during the course of an investigation is confidential unless there is a waiver previously obtained in writing. When the possibility exists that others, including family members, may obtain access to such information, this possibility, together with the plan for protecting confidentiality, is explained as part of the procedure for obtaining informed consent.

PRINCIPLE VI - RESPONSIBILITY TO THE PROFESSION

Marriage and family therapists respect the rights and responsibilities of professional colleagues and participate in activities that advance the goals of the profession.

6.1 Marriage and family therapists remain accountable to the standards of the profession when acting as members or employees of organizations. If the mandates of an organization with which a marriage and family therapist is affiliated, through employment, contract or otherwise, conflict with the AAMFT Code of Ethics, marriage and family therapists make known to the organization their commitment to the AAMFT Code of Ethics and attempt to resolve the conflict in a way that allows the fullest adherence to the Code of Ethics.

6.2 Marriage and family therapists assign publication credit to those who have contributed to a publication in proportion to their contributions and in accordance with customary professional publication practices.

6.3 Marriage and family therapists do not accept or require authorship credit for a publication based on research from a student's program, unless the therapist made a substantial contribution beyond being a faculty advisor or research committee member. Coauthorship on a student thesis, dissertation, or project should be determined in accordance with principles of fairness and justice.

6.4 Marriage and family therapists who are the authors of books or other materials that are published or distributed do not plagiarize or fail to cite persons to whom credit for original ideas or work is due.

6.5 Marriage and family therapists who are the authors of books or other materials published or distributed by an organization take reasonable precautions to ensure that the organization promotes and advertises the materials accurately and factually.

6.6 Marriage and family therapists participate in activities that contribute to a better community and society, including devoting a portion of their professional activity to services for which there is little or no financial return.

6.7 Marriage and family therapists are concerned with developing laws and regulations pertaining to marriage and family therapy that serve the public interest, and with altering such laws and regulations that are not in the public interest.

6.8 Marriage and family therapists encourage public participation in the design and delivery of professional services and in the regulation of practitioners.

PRINCIPLE VII – FINANCIAL ARRANGEMENTS

Marriage and family therapists make financial arrangements with clients, third-party payors, and supervisees that are reasonably understandable and conform to accepted professional practices.

7.1 Marriage and family therapists do not offer or accept kickbacks, rebates, bonuses, or other remuneration for referrals; fee-for-service arrangements are not prohibited.

7.2 Prior to entering into the therapeutic or supervisory relationship, marriage and family therapists clearly disclose and explain to clients and supervisees: (a) all financial arrangements and fees related to professional services, including charges for canceled or missed appointments; (b) the use of collection agencies or legal measures for nonpayment; and (c) the procedure for obtaining payment from the client, to the extent allowed by law, if payment is denied by the third-party payor. Once services have begun, therapists provide reasonable notice of any changes in fees or other charges.

7.3 Marriage and family therapists give reasonable notice to clients with unpaid balances of their intent to seek collection by agency or legal recourse. When such action is taken, therapists will not disclose clinical information.

7.4 Marriage and family therapists represent facts truthfully to clients, third-party payors, and supervisees regarding services rendered.

7.5 Marriage and family therapists ordinarily refrain from accepting goods and services from clients in return for services rendered. Bartering for professional services may be conducted only if: (a) the supervisee or client requests it, (b) the relationship is not exploitative, (c) the professional relationship is not distorted, and (d) a clear written contract is established.

7.6 Marriage and family therapists may not withhold records under their immediate control that are requested and needed for a client's treatment solely because payment has not been received for past services, except as otherwise provided by law.

PRINCIPLE VIII - ADVERTISING

Marriage and family therapists engage in appropriate informational activities, including those that enable the public, referral sources, or others to choose professional services on an informed basis.

8.1 Marriage and family therapists accurately represent their competencies, education, training, and experience relevant to their practice of marriage and family therapy.

8.2 Marriage and family therapists ensure that advertisements and publications in any media (such as directories, announcements, business cards, newspapers, radio, television, Internet, and facsimiles) convey information that is necessary for the public to make an appropriate selection of professional services. Information could include: (a) office information, such as name, address, telephone number, credit card acceptability, fees, languages spoken, and office hours; (b) qualifying clinical degree (see subprinciple 8.5); (c) other earned degrees (see subprinciple 8.5) and state or provincial licensures and/or certifications; (d) AAMFT clinical member status; and (e) description of practice.

8.3 Marriage and family therapists do not use names that could mislead the public concerning the identity, responsibility, source, and status of those practicing under that name, and do not hold themselves out as being partners or associates of a firm if they are not.

8.4 Marriage and family therapists do not use any professional identification (such as a business card, office sign, letterhead, Internet, or telephone or association directory listing) if it includes a statement or claim that is false, fraudulent, misleading, or deceptive.

8.5 In representing their educational qualifications, marriage and family therapists list and claim as evidence only those earned degrees: (a) from institutions accredited by regional accreditation sources recognized by the United States Department of Education, (b) from institutions recognized by states or provinces that license or certify marriage and family therapists, or (c) from equivalent foreign institutions.

8.6 Marriage and family therapists correct, wherever possible, false, misleading, or inaccurate information and representations made by others concerning the therapist's qualifications, services, or products.

8.7 Marriage and family therapists make certain that the qualifications of their employees or supervisees are represented in a manner that is not false, misleading, or deceptive.

8.8 Marriage and family therapists do not represent themselves as providing specialized services unless they have the appropriate education, training, or supervised experience.

This Code is published by: American Association for Marriage and Family Therapy

1133 15th Street, NW Suite 300 - Washington, DC 20005-2710

(202) 452-0109 - (202) 223-2329 FAX - www.aamft.org

APPENDIX B – ADDITIONAL ETHICS RESOURCES FROM THE AMERICAN ASSOCIATION FOR MARRIAGE AND FAMILY THERAPY

- Visit the American Association for Marriage and Family Therapy (AAMFT) website at *http://www.aamft.org*. There you will find the full text of the *AAMFT Code of Ethics*, and information about how ethical complaints are filed and processed.

- *http://www.FamilyTherapyResources.net* is a service of the American Association for Marriage and Family Therapy. At this site, you will find a searchable database of books, conference tapes, articles, fact sheets, and upcoming conferences. Many of these resources address ethical and legal issues in the practice of family therapy.

- Even the most ethically conscious clinician will experience ethical and legal quandaries. Hence, the AAMFT Legal Risk Management Plan was created as a free benefit of AAMFT membership. Through this program members can access numerous legal and ethical fact sheets, and consult with an attorney via telephone about legal matters relating to their professional practice. AAMFT members can also request a free ethical advisory opinion based on the *AAMFT Code of Ethics* and the experience of the AAMFT Ethics Committee. Professional liability insurance is available to AAMFT members at a group rate.